America's Songs

America's Songs

The Stories Behind the Songs of Broadway, Hollywood, and Tin Pan Alley

Philip Furia and Michael Lasser

Routledge
Taylor & Francis Group
New York   London

Routledge is an imprint of the
Taylor & Francis Group, an informa business

Published in 2006 by
Routledge
Taylor & Francis Group
270 Madison Avenue
New York, NY 10016

Published in Great Britain by
Routledge
Taylor & Francis Group
2 Park Square
Milton Park, Abingdon
Oxon OX14 4RN

Printed in the United States of America on acid-free paper
10 9 8 7 6 5 4 3 2 1

International Standard Book Number-10: 0-415-97246-9 (Hardcover)
International Standard Book Number-13: 978-0-415-97246-8 (Hardcover)
Library of Congress Card Number 2005032854

Library of Congress Cataloging-in-Publication Data

Furia, Philip, 1943-
    America's songs: the stories behind the songs of Broadway, Hollywood, and Tin Pan Alley / Philip Furia and Michael Lasser.
        p. cm.
    Includes bibliographical references (p.) and index.
    ISBN 0-415-97246-9 (hb)
    1. Popular music--United States--History and criticism. I. Lasser, Michael. II. Title.

ML3477.F87 2006
782.421640973--dc22   2005032854

Taylor & Francis Group
is the Academic Division of Informa plc.

Visit the Taylor & Francis Web site at
http://www.taylorandfrancis.com

and the Routledge Web site at
http://www.routledge-ny.com

To Laurie and Elaine

Table of Contents

Table of Songs

Songs listed in **boldface** type have an entry of their own or, if followed by the title of a Broadway musical or Hollywood film, are part of an entry for that musical. Songs in roman type are mentioned in the entry of another song. All entries are organized chronologically and alphabetically within each year.

Introduction

Song is the most beloved of the arts. People speak of "my song" or "our song" with a possessiveness they never feel for a painting or a novel. Yet just as we possess songs, they also possess us. Hearing a song evokes a time, a place, another person, an image of ourselves. It is little wonder that it stirs our curiosity. What inspired it? What does it say and how does it say it—in music and in words? We have tried to answer these questions by telling the stories behind many of the great songs of Broadway, Hollywood, and Tin Pan Alley.

Even though some of these anecdotes are probably apocryphal, they still reveal why the songs fascinate us. Did Jimmy McHugh and Dorothy Fields really rush off to write a song when they overheard a boy say to his girlfriend as they gazed into Tiffany's window, "Gee, honey, I wish I could get you one of them rocks, but right now I can't give you anything but love"? Regardless, the story reveals a deeper truth: song comes not only from its creators but also from us: our chance remarks, the lilt of our speech, the rhythms of our lives.

Besides telling the stories behind these songs, we have tried to suggest, simply and succinctly, what makes a song great. Frank Sinatra once said, "A Johnny Mercer lyric is all the wit you wish you had and all the love you ever lost." That combination of wit and sentiment, verbal by-play and ardent emotion, defines the classic American songs of Jerome Kern, Irving Berlin, Cole Porter, and other great composers and lyricists. These songwriters started out in Tin Pan Alley, the sheet-music publishing business that emerged in New York at the beginning of the twentieth century. They never forgot, as Irving Berlin put it, that "a good song is a song that sells."

Berlin and his contemporaries wrote for what he sometimes called "the mob," and he trusted its judgments absolutely.

The songwriters who gave us what has come to be known as the Great American Songbook were not writing about themselves; they were writing about us. They were "democratic populists" who gave voice to the American people. If it was on our minds or in our hearts, it soon ended up in a popular song. Our songwriters have given us an emotional history of our times by encapsulating our attitudes, values, and behavior for a hundred years. Somehow, these practical businessmen wrote songs of intricate artistry and urbane wit for Broadway musicals and Hollywood films: some debonair patter for Fred Astaire in top hat, white tie, and tails, on a penthouse balcony against the New York skyline or a gritty, street-smart number that sees through the hip-hooray and ballyhoo of Hollywood. Many of these songs have transcended their original heyday to become "standards," songs that sound as fresh today as when they were first composed.

Max Morath called a standard

> ... a song, words and music, that every professional musician and singer is supposed to know .... When I was a kid, playing jazz, I would do jobs where a phone rings and on the other end is a leader that maybe you have never even worked with, who says, "Hey Max, can you play the Hilton hotel on Saturday night?" .... So, you show up and you don't know these people—never worked with them before. The leader gets up and says, "Okay, let's open up with 'I Got Rhythm,' we'll do it in 'C', and then if we want to do a vocal we'll bring it into 'A' flat." Now, you'd better know the chord progression, you'd better know the melody, you'd better know where to go, or you're not going to get called again.

Such standards are miniatures, most of them only thirty-two bars long, each exploring a single point along love's endlessly changing line. Then, in the best songs, the writers ring witty changes on the most tired clichés of romance. Though songs are often extravagant in sentiment and expansive in emotion, good songwriters are masters of economy. Although they hardly thought of themselves as "artists," these rough-and-tumble craftsmen created what is widely regarded as one of America's greatest cultural achievements.

Musically, their songs drew upon European, Middle-Eastern, and African idioms to weave a distinctively American fabric. When lyricists wedded that music to the everyday speech of ordinary people, they made the American vernacular sing. Once the right words fit the right music, we cannot hear one without thinking of the other.

We also try to provide insight into the fascinating but mysterious process of collaboration. With lyricist Lorenz Hart, Richard Rodgers wrote the music first; with Oscar Hammerstein, he wrote it last. George and Ira Gershwin always worked—even lived—side by side. When Dubose Heyward collaborated with them on *Porgy and Bess*, he marveled at the way in which they "would get at the piano, pound, wrangle, swear, burst into weird snatches of song and eventually emerge with polished lyrics."

Yet a great song always transcends its creators. A film clip from the 1930s shows lyricist Mack Gordon singing, "Did You Ever See a Dream Walking?" while composer Harry Revel plays the piano. Gordon, weighing at least 300 pounds, is dressed nattily in a double-breasted suit and wing-tipped spectators. He is deadly serious; he is out there selling the song, but he has all the stock mannerisms of a bad lounge singer. He puts one hand in his side jacket pocket, sways to the rhythm of Revel's playing, and keeps smiling no matter what. He looks more than slightly ridiculous, but you do not laugh. After all, here is the guy who wrote it; somewhere, behind all the affectation, is something genuine. That something in each great song is what we hope to capture in this book.

America's Songs is a work of history, anecdote, analysis, and interpretation. It is organized chronologically, beginning after the first decade of the twentieth century, when songs such as "Some of These Days" and

Composer Harry Revel at the piano and lyricist and former vaudevillian Mack Gordon on top of it. Courtesy of Photofest.

"Alexander's Ragtime Band" established themselves as enduring standards. Our endpoint is the late 1970s, a generation ago, because a song becomes a standard only when it proves it can endure beyond the listeners who first embraced it.

For much of a century, these songs defined who we were, where we were, and how we thought and talked and felt. They managed to catch and hold our attention by how the composer and lyricist intuited what was happening in our world: an attitude, a slang expression, an elusive but universal feeling. To become popular, their songs needed to "agree" with us. They certainly were not going to tell us we were wrong or foolish. Rather, they were going to smile at our follies and confirm that what we wish were true is worth wishing for. That is what makes them the extraordinary social mirror that they are, a mirror in which, we hope, readers will see themselves. Ultimately, as the songwriter says, the song is you.

The Authors

Philip Furia is the author of *The Poets of Tin Pan Alley: A History of America's Great Lyricists* (Oxford, 1990), *Ira Gershwin: The Art of the Lyricist* (Oxford, 1996), *Irving Berlin: A Life in Song* (Schirmer Books/Simon & Schuster, 1998), and *Skylark: The Life and Times of Johnny Mercer* (St. Martin's, 2003), the first biography of the Savannah songwriter. He has also written about American popular song in *The American Scholar, In Theater, Style, Italian Americana*, and other journals and magazines. A native of Pittsburgh, Furia studied at Oberlin College (BA, 1965), the University of Chicago (MA, 1966), and the Iowa Writers Workshop (MFA, 1970). He received his PhD in English in 1970 from the University of Iowa and taught for twenty-five years (and twenty-five *winters*) at the University of Minnesota, where he was also chair of the Department of English and associate dean for faculty of the College of Liberal Arts. He is currently chair of the Department of Creative Writing at the University of North Carolina at Wilmington.

Furia's writings on American popular song have been lauded in *The New York Times, The London Times, The Atlantic Monthly, The New Yorker, American Music*, and other publications. He has spoken at the Library of Congress, the New York Historical Society, and at numerous universities in America and Europe. Furia has also appeared on *Larry King Live, The Turner Entertainment Report*, A & E's *Biography, The Studs Terkl Show, All Things Considered, Ben Wattenberg's Think Tank*, the PBS series *Broadway: The American Musical*, and *Fresh Air with Terry Gross*. In addition, he has written and emceed musical tributes to Cole Porter, Irving Berlin, the Gershwins, Harold Arlen, and other songwriters that have featured prominent jazz and cabaret performers in New York, New Orleans, and other cities.

Michael Lasser is a lecturer, writer, broadcaster, critic, and teacher. He has been the host of the nationally syndicated public radio show, *Fascinatin' Rhythm*, since November, 1980. The weekly program explores the history and themes of American popular music through a series of "radio essays" illustrated by recordings. Each week, it examines a different topic: a kind of song, a composer or lyricist, a kind of musical, a performer, theme, or image. In 1994, it won a prestigious Peabody Award for letting "our treasury of popular tunes speak (and sing) for itself with sparkling commentary tracing the contributions of the composers and performers to American society."

For twenty years, Lasser was the theater critic for *The Rochester Democrat & Chronicle*. He has spoken at universities and art and history museums in thirty-three states and also designs and narrates concerts for symphony orchestras.

Lasser has taught the history of the American musical at the University of Rochester and Nazareth College. A former teacher of English at The Harley School, an independent day school in Rochester, New York, Lasser has also taught at Rutgers University, St. John Fisher College, and Fairleigh Dickinson University. Lasser is a graduate of Dartmouth College, holds an MA from Brooklyn College, and has done additional graduate work at Rutgers University. He is married and has two grown children and one grandchild.

1910 – 1919

Composer and lyricist Shelton Brooks (second from left) onstage with, from the far left, W. C. Handy, Harold Arlen, and Irving Berlin during the San Francisco World's Fair of 1940. Courtesy of Photofest.

1910

Some of These Days
Lyrics and music by Shelton Brooks

"Some of These Days" is the first American popular song that clearly deserves to be called a "standard." Written in the same year as such dated barber shop quartet staples as "Let Me Call You Sweetheart" and "Down by the Old Mill Stream," "Some of These Days" is a distinctively *modern* song. Composer Alec Wilder called it a "landmark in popular music, perhaps *the* landmark song."

Like many songs of its era, "Some of These Days" portrayed African-Americans in comic and frequently suggestive racist caricatures. Although demeaning, such "coon songs," as they were unfortunately called, bristled with vernacular lyrics and rhythmical music—a refreshing change from lugubrious Victorian ballads. Some, such as "Hello, Ma Baby" (1899) and "Bill Bailey, Won't You Please Come Home?" (1902), have endured and shed their racist overtones. "Some of These Days" reflects its "coon song" heritage in its open avowal of passion ("You'll miss my hugging, / You'll miss my kissing"), its sexual innuendo ("For you know, honey, / You've had your way"), and its colloquial language. Its title gives a twist to the every-day catchphrase "one of these days."

Black songwriters, as well as white ones, created "coon songs." Shelton Brooks, a black vaudeville pianist, wrote "Some of These Days" and tried to demonstrate it for Sophie Tucker. A former "coon shouter" who had performed in blackface, Tucker refused to see him, but Brooks persuaded her maid to let him play the song for her. When Tucker heard "Some of These Days," she said she could have kicked herself for nearly losing such a treasure. "It had everything," she recalled, "and always audiences have loved it and asked for it."

1911

Alexander's Ragtime Band
Lyrics and music by Irving Berlin

As Irving Berlin was shaving one morning, a tune popped into his head. It had a sprightly rhythm in the popular style of ragtime, the syncopated music that had swept America after it was introduced at Chicago's 1893 Columbian Exposition, the same year that Berlin's family had fled Russia for America. The lyric he set to the melody branded "Alexander's Ragtime Band" as a "coon song" (the name "Alexander" was used in such songs because it was considered comically inappropriate for a black man to have such a "highfalutin" name). Yet, although he used black dialect ("It's just the bestest band what am"), Berlin's lyric contained no demeaning racial stereotypes. Instead, it celebrated "Alexander" as a musical camp-meeting revivalist and offered to take the listener "by the hand, up to the man, up to the man, who is the leader of the band." That friendly invitation dispelled the widespread image of ragtime as devilish music leading young people

Sheet music for "Alexander's Ragtime Band." Courtesy of David A. Jasen.

astray and undermining American society. In fact, Berlin's lyric even suggested that ragtime was part of the country's musical tradition when he promised "the 'Swanee River' played—in ragtime."

Although "Alexander's Ragtime Band" lacks true ragtime's syncopated style, Berlin "rags" the music against the words when, for instance, he uses musical accents to distort the pronunciation of "natural" so that it rhymes with "call":

They can play a bugle *call*
Like you never heard before;
So natur*al*
That you want to go to war

He also created subtle internal rhymes such as *"natu-"* and *"that you"* to give the song a catchy verve.

"Alexander's Ragtime Band" soon became the greatest hit Tin Pan Alley had yet seen, selling a million copies of sheet music in a few months, then another million in 1912. The song was heard everywhere, as Berlin found when he visited England and heard his cab driver whistling the melody with no idea that his passenger was the song's creator.

"Alexander's Ragtime Band" was Irving Berlin's first enduring hit, but it also set a standard he would strive to maintain for the rest of his life. "My struggles didn't actually begin until after I'd written 'Alexander's Ragtime Band'," he said. "It's been a struggle ever since to keep success going."

Everybody's Doin' It Now
Lyrics and music by Irving Berlin

When Irving Berlin performed at London's Hippodrome Theatre, he invited the audience to call out the titles of his songs for him to sing. Soon, they began calling out titles he had not written. Then it dawned on him: they thought he had written *every* ragtime song. Their confusion was understandable because most ragtime songs were quite similar. Many were about themselves—how ragtime and its shoulder-shaking dances made you feel. For "Everybody's Doin' It Now," Berlin said, "It was an idea out of the air. I wanted a dance song; everybody was doing it. I just sat down and wrote the thing as it was. It was the dance craze put to music and words."

In a single song, Berlin had crystallized the dance craze, with its exciting new mix of youthful vitality and sexual license—from the energetic dancing of "See that ragtime couple over there / Watch them throw their shoulders in the air," to the sexual innuendo of "Everybody's doin' it, doin' it, doin' it."

The dance craze first captivated America when dancers Vernon and Irene Castle tamed the smoldering tango and made such ragtime "animal dances" as the Grizzly Bear and the Turkey Trot respectable, even though they took the then controversial step of using a black bandleader, James Reese Europe, to provide their accompaniment. Irene was especially daring, though not intentionally so; she bobbed her hair and removed her corsets because she liked the look. She was the unlikeliest of revolutionaries. Although the Castles featured a lot of very modern shoulder shaking, they also performed with great charm. They were stylish, attractive people who made dancing glamorous and fashionable. They embodied the ideal—or at least the fantasy—of nearly every middle-class American woman: a romantic love affair lived out gracefully within marriage and crowned with fame and success.

Yet ragtime dancing remained controversial, at least for some. Young people pressed themselves together on the dance floor, and before long New York's Commission on Amusements and Vacation Resources for Working Girls found that "reckless and uncontrolled dances" could create "an opportunity for license and debauchery." In Boston, usually mocked for its prissy rectitude, a few young people who ragged at an unseemly moment were put on trial. However, when their lawyer sang Berlin and George Bottsford's "The Grizzly Bear" for the judge and jury, the whole courtroom joined in on the chorus.

Oh, You Beautiful Doll
Lyrics by Seymour Brown, music by Nat D. Ayer

Seymour Brown, an actor–lyricist writing sketches for the *Ziegfeld Follies*, told vaudevillian Nat D. Ayer that Florenz Ziegfeld wanted to mount a jungle ballet with the showgirls dressed as animals because Teddy Roosevelt had just returned from big game hunting in Africa. Once they collaborated on "Moving Day in Jungle Town" for the *Follies of 1909*, the two young men became songwriting opportunists. One day, they read a newspaper article about a wife named Gladys, who beat up her husband when he said "Mabel" in his sleep, and cranked out the still funny, "If You Talk in Your Sleep, Don't Mention My Name."

In July 1911, after a vaudeville matinee in St. Louis, the two men watched a pretty girl walk by. A theatre electrician remarked: "Say! There's some beautiful doll! I'd like to get my limbs 'round her!" Before the curtain went up that evening, they had finished writing "Oh, You Beautiful Doll," but, when audiences failed to respond to it, they dropped it from their act. The song got a second chance when composer A. Baldwin Sloane asked if Ayer had a song to fill a spot between scenes in *The Red Rose*. A dozen chorus girls were rehearsing the number until one day, Ian Whitcomb reports, one of them rested her foot on a footlight as she leaned over to chat with a musician in the pit. At just that moment, an electrician happened to flip on the lights, "throwing the girl's legs, thighs, and torso into silhouette" from below. That was all the song needed. "Oh, You Beautiful Doll" became a huge hit, averaging ten encores a night. "We made $24,000 off that in one year," Ayer remembered.

The lyric the chorines were singing was about a young man who is encouraging his girl to "turn out the light and come over here." However, like most inflamed love songs of its time, a bouncy melody undermines the passion, and the lyric feels duty bound to move from the implicit postcoital bliss of "In my arms, rest complete" to the obligatory pledge of fidelity: "If you ever leave me how my heart would ache."

1912

Mother Machree
Lyrics by Rida Johnson Young, music by Chauncey Olcott and Ernest R. Ball

Long forgotten Rida Johnson Young deserves a better fate, if only because she wrote the book and lyrics for what we usually call "Victor Herbert's *Naughty Marietta*." Although songwriting was very much a man's business, Young was not the only woman to write important songs in the early days of Broadway and Tin Pan Alley. Among the others were Carrie Jacobs Bond, the first professional woman songwriter, whose titles include "I Love You Truly" (1901) and "A Perfect Day" (1910), and former actress Dorothy Donnelly, who wrote the lyrics to Sigmund Romberg's music for *The Student Prince* (1924).

Working on *Barry of Ballymore*, Young needed a song for songwriter–performer Chauncey Olcott ("My Wild Irish Rose," 1899). She told an interviewer,

> There kept coming into my mind the picture of a mother I know, a mother who was suffering because the time had come when her boy had another love in his life besides hers …. And so, as I was thinking about this one day, the song came, because of that mother who was so like other mothers, and of that boy who was so like most boys. It happened that the song was Irish, because the play was Irish.

Young later confessed that the song's popularity surprised her. Occasionally a "mother song" makes it, she said, but then she added, "Why poor old Father can't get a look-in on this heart-interest business I don't know …. It seems that Father simply has to be the goat in song, story, play—and often in real life."

"Mother Machree" was a combination Irish song, mother song, and sentimental ballad. It was a classic tearjerker. In a song of praise to an aging mother, a son kisses "the dear fingers so toil-worn for me" and asks for God's blessing on her. Clearly, Young knew her trade; her lyric uses internal rhyme, alliteration, and antithesis effortlessly. She also wrote with a hint of an Irish brogue: "Sure I love the dear silver that shines in your hair."

The Irish began to appear in popular songs soon after they arrived in America, but their early portrayal in a song like "No Irish Need Apply" offered anything but a friendly welcome. By the 1880s, though, they had begun to write songs and perform them on Broadway and in vaudeville. In the early musical comedies of Ned Harrigan and Tony Hart, the popular image of the stereotypical Irishman—physically strong but not very bright, an imaginative liar with a gift of gab, a hard drinker, a brawler, and a weepy sentimentalist—had been transformed into the play's hero. At the same time, songs like "Sweet Rosie O'Grady" (1896), "When Irish Eyes Are Smiling" (1912), and "Peg o' My Heart" (1913) portrayed Americanized colleens as pure and open-hearted, feisty and independent.

My Melancholy Baby
Lyrics by George Norton, music by Ernie Burnett

In the years before World War I, songs were often about young lovers trying to spend some time cuddling close. The new conversational style made lyrics sound like extensions of everyday talk. Many songs were seductive even though the tone was playful rather than passionate. Although they seemed to belong more on the vaudeville stage than in the boudoir, there is no mistaking their sexual intentions. What keeps them from becoming erotic, among other things, is their use of childlike language (such as in "Cuddle Up a Little Closer": "Like to make you comfy cozy 'cause I love from head to toesy, lovey mine"), comic hyperbole (in "Put Your Arms Around Me": "When you look at me, my heart begins to float / Then it starts a rockin' like a motor boat"), or their echo of the sentimental ballad (in "My Melancholy Baby": "All your fears are foolish fancy, maybe / You know, dear, that I'm in love with you").

Of these three well-known cuddling songs, "My Melancholy Baby" is the most interesting because of its young man's capacity for empathy. Because the girl is so sad, he invites her to sit close. In the song's most suggestive line, given emphasis through alliteration, he first tells her that her fears "are foolish fancy." You have only to imagine the look she gives him to understand why he immediately adds, "maybe." The word adds a touch of comic realism. Eventually, she sits beside him to cuddle as he attempts to woo her gently ("Come on and smile, my honey dear, while I kiss away each tear") and then concludes with a lyrical twist that appeals to her capacity for empathy: "Or else I shall be melancholy too."

When the song first appeared, it was called "Melancholy," with lyrics by composer Ernie Burnett's wife, Maybelle E. Watson. When it was published again the next year as "My Melancholy Baby" with new lyrics by George A. Norton, it became an enormous hit.

Composer Ernie Burnett fought in World War I and was wounded on a battlefield in France. When medics found him, he had lost his dog tags and did not know who he was. A total amnesiac, he was placed in a field hospital. When his dog tags were found near other bodies, it was assumed he was dead. A piano player entertaining the wounded at the hospital noticed Burnett's name on the daily report of soldiers killed in action. He announced to the wounded the sad fact that the composer of "My Melancholy Baby" had died and then played the song in his memory. When Burnett heard the melody, he sat up and shouted, "I wrote that song," as his memory suddenly returned.

Waiting for the Robert E. Lee
Lyrics by L. Wolfe Gilbert, music by Lewis F. Muir

A few days after he savaged Lewis F. Muir and Edgar Leslie's "When Ragtime Rosie Ragged the Rosary" in a newspaper review, L. Wolfe Gilbert ran into Muir. "It's easy to criticize," Muir said. "Maybe you can write a better song by yourself." Gilbert replied, "If I couldn't, I'd quit." They wrote two songs that night, a summertime love ballad and a chorus for a Dixie song, and took them to music publisher Fred Mills. Mills was unimpressed, saying of the love song, "It stinks," and then he told them Dixie songs were passé, offering Gilbert copies of the kinds of songs his firm published. Gilbert left in a rage before realizing he had not taken them with him. When he went back, Mills told him he could not get the Dixie song out of his mind. A few weeks later, Al Jolson introduced it, and it became, along with "Alexander's Ragtime Band," one of the biggest ragtime hits.

Music historian David Ewen wrote, probably incorrectly, that Gilbert got the idea for the lyrics after watching black men unload freight from a Mississippi riverboat, the *Robert E. Lee*, at Baton Rouge. Most of these Jewish songwriters, born in Eastern Europe and living in Manhattan, had never been south of the Battery. Gilbert did not know, for instance, that there were no levees in Alabama, but he still wrote about "waitin' on the levee" for the *Robert E. Lee*.

The rest of the lyric is no more accurate, although it is certainly more troubling. The problem, as with all the best "coon songs," is that despite its demeaning racial attitudes, it is hard to keep from tapping your toes, especially when most of the people in the song seem to be having such a good time. The black workmen described in the first lines pass the time as they await the arrival of the riverboat, singing and dancing without weariness or resentment. At the same time, a black family ("There's Daddy and Mammy, and Ephraim and Sammy") joins them in the moonlight to shuffle to the syncopated twang of the banjos. Meanwhile, their white "betters" watch the "shufflin' throng." The call goes out to "take your best gal, your real pal / Go down to the levee" for the show that will probably continue until the riverboat arrives. Then the backbreaking labor of loading bales of cotton will begin.

America's sense of humor in the late nineteenth and early twentieth centuries was certainly racist from our perspective. Epithets and insults were common. Many songs used a word like "darkie" unselfconsciously and even affectionately. Although "coon songs" eventually passed from the scene and racial attitudes began to change, especially during the Great Depression, "Waiting for the Robert E. Lee" and other songs like it remained popular. Over the years, major performers began to sing it and other "coon songs" straight—that is, without the use of broad dialect. Eddie Cantor first sang it as a child performer in vaudeville and later as an adult, this time in, of all things, a southern Yiddish accent. Fred Astaire and Ginger Rogers danced to it in *The Story of Vernon and Irene Castle* (1939), their last movie together for RKO; Benny Goodman swung it; and Bing Crosby crooned it, but in 1940, Louis Jordan became the only significant black performer to record it.

When I Lost You; When the Midnight Choo-Choo Leaves for Alabam'
Lyrics and music by Irving Berlin

Irving Berlin married Dorothy Goetz in February 1912. She was twenty and the sister of songwriter E. Ray Goetz, best known as one of the lyricists for "For Me and My Gal." She and Berlin met when she went to his office to find a song. When another female performer tried to take the one she wanted, Dorothy slugged her. They swapped punches like a couple of prizefighters. Berlin said, "I had dreamed of people fighting for the right to sing my stuff, but this was the first time I saw that dream come true." He gave the song to the other singer but asked Dorothy for a date. They went to Havana on their honeymoon, where Dorothy contracted typhoid; she died five months later. Berlin was devastated, and Dorothy's brother took him to Europe to help him recover.

When they returned, Berlin tried to write some of his jingly ragtime songs, but the results were, in Edward Jablonski's words, "all limp and sorry." Instead, Berlin poured his anguish into a slow waltz that became his first important ballad: "When I Lost You." Although it lacks the ease and surprising sophistication of his later work, as in his finest songs, its simplicity is the source of its lucid emotionalism: "I lost the sunshine and roses, I lost the heavens of blue, / I lost the beautiful rainbow, I lost the morning dew." It was the only song he ever admitted reflected his own life. In his biography of Berlin, Alexander Woollcott wrote, "He had to write the song. It gave him his first chance to voice his great unhappiness in the only language that meant anything to him."

Once he had written "When I Lost You," Berlin could truly return to his work. His next song was "When the Midnight Choo-Choo Leaves for Alabam'," an ebullient ragtime song whose opening measures are reminiscent of plantation and minstrel songs. It portrays a black man about to leave a northern city to return home "when the midnight choo-choo leaves for Alabam'." The repetition that follows expresses his eagerness: "I'll be right there, I'll be right there." At a time when blacks were fleeing the South in record numbers, it is hard to understand why any would return, even if his "honey lamb" was waiting for him. To get back, he would still have had to ride in a separate railroad car. As playwright George S. Kaufman quipped, the train actually left at 12:19 a.m., and all the songwriters got off in Newark.

You Made Me Love You
Lyrics by Joseph McCarthy, music by James Monaco

Ask people of a certain age, "Who sang 'You Made Me Love You'?" and they invariably say Judy Garland. Most of them possess an indelible mental image of Judy in medium close-up, eternally young, writing a fan letter to Clark Gable and going gaga over his photograph. She made the song her own, partly by singing a new introductory verse, "Dear Mr. Gable," written by MGM arranger Roger Edens.

Nevertheless, "You Made Me Love You" was already twenty-five years old when Garland performed it and had originally been sung by Al Jolson. James Monaco wrote it as a ragtime song, but Jolson's initial recording slowed the tempo and transformed it into a bravura ballad. It was also the song in which he first dropped to one knee, to belt out the line "Gimme, gimme what I cry for." Jolson loved to spread the story that he went down on his knee because he had a painful ingrown toenail and then decided to keep doing it because the audience responded enthusiastically. Actually, he borrowed the gesture from another performer.

Even without its original ragtime syncopation, the song lends itself to the belting styles of Jolson and Garland. Though the opening use of the title line is almost matter of fact, the melody's reliance on a strong, insistent beat and the lyric's use of repetition intensify the mood until it becomes an outpouring of accusation and need. Each time the title line reappears, it emphasizes the word "made" to underscore the song's childishly helpless point of view. Perhaps that inherently childlike character of the song first appeared in Garland's rendition.

1914

Play a Simple Melody
Lyrics and music by Irving Berlin

Although Irving Berlin had established himself as Tin Pan Alley's "ragtime king," he had yet to write a score for a Broadway musical. Broadway scores were usually written by such classically trained composers as Victor Herbert for operettas in the Viennese tradition of Strauss and Lehár. They seldom produced hit songs, but their scores were considered superior to the wares of Tin Pan Alley.

Thus, when producer Charles Dillingham invited Berlin to write the score for a Broadway show, the self-taught, musically illiterate songwriter saw it as a breakthrough: the first time Tin Pan Alley made it to Broadway. The show, *Watch Your Step*, stretched Berlin's musical and lyrical muscles as he brought ragtime dance music to the Broadway stage. In "Ragtime Opera Melody," he "ragged" Verdi and Puccini with intricate parodies. He also wrote "Play a Simple Melody," the first of what he called his "contrapuntal" songs: duets in which two melodies, with two different sets of lyrics, are sung simultaneously. One singer yearns for "some simple melody / Like my mother sang to me," while the other demands, "Won't you play me some rag? / Just change that classical nag / To some sweet beautiful drag."

Berlin always said that the opening night of *Watch Your Step* was the greatest thrill of his life. He escorted his mother to the theater, and during the encores the audience called him to the stage with cries of "Composer! Composer!" *Watch Your Step* helped further George M. Cohan's campaign to "Americanize" the Broadway musical. The orchestras featured saxophones and banjos instead of violins, and Berlin's ragtime score provided audiences weary—and wary—of Germanic operetta with a jaunty American alternative.

St. Louis Blues
Lyrics and music by W. C. Handy

William Christopher Handy grew up listening to what he termed the "sorrow songs" of blacks up and down the Mississippi, but his father, a minister, frowned on blues. Handy received a classical musical education and performed with his band across the South, but white audiences asked him to play "his" kind of music. By inserting "flatted" minor notes into major-key melodies, Handy could create the feel of the blues in his renditions of popular songs.

Handy wrote his first original blues as a campaign song for the mayor of Memphis and then sold it for $50 to a music publisher after renaming it "The Memphis Blues." The publisher hired George Norton, who had written the words to "My Melancholy Baby," to add a lyric, and "The Memphis Blues" became the first successful blues song to reach the general public—even though Handy reaped none of its profits. From then on, he decided to publish his own songs.

Handy found inspiration on Memphis' Beale Street when he heard a woman from St. Louis complain about her cheating lover: "Stumbling along the poorly lighted street, she muttered as she walked, 'My man's got a heart like a rock cast in the sea.'" For "St. Louis Blues," Handy followed the AAB pattern of twelve-bar blues, in which an initial four-bar phrase is repeated with a slight variation in the music and words before a second four-bar phrase varies and completes the musical and lyrical idea:

(A) I hate to see de ev'-nin' sun go down,
(A) Hate to see that evenin' sun go down,
(B) 'Cause my baby, he done lef' this town.

In other sections of the song, however, Handy broke into a tango rhythm that he believed Moors brought to Spain and black slaves carried to America. Despite its unusual form, "St. Louis Blues" was an enormous success that established Handy on Tin Pan Alley and brought the "blues" into America's cultural mainstream. Sophie Tucker's recording in 1917 was the first blues to sell a million copies, and Bessie Smith sang it in her only film performance, a 1929 sound short entitled *St. Louis Blues*. In the fifty years after it was written, "St. Louis Blues" was the second most frequently recorded song in America—after "Silent Night."

They Didn't Believe Me
Lyrics by M. E. Rourke, music by Jerome Kern

Although "They Didn't Believe Me" was only an interpolation into the forgettable musical, *The Girl from Utah*, it became for the next half century the model for what a musical comedy love song should be. What is wondrous about it is the natural ease it still radiates after nearly a century. Its melody has an irresistible open-heartedness to which lyricist

M. E. Rourke (writing as Herbert Reynolds) fit words that sketch a pledge of affection and the dramatic complication that necessitates it.

Two lovers affirm the permanence of their love and their determination to marry. The song's drama lies in their mutual pledge, expressed against a background of skeptical family and friends. The lyric begins in the middle of a conversation to underscore the distress they feel because they have been unable to convince others of their mutual affection. The moment is especially touching because the song's melody is so direct and the first part of its lyric so persuasive. Kern's melodic line underlies the song's conversational quality. He is truly writing music to be sung as impassioned talk: "And when I told them how wonderful you are, they didn't believe me. / They didn't believe me."

Although the lyric's tone ranges from the directness of the title line to the overheated abstraction of the release—"Your lips, your eyes, your cheeks, your hair are in a class beyond compare"—Kern's melody keeps the emotions accessible throughout the song. His closing musical phrases, matched by Rourke's parenthetical lyric, have the feel of real people expressing recognizable emotions: "And when I tell them, For I cert'nly am going to tell them, / That you're the girl whose boy one day I'll be." The song had such a strong effect on a sixteen-year-old Tin Pan Alley song plugger named George Gershwin, when he heard it played at a wedding, that he began to write his music for the Broadway stage, convinced that songs that emanated from the musical theater could be markedly better than the average run of popular songs.

1915

I Love a Piano
Lyrics and music by Irving Berlin

Although Irving Berlin loved the piano, he could barely play it. He had taught himself to play when he worked as a singing waiter in a Chinatown saloon, and, like many neophytes, he gravitated toward the black keys. Eventually he learned to play in the key of F#, an unusual key for composition and singing, but one that featured primarily the black keys on the piano. Like many Tin Pan Alley songwriters, Berlin purchased a "transposing" piano (he called it his "Buick") so that, with a flick of a lever, he could continue to play in F# but hear how a tune sounded in other keys.

Even though he could not read music, Berlin heard melodies as well as harmonies in his head. When he had worked out a song, he would play it for his musical secretary, who would then take it down in musical notation

Irving Berlin. Courtesy of Photofest.

and laboriously play chords for Berlin, who would listen until he heard the chord that matched the one in his musical imagination.

"I Love a Piano" clearly expresses Berlin's love for his musical "Buick," as he gave a ragtime twist to the title line by crunching the three syllables of "pi-a-no" over two notes, so that the phrase comes out "I love a *pyan*-o." His love for the instrument takes a rather suggestive turn when he calls it a "baby" grand and lovingly talks of running his fingers "o'er the keys" while "with the pedal / I love to meddle." At the climax of the song, the very letters of the word elicit an ecstatic ejaculation: "Give me a P-I-A-N-O! Oh! Oh!"

1916

Poor Butterfly
Lyrics by John Golden, music by Raymond Hubbell

The first large numbers of Chinese landed in California to build the transcontinental railroad. An early song like "It's the Chinese, the Chinese, You Know" (1883) depicted them viciously: "For a crying disgrace is this abominable race, / It's the Chinese, the Chinese, you know." Before long, though, they began to look more appealing in such "Oriental" songs as "Chinatown, My Chinatown" ("Dreamy, dreamy

Chinatown, almond eyes of brown …," 1910). It was Tin Pan Alley's way of domesticating the mysterious East and transforming its sons and daughters into acceptable stereotypes. Nearly all the songs created a staccato effect by using parallel fifths, along with flowing melodies and bass chords, to simulate Asian music.

As the Japanese also began to immigrate, Tin Pan Alley turned its attention to them in such songs as "Poor Butterfly." Raymond Hubbell and John Golden wrote it for *The Big Show*, an extravaganza that featured ballet, ice skating, elephants playing ball, a giant minstrel show, and "Poor Butterfly." Producer Charles Dillingham wanted an Oriental number because he had arranged for a famous Japanese soprano, Tamaki Miura, to sing it. Puccini had called Miura the "ultimate Madame Butterfly," so Hubbell composed a typically phony Japanese melody inspired by the success of Puccini's opera, and Golden borrowed from a Westerner's idea of Japanese poetry ("Poor Butterfly, 'neath the blossoms waiting") that soon descended into Tin Pan Alley mawkishness ("But if he don't come back, then I'll never sigh or cry, / I just must die").

Unfortunately, Dillingham's deal with Miura fell through, so on opening night a Chinese–American vaudevillian introduced the song but was so bad that Dillingham replaced her with an American soprano, thus dropping all pretense to ethnic authenticity. Two months later, thanks to recordings by such artists as Francis Alda, Fritz Kreisler, Joseph C. Smith and His Orchestra, and the Victor Military Band, the country, in John Golden's words, "was 'Butterfly' mad." It might have been an unlikely song for survival, but singers with a wide range of styles have performed it since, from Sarah Vaughn to Vicki Carr, from Julie Andrews to Carmen McRae.

Pretty Baby
Lyrics by Gus Kahn, music by Tony Jackson and Egbert Van Alstyne

The story of the composition of "Pretty Baby" reads like an overplotted mystery, but remains a cautionary tale about the shady deals that regularly occur in American popular music. It is Egbert Van Alstyne's most famous song, but black ragtime pianist Tony Jackson is, without doubt, the song's original composer. According to Gus Kahn's son, Donald, Van Alstyne and Kahn first heard Jackson's song in a black nightclub in Chicago, although it was performed at a much slower tempo and was called "Jelly Roll Rag." A representative of the Shubert Brothers soon bought it from Jackson for $250 to use in the newest edition of the Shuberts' annual revue, *The Passing Show*.

Because Remick Music paid the Shuberts an annual fee to publish all their show tunes, the producers turned it over to the publisher, who in turn gave it to Van Alstyne and Kahn to rewrite. The Shuberts did not like the song's half-spoken verse or its bawdy lyric. Kahn cleaned up the words in a charmingly indirect lyric that relied heavily on the flirty repetition, "pretty baby, pretty baby." Meanwhile, Van Alstyne replaced Jackson's melody for the verse with his from a song he had written in 1915, "I Love to Tango with My Tea," because it fit the chorus and because there was no time to write new music. If Van Alstyne stole from anyone, it was from himself. It is probably fair to say that Jackson and Van Alstyne each wrote half of a substantially new song called "Pretty Baby."

What was bawdy in Jackson's lyric now begins as a bit of innocent teasing by a boy who falls for a girl because she is child-like. He is serious about her, but may not be sure how serious she is about him, especially when she complains about his teasing. He feels compelled to explain: "I really thought that I was pleasing you, / Oh you're just a baby to me." Although his explanation in the verse soon gives way to his profession of love in the chorus, the teasing remains light and effortless. Even though he is talking about how much he loves her, he tries to conceal the depth of his feelings so he does not scare her off: "Oh, I want a loving baby and it might as well be you, pretty baby of mine."

1917

For Me and My Gal
Lyrics by Edgar Leslie and E. Ray Goetz, music by George W. Meyer

"For Me and My Gal" is a charming little song, set on a wedding day, in which a groom idyllically imagines building "a little home for two or three or four or more, in Loveland, for me and my gal." Yet even though it is a generic song, the setting and the dream would have lent it a trace of poignancy when it was first sung during World War I, as they did when it was reprised by Judy Garland and Gene Kelly in the movie of the same name in 1942.

Until he published his first song, composer George Meyer was working as a bookkeeper in New York. With the song's success, he could marry Grace, his childhood sweetheart, an Irish girl who agreed to be married by a rabbi. "And what was your mother's name?" the rabbi asked. "Emma Jane O'Brien," Grace answered. George and Grace then had to be married at City Hall. "For Me and My Gal" soon became Grace's favorite song, so much so that Meyer had the title inscribed on her tombstone.

(Back Home Again in) Indiana
Lyrics by Ballard MacDonald, music by James Hanley

Returning to all that is precious—home, family, beloved—is as old as *The Odyssey*. Thus, there was nothing new about the idea when it became one of the central themes of American popular music after the Civil War, continuing into the 1920s and beyond. Though popular music has always been devoted to individual emotion, these songs also used a vividly drawn sense of place to create atmosphere. You discern it, for example, in Paul Dresser's hushed, elegiac, "On the Banks of the Wabash" (1895), in which the singer, who realizes he will never return to Indiana, recalls "the breath of new mown hay ... on the banks of the Wabash far away."

In the twentieth century, songs developed an expansive imagery of the American landscape as millions of people left the farm and village for the city and transformed the countryside into a lost paradise they longed for in a thousand popular tunes. James Hanley and Ballard MacDonald's "Indiana" also had a keener sense of longing when it was new because thousands of young men were at war in France, missing home, and eager to return. Yet Clayton Henderson, Paul Dresser's biographer, rightly calls "Indiana" a "shameless" borrowing. Dresser's lyric reads, "Thro' the sycamore the candle lights are gleaming"; MacDonald's is "The gleaming candlelight still shining bright through the sycamores." Dresser writes, "From the fields there comes the breath of new mown hay," and MacDonald follows along, "The new mown hay sends all its fragrance." Much of Hanley's melody also makes only small changes in what Dresser had composed.

"Indiana" is a good jaunty song, but "On the Banks of the Wabash" is one of our most deeply felt elegies. It's also the state song of Indiana, although most Hoosiers are unfamiliar with it or Paul Dresser. Ask them their state song and they will probably start to sing in a lively tempo: "Back home again in Indiana ... ."

Over There
Lyrics and music by George M. Cohan

George M. Cohan, an Irishman, a New Yorker, and a patriot, tipped his derby hat over one eye and strutted down Broadway as if he owned it. In the years before 1920, he was one of the first to free lyrics from the formal style and grand rhetoric of the nineteenth century. He made his songs slangy and that made them feel up to date. By 1917, he had long since learned to take the advice he once gave his protégé, young Irving Berlin, "The words must jingle, Irvy, the words must jingle." The night after Woodrow Wilson signed the declaration of war on Friday, April 16, 1917, Cohan closed himself in his study. When he emerged early Sunday morning, he had finished writing, "Over There," one of the most martial of our patriotic songs. It is also one of the jingliest.

His daughter Mary recalled that Cohan gathered his family in the living room to hear the new song: "We all sat down and waited expectantly because we loved to hear him sing. He put a big tin pan on his head, used a broom for a gun on his shoulder, and he started to mark time like a soldier" as he sang the famous opening call to action, "Johnnie, get your gun, get your gun, get your gun." Soon he was marching around the room, swinging his arms, and singing at the top of his lungs.

It is surprising that the family was not up on its feet, marching along. From the insistent march rhythms of the melody to the tight, sharp repetitions and packed rhymes of the lyric, this is a song designed to stir the heart and get the feet moving. "Over there," the chorus begins and then repeats, "over there." "Send the word, send the word," it continues, and then returns to the title to finish the second line, "over there." As the patriotic sentiments advance in two- and three-word bursts, Cohan completes the chorus by returning to his title yet again, this time spinning off a second definition of "over" to confirm his—and America's—determination: "And we won't come back till it's over over there."

Till the Clouds Roll By
Lyrics by P. G. Wodehouse, music by Jerome Kern

Between 1916 and 1918, the trio of Guy Bolton, P.G. Wodehouse, and Jerome Kern created a series of shows that virtually invented the modern American musical comedy. Because they staged most of them at the tiny Princess Theatre, they had to rely on the material to carry the show, rather than large chorus lines, big production numbers, and elaborate sets common to major Broadway productions. They used an eleven-piece orchestra (instead of the usual thirty to forty musicians); a sixteen-member chorus (some operettas featured ninety singers); two sets instead of the usual dozen; and contemporary characters (so they would not need expensive period costumes). The songs and stories dealt with modern American life rather than the "Ruritanias" of Viennese operetta, and mark the first serious attempt to write more or less integrated musicals with recognizable, contemporary characters who possessed verbal wit, the language and attitudes of the moment, and a light but insistent sexual eagerness.

The three-way collaboration began in 1915, when Wodehouse attended *Very Good Eddie*, a musical written by Bolton and Kern. After the show, Wodehouse praised Kern's music and Bolton's libretto, but said he thought Bolton's lyrics could stand improvement. Kern and Bolton pressed Wodehouse to join them as their lyricist, but writing lyrics seemed impossible to Wodehouse. Schooled in the tradition of Gilbert and Sullivan, where words came first, Wodehouse was dismayed to learn that in American songwriting the music usually did.

Nevertheless, he agreed to "have a go" at such an unorthodox method of collaboration and soon found that its constrictions opened up new possibilities for him. When the music came first, the notes created an irregular pattern that invited more colloquial, conversational lyrics rather than metrically regular poetry. It also opened up more subtle rhyming possibilities than the thumping end-rhymes of verse. Wodehouse's lyric for "Till the Clouds Roll By," the most popular of the songs he wrote with Kern, starts out with a perfectly vernacular expression that contains a clever rhyme: "What bad *luck!* It's coming down in *buckets.*" "Jerry generally did the melody first, and I put words to it," Wodehouse explained. "If I write a lyric without having to fit it to a tune, I always make it too much like a set of light verse, much too regular in meter. I think you get the best results by giving the composer his head and having the lyricist follow him."

In joining his talent to Kern's, Wodehouse found a partner with the most rigorous standards of artistic perfection. Early in his career, Kern disciplined himself to write a song a day, and when he was finished, he gave it one final acid test by using the eraser end of a pencil to tap out only the notes of the melody on the piano without the harmonic embellishments. Together, Wodehouse and Kern brought simplicity and sophistication to the American musical theater as they wove their songs into the fabric of characters and dramatic action.

The collaboration of Bolton, Wodehouse, and Kern lasted only a few years, yet their shows inspired young composers and lyricists. When a mutual friend introduced the sixteen-year-old composer Richard Rodgers to the twenty-three-year-old lyricist Lorenz Hart, Rodgers was overwhelmed by the gnome-like figure attired in tuxedo pants and a bathrobe, who launched into a diatribe against Tin Pan Alley lyricists who knew nothing about slant rhyme, eye rhyme, feminine rhyme, or any rhyme more complex than "slush" and "mush." Only P. G. Wodehouse was exempt from Hart's scorn, and when he put a song by Wodehouse and Kern on his Victrola, he found that Rodgers shared his love of the Princess Shows, and their collaboration was settled. "I left Hart's house," Rodgers said, "having acquired in one afternoon a career, a partner, a best friend, and a source of permanent irritation."

1918

After You've Gone
Lyrics by Henry Creamer, music by Turner Layton

Henry Creamer had previously collaborated with such important figures as Bert Williams, James Reese Europe, and Will Marion Cook, and he considered himself a man of the theater. Fifteen years his junior, Turner Layton was a talented piano player who wanted little more than to turn out hits. It is not surprising that their collaboration lasted only a short time, yet in their six years together, they wrote more than sixty songs, including their most important hit, a syncopated number called "After You've Gone."

Strangely enough, the last place "After You've Gone" became popular was New York City. In 1916, a musical called *So Long, Letty* had a so-so run on Broadway before beginning a successful road tour. Eventually, "After You've Gone" was added to the score and became very popular wherever the show played. However, nobody could buy it because the sheet music did not appear for another year. Both Bessie Smith and Sophie Tucker recorded it in 1927, and that finally made it a hit. In a business that usually measures success week by week, it took more than a decade for "After You've Gone" to become a standard.

We usually assume that happy songs will be up-tempo and sad songs slow, but a strange streak runs through our popular music largely before 1930: a batch of melancholy songs that insists on sounding good-natured. In "After You've Gone," the betrayed lover responds with a promise of retribution, set to the bounciest of tunes: "There'll come a time, don't you forget it, / There'll come a time when you'll regret it." Similarly, in "There'll Be Some Changes Made," (Billie Higgins and Ben Overstreet, 1924), a rejected lover vows to transform herself—"Ain't nothin' 'bout me gonna be the same"—and find a new man.

K-K-K-Katy
Lyrics and music by Geoffrey O'Hara

Katherine Craig Richardson, the "Katy" of the title, was a friend of Geoffrey O'Hara's sister, and her parents remembered his writing this song in their living room. O'Hara probably used the stuttering consonants for comic effect and to make the lyric fill out the melodic line: "When the m-m-m-moon shines, over the c-c-c-cowshed, / I'll be waiting at the k-k-k-kitchen door." The song became one of the biggest hits of World War I.

In "Katy's" first verse, a soldier named Jimmy and Katy, "a maid with hair of gold," flirt as he marches by. They agree to meet later that night.

The chorus is the song he uses to court her: "K-K-K-Katy, beautiful Katy, you're the only g-g-g-girl that I adore." Because it was popular during World War I, people thought of it as a song of parting even though its spirits are light and its hopes high. It doesn't mention Jimmy's eagerness to get to France until the middle of the second verse.

"K-K-K-Katy" is one of the few songs of wartime parting told almost entirely from the soldier's point of view. He wants to "see if he could make the Kaiser dance," but he assures her that despite his absence, he'll be thinking of her. The song certainly lacks the sadness we expect from this genre. "K-K-K-Katy" is also a "stuttering song" of a kind that fits the spirit of wordplay so important to lyricists who have to keep reinventing the same emotions with familiar imagery. The gimmick, pun, or turn of phrase that makes a song distinctive meant everything to them. Therefore, "stuttering songs" have lots of cousins in "spelling songs," tongue twisters, and, especially during the war, songs that delighted in fracturing French.

Perhaps the second best known stuttering song is composer Cliff Friend's and lyricist Billy Rose's, "You Tell Her, I S-t-u-t-t-e-r" from 1922. It is about a young man who lacks Jimmy's confidence. He wants to propose but asks the girl's brother to do it for him because he stutters. One of the first successful "spelling songs" goes back to 1915: Theodore Morse and Howard Johnson's "M-O-T-H-E-R" ("A name that means the world to me"). The best known tongue twister from the war years was actually written in 1914 but became a hit in 1917 when Al Jolson recorded "Sister Susie's Sewing Shirts for Soldiers" (R. P. Weston and Hermann E. Darewski). Finally, the doughboys mangled French until it resembled English, most famously in "Mademoiselle from Armentieres" (Edward Rowland and Glitz Rice, 1915), with its unforgettable tag line that turns French not only into English, but into nonsense as well: "Hinky dinky parlez-vous."

Oh! How I Hate to Get Up in the Morning
Lyrics and music by Irving Berlin

Irving Berlin, whose real name was Israel Baline, had emigrated from Russia to the United States in 1893 when he was five years old. Twenty-five years later, in 1918, when he was the most successful songwriter in America, he became a naturalized citizen. Shortly afterward, he was drafted. Stationed at Camp Upton in Yaphank, Long Island, Berlin found the army routine of marching and drilling arduous. An insomniac, he was accustomed to reveling in the nightlife of Broadway, then working long into the night until he was tired enough to sleep.

"There were a lot of things about army life I didn't like," he said, "and the thing I didn't like most of all was reveille. I hated it. I hated it so much

I used to lie awake nights thinking about how much I hated it." Berlin turned his frustration into a song that set words to the insistent call of the bugle: "You've got to get up! You've got to get up! You've got to get up this morning!" The success of "Oh! How I Hate to Get Up in the Morning" also helped Berlin avoid reveille forever. Hearing that the Navy had staged a successful fund-raising show on Broadway, Berlin approached his commanding officer and suggested that, with all the vaudeville and Broadway entertainers at Camp Upton, they put on a similar show for the Army. When General Bell gave him the go-ahead, Berlin said, "But here's the thing, General … I write at night. Sometimes I work all night when I get an idea. And I couldn't do that if I had to get up in the morning at five."

"Why, you don't have to get up at five," said the general. "You just forget about all that."

Berlin wrote and, for the first time, produced his own show, a revue called *Yip, Yip, Yaphank*, with blackface numbers like "Mandy" and spoofs of the *Ziegfeld Follies* with soldiers in drag. The highlight of the show, however, was Berlin, in uniform, singing "Oh! How I Hate to Get Up in the Morning" as two burly fellow soldiers dragged him, bleary eyed and yawning, out of his pup tent. In reality, however, Irving Berlin never had to heed reveille again.

Till We Meet Again
Lyrics by Raymond Egan, music by Richard Whiting

Singer Margaret Whiting said that her father, composer Richard Whiting, "was a shy man who never took his success for granted. And what happened with 'Till We Meet Again' is straight out of a Doris Day movie." With America's entry into World War I, everybody was writing war songs. Whiting and lyricist Ray Egan, both on the songwriting staff at Jerome H. Remick's music publishing company, were working on a number to enter in a war song contest in Detroit. When they finished, Whiting decided Egan's lyrics were too simple and his own little waltz was not stirring enough to win. He tossed the song in the wastebasket. After he had left for the day, his secretary noticed it. She smoothed out the paper, played a few bars, and took it to Remick. The publisher played the song, told the secretary, "Let's not tell Richard," and entered it in the contest. First, though, he changed the title. The secretary told him Whiting and Egan were calling it "Auf Wiedersehen"—an impossible title, given the anti-German sentiment of the day.

"What does that mean in English?" he asked.

"Till we meet again."

"That's it! That's it!"

The song won the contest and went on to become the most popular American ballad of World War I.

Typical of war songs, "Till We Meet Again" contrasts the melancholy of departure with the happiness of safe return in the familiar imagery of tears and smiles, clouds and sunshine. The simple little waltz is a perfect setting for a soldier boy's "whispers" of parting. He may ask her to smile as he promises to return "when the clouds roll by," and even anticipates the "wedding bells" that "will ring so merrily," but nothing can ease the two breaking hearts for now. The lyric is every bit as simple as Whiting feared, but that very simplicity made the song so appealing during difficult times.

1919

Alice Blue Gown
Lyrics by Joseph McCarthy, music by Harry Tierney

A sentimental story about an Irish working girl who marries a handsome millionaire, *Irene* was so successful that it established the pattern of the "Cinderella musical" that dominated musical comedy in the 1920s. Sweet-faced Edith Day was the perfect ingénue to portray a Cinderella described in *Irene*'s title song as "a dainty slip of rare completeness." From the time she sang her first number, the equally sweet and pretty "Alice Blue Gown," Day won the audience's hearts. During rehearsals, she told composer Harry Tierney that she needed a song to establish her character. She reminded him that she had first become known by singing a sentimental ballad, "Little Grey Home in the West," and asked if he could write her a similar number.

Tierney grumbled but eventually sat down at the piano and reversed the melodic line of the opening of "Little Grey Home" until it became, "In my sweet little Alice blue gown." In the lyric he set to the simple waltz, Joseph McCarthy dwelt first on the gown, "with little forget-me-nots placed here and there." The lyric then has her remember those self-conscious days when she "felt ev'ry eye," but also has her reveal that, even then, she had the spunk and self-possession we would soon come to admire, as "in ev'ry shop window I'd primp, passing by." Though the song appeared after the war, its waltz tempo and slightly archaic language ("Then in manner of fashion I'd frown") give it the feel of a sentimental ballad that hearkens back to prewar serenity before the frenzied freedom of the twenties.

Day's life had more than a little Cinderella to it as well, as this kid from Minneapolis found herself the toast of London when she opened in the British production of *Irene*. When she learned that barons and earls planned to honor her at a testimonial dinner, she wanted her father to attend even though he was only a mail carrier back in the States. How was she to introduce him to her new friends? When he arrived, she rose to the occasion. "This is my father," she announced, "an American man of letters."

I'm Always Chasing Rainbows
Lyrics by Joseph McCarthy, music by Harry Carroll

Shooting the breeze at the Friars Club one night, illustrator James Montgomery Flagg remarked to composer Harry Carroll and lyricist Joe McCarthy, "You songwriters are an unpredictable lot. You're up in the clouds one day and lower than all hell the next."

"You know why that is, don't you?" Carroll replied. "We're always chasing rainbows but we never catch up with them."

"Boy," said Flagg, "you've got a song title there. A sure hit!"

Before the night was out, Carroll and McCarthy had written a ballad that became a top seller. McCarthy crafted a lyric that relies on weather imagery and on a series of devices favored by lyric writers: repetition, internal rhyme, and several contrasting observations to express someone's frustration because he cannot find happiness. Even though he chases rainbows, he never catches them. He feels doubly low because "some fellows look and find the sunshine" while he finds only the rain, and "some fellows make a winning some time" whereas "I never even make a gain."

Carroll gets only part of the credit for the song's mournful melody because he based it on Chopin's *Fantasie Impromptu in C Sharp Minor*. That kind of wink-and-nudge lifting from the classics is as old as Tin Pan Alley itself. It was so common at the start of the twentieth century that lyricist Will D. Cobb ("Waltz Me around Again, Willie") commented wryly, "It's a wise song that knows its own father."

Filching a song covers everything from gentle borrowing to plagiarism so blatant the composer ends up in court. Probably the most notorious of the lawsuits concerned Vincent Rose, Buddy DeSylva, and Al Jolson's "Avalon," which became a hit after Jolson interpolated it into his 1920 Broadway show, *Bombo*. Its success prompted a lawsuit by Giacomo Puccini, who claimed the tune had been lifted from his score for *Tosca*. Puccini was awarded $25,000 in damages, but the success of "Avalon," to borrow a phrase from the song, continued to "travel on."

A Pretty Girl Is Like a Melody
Lyrics and music by Irving Berlin

Beginning in 1907, the *Ziegfeld Follies* was the most important of the extravagant annual revues that defined Broadway opulence for more than two decades. With their arms extended, their tall headdresses effortlessly balanced, and their spangles in perfect tactical array, the *Follies* Girls would float down glittering white staircases that seemed to descend from Ziegfeld's version of heaven. He designed elaborate production numbers around their costumes and the gracefully aloof but erotic way he taught them to walk. Movie star Paulette Goddard, a *Follies* Girl when she was still a teenager, wrote that in one show, all she had to do was sit on a cardboard moon and smile. She explained that "girls were far more frivolous then because … nothing was expected of them. I could tap but I was never given the chance. Ziegfeld used to say I was a great sitter."

Nothing was ever quite finished for the restless Ziegfeld. Though he had composers and lyricists on his staff, he hired additional songwriters to contribute extra songs. If a song from outside the *Follies* became a hit, he would build a new number around it and insert it to keep the current show fresh and up to date. That is why it was surprising to learn that Ziegfeld had hired one man to write the entire score for the *Ziegfeld Follies of 1919*, even if it was the redoubtable Irving Berlin. By opening night, Ziegfeld had also added a few songs by less talented songwriters, even though Berlin wrote what many theater historians think is the best of all the *Follies* scores.

By 1919, Ziegfeld had long since perfected his vision of the showgirl, but the *Follies* had no theme song until Berlin wrote it. Ziegfeld was planning a number in which tenor John Steele would sing well-known arias from the light classics as the girls paraded by. Although Berlin had finished the score and the show had gone to Atlantic City to be tested, Ziegfeld begged him for one more song. As he showed Berlin the drawings for the showgirls' expensive costumes, he said, "Look at these costumes. I have to have a song; my bookkeeper will kill me." The morning after Ziegfeld's impassioned plea, as Berlin and *Follies* star Eddie Cantor were being pushed along the Boardwalk in a rolling chair, the songwriter hummed a new tune and then sang the words he had written the previous night, "A pretty girl is like a melody …." He paused to ask, "Is this any good, Eddie?" "I don't know," Cantor replied, "but it'll certainly serve the purpose."

Although Berlin wrote the song to praise the showgirls' beauty, he also laid out the melody so that they could walk to its sweeping yet measured rhythms: "A pretty girl is like a melody / That haunts you night and day." Yet the music advances subtly and gracefully, and provides a lovely setting for the lyric's extended simile. First, the pretty girl is like an insistent melody that "haunts you night and day" until, in the end, "you can't escape" because, paradoxically, "she's in your memory." The song evokes the tantalizing ideal of the *Follies* Girl's seductive beauty.

In the same score, Berlin wrote "You'd Be Surprised," a song that was a lot bawdier. It became a signature song Cantor would perform for the next forty years. Though it appears to be a story song about somebody else, it is really Cantor singing about the lecherous innocent he often played. Set to an aptly bouncy tune, Berlin's lyric, writes Laurence Bergreen, "achieved its comic effects through juxtapositions between the unassuming suitor and his outsized passion," someone who "may not look very strong" until "you sit on his knee." At that point, in each of the song's choruses, Berlin uses the same innocent catchphrase to drive home his naughty point.

Swanee
Lyrics by Irving Caesar, music by George Gershwin

If a song became a big enough hit, every songwriter in town would try to cash in on it by crafting a copy that was just different enough. Over dinner with his friend George Gershwin, lyricist Edgar Leslie proposed what he called "an American one-step" so that it would be ready when the enormously popular "Indian" one-step, "Hindustan," began to fade. Gershwin immediately thought of Stephen Foster's "Old Folks at Home," although it was Caesar who eventually came up with the title. They rode the Fifth Avenue bus to the Gershwin family's apartment on 144th Street, working out the song along the way. Instead of India, the lyric would use the kind of southern setting that had been popular since the minstrel shows. By the time they arrived, they had blocked out the lyric and Gershwin had some ideas for the tune.

They finished the song while George's father, Morris, and his cronies were playing poker in the next room. Caesar later said

> In about fifteen minutes we had turned out "Swanee," verse and chorus. But we thought the song should have a trio and for a few minutes were deciding about this addition. The losers in the game kept saying, "Boys, finish it some other time," and the lucky ones urged us to complete the song right there and then. This we did, and old Gershwin lost not a moment in fetching a comb, over which he superimposed some tissue and George while I sang it over and over again at the insistence of the winning poker players.

The song was not immediately successful; in fact, it did not sell at all. However, one night Gershwin accompanied Buddy DeSylva to a party for

Al Jolson, who was in New York briefly during the national tour of his latest show, *Sinbad*. As always, George ended up at the piano, playing every song he had ever written. When Jolson heard "Swanee," he offered to add it to the tour and record it. Before long, it became a hit and went on to become the biggest selling of all George Gershwin's songs.

Even though little about the tune is recognizably "Gershwin-esque," it has drive and humor ("I'd give the world to be among the folks in D-I-X-I-E-ven now / My mammy's waiting for me...."), a surprising key change from F-minor to F-major as it goes from the verse to the refrain, and an unusual sixteen-bar trio that helps extend the music to a full eighty bars. Caesar's lyric adds even greater drive through staccato repetition: "How I love you! How I love you! ... Waiting for me! Praying for me!" When, in the penultimate line, Gershwin writes three consecutive emphatic notes, Caesar matches them to underscore the lyric's story of a young man who vows to return to his southern home: "The folks up *north will see* me no more."

1920 – 1929

1920

I'm Just Wild about Harry
Lyrics by Noble Sissle, music by Eubie Blake

The success of *Shuffle Along* ended more than a decade of systematic exclusion of blacks from the Broadway stage. Backstage at an NAACP benefit in 1920, Eubie Blake and Noble Sissle, one of the few major black attractions in white vaudeville, met the black comedy team of Flournay E. Miller and Aubrey Lyles. Though the two acts were familiar with one another, they had never met because white vaudeville houses never presented more than one black act on a bill. Miller told Sissle and Blake that the only way blacks could return to white theaters with any dignity was through musical comedy and then invited them to write songs for an all-black show.

The foursome put the show together quickly because it was little more than an expansion of their vaudeville acts. They had little money, so they could not afford scenery, costumes, or big-name stars, and they nearly closed before they got to New York. "We didn't have money for nothin'," Blake recalled. "It just seemed that we found everything just when we needed it." When the show reached New York, it was booked in a dilapidated, out-of-the-way lecture hall without a proper stage or orchestra pit. They also salvaged sets and costumes from two recent Broadway flops. Though the costumes still had sweat stains under the arms, they could not afford to have them cleaned.

Shuffle Along tells the story of a mayoral election in which all the candidates but one are corrupt. His name happens to be Harry. More significantly, the show broke the final taboo for black characters by showing romantic love between them. They could be sexually comic or even rambunctiously erotic, but an unspoken rule kept black characters from falling in love. "If anything

29

Sheet music for "I'm Just Wild about Harry." Courtesy of David A. Jasen.

approaching a love duet was introduced in a musical comedy, it had to be broadly burlesqued," recalled black poet and lyricist James Weldon Johnson. "The reason … lay in the belief that a love scene between two Negroes could not strike a white audience except as ridiculous."

Though Blake originally composed "Harry" as a Viennese waltz, Lottie Gee, the veteran performer who introduced it, said for her to make it work, it would have to be an up-tempo one-step. "That cut me to the quick," Blake remembered. "She was going to destroy my beautiful melody. I loved that waltz. Then Sissle went along with her …. 'All right,' I said, 'we'll make it a one-step.'" Sissle and Blake nearly dropped "I'm Just Wild about Harry" from the show because it was not scoring with audiences, but just before the New York opening, they replaced a sick chorus boy with a member of the singing ensemble. When the singer could not follow the dance steps, Sissle explained, "he dropped out of line and with a jive smile and a high-stepping routine of his own, he stopped the show cold."

"I'm Just Wild about Harry" lends itself to such shenanigans. It has the short melodic phrases—lighthearted but thumping on the beat—that were so popular in the 1920s. Its chorus is brief and its point about romantic reciprocity clear: "I'm just wild about Harry and he's just wild about me." Its slangy lyric matches the melody's good spirits as it offers little beyond exuberant abstractions and close rhymes ("The heavenly blisses / Of his kisses / Fill me with ecstasy"), along with a few familiar images of sweetness that border on comic hyperbole ("He's sweet just like chocolate candy And just like honey from the bee"), but the song as a whole is an infectious delight—so much so that it re-emerged in 1948 as Harry Truman's campaign song.

Look for the Silver Lining
Lyrics by Buddy DeSylva, music by Jerome Kern

Buddy DeSylva's father, Aloysius, had been a vaudeville performer whose stage name was Hal de Forest (the English equivalent of DeSylva). When he proposed to the love of his life, her father, the sheriff of Azusa, California, insisted his prospective son-in-law quit show business. Although he complied, Aloysius was determined that his son would be a star. By the age of four, Buddy was doing a song-and-dance routine in vaudeville, but his grandfather insisted he go to school and then enroll at the University of Southern California. There, Buddy and three classmates formed a singing group, "The Hawaiians," accompanying themselves on ukuleles. DeSylva wrote songs for the group, and when two of his numbers —"'N' Ev'rything" and "I'll Say She Does"—caught the ear of Al Jolson with their risqué lyrics, Buddy, while still a sophomore at USC, received a royalty check for $16,000. He promptly quit school and headed for New York, where he was teamed with some of the top composers: first, George Gershwin for the 1919 show *La, La Lucille*, then, in 1920, with Jerome Kern on *Sally*, one of the most successful musicals of its time.

The big hit from *Sally* was "Look for the Silver Lining." It was what was then called a "Pollyanna" song, named after the irrepressibly optimistic heroine of Eleanor Porter's 1913 novel. Pollyana songs were designed to cheer up a despondent heroine by reminding her that romantic gloom would pass away as surely as inclement weather (DeSylva would write another Pollyanna weather song, "April Showers," for Al Jolson in 1921). For "Look for the Silver Lining," one of Kern's most soaringly beautiful melodies, the young lyricist dropped his double entendre style for a simple, passionate lyric filled with long vowels and liquid and nasal consonants:

> A heart full of joy and gladness
> Will always banish sadness and strife.
> So always look for the silver lining
> And try to find the sunny side of life.

Such wholesome sentiments might have suited *Sally*'s star, Marilyn Miller, in her on-stage role; however, they were a far cry from her behavior backstage. One night, when producer Florenz Ziegfeld brought his daughter to meet Miller after a performance, she greeted them by saying, "Hello, you lousy son of a bitch!"

"You've heard me talk about Patricia," Ziegfeld said, pushing his daughter toward Miller in an effort to stem her tirade.

"Yes," Miller shot back, "To the point of nausea." She then shouted, "This piece of crap you call a costume ... you can take it and shove it."

In an effort to placate her, Ziegfeld provided Miller with a new costume every night and had her dressing room redecorated in satin and velvet. Still, nothing would calm the troubled waters of *Sally* during its spectacularly successful three-year run. Jerome Kern told a friend that "it was the only one of his hit shows that he actually hated."

1921

Say It with Music
Lyrics and music by Irving Berlin

Irving Berlin was as brilliant a businessman as he was a songwriter. "Talent and business are wedded in him," quipped lyricist Howard Dietz, "like his words and music." When Berlin started out as a songwriter on Tin Pan Alley, he quickly realized that it was not the composers and lyricists but the music publishers who reaped the most profit from the sale of sheet music because they controlled the copyrights. He soon became one of the most successful music publishers and thus one of the few songwriters who owned the copyrights of his songs.

Shortly after he began writing for the Broadway theatre, Berlin decided not only to become the producer of his own shows but also to build his own theater to mount them. He and producer Sam Harris built a lavish theater on 45th Street near Broadway, which Berlin dubbed The Music Box because it would be devoted exclusively to musical shows. To mount a revue would cost $200,000—three times the normal expense—and tickets cost $4 a seat, an exorbitant price in the early 1920s. Broadway insiders predicted that Berlin and Harris were building a tomb that would bury both men in financial ruin.

To save their investment, Berlin took it upon himself to write songs for a series of annual *Music Box Revues*. For the first, he wanted a song that would dedicate his new theater. In "Say It with Music," he crafted a sumptuous but spare melody of only fifty-two notes. It had just a touch of jazzy syncopation, and lyrics that evoked the classics but in such casual vernacular phrases as "Somehow they'd rather be kissed / To the strains of Chopin or Liszt." He also interwove long vowels—"Say it with music, beautiful music"—and subtle internal rhymes: "A melody mellow played on the cello / Helps Mister Cupid along."

Worried about the soaring expenses of his new theater, Berlin broke a cardinal show business rule by giving a jazz band a copy of "Say It with Music" before *The Music Box Revue* of 1921 opened. The song quickly became popular, so Berlin had to squelch it lest it sound dated when it appeared in the show. Despite doomsday predictions, *The Music Box Revue* of 1921 opened to rave reviews, sold out for months, and earned a profit of $400,000. The Music Box has delighted audiences to this day; it is still regarded as one of Broadway's "charmed houses."

Second Hand Rose
Lyrics by Grant Clarke, music by James Hanley

My Man
English lyrics by Channing Pollack, music by Maurice Yvain

Fanny Brice had a well-tuned ear for dialect and a sharp eye for the ridiculous. She would enter as Camille and sigh, in a rich Yiddish accent, "I've been a bad woman but such good company, *nu*?" Beyond mockery, though, she was attuned to pathos. What matters about the *Ziegfeld Follies of 1921* is Fanny Brice and the two remarkable songs she introduced, one in each act. Rarely has a star demonstrated such bravura versatility in a single evening's performance.

In the first act, Brice did what was expected of her. "Second Hand Rose" is the kind of comic dialect song on which her reputation rested, although it went much deeper into character than the typical shtick and shpritz of ethnic mockery. The song's joke is simple enough. Rose, a Jewish working-class girl from the Lower East Side, has never had "a thing that ain't been used," including the "piano in the parlor" and her pajamas, complete with "somebody else's 'nitials on them." Even her fiancé, Jake the plumber, "had the nerve to tell me / He's been married before." The song's comedy perches atop the darker reality of poverty and loss. Rose's sense of the ridiculous is too highly developed to be pathetic, but she is angry and resentful beneath her resilient resignation.

In the second act, Brice, clad in a plain dress under a streetlight, sang a weary lament forlornly and without gesture. Florenz Ziegfeld had originally intended "Mon Homme" for the French music hall singer, Mistinguett, but soon dropped her. At rehearsal one day, he handed Brice the sheet music and said, "Do you think you can make them cry?" He almost certainly chose the song for Brice because audiences would recognize its parallels to her very public "private" life. People would hear in her anguished confession ("Oh my man, I love him so!") a reference to her husband, gambler Nick Arnstein, who was serving time for stock fraud. They were not wrong. When Brice was onstage singing "My Man," she explained, "in my mind I think of Nick leaving and the tears just come." Determined to impress Ziegfeld at her first rehearsal, Brice appeared in a red wig, black velvet dress, sparkling earrings, and ballroom shoes. Ziegfeld said she looked like a female impersonator. He made her tousle her hair and had someone cut the skirt in half, tear it down the side, rip her stockings, and smear her costume with ashes. "Now," he told her, "sing it."

Channing Pollack's original lyric was a literal translation from the French, but he made it somewhat gentler and more sympathetic to suit Brice. Though the man "beats me, too," Pollack excluded his habit of taking the money she earns. In English, he is her lover; in French, he was her pimp. The carriage trade to which Ziegfeld catered was not looking for such gritty reality at the *Follies*.

The Sheik of Araby
Lyrics by Harry B. Smith and Francis Wheeler, music by Ted Snyder

Projecting smoldering mystery and erotic danger, Rudolf Valentino was the first great "screen lover." When he died in 1926 at only thirty-one, the 80,000 people at his funeral—mostly women—nearly caused a riot. Valentino's appeal was understandable, especially in a more repressed age. His features were sleek and almost feminine, but he also possessed daring, strength, and cat-like grace. In *The Sheik*, he rode across the desert on a great white stallion, and the leading ladies who initially feared him soon melted in his arms.

"The Sheik of Araby," written to capitalize on his popularity, became an overnight hit in the same year as the movie. It portrayed him as a man accustomed to having what used to be called "his way" with women, yet his seductive dominance would eventually lead to the happiest of marriages:

> I'm the Sheik of Araby,
> Your love belongs to me.
> At night, when you're asleep,
> Into your tent I'll creep ....
> You'll rule this land with me.
> I'm the Sheik of Araby.

Composer Ted Snyder had more than a little trouble with the song's melody. "I finally went into the Oriental," he told an interviewer, "and at last completed the song under the title of 'My Rose of Araby.'" Music publisher Harry Waterson suggested that the novel *The Sheik* was worth writing a song about because it had sold two million copies. Snyder "couldn't connect the sheik of the story with my 'Rose of Araby,'" but Waterson "showed the way and a few days after the song was written, the moving picture was announced. So it was an all-round fortunate combination of circumstances which helped to make the song a hit." In fact, like "Alexander's Ragtime Band" before it, it was so well known that it became the source of other songs, particularly a satire, "The Sheik of Avenue B," written the next year by Harry Ruby and Burt Kalmar for Fanny Brice.

1922

Chicago
Lyrics and music by Fred Fisher

After Fred Fisher emigrated to America from Germany in 1905, a black musician in a Chicago saloon taught him to play piano, and the next year he had his first hit, "If the Man in the Moon Were a Coon." He never lost his accent, but it did not take him long to pick up the rhythm and feel of Tin Pan Alley music and American speech. "Songwriting is a question of sounds, not sense," he told a group of fellow songwriters. "If you create new sounds, you make money. If you can't get new sounds, then you must write with passion."

One of Fisher's best "new sounds" was "Chicago," in which he gave the Windy City an impudent new moniker—"that toddlin' town"—and the label stuck. Fisher's tune was light but insistent, his lyric energetic and slangy. The premise is simple enough: someone who knows the city takes a visitor on a tour: "I'll show you around," he sings. "I love it." What Fisher managed to do was get a musical handle on Chicago in the 1920s, when it was wide open and hot. It was the home of Louis Armstrong and Al Capone, and it oiled itself on murder, sex, and bootleg liquor. Better than anyone else, immigrant songwriter Fred Fisher pegged it as the wicked town that even teetotaling evangelist Billy Sunday "could not shut down."

1923

Who's Sorry Now?
Lyrics by Burt Kalmar and Harry Ruby, music by Ted Snyder

Harry Ruby was a composer who was also good with words. He had a sense of humor and a flair for writing the kinds of tunes that seemed to invite lyrics made of slangy talk. For their Asian ethnic song, "So Long, Oo-Long," (1921), Kalmar, a serious amateur magician, came up with a bit of verbal prestidigitation that Ruby's bouncy notes almost insist upon: "So long, Oo-Long, / How long you gonna be gone." After the triple "ng" in the first six words, each anticipated by open *o* sounds, he flips the "g" to end the line with the alliterative "gonna be gone." It is a simple enough question, but the effortless blending of sound and sense is virtually perfect.

On infrequent occasions, Ruby also worked on lyrics. He and Kalmar wrote the words to a Ted Snyder tune they called "Who's Sorry Now?" A former lover sees that the one he loved is just as miserable as he. Is he sympathetic? Not on your life. The lyric bears witness to the sweetness of revenge. After asking several taunting questions—"Who's sad and blue, who's cryin', too, / Just like I cried over you?"—the lyric draws its self-satisfied conclusion: "You had your way, now you must pay, / I'm glad that you're sorry now."

Snyder once explained the song's origin:

> Well, everybody knows that song crazes go in cycles. All a publisher can do is try to feel what the public may want next. When I saw all those "cry" songs and none of them making the headway I thought they should, it made me feel that they had not hit on the right idea of that type of song. So I tried my hand and was lucky enough to get the right song. It was a number deliberately written to fit conditions which I felt were in the air. I thought the public wanted that kind of song.

1924

All Alone; What'll I Do?
Lyrics and music by Irving Berlin

Irving Berlin had a keen sense for changing tastes in popular music. He had started out when ragtime was the fashion, then, along with the rest of Tin Pan Alley, switched to patriotic songs during World War I. In the postwar years, however, Americans were becoming "consumers" rather than "producers" of music. Beginning in 1910, phonograph recordings vied with the piano as the source of home entertainment, and by the 1920s, a new medium, radio, was presenting songs aimed at the solitary listener, rather than at the group sing-along around the family piano. Americans wanted a different kind of song, something more personal and intimate that spoke to the many young women who were moving from small towns to large cities to work in offices, shops, and the new "department stores." Berlin first sensed this change when his 1921 song "All by Myself," sold more copies of phonograph records than it did of sheet music. He decided that what the public wanted were what he called "sob ballads," intimate romantic songs of sadness and yearning.

While working on *The Music Box Revue* of 1923, Berlin felt the show needed bolstering with an additional song. Part of the charmed circle of the Algonquin Round Table during those years, he showed up at a party thrown by Dorothy Parker with his work-in-progress and several bottles of champagne. Encouraged by fellow Algonquinites Alexander Woollcott and Robert Benchley, Berlin worked out the melody to his plaintive ballad. Rhythmic alterations between three-beat measures of waltz time and two-beat measures of modern dance music gave it the feel of a syncopated waltz.

When he started on the lyric, Berlin took a common catchphrase, "What'll I Do?" and set the first three syllables to the melody's opening triplet. He always claimed that one of the secrets of his success as a songwriter was that he knew how to "vocalize" the triplet by using contractions whose fluid syllables matched its musical lilt. Contractions also gave his lyrics a colloquial sound (as British listeners found when they inquired about the meaning of the word "whattle"). Berlin said he wanted to "syncopate for people's hearts as well as their toes," and in "What'll I Do?" he proudly claimed, "I established the syncopated ballad." "What'll I Do?" was introduced to the American public over the radio, and when Berlin interpolated it into his show, the song made *The Music Box Revue* of 1923 another success.

"All Alone" could not do the same for the next *Music Box Revue,* even though it is one of his finest songs. Berlin was incredibly persistent, with an absolute belief in his ability to get a song right and to recognize it when he had. Although he had completed a draft of "All Alone," he had a lingering sense that it was not quite finished. He had originally written, "All alone, / I am all alone." He struggled with the lyric for days until he made what looks to be one small change. "All alone," he now wrote, "I'm so all alone." The addition of that single contraction followed by "so" sharpened the opening and made the second line intensify rather than merely repeat the first. However, Berlin was also smart enough to underplay the word. The focus needed to remain on "all," on the completeness of the lover's desolation. This opening phrase also leads to the key line that tells the whole story in miniature: "All alone by the telephone, waiting for a ring, a ting, a ling." The rest is elaboration.

The song is also a textbook example of how deftly Berlin could work his title into the lyric: seven times in the course of thirty-two bars of music. His climactic use of the phrase came at the end, where the first two lyrical phrases, "Wond'ring where you are, / And how you are," neatly match the musical phrases, but then, as Gerald Mast points out, in a "syntactic surprise," the third lyrical phrase, "And if you are" leaves the thought—and the listener—dangling until Berlin returns once more to his title phrase: "All alone too."

"All Alone" was also introduced over the radio. Instead of hampering sales of recordings and sheet music (as some old-time Tin Pan Alley publishers had feared from radio's "free" performances), the broadcast prompted the sale of a quarter of a million records of "All Alone" within a month. Berlin promptly interpolated "All Alone" into *The Music Box Revue* of 1924, in which it was charmingly sung by the two stars, across the stage from one another, into telephones. However, this time the song could not save the show, which did poorly compared to the three previous *Music Box Revues* and brought Berlin's series of annual revues at his Music Box theatre to an end.

Indian Love Call
Lyrics by Oscar Hammerstein and Otto Harbach, music by Rudolf Friml and Herbert Stothart

Otto Harbach, born Otto Ables Hauerbach in Salt Lake City to Danish immigrants, went to New York to study literature at Columbia University. As he was riding on a streetcar one day in 1902, he saw a poster advertising Fay Templeton in a new musical. He went to the show and fell in love not only with Templeton but also with musical comedy. Abandoning his hopes to become a literary scholar, he teamed with a young immigrant composer, Karl Hoschna, on a series of musical comedies. Harbach's academic background made him a stickler for literate lyrics; he would have none of the false rhymes or imperfectly matched syllables that were all too common in Tin Pan Alley songwriting at the time. After Hoschna's death, Harbach went on to write successful operettas such as *The Firefly* (1912), with Czech composer Rudolf Friml, and musical comedies such as *Mary* (1920), with Louis Hirsch, which produced an enormous hit in "The Love Nest," a song of marital bliss whose popularity lasted even longer when it became the theme song of the George Burns and Gracie Allen radio and television shows.

In 1924, Harbach teamed with Oscar Hammerstein, a young lyricist named after his grandfather, the opera impresario and theater owner whose lavish ways sometimes left his sons, Arthur and William, in the red. Although he was determined to keep his son away from "the humbug of show business," William still named the boy after his father, but insisted he study law. At Columbia University, Oscar worked on musical productions, some with the young songwriting team of Lorenz Hart and Richard Rodgers. In 1917, he went to his Uncle Arthur, by then an established producer, to ask for a job. Faithful to his brother's mandate that Oscar stay clear of the theater, Arthur refused to help his nephew. However, when William Hammerstein died, Oscar again approached his uncle for a job, and this time Arthur relented and hired him as a stage manager, advising him to learn the craft of playwriting from the wings before he tried writing a script. After a year, Arthur decided his nephew needed more tutelage and assigned him to work with the established lyricist and librettist, Otto Harbach.

Harbach instilled in his young charge the belief that songs in a musical must grow out of character and dramatic situation. Such a commitment to integration was a rarity in the 1920s, yet Harbach and Oscar Hammerstein collaborated with composers Rudolf Friml and Herbert Stothart on *Rose-Marie*, one of the era's few integrated scores. The idea for the show was Arthur Hammerstein's; he had heard about a Canadian carnival where an enormous ice palace was constructed then melted down in a blaze of torches. The producer thought such a spectacular stage effect could be the climax of a musical and dispatched Harbach and Hammerstein on a research trip to Canada. Although the lyricists learned that the story of the ice palace was not true, they concocted a tale about Mounties, Indians, and something never before seen in American operetta: a murder.

Their working methods also differed from the standard practice of creating an operetta; rather than writing the lyrics first, the songwriters followed the Tin Pan Alley formula of writing music first. Harbach recalled how he and Hammerstein would listen as Friml played melodic fragments from "what he called his little sketch book—a book as thick as the Bible." When Harbach and Hammerstein heard something they liked, Friml would develop it into a melody. However, Friml liked to embellish his melody as he played it. "Friml filled the music so full of furbelows and frills that it was difficult to tell what the tune was," Harbach said. Therefore Harbach would get out his violin and play the tune as simply as possible. "This is the acid test," Friml would say, "If it sounds good with Otto playing the fiddle, it's bound to be good!" Although Harbach and Hammerstein would write lyrics to Friml's music, they tried, as Harbach observed, "to put words to it that would sound as though the words had been written first."

The biggest hit from *Rose-Marie* emerged from Harbach's request to Friml for

> … a song in which there would be a phrase, like a call in the mountains. In trying to tell him about that call, I *gave* him that call. We were in his car and he said, "What do you mean by a mountain call?" and I said, "Like you hear in the Swiss mountains—I want something where the voice is coming down."

With its yodel-like phrase "I am calling you-ooh-ooh-ooh-ooh," the heroine of *Rose-Marie* signals her Mountie lover that danger approaches. She sings "Indian Love Call" to warn him, Harbach explained, "to get the hell out of here because they're after you, under the pretense of just singing a song." It was, according to Stephen Citron, "the first truly generic song written as a plot device"—a culmination of Harbach's belief that song must be thoroughly integrated into the plot of a musical and a powerful lesson to the young Oscar Hammerstein, who would go on to further establish the principle of integration in such landmark musicals as *Show Boat* (1927) and *Oklahoma!* (1943).

It Had to Be You
Lyrics by Gus Kahn, music by Isham Jones

"It Had to Be You" is a model of beguiling simplicity, clarity, and directness. You hear it once and you can hum it; you hear it a second time and you have nearly learned the words. One of our most popular standards, it continues to give pleasure more than seventy-five years after composer Isham Jones first banged out the tune in less than an hour. Or so the story goes. For Jones' thirtieth birthday, his wife gave him a baby grand piano.

Within an hour, he supposedly composed four songs, including "I'll See You in My Dreams" and "The One I Love Belongs to Somebody Else," in addition to "It Had to Be You." Three standards in sixty minutes is pretty darned good work.

Kahn's lyric parcels itself out through a series of small increments that tell of the speaker's search for his ideal, his eventual recognition that nobody's perfect, and finally his satisfaction with what he's found. There's an almost blissful acceptance of her crossness and bossiness, of the way she sometimes makes him feel blue. His love makes him faithful, perhaps for the first time. When he finally chooses her, it isn't because she's perfect but because nobody else gave him a thrill. "With all your faults," he tells her in a backhanded compliment, "I love you still." We do not know how it happened; we don't need to. He's fallen head over heels in love, and now comes the more difficult problem of keeping her.

The song's mix of amiability and uncertainty—the amiability in the music and the uncertainty in the lyric—gives it more of an adult point of view than usually found in the 1920s. Typical of its time, it has a lot of close rhyming to fit its short melodic phrases, but it also develops with satisfying, if cryptic, logic.

LADY, BE GOOD!
Lyrics by Ira Gershwin, music by George Gershwin

"Wouldn't it be fun," George Gershwin said to Fred Astaire when they were teenagers, "if I could write the score of a Broadway musical and you could star in it?" At the time, Astaire was dancing in vaudeville with his sister Adele, as he had been since he was five years old. Gershwin was the youngest "piano plugger" on Tin Pan Alley, pounding out the latest songs from Remick Music all day long. When he offered his own compositions to the publisher, he was told "You're here to play songs, Gershwin, not write them."

However, in a few years, both men and their siblings were working on Broadway. George and Ira Gershwin were collaborating on their first Broadway musical, and the Astaires were set to star in it. George Gershwin saw the show, originally entitled *Black-Eyed Susan*, as an opportunity to infuse jazz into the Broadway musical. Initially, the script worried the Astaires with its hackneyed plot, but when Astaire heard the Gershwins' first song for *Black-Eyed Susan*, "Oh, Lady Be Good," his doubts were assuaged. Ira Gershwin had wedded his brother's plaintive, bluesy melodic line to a 1920s catchphrase that implicitly asked a lady to be not good but bad. The song was so enchanting that the show's title was changed to *Lady, Be Good!*

George (at the piano) and Ira Gershwin. Courtesy of Photofest.

The biggest hit to emerge from the show was "Fascinating Rhythm," which reflected the energetic pace of this quintessential Jazz Age musical. The music was part of a composition George had written as "Syncopated City," inspired by the dynamic energy of New York. When he played it for his brother, however, Ira was befuddled by the intricate and irregular melody, its brief rhythmic phrases between sudden, unexpected rests. "What kind of a lyric can I write for that?" he asked, then added, "still, it is a fascinating rhythm." Suddenly he had a title, but it was excruciating work to complete the rest of the lyric. The brothers argued over verbal and musical accents, but Ira managed to find such everyday catchphrases as "What a mess you're making" and "Won't you take a day off," as well as clever rhymes ("I'm all a-quiver" / "shaking like a flivver") that perfectly matched his brother's tricky melody. He always said "Fascinating Rhythm" was "the hardest song I ever had to fit words to."

Another song, a ballad, was cut from the score in tryouts because audience reaction suggested it slowed the show's all-important rhythmic pace. It had started out as the verse for a different song, but both brothers decided it was "a definite and insistent melody" that deserved to be a song in itself. Ira's ability to hear the emotional meaning in an abstract musical melody is nowhere more apparent than in his realization that his brother's melody was about yearning. His lyric describes a young woman's longing to find the man of her dreams, but the character Ira created is no love-struck ingénue. She is a pugnacious woman who is so sure of herself that she speaks of him in the present rather than future tense: "Someday *he'll* come along" but he's already "the man I *love*." The melody is one of George Gershwin's most passionately insistent, employing his characteristic way of beginning a phrase on a rest to give it more ardency. Ira's lyric underscores that ardency with subtle internal rhymes ("S*ome* day he'll c*ome* along") and rich long vowels: "M*ay*be T*ues*day will *be my* g*oo*d n*ews* d*ay*."

After it was cut from *Lady, Be Good!*, "The Man I Love" was placed in another show, only to be cut again. Then it was used in a third show, which never made it to Broadway. "The Man I Love" might have remained at the bottom of the Gershwin trunk of unused songs had not Lady Edwina Mountbatten heard George play it at a party and asked for the sheet music. London orchestras picked it up, the song passed to black jazz bands in Paris, and it quickly became so popular in Europe that it was published in America. "The Man I Love" was the only hit by the Gershwin brothers that did not emerge from the score of a Broadway show or Hollywood musical.

Somebody Loves Me
Lyrics by Buddy DeSylva and Ballard MacDonald, music by George Gershwin

"Somebody Loves Me" marked a turning point in George Gershwin's career. It would be the last time he would write a song for a revue. Instead, he wrote scores for musical comedy "book" shows and compositions for the concert hall. His first orchestral work was *Rhapsody in Blue*, performed by Paul Whiteman's Orchestra at New York's Aeolian Hall on February 12, 1924.

With its bit of syncopation and some unusual melodic intervals, "Somebody Loves Me" represents the last and one of the best of Gershwin's Tin Pan Alley songs. The lyrics by Buddy DeSylva and Ballard MacDonald give a clever twist to a traditional romantic theme. Beginning with the singer's exclamation that "Somebody loves me," they follow up with her befuddled admission, "I wonder who." Throughout the song, she expresses increasing frustration—"who he can be worries me"—and frantically accosts men in the street to find the one she knows, with daft assurance, loves her. The climax of the song comes, in a classic Tin Pan Alley "finish," when she coyly confronts the listener with "Maybe it's you!"

1925

Alabamy Bound
Lyrics by Buddy DeSylva and Bud Green, music by Ray Henderson

If You Knew Susie
Lyrics by Buddy DeSylva, music by Joseph Meyer

Like Irving Berlin's "When the Midnight Choo-Choo Leaves for Alabam'" (1914) before it and Harry Warren and Mack Gordon's "Chattanooga Choo-Choo" (1941) after it, "Alabamy Bound" is a train song and a song about returning home. When Americans, most of them young, left the small towns of the South and Midwest for Chicago and New York, they traveled by train. They reveled in big city life, but they also missed the villages they knew so well. They embraced jazz in Harlem and Bohemia in Greenwich Village, but they also yearned for the more settled life of the farm and countryside. Hundreds of songs expressed these contradictory attitudes, though most of them were about a young man's eagerness to return to the Midwest or South.

The song's title line, "I'm Alabamy bound," tells its theme, and the rest of the lyric is as direct and ebullient. Even the "meanest ticket man," who requires all the young man's money for an upper berth, cannot dampen his spirits. The train whistle tells him he will soon "cover ground"; all that remains is the exuberant holler, "Here I go / I'm Alabamy bound." Ray Henderson's tune has a driving train-like rhythm, and Buddy DeSylva and Bud Green's lyric revels in up-to-date slang. It parallels the young man's frenetic "heebie-jeebies" with the train's "choo-choo sound."

Though Al Jolson introduced the song, it soon became associated with Eddie Cantor, who interpolated it in the Broadway musical, *Kid Boots*. The same thing had happened earlier that year when Jolson introduced Meyer and DeSylva's "If You Knew Susie" in *Big Boy*. Once Jolson decided it did not suit him, he handed it over to Cantor, saying, "Eddie, I think this would fit you better than it does me." Jolson was right. Its naughtiness ("She wears long tresses / And nice tight dresses") was a perfect match for the character of the lecherous nerd that Cantor had perfected by the mid-1920s.

Always; Remember
Lyrics and music by Irving Berlin

"Always" supposedly originated when a young lady named Mona, the fiancée of Arthur Johnston, Irving Berlin's musical secretary, implored the two men to write a song for her. Berlin obliged by humming a melody along with the line, "I'll be loving you, Mona." Johnston dutifully wrote it down. Later, so the story goes, when Berlin was working with George S. Kaufman on the stage musical, *The Cocoanuts*, he changed "Mona" to "always." Kaufman, a cynic about all things romantic, noted that "always" was unrealistic and suggested Berlin change the lyric to "I'll be loving you, Thursday." Berlin did not use the song in the score for *The Cocoanuts*, where it could easily have been lost amid the antics of the show's stars, the Marx Brothers.

Soon, however, he had an excellent reason to return to it. After years of grieving over the death of his first wife in 1913, Berlin began courting Ellin Mackay, daughter of one of New York's most prominent Catholic families. The romance of the immigrant Jewish songwriter and the wealthy socialite was ballyhooed by the press and bitterly opposed by Ellin's father. Inspired by his love for Ellin, Berlin went back to work on "Always," which became one of his characteristically simple, yet intricate, ballads. The standard thirty-two bar chorus has an unusual ABCD structure so that not one of the eight-bar themes is repeated, a musical reflection of the enduring freshness of love pledged in the lyric. That lyric, with its primarily mono-syllabic words, took Berlin nearly two years to complete. Particularly trou-blesome was the closing line, which finally came to him in a single inspired moment: "not for just an hour, not for just a day, not for just a year—but always." Touché, Kaufman!

If "Always" reflects Berlin's ardent courtship of Ellin MacKay, "Remem-ber" registers his fears that her father would succeed in thwarting their romance. He also worked on "Remember" for nearly two years and was very pleased with "the little musical phrase that is coupled with the word 'remember' in the song." The word begins the chorus on a syncopated upbeat so that the waltz rhythm is slightly out of kilter, reflecting the sing-er's emotional consternation. The phrase and word repeat throughout the song, sometimes stretching over an octave and even beyond, always on an unresolved chord. Only when Berlin thought of the final "turnaround" final phrase—"You promised that you'd forget me not, / But you forgot to remember"—did he resolve the chord and complete the song.

The romantic fears expressed in "Remember" dissolved when Ellin forsook her prominent social position to elope with Irving in 1926. When her father disinherited her, Berlin gave her "Always"—and its royalties—as a wedding present.

California, Here I Come
Lyrics by Buddy DeSylva, music by Joseph Meyer

Toot Toot Tootsie
Lyrics by Gus Kahn, music by Ted Fiorito

As Americans became increasingly mobile in the 1920s, they began seeking ways to escape the East Coast's snowy winters. Like an up-to-date Ponce de Leon, they took the train overnight to Florida; like a latter day Balboa, they rediscovered the Pacific. Exploiting this interest in climes suddenly less remote, popular songs began to sound like promotional literature from a palm-bedecked chamber of commerce: "The flowers, the bowers, bloom in the spring. / Each morning, at dawning, / Birdies sing and everything."

The ebullience of "California, Here I Come" made it perfect for Al Jolson, who interpolated it into his 1921 hit, *Bombo*, after it went on the road. Lyricist Buddy DeSylva had told Jolson about his idea for a California song, and Jolson told DeSylva to get composer Joe Meyer to write the music. When DeSylva told Meyer about it, the composer said he went to a piano and "I just sat down and wrote 'California, Here I Come.' It was the greatest inspiration I ever had. Buddy got the song to Jolson, who was nuts about it."

In the same year, Jolson also sang composer Ted Fiorito's and lyricist Gus Kahn's "Toot Toot Tootsie," a song about leaving rather than returning. Instead of anticipating loneliness, its portrayal of parting comes close to being a joke: "Seven times he got aboard his train, / And seven times he hurried back to kiss his love again." The young beau tries to cheer up his beloved by pledging his fidelity but, once again, the song finds humor in the situation: "Watch for the mail, I'll never fail, / If you don't get a letter then you'll know I'm in jail."

Charleston
Lyrics by Cecil Mack, music by James P. Johnson

The New York Times wrote about this new dance craze sweeping the city:

> Debutantes are practicing it at the Colony Club; society matrons are panting over it in Park Avenue boudoirs; department store clerks are trying to master it in the restrooms at lunch hour; the models of the garment industry dance it together in the chop suey palaces at noon time .... Proprietors of employment agencies are being asked to supply cooks, waitresses, laundresses, and maids who can teach their employers to do it.

That same year, somebody else wrote, "Any lover of the beautiful will die rather than be associated with it. It is neurotic. It is rotten. It stinks. Phew. Open the window." The waltz was supposed to bring in social chaos, so was ragtime dancing. Now, so was the Charleston. Its flailing arms and flying knees characterize the most famous dance in American history.

Although black composer James P. Johnson wrote the particular Charleston tune that became *the* Charleston, the dance and its quirky rhythms originally grew up in black cabarets and spread across the country. Johnson first saw its basic step while playing piano at New York's Jungle Casino in 1913. The dancers were mainly longshoremen who had come north from South Carolina to find work on the docks. Johnson said, "It was while playing for these southern dancers that I composed a number of Charlestons—eight in all—all with the damn rhythm. One of them later became my famous 'Charleston' when it hit Broadway."

The Charleston craze did not begin until 1925 when Johnson dug the tune out of his trunk for the score to an all-black revue, *Runnin' Wild*, and Cecil Mack added words. Elisabeth Welch sang it and then chorus boys— known as "The Dancing Redcaps"—danced to it, accompanied by hand clapping and foot stomping that matched the music's complex rhythms. Poet James Weldon Johnson said, "It was the best demonstration of beating out complex rhythms I have ever witnessed; and I do not believe New York ever before witnessed anything of just its sort."

Dinah
Lyrics by Sam Lewis and Joe Young, music by Harry Akst

In 1925, Harry Akst, a thirty-year-old plugger for the Irving Berlin Publishing Company, took the train to Philadelphia where Eddie Cantor was appearing in *Kid Boots*. After the performance, Akst plugged Berlin's new song on a darkened stage lit only by a ghost light. Cantor thought it was simply awful but said only that it was not for him. After they had dinner together, Akst started to noodle around at the piano, eventually settling into a tune.

"Hey, *wait a minute*," Cantor interrupted, "what's that?"

"Oh, just a little thing of my own."

"Well, this I like, this I can do."

"You mean you want me to tell Berlin you don't want *his* song, you want *mine*. And what do I do for groceries?"

Cantor called Berlin the next morning to tell him what he wanted to do. Berlin replied, "Sure, Eddie. If it's Harry's, we'll publish it. Let him stay over as long as you need him to make the orchestration." Cantor introduced the song, "Dinah," that night and by the weekend it had become his finale.

Another performer who promoted the song was Ethel Waters, the first black female singer to succeed in white vaudeville. In the summer of 1924, black singing star Florence Mills left the revue at the Manhattan nightspot called Selvin's Plantation Club. Waters auditioned to replace her and said:

> Harry Akst and Joe Young asked me if I'd try a new one they'd written. And they sang it themselves for me, doing it fast and corny.
>
> "Is that the way you want me to sing it?" I asked ....
>
> "Why not sing it your way?" they said ....
>
> So that day I took the song home and worked on it ... .

When she returned the next day, she used a languorous delivery that gave the song's cute rhymes ("Why do I shake with fright / Because my Dinah might") a sexy edge.

"Dinah" combines a couple of common strains in the songs of the 1920s, including youthful good spirits expressed through playful rhyming and giddy comic hyperbole. Oh sure, a young fellow shakes "with fright" at the prospect that his explosive "Dinah might" leave him, but nobody really believes his promise to "hop an ocean liner" to recapture her.

Manhattan
Lyrics by Lorenz Hart, music by Richard Rodgers

Lorenz Hart and Richard Rodgers began collaborating in 1919, but Broadway producers dismissed their witty, sophisticated songs as "too collegiate." By 1925, Rodgers was so discouraged he considered accepting a job running a wholesale children's underwear business for fifty dollars a week. Jazz Age prosperity, however, enabled more people to attend college. To reach this new "smart-set" audience, the Theatre Guild staged a benefit performance at the Garrick Theatre. At their audition to write the score, Rodgers and Hart demonstrated a new song, "Manhattan," and their listeners flipped.

The audience on opening night called for encores. Then, at the end of the show, Rodgers, who conducted the orchestra, turned around to see everyone

> ... standing and clapping, cheering, yelling, stomping, waving and whistling. I turned back to the orchestra and had the boys strike up "Manhattan." The cast sang it. The musicians sang it.

Richard Rodgers (seated on the desk) and Lorenz Hart. Courtesy of Photofest.

Even the audience sang it. After about ten curtain calls, the house lights went on, but still no one wanted to go.

Afterward, Rodgers encountered Hart, who was "jumping up and down, rubbing his hands together and screaming, 'This show's gonna run a year! It's gonna run a year!'"

"If one song can be said to have 'made' Rodgers and Hart," Rodgers said, "it surely was 'Manhattan.'" Hart's rhymes were complex: "Summer journeys to Ni*agra* and to other places / *Aggra*vate all our cares"; subtle: "*what street* compares with *Mott Street* in Ju*ly*? / *Sweet* pushcarts gently gli*ding by*"; and hilarious: "The city's clamor can never *spoil* / The dreams of a boy and *goil.*" According to William Hyland, "Rodgers humorously claimed that Hart had not really worked on polishing 'Manhattan' but had written it in four minutes and twelve seconds on the back of a dirty envelope."

In a newspaper interview, Hart expressed surprise that a song with such "intricate and elaborate rhymes" was the hit of the show, because "the song hit of a show is usually a very simple one with monosyllabic words." Even more surprising to him was that "Manhattan" had become enormously popular through Tin Pan Alley's sheet-music sales; the music publishers usually made their royalty money from "banal lyrics." Things were clearly changing, however, and by the end of the year *Variety* took official note of a lyrical renaissance. Although lamenting that most popular songs were still "stupidly worded," the editorial singled out the lyrics of Hart, openly comparing him to W. S. Gilbert, but also praised other young lyricists, such as Ira Gershwin. A golden age in songwriting had arrived.

NO, NO NANETTE
Lyrics by Irving Caesar, music by Vincent Youmans

No, No Nanette's beginnings were hardly promising, yet it soon became the avatar of the frothy musical comedies of the 1920s. In the course of its pre-Broadway tryout, producer Harry Frazee replaced the director with himself, fired cast members helter-skelter, and tossed five songs from the score, only to replace them with, among others, "Tea for Two" and "I Want to Be Happy." He hired Otto Harbach to write the lyrics and cowrite the book, but Harbach soon asked for help from lyricist Irving Caesar, a strange match. Harbach made his name by cowriting operetta lyrics with Oscar Hammerstein, but *Nanette* was far removed from princes and bar maids. Caesar, by contrast, was known for writing simple but bouncy lyrics, without frills or reflection.

First Caesar dumped most of Harbach's lyrics and replaced them with words that matched Youmans' punchy melodies with a punch of their own. Youmans and Caesar were working late one night at Caesar's apartment, but Caesar wanted to nap before they left for a party at the apartment of English star Gertrude Lawrence, who would soon become the toast of Broadway by singing Joseph Meyer, Al Dubin, and Billy Rose's "A Cup of Coffee, a Sandwich, and You" in *Andre Charlot's Revue of 1926.* Youmans soon woke Caesar to hear a new melody and insisted Caesar put words to it then and there. Although he later said he thought the tune was "monotonous," the still groggy lyricist let himself be dragged to the piano to write a dummy lyric that he could rework the next morning. He told Youmans, "It stinks," but the composer kept urging him on. In a little more than five minutes, they had a finished song entitled "Tea for Two." "Sometimes I write lousy," Caesar often said, "but I always write fast."

Caesar was dead wrong about his lyric, with its skillful and very 1920s use of internal rhyme, assonance, repetition, and antithesis ("Just me for you and you for me alone") that conjured up two young lovers who anticipate the intimacies of marital bliss. Youmans liked the song so much that he refused to let Caesar change a single word. That may explain why the title line appears only once—in the second line.

After hearing "Tea for Two," Frazee ordered it inserted into the show and told Youmans and Caesar to give him more songs, this soon after he threatened to replace them if they didn't get cracking. He specifically requested what he called a "sunshine" song for a cheerful, girl-chasing, middle-aged man to sing. Though the collaborators were initially stuck, Youmans suggested a title for Caesar to work with. The result, "I Want to Be Happy," relies on permutations of the title line—"I want to be happy but I won't be happy till I make you happy, too"—to link personal happiness with making other people happy as well.

Sweet Georgia Brown
Lyrics by Kenneth Casey and Ben Bernie, music by Maceo Pinkard

Most songs about waiting for someone to arrive are set in the city, often on train platforms. One of the best of them is Maceo Pinkard and Kenneth Casey's "Sweet Georgia Brown." Ben Bernie's name also appears on the sheet music as a co-lyricist, even though he did not write a word; the popular bandleader apparently got an advance look at the song, smelled a hit, and cut himself in.

Pinkard is unique among black songwriters because he worked exclusively with white lyricists. He also differed from such black composers as Duke Ellington, Fats Waller, and Eubie Blake because he was never a performer. Instead, he stuck to writing mainstream popular hits, including "Gimme a Little Kiss, Will Ya', Huh?," "Sweet Man," and "Them There Eyes."

Georgia is clearly black ("No gal made has got a shade on Sweet Georgia Brown"), and nothing is the same once she arrives: "She just got here yesterday, / Things are hot here now, they say." At the same time, Casey fit the lyric to Pinkard's unusually complex melody but, David Jasen writes, the song sounds "as offhanded as an improvisation by an idle whistler." Even people who do not recognize the title will start whistling almost immediately because the Harlem Globetrotters have used it as their theme song for years.

Yes Sir, That's My Baby
Lyrics by Gus Kahn, music by Walter Donaldson

Gus Kahn wrote "Yes Sir, That's My Baby," sitting in Eddie Cantor's living room. Cantor's daughter Marilyn had a toy mechanical pig. After dinner, Kahn sat on the floor with her, winding its tail so that it would waddle across the room. Cantor remembered that it made "a funny whiny noise … when the tail unwound, and the next thing you knew, Gus was making up words to the whine." Relying on incremental repetition, Kahn reduces the title of "Yes Sir, That's My Baby" almost to nonsense as he flips from "yes sir" to "no sir" and back. Then, in the midst of rhyming "baby" and "maybe" six different times, he tosses in an amusing triple half rhyme in the brief second chorus: "Yes ma'am, we've *decided*, / No ma'am, we won't *hide it*, / Yes ma'am, you're *invited* now." When Kahn got his first royalty check, he showed it to Cantor, "Remember that night at your house, Eddie? This is a lot of money for a Jewish boy to make out of a pig's tail."

1926

Blue Skies
Lyrics and music by Irving Berlin

On a December night in 1926, Irving Berlin received a panicky phone call from vaudevillian Belle Baker. "Irving," she said, "I'm opening in a show tomorrow night, and there isn't a 'Belle Baker' song in the score." The show was Rodgers and Hart's *Betsy*, one of the new "book shows" in which songs were woven into the story rather than presented as "numbers" designed for star performers. "I'm so miserable," Baker wailed, "What can I do?"

Berlin resented the interpolation of songs by other composers into the scores of his shows, but he must have been delighted by the chance to work one of his songs into a score by the young songwriting team who were already being compared to Gilbert and Sullivan. "Belle, I'll be very honest with you," Berlin said. "All I have is a song in my trunk. I've often thought it would be great for you, but I never got around to finishing it." Baker pleaded with Berlin to bring it to her immediately: "Even something half-finished by you is better than what I've got now."

When he arrived at Baker's home, Berlin had only the eight-bar A-section of the melody, but because that melody was repeated three times in the song's AABA structure, all he had to do was complete the "bridge." Those eight bars, however, took him all night. Finally, at six in the morning he had it, one of the most brilliant bridges he ever created. The first two A-sections exult over "blue skies" and "bluebirds," but the bridge shifts to a minor key as the singer realizes that "when you're in love" the days go "hurrying by" so that her current happiness may be as fleeting as her recent gloom. The final A-section opens with "blue days," but the "blue" here is the hue of the "blues" rather than "blue skies" and "bluebirds." Although the song ends on a note of affirmation that such blue days are "all of them gone," that lingering melancholy underscores the singer's awareness that her "blue skies" may be as transient as her former "blue days."

Belle Baker took "Blue Skies" to Florenz Ziegfeld, producer of *Betsy*, who had the show biz savvy to recognize a great song. Without telling Rodgers and Hart, he authorized Baker to interpolate it into *Betsy*, and "Blue Skies" stopped the show as the audience demanded encore after encore. On one encore, Baker blanked on the lyric, at which point Irving Berlin, rose from his seat in the audience and belted out the song. Rodgers and Hart were furious at the surprise interpolation, and the success of "Blue Skies" made them feel the failure of their score for *Betsy* all the more keenly.

Bye Bye Blackbird
Lyrics by Mort Dixon, music by Ray Henderson

With its sentiment of returning home, "Bye Bye Blackbird" may reflect Mort Dixon's peripatetic life. The child of stage parents who could trace his ancestry back to the Mayflower, Dixon hit the rails after high school and worked at odd jobs, from zither salesman to pool room manager. One day a bantamweight pool shark named Billy Rose walked into Dixon's pool hall. He wanted to give up his day job as a court stenographer to become a songwriter. Together they sought out a young composer named Ray Henderson and wrote one of the most popular songs of the 1920s: "(Those Wedding Bells Are Breaking Up) That Old Gang of Mine" (1923).

Most of Dixon's songs are period pieces; the exception is "Bye Bye Blackbird," which endures as a universal expression of the longing to pack up all one's cares and woes and return to "where somebody waits for me." With wonderful idioms, Dixon captures the feeling of homesickness in strange surroundings—"No one here can love and understand me, / Oh, what hard luck stories they all hand me"—and the comfort of returning home. In Dixon's simple terms, going back home requires only the ebullient announcement to "Make my bed and light the light, / I'll arrive late tonight."

Someone to Watch Over Me
Lyrics by Ira Gershwin, music by George Gershwin

As George and Ira Gershwin were working on songs for *Oh, Kay!* George created a rhythmic melody that, the brothers agreed, would make a dynamic dance number. Because the book was not yet finished, they decided to hold the song until they knew where it would fit. "Then one day," Ira recalled, "for no particular reason and hardly aware of what he was at, George played the dance tune in a comparatively slow tempo." Suddenly both brothers realized that the melody was not a "rhythm tune but rather a wistful and warm one to be held out until the proper stage occasion arose for it."

Before they could work on it, however, Ira was rushed to the hospital for an emergency appendectomy. Confined to his bed for six weeks, he begged his doctors to release him: "They're waiting for me to finish the lyrics." Meanwhile, lyricist Howard Dietz was brought in to help and contributed a title for the wistful ballad. After trying several phrases to match the seven-note musical theme, Dietz came up with "Someone to Watch Over Me." Ira, who always complained that coming up with a title was the lyricist's most difficult task, snatched up Dietz's phrase and went off to work on the rest of the lyric by himself.

He gave the romantic plea a comic twist by having the heroine carry a torch for a man she has yet to meet: although she has been "lookin' everywhere" for him, she hasn't "found him yet"; still, "He's the big affair I cannot forget / Only man I ever think of with regret." Ira also created subtly clever rhymes such as "he may not be the *man some* girls think of as *handsome*." What is most moving about the song, however, is its combination of brassy aggressiveness—"Won't you tell him please to put on some speed, follow my lead"—and helpless yearning—"Oh, how I need someone to watch over me."

1927

Ain't She Sweet?
Lyrics by Jack Yellen, music by Milt Ager

Nobody ever had more oomph than the flapper, that "hotcha" hoyden from the 1920s, who managed to be dazzlingly feminine even though she appeared to be constructed like a twelve-year-old boy. Nothing says the Jazz Age like the hundreds of songs that reveled in the flapper's pursuit of love, sex, and pleasure for their own sakes—until the Great Depression wiped them away in a single swipe.

None of these songs did more to define the type than composer Ray Henderson and colyricists Sam Lewis and Joe Young's 1925 hit, "Five Foot Two." A young fellow, trying to find his missing girlfriend, describes her to somebody else, but everything he says soon turns to talk about sex: "Could she love, could she woo," he says, as the lyric escalates to the euphemistically climactic, "Could she, could she, could she coo," a line that immediately hits the ear as the silly but suggestive "Cootchy cootchy cootchy coo." Although she isn't "covered" with furs or diamond rings, she's very much "a flapper, yes sir, one of those." Anybody who bobbed her hair, knew the right dance steps, and could slug a little bootleg hooch could be one. The flapper was democratic. She was as self-made as any rags-to-riches millionaire.

Among the most buoyant of these Flapper songs was "The Best Things in Life Are Free" from the 1927 "college musical," *Good News.* Coed Connie Lane is from a lower social class than halfback Tommy Marlowe, so he reassures her that a lot of things make up for a lack of money. "The moon belongs to ev'ryone," he tells her, then adds stars, flowers, robins, and sunbeams to the list. It is not until just before the end that he gets to what is really on his mind: "And love can come to ev'ryone, / The best things in life are free."

Of all these songs, none has lasted longer than "Ain't She Sweet?" Its charm rests on the enthusiasm of a young man watching his sweetie approach and inviting someone confidentially to "look her over once or twice." Like many of the "flapper songs," it is actually a dramatic monologue in which a smitten swain boils over as he repeats the short, ungrammatical title phrase that creates the song's youthful delight. The lyric then contrasts that simple phrase with the few longer words that form its climax without ever losing its slangy drive: "Just cast an eye in her direction, / Oh me, Oh my, ain't that perfection?" Milt Ager was especially fond of the lines, "Now I ask you very confidentially, 'Ain't she sweet?'" with "confidentially" in the midst of all those short words.

Me and My Shadow
Lyrics by Billy Rose, music by Dave Dreyer

Billy Rose was best known for giving another lyricist a title or an odd word, then claiming credit on the sheet music and a share of the royalties. At his best, he was a musical gadfly. Composer Harry Warren said,

> Billy could be cruel, but he was a great feeder. He'd sit with the boys and say, "Now come on, you can do better than that." He'd ask for another line, or he'd come up with a clause himself. He'd make a thrust at a phrase; but he stimulated the real lyricists to produce. Somehow a song would get done but he couldn't easily work without another lyricist.

Of all his songs, Rose's favorite was "Me and My Shadow." Yet even here, somebody unknown approached him with the title. Billy bought it for fifteen dollars and set a crude lyric to it. Then he took it to Dave Dreyer because the young composer knew Al Jolson. Dreyer composed a melody and rewrote the lyric overnight. When he saw it, Rose changed a single word and wrote his name at the top of the page. It was ready to show to Jolson.

Regardless of who wrote what, the lyric relies on one of those conceits so common in popular songs: a witty treatment of solitude that uses one's shadow to provide companionship as a way to ease the pang of being alone, especially in your own bedroom. The effect of the song also lies in how having your shadow as your only companion intensifies the loneliness. The chorus begins innocently but soon reveals the singer's plight: "Me and my shadow, strolling down the avenue / Me and my shadow, not a soul to tell our troubles to."

My Blue Heaven
Lyrics by George Whiting, music by Walter Donaldson

Walter Donaldson first wrote songs as a boy, when he and his sister belted them out on Brooklyn street corners until the neighborhood cop sent them home with a warning about "disturbing the peace." Even though he wrote as deliriously as everybody else in the 1920s, some of his best songs from those years had a tender, wistful quality. He composed simple melodies for lyrics that express the sorrow of missing someone in "My Buddy" (lyric by Gus Kahn, 1922) and the quiet joy of anticipating a loved one's return in "At Sundown" (lyric by Donaldson, 1927). However, even here he relied on the short melodic lines and close rhymes typical of the time: "In a little cottage cozy, the world seems rosy at sundown / Where a loving smile will greet me and always meet me at sundown."

"My Buddy," the first of more than one hundred songs Donaldson wrote with Kahn, marked the start of an important collaboration and lifelong friendship. The song was Donaldson's most personal. At a time when songwriters usually worked within Tin Pan Alley's formulas, the poignant strains of "My Buddy" were an expression of Donaldson's grief at the death of his fiancé, not unlike those of Irving Berlin's "When I Lost You."

Donaldson apparently wrote the melody for "My Blue Heaven," another atypical 1920s song, in the billiard room of New York's famous Friars Club. Vaudevillian George Whiting heard it, wrote a lyric, and introduced it in his act. However, it was not until Gene Austin crooned it that it became an enormous hit. His effortless singing suits the lyric's anticipation of idyllic domesticity. Despite his talk about haste, the song's hero focuses on the more serene joy he will feel when he sees "A smiling face, a fireplace, a cozy room, / A little nest that's nestled where the roses bloom."

Even though many songs in the 1920s were about the new sexual freedom of the young, a surprising number brought the same giddy sense of pleasure to marriage. As early as 1921, Richard Whiting, Gus Kahn, and Richard Egan's "Ain't We Got Fun?" let the "happy chappy, and his bride of only a year" speak for themselves: "Ev'ry morning, ev'ry evening, ain't we got fun? / Not much money, oh but honey, ain't we got fun?"

SHOW BOAT
Lyrics by Oscar Hammerstein, music by Jerome Kern

When Jerome Kern first met Edna Ferber, he said he had been trying to read her best-selling novel, *Show Boat*, "but I had to keep putting it down." Before she could take offense, he explained, "I had to keep putting down the book and go to the piano to work out the melodies that kept

A stage still from the 1931 revival of Show Boat with Charles Winninger reprising his original 1927 portrayal of Cap'n Andy and Norma Terrell reprising Magnolia. Courtesy of Photofest.

popping into my head." He then asked if she would allow him to turn *Show Boat* into a musical. Ferber's novel, set on a Mississippi showboat late in the nineteenth century, dealt with racism, marital abandonment, and alcoholism—hardly the stuff of musical theater in the 1920s. Yet Ferber said, "If you are crazy enough to try it, I guess I am crazy enough to let you have the rights."

Kern then sought out Oscar Hammerstein, who fashioned from a novel that spanned five decades and thousands of miles a thoroughly integrated libretto where songs grew out of dramatic situations and defined three-dimensional characters. "Can't Help Lovin' Dat Man," for example, advances the plot by giving the first hint that Julie LaVerne, the star of the riverboat troupe, is a mulatto. The black characters are surprised that she knows a song whose twelve-bar blues structure, vernacular language— "Fish gotta swim, birds gotta fly"—and sensuous sentiments—"Ah even loves him when his kisses got gin"—reflect its racial heritage.

By contrast, the songs for the white lovers—"Why Do I Love You?" "Make Believe," and "You Are Love"—have a more elevated style in which lips blend in spiritual rather than physical "phantom" kisses, and lovers address one another with such genteel images as "bud of romance unfurl'd." The disparity in idioms reflects the late nineteenth-century setting of the show, where songs portrayed black lovers in vernacular "coon" songs and white lovers expressed their more refined sentiments in such formal waltzes as "After the Ball," an 1893 song interpolated into *Show Boat* to give it period flavor.

The score's other interpolation was "Bill," a "My Man"-like torch song that had originally been written by Kern and P. G. Wodehouse for an earlier musical but was recycled, with revised lyrics by Hammerstein, into *Show Boat*. While Julie relished gin-soaked kisses in "Can't Help Lovin' Dat Man," when she sings "Bill" she sounds like a befuddled maiden, wondering, "I can't explain—it's surely not his brain—that makes me thrill." Ironically, when she sang "Can't Help Lovin' Dat Man," she was expressing her true love for another member of the showboat company; when she sings "Bill," she is a broken-down alcoholic working in a nightclub.

The centerpiece of the score is "Ol' Man River," which makes the Mississippi River a major character. In addition to reading and rereading Ferber's novel, Kern and Hammerstein steeped themselves in the work of Mark Twain, especially *Life on the Mississippi*. Once Kern had created a melody that captured what Elizabeth Montgomery describes as "the omnipresence and power of the Mississippi River," Hammerstein envisioned the character of Old Joe, a black stevedore, as a "rugged and untutored philosopher" who gives voice to his feelings of racial oppression in a "song of resignation with protest implied."

"Ol' Man River" is a good example of how Hammerstein's lyrical talent differed from that of Lorenz Hart, with whom he is frequently compared. Hammerstein praised the "rhyming grace and facility" of Hart, whom he put on a par with W. S. Gilbert, but added "I would not stand a chance with either of them in the field of brilliant light verse. I admire them and envy their fluidity and humor, but I refuse to compete with them." Hammerstein's genius lay in creating a sense of character and drama in a lyric. To achieve it, he felt he had to avoid pyrotechnical rhymes. "Rhyme should be unassertive, never standing out too noticeably," he cautioned, "for if a listener is made rhyme conscious, his interest may be diverted from the story of a song." In "Ol' Man River" he never rhymes the title phrase, and only after ten lines of the chorus do we get a rhyme with "cotton" and "forgotten."

Yet Hammerstein has his subtle sound effects to give voice to the prosaic character who sings the song. He subtly weaves a pattern of similar sounds in "Ol'," "rollin'," and "along." He also creates counterpoint with verbs: humans "bend," "bow," "pull," "sweat," "strain," "tote," and "lift," while the river is almost passive: "don't plant 'taters ... don't plant cotton." In the final A-section of this surprisingly standard thirty-two bar AABA chorus, Hammerstein characterizes humans desperately "tryin'," "livin'," and "dyin'," while the river inexorably "keeps rollin' along."

With their score and libretto completed for the first act, Kern and Hammerstein approached Florenz Ziegfeld. The impresario was deeply moved by what he heard; however, accustomed to success with frothy girlie shows, he complained that *Show Boat* was simply not "commercial." Still, he agreed to back the production even though he lamented, "It's just plain suicide for me." He then poured his usual lavish expenses into sets and costumes even though, when the curtain went up, he was certain he had squandered his money on a flop. However, audiences and critics embraced this new kind of musical, and Ziegfeld found it to be the most successful production of his career.

Side by Side
Lyrics and music by Harry Woods

Even though Harry Woods was born without fingers on his left hand, his mother encouraged him to study piano. After Harvard, he was a gentleman farmer until he began writing songs, but he did not write full time until the success of "When the Red, Red Robin Comes Bob, Bob, Bobbin' Along" in 1926. In addition to his hits, Woods was known for his drinking and his violent temper. He once got into a barroom brawl that was so bad somebody called the police. They found Woods sitting astride his adversary, clutching him by the throat with his good hand and pounding the man's head with his stump. A woman entering the bar was appalled by what she saw. "Who is that horrible man?" she asked. One of Woods' drinking pals piped up, "That's Harry Woods. He wrote 'Try a Little Tenderness'."

Even though he wrote "Side by Side" in 1926, it sounds like one of those Depression songs that treats poverty with high spirits. Occasionally, songs from the 1920s also asserted that money did not matter as long as there was love. In "Side by Side," the jaunty response to being on the open road is possible only because they love each other, especially in the final lines just before the chorus: "We're sure we love each other / That's the way we'll always be."

Star Dust
Lyrics by Mitchell Parish, music by Hoagy Carmichael

When Paul Whiteman recorded "Washboard Blues," an early song by a young lawyer named Hoagy Carmichael, Carmichael returned to his home in Bloomington, Indiana, where, he wrote, "I finished off Hoagland Carmichael, Attorney-at-Law. RIP." With little to do but pass the time, he visited an old girlfriend because she had a piano. As he played for her and teased her about her legs ("They were the sexiest legs I ever saw ...."), he was thinking about another Bloomington girl, Dorothy Kelly, because he was in love with her. Later on that hot night, strolling on the campus of the Indiana University, he sat on what students referred to as "the spooning wall." As he thought about Dorothy, he "looked up at the sky and whistled a tune" that became *Star Dust*.

Intent on getting the song down, Carmichael raced to a nearby college hangout called The Book Nook to use a piano before closing time. "The notes sounded good," he wrote, "and I played till I was tossed out, protesting, still groping for the full content of my music." When he played the single chorus he had written for his friend Stuart Gorrell, Gorrell inadvertently provided the title. He said the song reminded him "of the dust from the stars drifting down through a summer night." Carmichael wrote, "I had no idea what the title meant, but I thought it was gorgeous."

After touring with Jean Goldkette's and Don Redman's bands, Carmichael was back in Bloomington, adding a verse, a piano interlude, and a clarinet passage to the chorus he had previously written. At the same time, Irving Mills was establishing himself as a music publisher and band manager in New York, specializing in jazz musicians, most notably Duke Ellington. By 1929, Mills was circulating "Star Dust" among jazz bands, but the general public was unfamiliar with it. Mills decided the tune needed a lyric, and assigned the task to staff lyricist Mitchell Parish. Yet Carmichael disliked Parish's lyric when he first heard it. "It didn't seem a part of me," he thought.

Carmichael's tale of how he came to write "Star Dust" is appealingly romantic, although much of it is not true. His biographer, Richard M. Sudhalter, makes it clear that the composer had been working on the melody in 1926 and maybe even earlier. Carmichael even wrote his own lyric but soon discarded it. Parish set his complex lyric to a melody that follows a conventional thirty-two-bar AABA pattern but, according to Alec Wilder, feels more like an instrumental than a vocal, and, in the bargain, an instrumental that feels like an improvisation. "And this fact makes its huge success as a song all that more remarkable," Wilder notes. Most commentators, notably Will Friedwald, acknowledge the lushness of the lyric but conclude that its "sensitive, introspective" quality fits "the dreamy, somewhat meandering melody." Others may conclude that it is simply purple.

A young man looks up at the stars at twilight made distinctive by the way "the purple dusk of twilight time steals across the meadows of my heart." This is an excessively florid line, but, Friedwald suggests, it reveals that Parish knew about Gorrell's comment. The young man then reflects on a lost love and hums a song that "haunts my reverie and I am once again with you."

What is most interesting about the refrain is its use of layers of awareness as the melancholy lover thinks and dreams before he can sing. It opens with the song's most famous line, "Sometimes I wonder why." Before he can sing, he dreams, and then he thinks about why he dreams. It is as if he must justify the dreaming, as dream and song—his "star dust melody"—remain silent but eventually become one. Surprisingly, the lyric uses the words, "star dust," only twice, but each time they enrich the song as Parish exploits their inherent mystery. He writes about "the star dust of a song" and "my star dust melody," in both cases creating a metaphor for love that combines the heavens with the lover's unuttered song.

'S Wonderful
Lyrics by Ira Gershwin, music by George Gershwin

Ira Gershwin always complained that his brother's music gave a lyricist little room to "turn around." Unlike the long, melodic lines of Jerome Kern and Richard Rodgers, George Gershwin's syncopated, staccato bursts forced a lyricist to work with very few syllables. For "That Certain Feeling," written for their 1925 musical *Tip-Toes*, Ira shrewdly solved the problem by collapsing two syllables onto a single note: "That certain feeling / *The first* time I met you!" Still, he complained that most singers missed "the rhythmic point" and sang "That certain feeling / The first time I met you."

Two years later, Ira set a lyric to another of his brother's truncated melodies by following current slang. Flappers not only shortened their dresses, but also shortened words by clipping syllables in such expressions as "Don't be ridic'" and "positively sil'." Ira started out, "Don't mind telling you, in my humble fash' / That you thrill me through with a tender pash." He then carried his syllable clipping to a wonderfully absurd end to fit George's musical repetition of an abrupt three-note phrase: "'S wonderful!' 'S marvelous!' 'S awful nice!' 'S paradise!' 'S what I love to see!" This perfect fit of lyrical and musical imbalance registers the giddiness of romantic bliss. Ira also resented singers who ignored such clever compression by blithely singing "It's wonderful! It's marvelous!"

Thou Swell; My Heart Stood Still
Lyrics by Lorenz Hart, music by Richard Rodgers

Even though Rodgers and Hart had proved that such witty, sophisticated songs as "Manhattan" and "Mountain Greenery" could become popular, producer Lew Fields balked at one of their songs for *A Connecticut Yankee*, a musical version of Mark Twain's novel about a modern American who finds himself transported to King Arthur's court. "Thou Swell," Fields complained, was too clever for a musical, with its mix of archaic diction and modern slang: "Thou swell! Thou witty! / Thou sweet! Thou grand! … Hear me holler I choose a / Sweet lolla/ Palooza / In thee." Fields agreed to keep the song for opening night, but then, if the audience didn't like it, it was out.

When they were no more than eight bars into its refrain, Rodgers, who conducted the orchestra on opening night, recalled, "I began to feel something on the back of my neck …. The audience reaction was so strong that it was like an actual blow …."

Also in *A Connecticut Yankee* was "My Heart Stood Still," a song originally written for a British revue called *One Dam Thing after Another*. Unlike "Thou Swell," it was an utterly simple ballad whose inspiration supposedly came to Hart as he and Rodgers and two women were racing across Paris in a taxi. After a near collision, one of the women said, "Oh, my heart stood still!" Hart asked Rodgers to make a note of it as a title and, although Rodgers was amazed that Hart could be thinking of songwriting at such a perilous moment, the composer dutifully took it down. Months later, Rodgers found the phrase in his notebook and wrote a melody to it. When he played it for Hart, the lyricist had completely forgotten the taxicab incident and complimented Rodgers on the title phrase.

Larry Hart would frequently cite "My Heart Stood Still" to defend himself against charges about his outlandish rhymes. (Howard Dietz once quipped, "Larry Hart can rhyme anything—and does!") "Now just take a look at this lyric," Hart would counter. "'I took one look at you, that's all I meant to do, and then my heart stood still.' I could have said, 'I took one look at you, I threw a book at you,' but I didn't."

1928

I Can't Give You Anything But Love
Lyrics by Dorothy Fields, music by Jimmy McHugh

Dorothy Fields and Jimmy McHugh supposedly took their inspiration for this song from a romantic couple gazing at jewelry in the window of Tiffany's. When the man said, "Gee, honey, I'd like to get you a sparkler like dat, but right now, I can't give you nothin' but love," the two songwriters had their title and the beginning of their first big hit. It is more likely that the song had a more complicated and shadier history. McHugh first used the tune with a lyric about Charles Lindbergh in a Broadway revue called *Harry Delmar's Revels*. Delmar hated it and ordered it cut. Then, with a new lyric by Dorothy Fields, it turned up in the all-black *Blackbirds of 1928* and became a great hit.

Ironically, the rumor began to spread that McHugh, who was working for Mills Music in those days, had bought the song from Fats Waller and Andy Razaf a few years earlier. A Mills employee said, "It's true, the white guys often got offices while the black guys would just come and sell their songs ...." For a newspaper article in 1929, an interviewer reported that Waller told him that "it was easy to sell tunes to white songwriters who would vary them slightly and resell them as their own." Nobody actually saw McHugh buy the song but the rumor persists to this day, and bandleader Don Redman's widow reports that when she asked Razaf, on his deathbed, to sing his favorite song, he responded with "I Can't Give You Anything But Love."

McHugh had started in the music business as a "bicycle plugger," pedaling around Boston with a small piano keyboard on his handlebars and playing the songs of Irving Berlin's music firm to drum up business. Fields was the daughter of the great vaudevillian Lew Fields, of the Weber and Fields comedy team ("Who was that lady I saw you with?" "That was no 'lady'—that was my wife!"). Her parents tried to keep her out of show business, but Dorothy worked her way into writing lyrics for Mills Music, where McHugh had risen to the position of music manager. She became known as "The Fifty-Dollar-a-Night Girl" because of her ability to write words to a melody overnight. Fields demonstrated that she had a knack for fitting punchy, vernacular phrases to McHugh's jazzy, driving melody: "Gee, I'd like to see you looking swell, baby," and the title phrase with its follow-up rhyme, "I can't give you anything but love, baby / That's the only thing I've plenty of, baby."

When she told her parents she and McHugh were going to write songs for all-black revues at Harlem's Cotton Club, her father exploded. "Ladies don't write lyrics!" he said. "I'm no lady," Dorothy snapped back, "I'm your daughter." "I Can't Give You Anything But Love" has endured in popularity by being interpolated into several revues and more than half a dozen movies, including *Stormy Weather* and *Bringing Up Baby*.

Let's Do It
Lyrics and music by Cole Porter

Long dismissed on Broadway and Tin Pan Alley as a wealthy dilettante, Cole Porter wrote his witty, elegant songs to entertain friends at lavish parties he threw in New York and in various European cities. At one party, Porter sang parodies of current popular hits, but then, a friend recalled, his "face grew somber and he said, 'But do you know? I wish I could write songs like that.'" Socialite Elsa Maxwell tried to console him by saying, "The wit and poetry of your lyrics are far beyond the people. But one day," she prophesied, "you will haul the public up to your taste."

That day finally came in 1928 when Porter was invited to write songs for the musical *Paris*, which featured the "French doll" Irene Bordoni, whose specialty was delivering risqué lyrics with sensuous charm. For her, he crafted the first of his great "catalog" songs, "Let's Do It," with a lyric that is essentially a list of witty images and allusions reminiscent of a Gilbert and Sullivan patter song. Porter's song, however, was not simply a list but an outpouring of images that mirrored nature's fecundity. Through its six refrains, Porter details how various kinds of creatures "do it": first, humans, not the typically romantic French and Italians, but the stolid Dutch, Finns, Lithuanians, and, in a pun on his title, "Letts" do it. As the lyric ranges through a biological bestiary, goldfish "in the privacy of bowls do it," "old sloths who hang down from twigs" do it "though the effort is great," and "Moths in your rug do it / What's the use of moth balls?"

Just as she had with Buddy DeSylva and George Gershwin's "Do It Again," in 1922, Bordoni breathed into Porter's innocent title phrase so much suggestiveness that it had to be subtitled "Let's Do It (Let's Fall in Love)" to get past the radio censors. Porter underscored the eroticism musically by dropping chromatically to a G flat on "do," a musical off-color wink that, as Alec Wilder notes, "gives immediate character to the melody."

Lover, Come Back to Me
Lyrics by Oscar Hammerstein, music by Sigmund Romberg

When Oscar Hammerstein was working on *Show Boat* with Jerome Kern, he was also working on *New Moon* with Sigmund Romberg. *Show Boat* was a great success; however, *New Moon* played only a week in Philadelphia before it closed for massive doctoring. To compound Hammerstein's woes with revising *New Moon*, his romantic life took a downward turn when Dorothy Jacobson, a married woman with whom he was having an adulterous affair, broke off their relationship. Nevertheless, he did a complete overhaul of the book for *New Moon* and cut half its songs. One of the new songs he wrote for it was "Lover, Come Back to Me," which may reflect his tormented love life in such aching lines as "Rememb'ring every little thing you used to say and do, / I'm so lonely."

According to some accounts, Romberg wrote the very complicated melody and, in their usual collaborative fashion, gave it to Hammerstein to set with a lyric. Like most operetta composers, who think their melodies are what audiences cherish, Romberg was barely interested in Hammerstein's words. Supposedly, he took the lyric sheet from Oscar's hands, propped it on the piano, and, after playing it through, simply said, "It fits."

Other songs in the score reflected Romberg and Hammerstein's florid operetta style: "Wanting You," which included lines like, "longing to hold you close to my eager breast"; "Softly, as in a Morning Sunrise," which had critics asking "as distinguished from an *evening* sunrise?"; and "Stouthearted Men," which, as Stephen Citron notes, "rhymes the most nonmasculine verb 'adore' with 'ten thousand more.'" Still, when *New Moon* was mounted again in 1928, it had a successful Broadway run.

In real life, too, Oscar Hammerstein's lover came back to him. Dorothy ended her marriage, but when Oscar asked his wife, Myra, for a divorce, she refused. Hammerstein plunged into his work with such fervor that he was soon hospitalized with a nervous breakdown. When he recovered, Myra relented; Oscar and Dorothy married in the spring of 1929.

She's Funny That Way
Lyrics by Richard Whiting, music by Neil Moret

"She's Funny That Way" has four different twists to unravel. First of all, its largely forgotten composer, Neil Moret, was born Charles Daniels. He hid behind pseudonyms for most of his songs, including "Moonlight and Roses" and "Sweet and Lovely." The second twist: his lyricist was composer Richard M. Whiting, who wrote the music for dozens of hit songs but only this one lyric, perhaps because he felt he owed the older man a debt of gratitude. When Moret was an executive for music publisher Jerome Remick, he served as a mentor for the still unknown Whiting. The third twist is in the lyric. It begins self-deprecatingly—"I'm not much to look at, I'm nothing to see"— but at the end of each chorus, it affirms the lover's good fortune: "I've got a woman crazy 'bout me, she's funny that way."

Although it's a torch song, it's written from the man's point of view; that is the final twist. Most torch songs portray a woman betrayed or abused yet still devoted to the man who caused all her misery. In this song, the man is loyal and honest. He considers leaving her only because he feels unworthy, but then he's smart enough to think better of it: "She'd be unhappy without me I know."

WHOOPEE
Lyrics by Gus Kahn, music by Walter Donaldson

When entrepreneur Florenz Ziegfeld collided with the American West, the result was *Whoopee*, a musical comedy that shouted its name as loudly as the *Ziegfeld Follies* shouted his. No one but he could have produced it, even though the original idea was Eddie Cantor's. The frenetic star persuaded Ziegfeld to hire the songwriting team of Walter Donaldson and Gus Kahn to write their first Broadway score.

Although the score more or less fits the story and characters, neither of its two most important songs has anything to do with the main plot. "Makin' Whoopee" lacks the pop-eyed cavorting we usually associate with Cantor. His restrained performance even underplayed the title's slangy reference to sex. Donaldson's melody beguiles and teases as Kahn's lyric lays out an amusingly cynical tale of marital and extramarital "whoopee," divorce courts with unsympathetic judges, and women who outsmart men at every turn. Its outlook is very up to date, vintage 1928, as it affirms with rueful humor that there is always "another season, another reason, for makin' whoopee."

Ruth Etting, the show's other lead, played a movie star who wanders onstage from time to time, utters a few lines of dialogue, and sings; one of her songs was the great torch ballad, "Love Me or Leave Me." Torch singers never portray cynics, only bruised romantics whose eagerness to love and be loved blinds them to what everyone else can see. They may not survive gracefully, but survive they do—to sing again the songs of broken love and shattered hopes, women of spirit offering their tribute to the fragility of all that is precious.

The woman in "Love Me or Leave Me" faces a choice between being alone or, even worse, being "happy with somebody else." Donaldson's melody is melancholy, but Kahn's lyric employs all the tricks we usually associate with the hot and happy songs of the 1920s. He uses short, tight phrases with open vowels to suggest the trap in which she finds herself and the surging emotion that she feels: "Love me or leave me and let me be lonely." Despite Kahn's uses of everything from internal rhyme to half rhyme to alliteration to repetition, the song is a convincing portrayal of deep sadness.

1929

Ain't Misbehavin'; Black and Blue; Honeysuckle Rose
Lyrics by Andy Razaf, music by Thomas "Fats" Waller

Asked in school what his father did for a living, one of Fats Waller's sons answered, "He drinks gin." Waller, who died before his fortieth birthday, was an irrepressible man of prodigious appetites and equally prodigious talents: musician, composer, and singer. He wrote most of his songs on the fly, often selling the same melody to several different publishers to get enough money for another bottle. The going rate, he said, was $250 per song.

Thomas "Fats" Waller. Courtesy of Photofest.

Jazz pianist Mary Lou Williams once described sitting in the theatre, watching Waller, his derby perched jauntily on the side of his head, work on a song for a Broadway show:

> [He] sat overflowing the piano stool, a jug of whiskey within easy reach. said, "Have you anything written for this number, Fats?" And Fats would reply, "Yeah, go on ahead with the dance, man." Then he composed his number while the girls were dancing …. Meanwhile he bubbled over with so many stories and funny remarks that those girls could hardly hoof it for laughing.

His most important collaborator, lyricist Andy Razaf, found that the hardest thing about getting Fats to settle down to work was just that— getting Fats to settle down to work. Waller once said about playing piano, though he might just as well have been talking about songwriting, that you had to "concentrate on the melody. You got to hang on to the melody and never let it get boresome." That desire never to be "boresome" underscored the ebullience and joy in most of his songs.

The Immerman Brothers, a couple of former butchers who ran Connie's Inn, a Harlem nightclub second in importance only to the Cotton

Club, hired Waller and Razaf to write the score for *Connie's Hot Choco-lates*, a lavish all-black revue that would play on Broadway and then be repeated in Harlem after midnight. Even though the performers in these shows were black, white songwriters such as Harold Arlen, Ted Koehler, Jimmy McHugh, and Dorothy Fields typically wrote the scores. This time, though, the score would include Waller and Razaf's "Ain't Misbehavin'" and "Black and Blue."

At the time, Waller was in jail because he owed $250 in alimony payments. He sent his lawyer to get "a miniature piano" so he could write "Ain't Mis-behavin'," which he always referred to as his "alimony jail song." He wrote it in two days, and his lawyer immediately sold it for the amount Fats owed so that he could get out of jail. Razaf had a different version. When he showed up at Waller's apartment at noon, Fats, still in his pajamas, went to the piano to play what Razaf called "a marvelous strain, which was complicated in the middle. I straightened it out with the 'no one to talk with, all by myself' phrase, which led to the phrase, 'ain't misbehavin',' which I knew was the title. The whole thing took about forty-five minutes." Razaf added that as they were walking down Broadway with the manuscript in hand, a pigeon with perfect aim soiled the sheet. The irrepressible Waller cried, "That's good luck! That's good luck! But I'm sure glad elephants ain't flyin'!"

The score's great surprise was the powerful "Black and Blue," which originated when mobster Dutch Schultz, who was backing the show, approached Razaf to say he thought it would be funny to have a scene in which a dark-skinned woman was seen lying on white sheets in an all-white room. Razaf was to write a comic song about being too black and losing men to lighter skinned women. When Razaf said he could not possibly write a song like that, Schultz put a gun to his head: "You'll write it or you'll never write anything again."

Although the incident left him shaken, Razaf told Waller he intended to write a comment on racism in the form of a popular song. Fats wrote a mournful melody that echoed memories of torch ballads, spirituals, and the blues, its offhanded quality matched in spirit by Razaf's spare, elliptical lyric. It was the first racial protest song ever sung on the Broadway stage. On opening night, though, Razaf found himself standing at the back of the theater, next to Dutch Schultz. As Edith Wilson began to sing "Black and Blue," the audience was laughing and Schultz was smiling: "Gentlemen prefer them light / Browns and yellers all have fellers." Then she sang, "I'm so forlorn, life's just a thorn, / My heart is torn, why was I born," and Dutch stopped smiling. Razaf later said he believed his life rested on the audience's reaction. When the song ended, there was a hush before the opening night crowd was on its feet cheering. Schultz slapped Razaf on the back and disappeared.

Connie's Hot Chocolates was so successful that the Immermans hired Waller and Razaf to write songs for a second revue to be called *Load of Coal*. The contract called for at least three songs, but Razaf knew Waller would want to celebrate after the success of *Hot Chocolates*. To get him away from Harlem's temptations, he lured him to his mother's house on the Jersey Shore with the promise of home cooking. Waller walked through the door and started to eat, pausing now and then to return to the piano for a new musical phrase. He and Razaf had finished two songs and had written half a chorus for the third when Waller said, out of nowhere, "I gotta go," and was gone.

Determined to finish the song even if he had to do it alone, Razaf remembered another song he had written five years earlier: "Why not rewrite that unpublished oldie of mine, 'Honeysuckle Rose'? Its title was too good to be wasted." Working from both songs, Razaf finished Waller's chorus, added a verse, and then tracked Waller by phone to a noisy Harlem gin mill. Fats had forgotten the melody, so Razaf sang it to him. By now both of them had forgotten the release, so Waller devised a new one then and there. After the two of them shouted the song back and forth, Razaf went to the piano for a minute to try out what they had written. When he got back, Waller had hung up.

Am I Blue?
Lyrics by Grant Clarke, music by Harry Akst

Ethel Waters was the first to cross over: the first black singer with a background in the blues to appeal mainly to white audiences. Even when she sang the blues, her manner was suggestive rather than explicit, and her voice lacked the rough-edged sound we associate with the great blues singers. Eventually, several show business friends urged her to add standard tunes to her repertoire and perform them for white audiences. "White people would love you for the rest of your life," a friend told her, "You don't have to sing as you do for colored people." Waters' voice was smooth and melodious and her pronunciation impeccable, but she had a sure rhythmic sense she had learned from the blues and her own intensely dramatic way with a lyric. She said, "I could riff and jam and growl, but I never had that loud approach."

In 1929, she was appearing at the Orpheum Theatre in Los Angeles when composer Harry Akst told her he was writing a score with lyricist Grant Clarke for a new Warner Bros. musical, *On with the Show*. The movie needed a hit song, and he thought he had it in "Am I Blue?" Waters wrote in her autobiography that she and Akst "worked on the song together." When they finished, Akst took her to meet the studio's production chief, Darryl F. Zanuck. He listened and said, "This is it!" He also hired Waters to sing the song in the movie. "Am I Blue?" is not really a blues, but rather a "blues song," a conventional popular song influenced by the subject matter and the musical style of traditional blues. Like so many blues, "Am I Blue?" is a study in betrayal and its immediate aftermath: "Am I blue? Ain't these tears in my eyes tellin' you?". Typically, it is set at dawn as it provides emotional testimony from a woman who "woke up this morning along about dawn, / Without a warning I found he was gone."

Button Up Your Overcoat
Lyrics by Lew Brown and Buddy DeSylva, music by Ray Henderson

With the passage of the Eighteenth Amendment in January 1919, large numbers of people awaited with dismay the closing of saloons and the loss of tipsy conviviality. Beginning in that same year, popular songs offered tongue-in-cheek suggestions for how to make the best of things, perhaps by sailing for Havana, where there was no Prohibition to cramp one's style (Irving Berlin's spelling song, "I'll See You in C-U-B-A"). Harry Akst and Howard E. Rogers wrote "You Don't Need the Wine to Have a Wonderful Time" for Eddie Cantor, whose innocently lecherous character always preferred sex to booze anyway: "Lots of people like a cordial after dessert, / But give me someone cordial wrapped in a skirt." As Prohibition continued, popular music soon found itself caught up in the free-for-all 1920s, when song lyrics were filled with references to illegal hooch.

After writing *Good News* (1927), about college football and love, and *Hold Everything* (1928), about professional boxing and love, Ray Henderson, Lew Brown, and Buddy DeSylva continued their streak with *Follow Thru* (1929), about golf and love. "Button Up Your Overcoat," the musical's show-stopping hit, is filled with *mock* good advice about taking care of yourself. Like "You're the Cream in My Coffee" before it, "Button Up Your Overcoat" reflects what Ethan Mordden calls a musical comedy world of "unabashed happiness." Critic Gilbert Gabriel wrote about the three collaborators: "They seem dedicated to the task of making youth flame and love shout out, with crisp, crazy, lusty, ankle-loosing, hip-seizing songs, and lyrics that give this whole razzing, jazzing society circus its cue to get gay." He might have added that the whole thing was fueled by booze. Lyricists Brown and DeSylva wrote as part of the song's cautionary lyric: "Keep away from bootleg hooch when you're on a spree, / Take good care of yourself, you belong to me."

Get Happy
Lyrics by Ted Koehler, music by Harold Arlen

Harold Arlen, born Hyman Arluck, the son of a cantor, grew up in Buffalo with a deep admiration of his father's singing style. He called

Standing, left to right: lyricist Lew Brown, lyricist Buddy DeSylva, and composer Ray Henderson; seated: producer Robert Crawford. Courtesy of Photofest.

him, "the most delicious improviser I ever heard." By the age of seven, Hyman was singing in the synagogue choir, but he also listened to Bessie Smith and Louis Armstrong records. Arlen always believed that his father's cantorial style and the style of blues and jazz came from the same African–Middle-Eastern roots. Once when he played a Louis Armstrong "hot lick" for his father, the cantor asked, in Yiddish, "Where did *he* get it?"

Instead of going to college, Arlen formed his band, "The Buffalodians," in which he played piano, wrote "hot" arrangements of popular songs, and sang. Eventually, Arlen decided to try to make it as a singer in New

York. He got a singing role in Vincent Youmans' 1929 show *Great Day*, but during rehearsal, the show's regular pianist, Fletcher Henderson, was sick, so Arlen offered to sit in. He improvised a catchy vamp, a repeated musical phrase, to signal to the dancers that their number was about to begin. The show's choral director, the great Will Marion Cook, told Arlen he had better turn that piano vamp into a popular song, adding pointedly, "'fore somebody steals it off you." Arlen said:

> I didn't know I was composing anything. I was just improvising naturally. And one day along comes a guy I've met named Harry Warren and he introduces me to a guy named Ted Koehler, who writes lyrics. Koehler sits down and writes a set of words to my little vamp, and he calls it "Get Happy." I didn't seek it out, or ask for it—it just *happened*.

After the onset of the Great Depression, the song's ebullient sentiments cheered Americans who longed to "forget your troubles and just get happy."

Happy Days Are Here Again
Lyrics by Jack Yellen, music by Milton Ager

Along with "Brother, Can You Spare a Dime?" "Happy Days Are Here Again" embodied the Great Depression for millions of Americans. Yet initially, Ager's bouncy tune and Yellen's feel-good lyric had nothing to do with the Depression. The movie musical *Chasing Rainbows* was nearly complete when Irving Thalberg, MGM's head of production, told Yellen he wanted a song for a new scene in which World War I doughboys celebrate the armistice. Ager grumbled about having to collaborate on another song because his relationship with Yellen had soured, but he agreed to stop at Yellen's house that afternoon. "Got a title?" he groused. "Happy Days Are Here Again," Yellen answered. He later swore that the words came to him at that moment. A half hour later, they had finished the song. Two days later, MGM filmed the scene even though the movie was so lame it was not released for several years.

Ager and Yellen published the song anyway, and a New York song plugger took it to George Olsen, whose orchestra was playing at the Hotel Pennsylvania on Black Thursday, the day the stock market crashed. Yellen later wrote about the reaction:

> In the big dining room of the hotel, a handful of gloom-stricken diners were feasting on gall and wormwood. Olsen looked at the title of the song and passed out the parts. "Sing it for the corpses,"

he said to the soloist. The diners broke into a roar of laughter. The band played on, and one couple after another rose from their tables, stomped to the bandstand, and sardonically yelled the words with the vocalist …

A perky tune often played in a staccato manner to fit its jaunty words, "Happy Days Are Here Again" was soon joined by a legion of cheer-up songs that typified the Depression's insistent public optimism, among them Richard Whiting and Leo Robin's "Beyond the Blue Horizon" and Harry Warren and Al Dubin's "We're in the Money." Perhaps the success of "Happy Days Are Here Again" as a Depression anthem and as a campaign song for the Democrats derives from its directness and naiveté. The brief lyric has only two words of more than one syllable. Its sentiments are as simple as its words, but its bubbly assertion of good times in the face of the evidence soon has us singing along. Its narrow melodic range, its insistent repetition of the title line, and its triple rhymes then zip us through its infectious chorus.

I Guess I'll Have to Change My Plan
Lyrics by Howard Dietz, music by Arthur Schwartz

Like most of the lyricists and composers of their era, Howard Dietz and Arthur Schwartz were first-generation New Yorkers, the sons of Jewish immigrants from Eastern Europe. In many immigrant homes, music was cherished, but not in the home of Solomon Samson Schwartz. In Russia, he had been a lawyer; in America, he had to sew buttonholes for a living. Solomon was determined that his son would enter the legal profession. Despite Arthur's obvious love of music, he received no lessons, so he learned to play on his own, progressing from the kazoo to the harmonica and finally, self-taught, to the piano. While he was still in grade school, he was good enough to be hired to play piano accompaniment for silent movies at a nickelodeon in Flatbush.

Arthur dutifully went to law school, but in 1924, after admission to the bar, he worked at a summer camp in the Adirondacks. There he met and wrote musical shows with a young lyricist named Lorenz Hart. Schwartz would have given anything to collaborate with Hart, but Hart was already paired with another young composer named Richard Rodgers. Still, Hart gave Schwartz a piece of advice: "Give up your legal practice for one year and devote all of your time to music."

Schwartz then set out to search for a lyricist and found his ideal opposite in Howard Dietz. In his twenties, Dietz was rubbing elbows with such literati of the Algonquin Round Table as Dorothy Parker and

Lyricist Howard Dietz (standing) and composer Arthur Schwartz (right), with performers Beatrice Lillie and Jack Haley. Courtesy of Photofest.

Alexander Woollcott, and he was invited by Jerome Kern to write lyrics for a Broadway musical. If Arthur Schwartz was a brooding, melancholy man, Howard Dietz was the epitome of the flippant, debonair New Yorker.

Schwartz pursued Dietz. He began by writing him a letter on his law firm's stationery proposing a collaboration. Schwartz, despite his Russian Jewish roots, affected British mannerisms and spoke with a slight English accent. "My dear Dietz," his letter began, "I think you are the only man in town to be compared to Larry Hart."

Howard Dietz shot back:

> My dear Schwartz: As I have written a first show in collaboration with a well-established composer, I don't think our collaboration is such a good idea. What I would suggest is that you collaborate with an established lyric writer. In that way, we will both benefit by the reputation of our collaborators. Then when we both get famous, we can collaborate with each other.

One day in 1929, Dietz overheard two men in a speakeasy talking about producing a revue called *The Little Show*. Unlike most revues of the 1920s, it was to be "topical and artistic, a witty travesty" of modern American life in sophisticated songs and sketches. Dietz tried to discourage the men from mounting a Broadway show. He told them of his bad luck on Broadway, even writing with the great Jerome Kern. After a few more drinks, however, he agreed to write sketches and lyrics for *The Little Show*. The producers told him it would feature the wry Fred Allen, the urbane Clifton Webb, and the sultry Libby Holman. It was only then that Dietz thought to ask who would be writing the music. When the producers named Arthur Schwartz, Dietz figured their collaboration was fated.

"I Guess I'll Have to Change My Plan" was the big hit of *The Little Show*. Originally, it had been one of the camp songs Schwartz had written with Lorenz Hart. Hart had written a wistful lyric about the joys of sleeping in the great outdoors. As Howard Dietz listened to "I Love to Lie Awake in Bed," however, he thought of something the debonair Clifton Webb could sing in top hat, white tie, and tails. Taking the same opening seven notes for his title, Dietz built his lyric around the catchphrase, "I Guess I'll Have to Change My Plan." The opening words, "I guess," capture disappointment with a stoical, urbane shrug as the key word, "guess," falls on the down-beat and registers the singer's frustration at learning the woman who has caught his eye is married.

Dietz's lyric also had risqué touches, as when the singer wonders, "Why did I buy those blue pajamas before the big affair began?"—a line that gave "I Guess I'll Have to Change My Plan" notoriety as the "blue pajamas song." Even more daring was the singer's worldly decision to change his plan yet again to pursue the married woman, reflecting that the prospect of adultery would add spice to the affair. Schwartz's melody thus went from a wholesome camp song to a sophisticated, salacious meditation. Its success, together with that of *The Little Show*, cemented the partnership of Howard Dietz and Arthur Schwartz.

Liza
Lyrics by Ira Gershwin, music by George Gershwin

After George and Ira Gershwin had begun writing songs for Florenz Ziegfeld's production of *East Is West*, a musical about Americans in China, Ziegfeld read a novel about a young actress who aspires to become a star in the *Follies*, and he decided it should be the basis of a musical. Summoning the Gershwins into his office, he told them to shelve their work on *East Is West* and start on *Show Girl*, which would go into rehearsal in two weeks. The brothers were flabbergasted, but Ziegfeld simply advised George to dig down into his "trunk" of unused songs "and pull out a couple of hits." To Ira, Ziegfeld was more generous: he would have help from veteran lyricist Gus Kahn.

As *Show Girl* headed to Boston for out-of-town tryouts, Ziegfeld told the songwriters he wanted "a minstrel number in the second act with one hundred beautiful girls seated on steps that cover the entire stage." They came up with a winsome song with subtle internal rhymes: "L*iza*, L*iza*, sk*ies a*re gr*ay*, / But if you sm*ile* on me *all* the clouds*'ll* r*oll* aw*ay*." They assumed the song would be sung by the female lead, Ruby Keeler, who had recently married Al Jolson. What Ziegfeld did not tell them was that Jolson would be sitting in the third row of the theater and would suddenly rise and sing "Liza" to his new bride. "It caused a sensation," George Gershwin recalled, "and it gave the song a great start!"

Louise
Lyrics by Leo Robin, music by Richard Whiting

Leo Robin went to New York in 1923 with a dream of becoming a playwright and a letter of introduction to George S. Kaufman. After reading his work, Kaufman tried to persuade him to go back home to Pittsburgh, but Robin persisted until Kaufman agreed to look at some of his lyrics as well, including a song called, "My Cutey's Due at Two to Two Today." Kaufman took one look: "That's it—*That's* what you should be doing!"

Six years later, when music publisher Max Dreyfus teamed Robin with Richard Whiting, Robin said, "I nearly fell over, because, to me, practically a beginner in the business, the name of Dick Whiting had a prestige and a glamour and an aura that floored me." Paramount Studios assigned Robin and Whiting to write for a newly-signed French star named Maurice Chevalier.

These were the early days of talking pictures. Paramount did not even have a sound studio. Instead they hung huge rugs to muffle sound and filmed the musical numbers at 2 a.m. Everyone was there, including studio boss Adolph Zukor. As Chevalier sang "Louise," Robin noticed that he used identical gestures in both choruses. The lyricist realized it would make the second chorus anticlimactic, but Chevalier was the star and Zukor was standing there watching. Robin and Whiting were afraid to say anything, but the director ordered Robin to tell him. Chevalier looked at him and said only, "Mr. Ro*ban*, you are wrong."

Robin went and hid—literally. From his hiding place, he heard Chevalier singing until, halfway through the chorus, the director yelled "Cut!" Chevalier called out, "Ro*ban!*" He was nowhere to be found. Finally, he crawled out. Chevalier saw him, "Ro*ban*, you are right!"

The song looks like the soul of spontaneity, but its transparently effortless technique is what makes it so inviting. In its weave of rhyme, internal rhyme, and assonance—all using the long "e" sound from the title—the lyric is close to a *tour de force*: "Every little breeze seems to whisper Louise." In addition, Chevalier, with his French accent, pronounces "little" as "leetle" and "whisper" as "wheesper."

When a Hollywood trade paper printed the top songs of the week, there was "Louise" first on the list. However, a copy editor missed a typo. He left out the "i." Number One in Hollywood that week was "Louse."

Tiptoe through the Tulips; Dancing with Tears in My Eyes
Lyrics by Al Dubin, music by Joseph Burke

Once movie studios started making musicals, they lured songwriters west with pots of money and endless sunshine. Among the first to succumb were composer Joe Burke and lyricist Al Dubin, but both men soon learned that in Hollywood songwriters had no say in how their songs were used. The studios paid you a lot of money to crank them out as quickly as you could and to be sure you wrote some hits. In that environment, Dubin and Burke set to work on the songs for *Gold Diggers of Broadway* (1929), the first of what became a series of "Gold Digger" movies that still remain an indelible part of how we perceive the Great Depression. They wrote a whimsical little song that felt as if it belonged more to the past than the future. There is nary a sign in "Tiptoe through the Tulips" of the moxie and grit of "Forty-Second Street" or "Lullaby of Broadway," the songs that defined the Warner Bros. musicals of the 1930s. Burke and Dubin's first movie hit envisioned pretty gardens, not honking taxis. Dubin got the idea for the lyric from "The Bells," by Edgar Allan Poe, his favorite poet. He wrote the lyric as a conscious exercise in alliteration.

Crooner Nick Lucas introduced "Tiptoe through the Tulips" in the movie as he sang the song's frothy little invitation in a high, pretty voice: "Tiptoe from your pillow to the shadow of a willow tree and tiptoe through the tulips with me." Nothing ever sounded quite so innocent, though, in fact, the young suitor wants the girl he is serenading to sneak out in the middle of the night. Everything will be swell as long as no one finds them. This is strictly forbidden fruit, as he encourages her to come tiptoeing "knee deep in flowers." Clever lad that he is, he even lets her know almost bashfully that he plans on stealing a kiss or two and asks disingenuously, "Will you pardon me?" He may just be a little shrewder than he lets on.

It turns out that the song had legs beyond all likelihood. In 1968, it became a hit all over again, revived by the improbable Tiny Tim who sang his trilling falsetto rendition, heard most frequently on the *Tonight Show Starring Johnny Carson*, where Carson treated him with bemused but affectionate condescension.

Before they parted company in 1931, Dubin and Burke also wrote "Dancing with Tears in My Eyes." Burke's mournful, torch-like melody may reflect his admission that he wrote his best music when he was carrying the torch. "The trouble then," he observed, "is to get a lyric writer in the same romantic boat." Dubin said he found his inspiration from a night on the town at the famous Hollywood restaurant, The Coconut Grove. He noticed many young women dancing with men old enough to be their fathers: gold diggers out on the town with their sugar daddies. Dubin wondered if he was seeing true love or whether they were together because the men could support the young women in luxury, especially during the Depression. Take any one of the women, though; surely, there was a young man somewhere she really loved. Dubin wrote the lyric from the point of view of the young woman, who speaks apostrophically to the boy she misses: "For I'm dancing with tears in my eyes 'cause the boy in my arms isn't you."

What Is This Thing Called Love?
Lyrics and music by Cole Porter

Still struggling to find success as a songwriter, Cole Porter was performing his sophisticated songs at a party in his Venetian *palazzo*. Among the guests was Richard Rodgers, who had only recently established himself on Broadway after his frustrating attempts at musical comedy. To encourage Porter, Rodgers told him how good his songs were. Porter then confided to Rodgers that he had found the secret to songwriting success. "As I listened breathlessly for the magic formula," Rodgers recalled, Porter explained

Cole Porter. Courtesy of Photofest.

that because most successful songwriters, such as Irving Berlin, George Gershwin, and Rodgers were Jewish, the secret was "simplicity itself: I'll write Jewish tunes."

As Rodgers interpreted that remark in the light of the successful songs that followed, it signaled a shift in Porter's music toward minor-key, chromatic melodies that sounded "unmistakably Mediterranean." "What Is This Thing Called Love?" from the revue *Wake Up and Dream* is a perfect example of Porter trying to "write Jewish." The melody shifts dramatically between major and minor keys, and lyrically Porter indulges in such melodramatic and brooding images as "You took my heart—and threw it away."

"It is surely one of the ironies of the musical theatre," Rodgers later observed, "that despite the abundance of Jewish composers, the one who has written the most enduring 'Jewish' music should be an Episcopalian millionaire who was born on a farm in Peru, Indiana."

With a Song in My Heart
Lyrics by Lorenz Hart, music by Richard Rodgers

Richard Rodgers detested the notion of inspiration. He regarded the composing of music as his *job* and went about it in a workmanlike fashion. Once at a dinner party, a woman asked him how he wrote music, but Rodgers could sense she was disappointed as he described getting up early every morning to compose while his mind was fresh. Finally he said, "Look, I've been lying to you. I never get to work before two in the morning. I have to be blind drunk before I get any kind of idea, and on top of the piano I always place a small naked girl."

The closest that Rodgers ever came to writing from inspiration was when he took his first airplane ride in 1929. He was staying on Long Island when a friend offered to fly his seaplane to Manhattan so they could attend a party in the city. "Never having flown before, I felt tremendously stimulated by the flight," Rodgers recalled. When he arrived at his parents' apartment to dress for the evening, he said, "I did something I rarely do. I walked over to the piano and began improvising a melody, which to my surprise sounded good." Later, at the party, he played it for producer Alex Aarons, who leaned over, kissed Rodgers on the forehead, and said, "This has got to be in our new show."

For Rodgers' soaring melody, Larry Hart crafted an utterly straightforward, rapturous lyric: "At the sound of your voice, Heaven opens its portals to me." "With a Song in My Heart" became the hit song from *Spring Is Here*. For once, at least, inspiration had worked for Richard Rodgers.

Without a Song; Great Day; More Than You Know
Lyrics by Edward Eliscu and Billy Rose, music by Vincent Youmans

In 1929, fed up with Broadway producers, composer Vincent Youmans decided to produce his own show, to be called *Great Day*. Only a month before tryouts, he hired lyricists Edward Eliscu and Billy Rose, but Rose had little feel for Youmans' music. For an especially warm melody, he wrote that love was "like a slug in the nose." Youmans was so angry he threw him out and asked Eliscu to write a lyric for what became "Without a Song." Things were not always smooth between Youmans and Eliscu, however. Youmans drank heavily and rarely got down to work before midnight; Eliscu had regular habits and was an early bird.

American popular music is a vast pastiche. Songwriters borrow what they need, sometimes going as far afield as hymns and spirituals to lend a song a sense of uplifting jubilation—even though such borrowings as "Without a Song" and "Great Day" are secular rather than religious. As dignified in its way as "Swing Low, Sweet Chariot," "Without a Song" proclaims, in Gerald Bordman's words, "the transcendent power of melody." Hearing a citified crooner like Bing Crosby or Frank Sinatra sing "That field of corn would never see a plow" feels dislocating, but the line fits the song's allusions to elemental nature: "I've got my trouble and woe, but sure as I know, the Jordan will roll."

Closer in content and theme to traditional spirituals than "Without a Song," "Great Day" also sets religious imagery to its melody, a driving song of promise: "Gabriel will warn you / Some early morn, you will hear his horn." In that same way, it resembles Youmans, Leo Robin, and Clifford Grey's "Hallelujah" from *Hit the Deck* (1927), although the resemblance of "Hallelujah" to a typical 1920s cheer-up song suggests a borrowing from the white revivalist tradition rather than black spirituals: "Satan lies a-waitin' and creatin' skies of gray / But hallelujah, hallelujah, he helps to shoo the clouds away."

"More Than You Know," the most conventional of the important songs from *Great Day*, relies on permutations of a single line as, in Bordman's words, it "poignantly wails its protestations of enduring affection," no matter what. The five-line first chorus begins with the title line repeated in lines two and five, again with a slight variation for emphasis just before the release ("More than you'll ever know"), and then incrementally at the very end to link the singer and the one he loves: "More than I'd show / More than you'd ever know."

You Do Something to Me
Lyrics and music by Cole Porter

Although Cole Porter was the master of the witty, literate catalog song, he could also write beautifully simple songs whose artistry is barely noticeable. Hearing three subtle rhymes in the catchphrase "*You do* something *to* me," he wove a song of magical entrapment that has touches of his characteristically arch society diction, such as "something that *simply* mystifies me" and "*do* do that voodoo that you do so well." The latter line, years later, inspired Johnny Mercer to create an entire song based on the bewitching power of love: "That Old Black Magic."

Although "You Do Something to Me" was the hit of *Fifty Million Frenchmen*, Porter's first full score for a major Broadway musical, the show got mixed reviews from the critics. Star comedienne Helen Broderick was so incensed that she confronted a critic in a hotel lobby and asked him if he knew why critics were like eunuchs. "Critics are like eunuchs," she said, "because they tell you how to do things they can't do themselves." Also rising to Porter's defense was Irving Berlin. The two men had become friends in Europe while Berlin was honeymooning with his bride, Ellin MacKay. Although many of Ellin's society friends had shunned her for marrying a Jewish songwriter, Porter and his equally fashionable wife, the former Linda Lee Thomas, befriended the newlyweds. Berlin may have been repaying the kindness when he took out a newspaper ad to proclaim that *Fifty Million Frenchmen* was "the best musical comedy I have seen in years" and "It's worth the price of admission to hear Cole Porter's lyrics."

1930 – 1939

1930

Beyond the Blue Horizon; My Ideal
Lyrics by Leo Robin, music by Richard Whiting

One of the major themes in any history of the musical is the move toward integration of plot and songs, especially the ways in which each song reveals character or moves the plot forward. The pattern is less clear in the movies than on Broadway—although Ernst Lubitsch was the first movie director to integrate songs into the story line. He told lyricist Leo Robin, "I like your style of writing because you don't turn my characters into performers."

In *Monte Carlo*, Jeanette MacDonald starred as a spunky but down-on-her-luck countess who leaves her feckless husband and eventually falls for a dapper count. "Beyond the Blue Horizon," the song Robin and Richard Whiting wrote for her flight from her marriage, is supposed to show her spirit and her determination to rise above her financial problems, something bound to appeal to audiences during the Depression. Robin's optimistic lyric about "a rising sun" lying just "beyond the blue horizon" certainly does the trick, but even more interesting is how Whiting's melody works within the movie. The song has to dramatize what the countess is thinking and, because she is on a train, the music has to fit its rhythms. When MacDonald opens her compartment window and sees farmers working in the fields, they join in the song as the train whizzes by. You will have to look elsewhere for realism.

Even though "Beyond the Blue Horizon" broke new ground in the movies, in that same year Whiting also wrote "My Ideal," the song his daughter, singer Margaret Whiting, said "he loved better than any other song he'd written." Maurice Chevalier sang it in *Innocents of Paris*, where he played a waiter who inherits a fortune but finds it does not bring happiness. The lyric is the soul of brevity, as the song defines the character's speculation about his future, grounded in reality even as it expresses hope: "Maybe she's a dream, and yet she might be / Just around the corner waiting for me."

Margaret remembered that when she was only five, "if I cleaned my plate, I could go to the piano with Daddy to run through songs he'd written. One night he played a wistful melody. 'Are there words?' I asked. He sang them in that halting half-spoken way that songwriters have." When he finished, Margaret remembers saying, "Oh, Daddy, that's the best one you ever wrote." Whiting thought so, too. Every time he had a new song to write, he had a habit of playing "My Ideal" before he got started, "as if," his daughter said, "he had written one thing he really approved of." From time to time, she would hear him mutter, "Jesus Christ, will I ever write another one like that!"

When Margaret first met lyricist Johnny Mercer, another of her father's collaborators, she came downstairs in pajamas and bunny slippers to sing "My Ideal" for him. Years later, in 1943, he recruited her for Capitol Records and wanted her to record it. She protested. Her father had written it for Chevalier more than a dozen years earlier, and other singers had recorded it as well. "I don't care," Mercer responded, "I love this song more than any other song, and I loved your father, so damn it, you're going to sing this song." Whiting's recording was a major hit and launched her career as a singer.

Body and Soul
Lyrics by Edward Heyman, Ed Sour, and Frank Eyton, music by Johnny Green

No 1930s torch ballad is darker than "Body and Soul." It combines self-doubt with weary desperation to conclude reluctantly, "It looks like the ending," though its mournful melody and oddly blue-collar lingo still manage to affirm, "I'm all for you body and soul."

Producer Max Gordon bought the song's rights so Libby Holman could sing it in *Three's a Crowd*, even though the revue's score was by Arthur Schwartz and Howard Dietz. Dietz, for one, did not regret its use. He called it "solid material for Libby" and even admitted to having written some of the words at Holman's request. There was a problem, though. Her performance during the Philadelphia tryouts was so bad that she changed the show's publicity poster to read, "Clifton Webb and Fred Allen in *Two's a Crowd*," and pinned it to her dressing room wall. With Green's permission, Dietz called on Ralph Rainger, composer of Holman's other great torch hit, "Moanin' Low," to work with her. They did not find an approach to the song that worked until the last performance in Philadelphia. On opening night in New York, Dietz wrote, "'Body and Soul' was a show stopper."

Dancing on the Ceiling
Lyrics by Lorenz Hart, music by Richard Rodgers

"Dancing on the Ceiling" was originally written for *Simple Simon*, but producer Florenz Ziegfeld insisted it be dropped from the show. Ziegfeld's peculiar judgments were legendary. Sitting next to Hart at the opera one night, he turned to him after an aria and said, "That's the greatest voice I ever heard—isn't it?" At a rehearsal of an orgy scene in a musical where harem girls danced erotically around their sheik, Ziegfeld stormed down the aisle screaming, "What's that sonofabitch doing on the stage? Get him out of there so those girls can have their goddamned orgy by themselves!"

However, Rodgers and Hart had faith in the cut number. Rodgers recalled that when he played the melody for Hart, "there was something about it that gave Larry the feeling of weightlessness and elevation. This in turn led to the notion of a girl imagining that her dream lover is dancing on the ceiling above her bed." The composer speculated that his sudden intervals of nearly an octave may have inspired Hart to such oscillating lines as "He dances overhead on the ceiling—near my bed." Hart also managed to give the lyric a suggestive edge, as the singer whispers intimately, "Go away, my lover, it's not fair" but then coyly confides "I'm so grateful to discover he's still there."

When British producer Charles Cochrane invited Rodgers and Hart to write the score for *Ever Green*, they decided to include "Dancing on the Ceiling." Rodgers wrote that a huge inverted chandelier "rose from center stage like an incandescent metal tree" and created the impression that the singers were really dancing on a ceiling. "The song easily became the most popular number in the show," Rodgers said, "done as it should be, which is a rare experience for me."

Fine and Dandy
Lyrics by Paul James, music by Kay Swift

In the first half of the twentieth century, most female songwriters were lyricists. Noteworthy female composers did not appear until the late 1920s and early 1930s. Among them were Ann Ronell, Dana Seusse, Ruth Lowe, Kay Swift, and especially Mabel Wayne, who with Abel Baer composed the first hit song by a woman, the now forgotten "Don't Wake Me Up and Let Me Dream."

The most interesting of this generation was Kay Swift, whose lyricist was her first husband but whose great love was George Gershwin. In 1918, she had married James Paul Warburg, a member of the great banking family. When he became her lyricist to try to ease the strain in their marriage caused by her affair with Gershwin, he called himself "Paul James." Four years later, the marriage ended, and two years after that George left for Hollywood. "We said goodbye and he walked up the ramp," she later wrote. "And I knew for sure I'd never see him again. I didn't know why, but I knew that was all, that was it." Her best known song would have served the occasion well.

She had written "Fine and Dandy" in 1930 as the title song for the only Broadway musical the husband-and-wife team wrote together. More important, it was the first full-scale musical with a score by a woman. "Fine and Dandy" appeared right after two lovers have a spat, and it reflected the uncertainty common to such moments. Even though Swift and James wrote it during the Depression, it feels more like a flapper song from the 1920s, with lyrics like: "Please forgive this platitude / But I like your attitude." What makes it distinctive, though, is a slowly emerging sense of poignancy; they can never be quite sure about one another. He tells her that when they are together, he sees only "the sunny side," but he also adds, "Even trouble has its sunny side." "It's fine and dandy," he tells her in his slangy way, but then he flips his ebullient confidence into an echoing question of unanswered doubt, "But when you're gone / What can I do?"

Georgia on My Mind
Lyrics by Stuart Gorrell, music by Hoagy Carmichael

In the early 1930s, Hoagy Carmichael was living in what he called "an old, creaky walk-up" because "it had a grand piano in it, the first I ever had in my own place." He was constantly at it, doing what he called "finding" tunes. His friend, saxophonist Frank Trumbauer, said to him, "Nobody ever lost money writing songs about the South." Carmichael took Trumbauer's advice. A fellow Indianan, Stuart Gorrell, worked on the lyric and got credit for it on the sheet music though Carmichael wrote most of it.

Entitled "Georgia on My Mind," the song was the first full expression of one of Carmichael's central themes, what he called "the idea of home." Biographer Richard M. Sudhalter defines it as "a place where wandering ceases and the heart comes to rest. It need not be any specific place ... but it must be what thought and emotion perceive as home." Carmichael had never been to Georgia when he wrote "Georgia on My Mind." The emotional tie in these "home songs" could be imagined as well as real,

Hoagy Carmichael. Courtesy of Photofest.

though it always derived from Carmichael's own deep affection for Indiana.

The lyric to "Georgia on My Mind" is elegiac yet ambiguous. The lyric's defining use of apostrophe heightens the ambiguity in the opening lines and continues without resolution to the end: "Georgia, Georgia, no peace I find / Just an old sweet song keeps Georgia on my mind." What makes the ambiguity so poignant is the precision of the memory and its inseparability from "a song of you" that "comes as sweet and clear as moonlight through the pines." Always there is the bluesy tolling of the name, "Georgia, Georgia."

GIRL CRAZY
Lyrics by Ira Gershwin, music by George Gershwin

Girl Crazy, the last of a series of frothy, Jazz Age musicals by George and Ira Gershwin, produced the greatest array of hits of any of their shows. When the curtain rose, it revealed, not the usual bevy of chorus girls, but four cowboys with ukuleles, singing "Bidin' My Time." The song had started out back in 1916 as a bit of light verse by Ira:

A desperate deed to do I crave,
  Beyond all reason or rhyme;

Some day when I'm feeling especially brave,
   I'm going to bide my time.

When he reworked the poem into the lyric for "Bidin' My Time,"
George's melody inspired him to such witty touches as stretching a
syllable, lazily, over two notes: "I'm bidin' my ti—me, / 'Cause that's the
kinda guy I'—m."

George's abrupt and uneven melody for another of *Girl Crazy*'s songs
also inspired Ira to create intricate rhymes. Like so many Gershwin songs,
it started on a rest, so that music—and lyric—begin on the upbeat, giving
the melody an insistent drive, which Ira matched with the ardent phrase
"—Embrace me!" When George abruptly threw in two more rests, Ira
followed with a wryly playful "my sweet embrace—able you." He used
the same disruptive musical pattern to suggest the giddiness of romantic
passion: "My heart grew tip—sy in me" and "You and you alone bring out
the gyp—sy in me."

"But Not for Me," *Girl Crazy*'s other romantic ballad, introduced a
newcomer to the Broadway musical: Ginger Rogers, as a tough-talking,
gun-toting cowgirl. The Gershwins gave her a pugnacious torch song that
begins with her telling "Old Man Sunshine" not to try to comfort her with
such romantic clichés as "Dreams Come True" or "Fate Supplies a Mate."
She dismisses all these palliatives with a Winchellesque, "It's all bananas!"
Beneath her feisty exterior, however, Rogers' character is wrenchingly
poignant as she catalogs the clichés of theatrical love stories, culminating
in her final observation that a love plot should end in a marriage knot,
"But there's no knot for me." It is one of Ira Gershwin's cleverest puns
and shows that even when writing a romantic lament he never forsook
linguistic playfulness.

In contrast to the witty lyrics of "Embraceable You" and "But Not for
Me," "I Got Rhythm" is a deceptively simple song that further reveals how
closely the Gershwin brothers wove words and music together. George had
sketched out the melody as a slow ballad for an unproduced 1929 musical, *East Is West*. For *Girl Crazy*, he quickened its pace and suddenly the
tune came to life. Its bone-simple, four-note phrases came in on the upbeat
after a rest; however, when Ira tried to put a lyric to the phrases, it had
what he called a "jingly Mother Goose quality," which he illustrated with
a dummy lyric: "Roly Poly / Eating solely / Ravioli— / Better watch your
diet or bust!" When he abandoned rhymes, however, he found George's
tune could "throw its weight around": "I got rhythm, I got music, / I got my
man, who could ask for anything more?"

Although he cut the normal end-rhymes, Ira slipped in some internal rhymes, including *for* and *more* in the vernacular catchphrase, "Who could ask *for* anything *more*?" Because he repeated the line four times, Ira thought about calling the song "Who Could Ask for Anything More?" but he loved the slang of "I Got Rhythm" and resented singers who "corrected" his grammar by singing "*I've* Got Rhythm."

"I Got Rhythm" was sung by another newcomer making her Broadway debut, Ethel Merman. While working as a stenographer, she also sang in movie theaters, including the cavernous Brooklyn Paramount, where her voice filled the room and caught the ear of Broadway producer Vinton Freedley, who whisked her over to George Gershwin's apartment. After Gershwin heard her sing, he asked whether she had ever taken voice lessons. When Merman said she had not, he said, "Good. Don't ever take one." Gershwin offered to make changes in his songs for her, but she brassily told the famed composer, "No, Mr. Gershwin, they'll do very nicely."

Girl Crazy shrewdly held off her first song until late in the first act, by which point the audience had assumed Ethel Merman was a nonsinging actress. When she did finally belt out a song, they were doubly bowled over. "I Got Rhythm" rang down the curtain on Act One, with Merman holding the last note for eight bars. It was the last glorious musical gasp of the Jazz Age.

Memories of You
Lyrics by Andy Razaf, music by Eubie Blake

When producer Lew Leslie learned that Eubie Blake and lyricist Noble Sissle had split, he went to Blake's house in Harlem to ask him to write the music for his second Broadway edition of the *Blackbirds* all-black revue. The composer had only one question, "Who's your publisher?" He knew that a solvent publisher's financial commitment to a show would guarantee his payment. Leslie gave him a $3,000 advance and Blake agreed to write *twenty-eight* songs. Leslie then hired Andy Razaf, who usually worked with Fats Waller.

Razaf felt freer writing with Blake than with Waller. He later said, "There no way to write for Waller without being aware all of the time that he's the one who's going to perform what you write." Blake in turn said he had never seen anyone who could write a polished lyric so quickly: "He will hear a tune once through, sit right down, and write out the lyric in one sitting. In all the time we worked together—and we wrote four shows together—once he wrote a line it was down there. I never saw him change a line with me."

Razaf pressed Blake to write a song for his lover, Minto Cato, a beautiful singer in the *Blackbirds* cast. Blake responded with a melody designed to suit Cato's unusual vocal range. The composer was best known as a writer of rags and Razaf as a writer of double-entendre lyrics, but Blake wrote a soaring melody to which Razaf set a lyric that captures, in Barry Singer's words, "this sense of wistful flight with straightforward, unerring poignancy." For a chorus that rises precipitously through the first four bars before dropping in the second four, Razaf wrote with what must have been perfect assurance: "Waking skies at sunrise, every sunset too, / Seem to be bringing me memories of you." It was the best ballad either man ever wrote.

On the Sunny Side of the Street; Exactly Like You
Lyrics by Dorothy Fields, music by Jimmy McHugh

Lew Leslie's International Revue was one of four revue scores Jimmy McHugh and Dorothy Fields wrote in 1930 and 1931, an effort that taught Fields she eventually wanted to write book shows. Fields explained, "Writing for a revue, you start from scratch twelve or fourteen times. After writing all those extraneous songs—pop songs, which was hard—I always thought writing a book show would be heaven."

She and McHugh were indeed writing "pop songs," none more popular than "On the Sunny Side of the Street." It is the very best of the breezy urban cheer-up songs of the Great Depression. The first measures of McHugh's melody have the staccato verve of a jazzy bugle call. Field's first line, "Grab your coat and get your hat," combines two imperative outbursts with alliteration and cacophony to turn the slangy "pitter pat" of spontaneous American talk into a lyric. To write words that never lose their tie to everyday speech, Fields also uses internal rhyme ("hat" and "pitter pat," "parade" and "afraid," and "rover" and "over") and assonance ("you," "tune," and "used," leading to "blues"). She also limits her end-line rhymes mainly to the incrementally repeated refrain that initially includes the mock formal "direct" in the effortlessly slangy: "Just direct your feet to the sunny side of the street."

Fields and McHugh's other hit song from *Lew Leslie's International Revue* felt more like a charm song than a romantic ballad. "Exactly Like You" makes you smile rather than sigh. Even though its range exceeds an octave, its light touch makes it a testament to quiet joy. Fields' lyric rises from the chatty to the grand, the ordinary to the unique. She takes us from watching a movie to "love scenes" of our own, from the abstraction of "You make me feel so grand" to the wittily precise "I want to hand the world to you," and from "schemes I'm scheming" up to "dreams I'm dreaming."

There may be lots of good lovers out there but no one else is "exactly like you."

Puttin' on the Ritz
Lyrics and music by Irving Berlin

Ever since "Alexander's Ragtime Band" in 1911, Irving Berlin had "ragged" words against music, so that musical accents disrupted or underscored individual syllables. "Puttin' on the Ritz" carries this principle to the extreme: "*Spang*led *gowns* up*on* a *bevy of* high *browns* from *down* the *lev*ee / *All* mis*fits putt*in' on the *ritz*." Berlin compounds this misfit of musical and lyrical accents with an equally discordant clash of highbrow and slangy diction, from "swell beaux" to "see them spend their last two bits." His artistry was wasted in the movie for which "Puttin' on the Ritz" was the title song. After the initial flurry over the novelty of musical pictures, customers were going to theater box offices, asking "Is this a musical?" and walking away if it was. Studios cut back severely on musical films and sometimes cut songs out of musical films already in production.

Nonetheless, with the development of a silent camera and boom microphones that could follow performers from above the frame, Berlin and other songwriters found that songs in films could now be presented more spectacularly and more intimately than they could ever be rendered on the live stage. No performer put over a song on the screen better than Fred Astaire, so when Berlin was commissioned to write the score for *Blue Skies* in 1946, a film that was to be Astaire's swan song before going into retirement, Berlin recycled "Puttin' on the Ritz."

First, however, he revised the lyric. The original lyric was about blacks parading in their finery on Harlem's Lennox Avenue, but by the 1940s the NAACP objected to such racial stereotyping. Realizing that it was no longer acceptable, Berlin, who had started out in the era of ragtime "coon" songs, rewrote "Puttin' on the Ritz" to make fun of the "well-to-do" strutting on "Park Avenue" with "their noses in the air." Amazingly, he was able to recreate the same clash of music and lyrics in such lines as "*Come* let's *mix* / Where *Rock*-e-*fel*lers / *Walk* with *sticks* or *umbe*rellas / *In* their *mitts*."

Ten Cents a Dance
Lyrics by Lorenz Hart, music by Richard Rodgers

During the Boston tryout for *Simple Simon*, producer Florenz Ziegfeld supposedly said to Richard Rodgers and Lorenz Hart, "Everything you fellows write is clever. Everything is fancy. Why can't you just write me a nice, simple hit." Stung by the faint praise, the team decided to do just that.

By nightfall, they'd finished "Ten Cents a Dance," the plaintive lament of a weary dance hall hostess. It became one of Rodgers and Hart's most enduring songs, even though it was at odds with the rest of the show.

Ed Wynn and Guy Bolton had written the book for the musical to serve as a vehicle for Wynn, "The Perfect Fool," who would gallop into a forest brandishing a sword as big as he was and lisping in a goofy falsetto, "I love the woodth! I love the woodth!" As Richard Rodgers explained, he "looked on the world with a wide-eyed childlike innocence that made everything he did seem uproarious."

In the midst of this fractured fairy tale, "Ten Cents a Dance" was a despairing torch song for Ruth Etting as a tough but teary taxi dancer. The song is her relentless portrait of herself, but also of a demi-monde populated by "pansies and rough guys, tough guys who tear my gown." The emotions in "Ten Cents a Dance," Richard Rodgers wrote, are those "of a person caught up in one of the more unsavory areas of employment." The ultimate expression of that strain of torch ballads came later in the same year, when Cole Porter portrayed a streetwalker in "Love for Sale."

Three Little Words
Lyrics by Burt Kalmar, music by Harry Ruby

Composer Harry Ruby always wanted to be a professional ballplayer. Max Wilk writes that one day, over lunch in the MGM commissary, producer Joe Mankiewicz put it to Ruby:

> Let's assume you're driving along a mountain road, high up. You see a precipitous cliff with a sheer 600-foot drop. Two men are hanging there, desperate. One of them is Joe DiMaggio, the other is your father. You have time to save only one of them. Which one do you save?

"Are you kidding?" Ruby replied, "My father never hit over .218 in his life!" Ruby also loved Gilbert and Sullivan's comic operas, but the engaging little songs he and Burt Kalmar wrote together were simple rather than complex and witty. Most songwriters tried to avoid the phrase "I love you," so Kalmar counted up the words and letters to write a playful little lyric about the essential "three little words."

Once asked if he regretted writing any of his songs, Ruby told an audience, "Three Little Words." Soon after it became a success, the manager of the Washington Senators asked him to play in an exhibition game. "I did what any sensible man would do," Ruby said. "The very next day I reported, spike shoes, sweatshirt, sliding pads and all." He took the field in the seventh inning as the loudspeaker announced, "Harry Ruby now playing second base for Buddy Meyer." Ruby called it the biggest moment of his life. Then Al Schacht, the third base coach, announced that Ruby had written "Three Little Words" and used a bat to conduct the fans in singing the song. Ruby said

> Right then and there, I went to pieces. I wanted them to think I was a real baseball player …. The inning started. The first Oriole hit a single. The next man up hit a grounder to Ossie Bleuge. Ossie was about to throw to me at second, when he saw that I wasn't there. I hadn't covered the bag to complete the double play. I was glued to the spot, telling Al Schacht what I thought of him …. The next day the following banner line appeared in the sports section of the *Washington Post*: SONGWRITER MISSES DOUBLE PLAY. And that, folks, is why I am sorry I wrote "Three Little Words."

Time on My Hands
Lyrics by Harold Adamson and Mack Gordon, music by Vincent Youmans

With solid hits such as "Tea for Two" and "I Want to Be Happy" behind him, Vincent Youmans was an established composer, but lyricists Harold Adamson and Mack Gordon were neophytes. When the three men were having lunch in a restaurant, Youmans jotted down the notes of a melody while his date went to the ladies room. Adamson and Gordon went to work on a lyric and, even though Youmans' melody was laced with triplets—the most difficult musical figure for lyricists to set—they found an everyday catchphrase that fit the triplet and the long note that followed it: "Time-on-my hands." They then concocted the perfect turn around matching phrase: "You-in-my arms."

Youmans took the song to the great Ziegfeld, who was producing a musical called *Smiles*, starring Marilyn Miller. When she refused to sing it, Ziegfeld mollified her by decreeing that Paul Gregory would sing it *to* her. Eventually, Miller did agree to sing one chorus of Youmans' melody but only to a lyric by Ring Lardner that fitted the triplet clumsily with "What-Can-I Say?" The lyric that endured, however, was "Time on My Hands."

1931

All of Me
Lyrics by Seymour Simons, music by Gerald Marks

Composer Gerald Marks says most hit songs are accidents. Because he and lyricist Seymour Simons had a song they believed in, Marks traveled to New York from Saginaw, Michigan, with enough money to last him a week. "I peddled my song ... up and down the street and every single pub-lisher turned it down." When he got back to Michigan, he arranged to play it for vaudevillian Belle Baker. "The first accident was that she had a piano in her dressing room, and I played it for her while she put on her makeup. When I got to the line, 'Your goodbye left me with eyes that cry,' she became hysterical." The line itself was the second accident. "Later," Marks recounted, "I learned it was the anniversary of her husband's death. From then on, she plugged my song and made it a hit all by herself."

Though "All of Me" is a Depression song, it sings about a break-up in the jauntiest possible way, even with a modicum of cleverness. The title line leads the singer to dissect himself emotionally, offering up his lips, his arms, his eyes, and ultimately his heart because they are no good to him without her: "You took the part that once was my heart / So why not take all of me."

Dancing in the Dark
Lyrics by Howard Dietz, music by Arthur Schwartz

Like most of the songs of Howard Dietz and Arthur Schwartz, "Dancing in the Dark" emerged from a Broadway revue, *The Band Wagon*, arguably the greatest of the "little" revues of the 1930s. The intimate revue was per-fectly suited to Howard Dietz, for whom songwriting was only a sideline. He had started out in advertising, and later became director of advertising and publicity for Metro–Goldwyn–Mayer. Among other brainstorms, Dietz managed the brilliant public relations campaign for *Gone with the Wind* that had all of America guessing which star would play Scarlett O'Hara; then, when Clark Gable returned from World War II to star in a film with Greer Garson, Dietz concocted "Gable's Back and Garson's Got Him."

Many of Dietz's lyrics have the qualities of a good ad: They grab the listener's attention, make their point quickly, and involve a clever twist—the perfect formula for the snappy songs and sketches of a loosely structured revue. Arthur Schwartz, however, longed to write scores for more dra-matic musicals in which songs were closely integrated into the story and characters. A lover of classical composers, Schwartz crafted intricate, passionate compositions that sometimes bordered on art song.

When Dietz articulated the latent emotional power of Schwartz's com-plex melodies in a lyric, the song could be ambiguous and mysterious—but also, at times, bombastic or melodramatic. Their best songs in this style are "Alone Together" (1932), "You and the Night and the Music" (1934), and, of course, "Dancing in the Dark." The melody for the latter came to Schwartz in a sudden inspiration. He and Dietz frequently worked in New York hotel rooms that came equipped with a piano. When their all-night sessions brought complaints from other hotel guests, they were asked to leave. "It must be your melodies," Dietz quipped to the dour Schwartz. "They never complain about my lyrics." However, at the Edison Hotel one night, Schwartz sat down at the piano and played the insistent melody that became "Dancing in the Dark" "as if," his son Jonathan Schwartz recalled, "it had already existed."

When Dietz heard the melody, he brought out its brooding undertones in another of his emotionally complex and mysterious lyrics. He used very few rhymes (there are no rhymes in the lyric for "dark"), but relied instead on alliteration and repetition to match Schwartz's swirling melody ("waltzing in the wonder of why we're here"). The title is a brilliant metaphor for what it felt like to live in such uncertain times as the 1930s. As Thomas Hischak says, "The picture of two lovers waltzing in the dark is highly romantic, but there is also a sense of foreboding, a feeling that when the music inevitably ends there will be just darkness."

I Surrender, Dear
Lyrics by Gordon Clifford and Bing Crosby, music by Harry Barris

Bing Crosby's emergence as a star is inseparable from two songs by composer–singer Harry Barris. Crosby's career moved from jazzily singing "Mississippi Mud" with a trio, to crooning "I Surrender, Dear" as a soloist. When he and Al Rinker joined Paul Whiteman's Orchestra as a vocal duo in 1926, they flopped so badly the theatre manager asked Whiteman to drop them. Instead, Whiteman added the cocky young Barris to the duo and renamed them The Rhythm Boys. To the recording of "Mississippi Mud," the trio's first hit, Barris added a hand-held cymbal and the breathy "Hhhaaaa!" that characterized its irreverent, jazz-flavored style.

Meanwhile, the three young performers combined stylish singing with after hours hell-raising. When Crosby got drunk, cracked up his car, and was taken off to jail, Whiteman fired all three of them. Bandleader Gus Arnheim immediately hired them but soon began to push Crosby as a soloist. In 1931, Bing recorded "I Surrender, Dear," the hit that established him as a solo singer. Barris wrote it after hearing Crosby sing a variation on Sigmund Romberg's lush, "Lover, Come Back to Me."

Crosby's singing transformed a routinely purple ballad of suffering— "When stars appear and shadows fall / It's then you'll hear my poor heart call"—into a combination of tenderness and sexual heat. Crosby biographer Gary Giddins writes that the song all but buried The Rhythm Boys because audiences, mainly female, wanted to hear "that astonishing singer with the throb in his voice, not a trio of hepcats."

That throb was what it was all about. Before Crosby and Russ Columbo, crooning was light and charming but lacked intimacy and sexuality. With Columbo's death in a freak shooting in 1934, Crosby emerged as one of the most influential singers in American music. He became a radio star soon after William S. Paley, the head of CBS Radio, heard a phonograph record as he was walking the deck of an ocean liner on his way to Europe. Paley read the label, "I Surrender, Dear, Vocal Chorus by Bing Crosby," and immediately cabled his office, "Sign up singer named Bing Crosby." Within weeks, Crosby was radio's hottest new sensation.

Before his first broadcast, Crosby had to choose a theme song. He eventually settled on Fred Ahlert and Roy Turk's "Where the Blue of the Night (Meets the Gold of the Day)." Barris' daughter said it broke her father's heart when Crosby did not select "I Surrender, Dear."

Life Is Just a Bowl of Cherries
Lyrics by Lew Brown, music by Ray Henderson

By 1931, the songwriting threesome of Buddy DeSylva, Lew Brown, and Ray Henderson was breaking up. The sirens of Tinsel Town lured DeSylva from songwriting to producing, so Brown and Henderson moved back to New York to work on *George White's Scandals of 1931*, starring Ethel Merman and crooner Rudy Vallee. The big hit from the show was "Life Is Just a Bowl of Cherries." Unlike the "Polyanna" songs of optimistic uplift written during the Depression, "Life Is Just a Bowl of Cherries" takes a stoical look at material loss: "You work, you save, you worry so, but you can't take your dough when you go, go, go." The title is a surreal metaphor for life as a pleasant but transient experience: "The sweet things in life to you were just loaned so how can you lose what you never owned?"

Minnie the Moocher
Lyrics and music by Cab Calloway, Clarence Gaskill, and Irving Mills

Talent manager Irving Mills went to Chicago to audition singer Blanche Calloway, but she said she would not go to New York unless her brother could go too. "He sings a good song and he dances very good," Blanche told Mills, "but the proprietor didn't want to use him in the revue so he made him a bus boy." After an audition late that night, Mills signed both Calloways. Fronting his own band at the Cotton Club when Duke Ellington was unavailable, the irrepressible Cab Calloway soon developed his signature habits of wearing white silk tails and speaking a wildly improbable jive lingo that appealed to the "hepcats" of the day.

As Calloway became well known, Mills decided he needed a theme song. The band had been using the dirge-like blues, "St. James Infirmary," as a theme, so Calloway and Mills "figured that we ought to try to write something that would have the same feeling, and a melody that wasn't too different." They adapted the idea for the title and the lyric from two songs of the day: "Minnie the Mermaid" and "Willie the Weeper." Right from the start, "Willie" sounded more than a little like "Minnie the Moocher": "Have you heard the story, folks, of Willie the Weeper? / Willie's occupation was a chimney sweeper." Calloway and Mills' song told a darker tale about a rough, tough prostitute, "a real hot hoochy-coocher," who also has "a heart as big as a whale." Despite its boisterousness, Calloway and Mills gave the song an underlying melancholy by writing in a minor key. Minnie lives a degrading life in which her pimp introduces her to cocaine and opium ("He took her down to Chinatown and showed her how to kick the gong around").

Calloway wrote in his memoir that the "hi-de-ho" came slightly later. During a national broadcast of a Cotton Club show, "the damned lyrics went right out of my head …. I had to fill the space, so I just started to scat-sing the first thing that came into my mind." The crowd loved it, "and I went on with it—right over live radio …. Then I asked the band to follow it with me and I sang, 'de-dwaa-de-dwaa-de-doo.'" People in the audience began to join in and "we went on and on for I don't know how long, and by the end the rafters were rocking and people were standing up and cheering."

OF THEE I SING
Lyrics by Ira Gershwin, music by George Gershwin

The Gershwin brothers were ambitious: George wanted to write classical works; Ira wanted to write satirical operettas in the style of Gilbert and Sullivan. With the onset of the Great Depression, American audiences seemed more receptive to political satire. Teamed with playwrights George S. Kaufman and Morrie Ryskind, they set out to write *Of Thee I Sing*, a political satire that lampooned the presidential election. They saw it—and even more the election of a vice-president—as just the sort of quirky political institution that Gilbert and Sullivan had satirized in Britain's House of Lords. The American presidency had never been mocked from the musical stage before.

The Gershwins, Kaufman, and Ryskind built their satire about the election of John P. Wintergreen, "the man the people choose—He loves the Irish and the Jews." The title song simply added Tin Pan Alley's favorite form of address—"Baby"—to a patriotic slogan, and "Love Is Sweeping the Country" mingled the clichés of love with those of politics: "Waves are hugging the shore; / All the sexes from Maine to Texas have never known such love before."

Again, the Gershwins sprinkled some love songs into the long stretches of Gilbert and Sullivan pastiche. For one of George's most winsome melodies, Ira constructed a Depression-era pledge of love in the face of economic catastrophe: "Who cares if the sky cares to fall in the sea? / Who cares what banks fail in Yonkers, long as you've got the kiss that conquers?" When Kaufman, who thought romantic love the silliest of artifices, objected to the addition of these songs, George Gershwin said, "Don't knock love, Kaufman; without it, we'd be out of business."

1932

April in Paris
Lyrics by E. Y. "Yip" Harburg, music by Vernon Duke

Although some songs written in the Great Depression reflected its grim realities, "April in Paris" conjured up a world of elegance about which most Americans could only dream. Yet it had its roots in the economic hard times. The producer of *Walk a Little Faster*, one of the few musicals mounted in the early years of the Depression, managed to acquire a second-hand Parisian set and called upon his songwriters to write a number to go with it.

The composer Vernon Duke was a Russian émigré born Vladimir Dukelsky, who had lived in Paris in the 1920s. Surrounded by his literary cronies at a fashionable New York restaurant, Duke tossed off the haunting melody of "April in Paris" on an old upright piano. Lyricist E. Y. Harburg also had Russian roots, but his parents were poor immigrants who had settled on New York's wretched Lower East Side. Having never been abroad, Harburg went to Cook's travel agency, picked up some brochures, sat in a New York deli, and tried to imagine what it was like to be in Paris.

Harburg, like most of the great lyricists, prided himself on subverting romantic clichés. He started with a hackneyed scene—a woman drinking a glass of wine in a Paris café in the spring—but instead of having her recall an old flame, Harburg gave the cliché a twist by portraying her as a woman who has never been in love. Then, in a tribute to the power of Paris in the spring, she wishes she *had* had a lover just so she could recall him at this romantic moment. Harburg's lyric matched Duke's simple but harmonically complex melody with striking imagery ("chestnut in blossom"), literate sophistication ("Whom can I run to?"), and subtle internal rhymes ("holi*day ta*bles," "*till* April in Paris").

Brother, Can You Spare a Dime?
Lyrics by E. Y. "Yip" Harburg, music by Jay Gorney

When the Depression destroyed his thriving electrical appliance business, E. Y. "Yip" Harburg said he had nothing left but a pencil. That's when his boyhood friend Ira Gershwin suggested he try writing lyrics. "You've got your pencil," Gershwin told him. "Get your rhyming dictionary and go to work." Gershwin also introduced him to his first collaborator, composer Jay Gorney. At the age of thirty-three, Harburg announced with typical puckishness, "I decided to give up this dreamy stuff called business and do something realistic like writing lyrics." He and Gorney wrote, "Brother, Can You Spare a Dime?"—their first important song—for *Americana*, a satiric revue that closed after only two performances. Despite the show's failure, the song was a huge success as Bing Crosby's muscular recording swept the country and soon rose to the level of anthem. No other popular song caught the spirit of its time with such urgency.

Harburg told Studs Terkel that he got the idea for the lyric from the breadlines he saw in New York City and from the common experience of being approached on the street and asked, "Can you spare a dime?" Gorney intended the melody as a torch ballad and Harburg had already written a lyric for it, but the lyricist was determined to write about current conditions. He asked Gorney, "Jay, is this lyric wedded to this tune?" "Well," Gorney answered, "we can get a divorce if you have the right tactics." Before long, the torchy opening lines, "I could go on crying big blue tears," had become the bitter, "Once I built a railroad, made it run."

What makes the lyric unusual is its reliance on a story rather than imagery or the direct expression of emotion. A panhandler recognizes the man he's asking for a dime. The recognition brings on a poignant, bewildered remembrance. Here is someone who kept faith with America and now America has betrayed him. He even went to war, "slogging through hell" in 1917, and then returned to work hard in a time of prosperity, a working stiff who found satisfaction in the fields he plowed, the bridges and skyscrapers he helped to build, and the camaraderie that came with the work. "They called me Al," he reminds his former "buddy," "it was Al all the time." Now, three years into the Great Depression, he's out of work, stripped of his pride, and reduced to begging in the streets.

The song reveals the depth of Al's feeling of betrayal as it returns to the anguished confession of failure in the title line. Although much of it is in a minor key, Gorney's melody is plaintive and increasingly bold as the lyric expresses not only confusion but also quiet rage. Once Al "built a tower up to the sun"; now he can only beg. In his troubled response to bad luck and bad times, people heard their confusion about their lives and about the nation.

How Deep Is the Ocean?; Say It Isn't So
Lyrics and music by Irving Berlin

As America sank deeper into the Depression, Irving Berlin was mired in the worst crisis of his career. Like many Americans, he had lost almost all of his fortune in the stock market crash. His fairy-tale marriage to the elegant socialite Ellin MacKay turned tragic when their infant son, Irving Berlin, Jr., died suddenly on Christmas Day—punishment, Ellin's former friends said, for marrying a Jew. On top of these losses, Berlin feared he had lost his talent. "I had gotten rusty as a songwriter," he said. "I developed an inferiority complex. No song I wrote seemed right. I struggled to pull off a hit."

One of the songs he struggled with in these years was "Say It Isn't So," a poignant ballad built around an ordinary vernacular catchphrase. Berlin decided it was not even worth publishing. "There were times between 1930 and 1932," he said, when he "... got so I called in anybody to listen to my songs—stock room boys, secretaries. One blink of the eye and I was stuck."

Fortunately, Max Winslow, one of his music publishing associates, took "Say It Isn't So" to radio crooner Rudy Vallee. "Irving's all washed up, or at least he feels like it," Winslow told Vallee. "He thinks he's written out as a songwriter. But there's a song of his I'd like you to look at and please, sing it for him." Vallee, who was going through his own heartache in a divorce, was deeply moved by "Say It Isn't So": "Here was I singing that song about my girl seeing someone else, and going away—it was all true and happening to me."

The success of "Say It Isn't So" prompted Berlin to reexamine another song he had recently discarded, "How Deep Is the Ocean?" In writing it, he had taken bits and pieces out of other songs, and cast the lyric as a series of questions: "How much do I love you? .... How deep is the ocean? How high is the sky?" When "How Deep Is the Ocean?" became a hit, Berlin began to overcome his creative depression. "Those two songs came at a critical time," he said, "and broke the ice."

Isn't It Romantic?
Lyrics by Lorenz Hart, music by Richard Rodgers

Love Me Tonight was one of several musicals Paramount made that did not present songs as "performances" by actors playing the parts of singers. Instead, it presented them dramatically, as in operetta, and its European setting made it easier for American audiences to accept that ordinary characters suddenly burst into song.

When songwriters Richard Rodgers and Lorenz Hart were hired to write songs for *Love Me Tonight*, Hart thought it would make the transition from talking to singing even more believable if he wrote rhymed dialogue. In one of the most innovative sequences in musical film, Maurice Chevalier, playing a Parisian tailor, begins speaking in rhyme, then launches into "Isn't It Romantic?" in which he dreams, in very practical and "unromantic" terms, of a wife who will cook him onion soup and scrub his back in the bathtub.

A customer sings the song as he leaves the tailor shop and then a composer picks it up as he heads for the train station. Aboard the train, the composer continues singing the song surrounded by soldiers; then we see the soldiers marching across the countryside singing even more "unromantic" lyrics about all the girls they have left behind them. A gypsy boy who overhears their bawdy chorus rushes back to camp, grabs his violin, and sweetly plays the melody around the campfire. From there it drifts up to the balcony of a castle where Jeanette MacDonald sings the truly romantic lyrics that invoke "music in the night" and a prince in shining armor.

Love Me Tonight also utilized a new technology—the playback—that let singers record a song beforehand, then lip-synch to their recording on the set. The playback helped songwriters escape the confines of writing for the theater, in which composers and lyricists had to give singers plenty of long notes and long vowels so they could project a song to the back of the balcony. Because they knew singers would be prerecording songs into a microphone, composers could use shorter notes and lyricists could match them with short vowels and crisp consonants closer to speech. Although the alliterative "Isn't It Romantic?" would be difficult for a stage performer to project, it works in a film thanks to the playback system, and Rodgers and Hart could add other perfectly conversational songs such as "Lover" and "Mimi" to *Love Me Tonight*.

I've Got the World on a String
Lyrics by Ted Koehler, music by Harold Arlen

In the early years of the Depression, Harold Arlen and Ted Koehler worked on songs for shows at Harlem's Cotton Club, where white patrons— the "Mink Set," as Arlen called them—came in taxis and limousines to be titillated by racy shows with black performers. Like most great songwriting teams, Koehler and Arlen were opposites in temperament: Arlen was intense and driven; Koehler was laid-back and easygoing. Arlen would sit at the piano for hours, spontaneously creating short segments of music—he called them his "jots"—then weaving these bits together, bar by bar, stanza by stanza, until a completed song emerged.

All this time Koehler would be lying on the couch listening, though Arlen sometimes angrily accused him of sleeping on the job. Once the melody was finished, Arlen would play it over and over for Koehler, who would search for verbal phrases from everyday speech to match Arlen's notes. Instead of using clever rhymes and witty allusions, he matched Arlen's complex, driving melodies with slang phrases and punchy alliteration in "(You've Got Me in) Between the Devil and the Deep Blue Sea" (1931), "I Love a Parade" (1931), and "I Gotta Right to Sing the Blues" (1932).

Their greatest rhythm number was "I've Got the World on a String," written for the *Cotton Club Parade* of 1932. The "got" (one of Koehler's favorite words) falls percussively on Arlen's downbeat, as does the alliterative "string." However, he could also deftly shift from such guttural consonants to a softly mellifluous phrase: "I'd be a silly so-and-so / If I should ever let it go." The result is one of the most aggressively cheerful songs to come out of America's most dismal decade.

It's Only a Paper Moon
Lyrics by E. Y. "Yip" Harburg and Billy Rose, music by Harold Arlen

Billy Rose, the producer of a show called *The Great Magoo*, asked lyricist Yip Harburg to come up with a song for a jaded carnival barker who regards all of life as a tissue of lies and artifice—until he falls in love. Suddenly he wants to believe in the very stuff he has hitherto regarded as hokum. Harburg knew a composer, Harold Arlen, who had a melody that would be perfect. Rose liked the tune and suggested they all work on it. "When Billy Rose said, 'Let's sit down and do it,'" Harburg later recalled, "he's the producer of the show; he's paying you an advance; you're a neophyte; what are you going to do? You sit down."

What Rose wanted was a "cut-in," songwriting slang for placing someone's name on the copyright of a song so he could get a share of its royalties, although Harburg actually crafted the unusual lyric. "I got an idea," he said, "there's a guy, who sees the lights of Broadway, thinks the whole world is that, that the moon is a paper moon, everything is a Barnum and Bailey world." Weaving a list of tawdry versions of traditional romantic images—paper moon, cardboard sea, canvas sky, and muslin tree—Harburg revealed that the barker regarded the world as fakery made from the cheapest materials. Yet even as he derides that romantic world as a "honky-tonk parade," the barker insists that it would not be "phony" "if you believed in me"—a catchphrase that was the original title of the song.

Such a clever love song was characteristic of Harburg, who said, "I doubt that I can ever say 'I love you' head on—it's not the way I think. For me the task is never to say the thing directly, and yet to say it—to think in a curve, so to speak."

Night and Day
Lyrics and music by Cole Porter

With Fred Astaire on board for a new show to be called *The Gay Divorce*, Cole Porter set out to write a song tailored to the dancer's limited vocal range, with a forty-eight measure melody that still stayed within Astaire's vocal range of an octave and a half and revolved around easily sung repeated notes.

Writing the music first was a departure from Porter's normal way of creating a song by deciding upon a rhythm, writing the lyric, then composing the melody. As he was working on the song, his old friend from Yale, Monty Woolley, dropped by, listened, and, according to George Eels, "announced that he had no idea what Cole was trying to do but that it was terrible and he should give it up." Woolley's disparaging comment undermined Porter's efforts to come up with a lyric until the next weekend, which he spent with the Astors. As they were having lunch on the porch during a rainstorm, Mrs. Astor complained about a broken eave spout: "That drip, drip, drip is driving me mad!"

"I think that will work!" Porter exclaimed as he rushed to the piano to try out the lyrical idea. By adding the "tick tick tock" of a clock and the "beat, beat, beat" of a tom-tom, Porter had the perfect sequence of aural images to fit the repeated note sequences of the verse. Yet he preferred to tell the story that "Night and Day" was inspired by a Mohammedan chant that he had heard in a mosque in Morocco.

Although Porter was exultant over his completed song, Astaire doubted that he could sing it and complained to one of the show's producers that he feared his voice would crack. The producer suggested the song be cut, but Porter insisted he had written it for Astaire's voice. The song stayed in the show even though nobody but Porter liked it.

It was also the only song from Porter's score used in the movie version of the show, retitled *The Gay Divorcee*, to avoid the censors (who would object to the idea that divorce could be "gay" but knew that divorcees could—because even "widows" could be "merry").

It is clear now how important "Night and Day" was for Porter, for Astaire and Rogers, and for RKO; however, at the time, the song was overshadowed in *The Gay Divorcee* by "The Continental," another group dance, like "The Carioca," written by Herb Magidson and Con Conrad. "The Continental" was featured in a huge production number that ran for seventeen minutes; promotional ads in newspapers diagrammed its steps, and the song won the Academy Award in 1935—the first year an Oscar was given for best song. However, it is Porter's "Night and Day" that has endured as one of the greatest standards.

The Song Is You; I've Told Ev'ry Little Star
Lyrics by Oscar Hammerstein, music by Jerome Kern

During the 1930s, for successes and failures alike, Jerome Kern and Oscar Hammerstein wrote scores that were blessed with remarkable songs. "The Song Is You" was Kern's personal favorite, though he always called it "I Hear Music." As soon as he finished writing it, he called Hammerstein to play it for him. Kern's dazzling harmonies carry the listener through a dramatic melody sometimes barely whispered, sometimes soaring to a moment of impassioned reverie: "Why can't I let you know the song my heart would sing / A beautiful rhapsody of love and youth and spring."

The song is intensely romantic from its opening line: "I hear music when I look at you / A beautiful theme of ev'ry dream I ever knew." Within the show, it is also part of a sophisticated comic scene between two worldly lovers who acknowledge that the man uses the song to seduce other women. When composer Arthur Schwartz heard it at rehearsal, he asked Kern, "How can you sacrifice this sensational melody which will not be heard by anybody with all this physical stuff going on?" Kern did not take kindly to questions about his songs. He replied only, "The scene calls for it."

Though it sounds like a corny movie plot, Kern's melody for the trilling "I've Told Ev'ry Little Star" was actually inspired by a bird's song. This particular bird woke Kern during a visit to Nantucket. After the bird flew off, Kern sang the melody to himself and went back to sleep. Later that morning, he was unable to recreate what he had heard. Fortunately, the bird reappeared early the next morning, as if by appointment. Kern listened for a while before grabbing a pencil and an index card. When he finished, he wrote at the bottom, "6 a.m. Bird song from the willow tree outside east window. J. K." He later observed, "It was a complete phrase and a perfectly rounded melodic treatment." Kern did not reproduce the bird's song literally but used it as the basis for the song's melodic theme.

Unlike Kern, Hammerstein got no extra help. Despite the melody's lilt, the lyric proved extremely difficult to write. Hammerstein later remembered his frustration: "There were times during those hot August days when I wished the sparrow had kept his big mouth shut!"

Fourteen years later, on November 5, 1945, Jerome Kern collapsed on a sidewalk in New York City. Oscar Hammerstein sat at his friend's bedside until, on November 11, Kern died. Maintaining his vigil to the end, Hammerstein remembered Jerry's fondness for "I've Told Ev'ry Little Star." He lifted the oxygen tent and sang it softly in his ear. Only when he had finished and Kern failed to respond did Hammerstein begin to weep.

Willow Weep for Me
Lyrics and music by Ann Ronell

As music editor of the campus magazine, *The Radcliffe,* Ann Ronell asked George Gershwin for an interview. She played him some of her songs and he encouraged her to go into musical theater. "Look," he said, "There are only two ways to get into Broadway musicals—by dancing in the chorus or playing piano for rehearsals. Come on over to a rehearsal and I'll show you." She worked as a rehearsal pianist for Gershwin's *Show Girl* and Vincent Youmans' *Great Day*, but got nowhere with her songs. As a woman, she was brushed off by music publishers, but when an arranger demonstrated one of her songs, it got noticed. "That's a good tune," the publisher said. "Who wrote it?"

"That little girl that hangs around here every day," said the arranger.

The next day, the publisher took Ann and her song, "Baby's Birthday Party," to Rudy Vallee and Guy Lombardo, both of whom liked it. "It was lucky enough to be a hit," Ronell recalled, "and that's how I got started. Pure chance—a shot in the dark."

Her most complex and sophisticated song, "Willow Weep for Me," caught the ear of Irving Berlin, even though it had an unusual cross rhythm—the right and left hands playing in different time signatures on the piano—that would have taxed Berlin's limited musical abilities. Writing lyrics and music, Ronell underscored the dramatic octave drops and triplets that dominate the melody with assonance and alliteration: "Willow weep-for-me / Bend your bran-ches-green a-long-the stream that runs-to-sea." Berlin even allowed Ronell to dedicate "Willow Weep for Me" to George Gershwin on the sheet music—a violation of Tin Pan Alley practice.

The success of "Willow Weep for Me" earned her the assignment to write lyrics to Frank Churchill's melody, "Who's Afraid of the Big Bad Wolf?" for the Disney cartoon, *The Three Little Pigs*. "It came out in the depths of the Depression," Ronell recalled, "and I think people liked it because it was the song of the little guy laughing at the big, bad guy. I like to write music for the little guy."

1933

AS THOUSANDS CHEER
Lyrics and music by Irving Berlin

George S. Kaufman wittily remarked that "Satire is what closes on Saturday night," but the success of *As Thousands Cheer* proved him at least partly wrong. Playwright Moss Hart said that he and Irving Berlin quickly "hit upon the idea of writing a topical show right off the front pages of the newspapers." Each of the sketches and songs came from a different part of the paper—the society page, the comics, the weather report, and advice to the lovelorn, as well as the news pages—and each began by flashing a headline across the proscenium arch. "Heat Wave Hits New York" led to the sexy comic number, "Heat Wave," and, in a strikingly different mood, "Unknown Negro Lynched by Angry Mob" led to the powerfully dramatic "Supper Time." Both were sung by Ethel Waters. Berlin hired Waters after hearing her sing at the Cotton Club. That made her the first black star to receive equal billing with whites, and it made *As Thousands Cheer* Broadway's first truly integrated musical as Waters appeared in sketches with white cast members.

The simplest and cleverest of her four songs, "Heat Wave" is a tropical number about a sizzling woman who reached Manhattan from Martinique and promptly "started a heat wave / By letting her seat wave."

The dancing stars of Irving Berlin's *As Thousands Cheer,* Marilyn Miller and Clifton Webb. Courtesy of Photofest.

Berlin's trick was to pick up the long vowel "e" from "heat," the song's most important word. He lets it play through the lyric, at one point rhyming it three times in three lines. In addition, the rhythm shifts the emphasis to the last syllable, transforming it from feminine to masculine, and making it emphatic and funny. "Gee," he begins, "her anato*my* makes the mercu*ry* jump to ninety-*three—ee.*"

When Hart first heard Berlin play the song, he thought it "sounded terrible." He asked Berlin to play it again. "It sounded even more terrible." Then it occurred to him that the problem might not be the song but rather Berlin's singing and playing. He asked him to play "Always," which Hart loved, and found the results every bit as bad. So his confidence in Berlin was restored.

"Harlem on My Mind," another Waters solo, was a chic bluesy lament, one of hundreds of songs about Harlem from the 1920s and 1930s. It purports to reveal the ambivalent feelings of the expatriate singing star, Josephine Baker, who appeared in the *Folies Bergere* clad in a short skirt made of bananas—and nothing else. Though the character in the song appears on the arm of a marquis, she misses home, as her "lips begin to whisper 'Mon Cheri' / But my heart keeps singing 'Hi-de-ho.'" The song is poignant and sympathetic, but it also satirizes the sophisticated *hauteur* Baker had picked up in *Paree* and that alienated many blacks. There is a story about an encounter between Baker and Lorenz Hart's outspoken maid, Mary Campbell. In the course of a *soiree*, Baker spoke to her imperiously, "*Donnez-moi une tasse de cafe, s'il vous plait.*" Campbell replied, "Honey, talk the way your mouth was born."

After hearing Waters at the Cotton Club, Berlin told her agents, "We're going to try to inject a serious note into this musical." He was referring to "Supper Time," a song so troubling it was hard to know where to put it in an otherwise comic show. If someone without Berlin's clout had written it, it almost certainly would have been cut. However, Berlin was determined. A wave of lynchings sweeping the South had appalled him. Years later, he said, "People told me I was crazy to write a dirge like that," but he was convinced a musical about the news needed at least one serious song. Waters wrote in her autobiography:

> If one song can tell the whole tragic history of a race it was that song. In singing it, I was telling my comfortable, well-fed, well-dressed listeners about my people …. When I was through and that big, heavy curtain came down, I was called back again and again. I had stopped the show with a type of song never before heard in a revue.

The song is so understated it never mentions the lynching. A mother in a rural cabin is preparing dinner for her children when she learns that her husband has been lynched, yet she must continue the mundane task of cooking a meal. Berlin transforms the frequently repeated title line into a penetrating wail in a melody that combines the feel of a dirge with echoes of spirituals: "How can I be thankful when they start to thank the Lord, Oh, Lord!" Unlike "Strange Fruit" (Lewis Allen, 1939), the other great song about lynching, "Supper Time" relies on narrative and a character's overwhelming emotion rather than imagery. Instead of the haunting image of "strange fruit / Blood on the leaves, blood at the root," Berlin's lyric dramatizes the moment of impenetrable grief: "Supper time, I should set the table 'cause it's supper time."

As great as "Supper Time" is, it was not the score's most important song. In 1917, Berlin had written "Smile and Show Your Dimple" a little wartime cheer-up song designed to brighten those sad maidens whose doughboys had just left for France. In 1933, he rewrote it because, he explained, he needed an Act One finale: "We wanted a big Fifth Avenue number. I wanted an old-fashioned type song, but I couldn't come up with anything." Then he remembered "Smile and Show Your Dimple." He kept the catchy opening, recast the rest of the melody, and wrote a new lyric. He also changed the title to "Easter Parade." "A song is like a marriage," Berlin later explained, "It takes a perfect blending of the two mates, the music and the words, to make a perfect match. In the case of 'Easter Parade,' it took a divorce and a second marriage to bring about the happiest of unions."

The number portrayed people anticipating their stroll along Fifth Avenue on Easter Sunday, everyone dressed in brown to simulate the sepia tones of a newspaper's rotogravure. The irony here is that the Easter Parade is mainly for the upper crust who belong on Fifth Avenue. Popular songs are usually democratic, even classless, but class differences sharpened during the Depression, even in songs. In "Easter Parade," Berlin portrays a fellow who thinks the most beautiful "bonnet" is the one "with all the frills upon it," hardly a definition of elegance. He and his girl puff up with pride when he imagines that "You'll find that you're / In the rotogravure." These are good-humored working-class people, heading for what may be their very first Easter Parade.

The show's satiric approach took on a surprisingly bitter note backstage. During the show's tryout in Philadelphia, Marilyn Miller, Helen Broderick, and Clifton Webb told Berlin they would not take bows with Ethel Waters. Berlin said he would, of course, respect their feelings, only then there would be no bows at all. The next night, all four stars bowed together.

FORTY-SECOND STREET
Lyrics by Al Dubin, music by Harry Warren

The smart, savvy songs Harry Warren and Al Dubin wrote between 1933 and 1938 helped to define the Warner Bros. musical by capturing the dark, driven feel of the Great Depression. In drafty dressing rooms and cramped apartments overlooking concrete courtyards, the lovable smart alecks in the Warner Bros. backstagers sang the quick, in-your-face songs by Warren and Dubin that gave voice to their pursuit of stardom or love.

Warren and Dubin wrote four songs for the legendary musical, *Forty-Second Street*: the title song and "You're Getting to Be a Habit with Me," "Shuffle Off to Buffalo," and "Young and Healthy." They wrote them to be show-stopping performance numbers, with Warren's sharp rhythms and repeated melodic phrases especially well suited to Busby Berkeley's camera-driven choreography. The movie told the familiar story of an over-bearing star who breaks her ankle just before opening night. Unless the show opens, the director, played by Warner Baxter, will be ruined. Ruby Keeler, as a chorine in her first show, steps in to save the day, going out there a youngster but coming back a star.

"You're Getting to Be a Habit with Me" was one of those songs that grew from a casual remark. Warren explained that "Dubin liked to kid around

Harry Warren (at the piano) and Al Dubin. Courtesy of Photofest.

with the girls. One of them … was going around with a certain fellow, and Dubin asked her why. She said, 'Oh, I don't know. He's getting to be a habit with me.' We used it right away." The song is much more pointed than the remark that sparked it. It gives a streetwise twist to Hollywood's typical ways of saying "I love you" as it uses Warren's insistently repeated triplets to suggest that love's a metaphoric addiction. The helpless lover complains, "Ev'ry kiss, ev'ry hug seems to act just like a drug." By the time he admits he "couldn't do without my supply," the drug metaphor has paved the way for the brazen proposal, "I must have you ev'ry day."

For Warren's punchy urban melody to the title song, Dubin wrote brief, vivid sketches, characterized by internal rhymes that make his lyrical lines feel even shorter than they are. The language is hip and ironic, and the song revels in its New York point of view: "Little nifties from the Fifties, innocent and sweet; / Sexy ladies from the Eighties, who are indiscreet." Ruby Keeler sings and then tap dances in her girlishly lumbering way atop a taxicab as the camera pulls back to reveal a dizzying phantasmagoria of New York City street life played out against a wildly distorted Manhattan skyline that suddenly turns into dancing chorines.

Lazybones
Lyrics by Johnny Mercer, music by Hoagy Carmichael

One day in 1933, Johnny Mercer, in Hoagy Carmichael's words, "a young, bouncy butterball of a man from Georgia," climbed the stairs to Carmichael's apartment to announce, "I'd like to write a song called 'Lazybones.'" All he had in mind was that single word. Soon Carmichael had built a melody from a phrase he had used in "Washboard Blues" in 1926. That first day, they worked out the first sixteen bars, a month later they got the bridge, and three months after that, they got the ending. Then Carmichael came up with the line, "You never heared a word I say." Mercer said, "Well, of course, I got credit for it because my name was on the lyric."

The entire song took about a year, and Mercer was astonished at how much hard work it involved even though there was a story going around that they finished the entire song in twenty minutes. "Oh, God!" Mercer remembered, "It took a long time. Hoagy suffered through long months of waiting until I came up with the lyrics." Soon, "Lazybones" was selling fifteen thousand copies a day, perhaps because something about its languid melody and colloquial lyric touched a chord during the Depression. Mercer had created a character blissfully unaware of the terrible need to work.

Like Carmichael and Sidney Arodin's "Lazy River" before it (1931) and Nick and Charles Kenny's "Gone Fishin'" after it (1950), "Lazybones" embraces laziness as a way of life, as do many songs that conjure up the heat of a Southern or prairie summer. Mercer's lyric portrays someone who scolds a youngster for whiling away the time: "Lazybones, sleepin' in the shade, how you 'spect to get your cornmeal made?" The use of dialect, unusual by 1933, makes it clear the characters are black. Some have found the song patronizing, but Mercer writes with sympathetic good humor: "When taters need sprayin', I bet you keep prayin' the bugs fall off the vine."

Let's Fall in Love; Stormy Weather
Lyrics by Ted Koehler, music by Harold Arlen

"Let's Fall in Love" has to be one of the most unusual ways to say "I love you" in thirty-two bars. After the romantic plea of the title, the lyric turns disputatious, with the singer challenging his lover, "Why shouldn't we fall in love?" as if they were arguing. The song is another instance of how Ted Koehler was able to match Harold Arlen's rhythmic melodies with lyrics that echoed the vernacular of the streets.

For Arlen, however, the Tin Pan Alley formula of a thirty-two bar chorus soon became too confining. He originally wrote one of his most innovative departures from the formula for Cab Calloway but eventually gave it to Ethel Waters. When Waters sang "Stormy Weather" in *Cotton Club Parade*, under a lamppost lit with a blue spotlight and backed by Duke Ellington's orchestra, the song became her trademark.

Not only did Arlen push beyond the limits of the thirty-two bar pop song formula, he also veered from the standard way of creating a Tin Pan Alley melody by repeating the same melodic phrase over and over at higher or lower intervals; however, he did not realize it until George Gershwin pointed it out to him. Arlen recalled, "He said, 'You know, you didn't repeat a phrase in the first eight bars?' And I never gave it a thought."

Koehler wove truncated vernacular phrases into a relentless lament by using very subtle rhymes: "Can't *go on*, ev'rything I have is *gone*." A song of romantic loss, "Stormy Weather" captured the universal gloom many Americans felt in the depths of the Depression and even gave expression to Ethel Waters' personal suffering. "When I got out there in the middle of the Cotton Club floor," Waters said,

> I was telling the things I couldn't frame in words. I was singing the story of my misery and confusion, of the misunderstandings in my life that I couldn't straighten out, the story of the wrongs and outrages done to me by people I had loved and trusted. I sang "Stormy Weather" from the depth of the private hell in which I was being crushed and suffocated.

Because Arlen never wrote an enduring Broadway musical, his name is not as well known as Irving Berlin, George Gershwin, and Cole Porter. He loved to tell the story of how he got into a taxicab one day and found that the driver was whistling "Stormy Weather."

"Do you know who wrote that song?" Arlen asked.

"Sure," the cabbie replied, "Irving Berlin."

"Wrong," Arlen said, "But I'll give you two more guesses." After the cabbie guessed Richard Rodgers and Cole Porter, Arlen said, "No, you're wrong again. I wrote that song."

"Then who are you?" the driver asked.

"I'm Harold Arlen."

The cabbie drove another half block, then stopped, turned around, and asked, "Who?"

Smoke Gets in Your Eyes; Yesterdays
Lyrics by Otto Harbach, music by Jerome Kern

It seems unjust that Otto Harbach, who wrote books and lyrics for more than forty musicals and at one point in 1925 had five different shows playing on Broadway simultaneously, is primarily remembered today for only two songs, "Smoke Gets in Your Eyes" and "Yesterdays," from *Roberta*, his last successful show with composer Jerome Kern. Harbach's book for *Roberta*, originally entitled *Gowns by Roberta*, was a fluffy tale of an American football player who inherits a Parisian dress shop, but among its other songs are "The Touch of Your Hand" and "You're Devastating."

The melody for "Smoke Gets in Your Eyes" was one Harbach came across as he was looking through Kern's trunk of unused songs. Kern had written it as a tap-dance number for *Show Boat* but never used it. Looking at the rapid-fire eighth-notes, Harbach asked Kern if they could be slowed down to form the melody of a ballad. When Kern reworked the melody, the lyricist created one of his most poetic songs by comparing a fading romance to a dying fire whose smoke brings tears to a lover's eyes. Part of an older generation of operetta lyricists, Harbach was comfortable using such archly "poetic" terms and expressions as "laughing friends deride" and "so I chaffed them and I gaily laughed."

Harbach used the same elevated vocabulary in "Yesterdays," in which he rhymed "yesterdays" with "happy, sweet sequester'd days" and "gay youth was mine, Truth was mine, / Joyous, free, and flaming life forsooth was mine." Despite that "forsooth" and the other flashes of archaic diction, "Yesterdays" and "Smoke Gets in Your Eyes" became enormously popular. It was fitting that the star of *Roberta* was Fay Templeton, whose picture on a theater poster, thirty years earlier, had inspired Otto Harbach to abandon literary studies for Broadway.

Alan Jay Lerner, one of the songwriters most deeply influenced by Harbach, related a story about the lyricist in his last years. Nearly blind and confined to a wheelchair, one morning Otto Harbach told his son he had not been able to sleep because he had struggled all through the night trying improve his lyric to "Smoke Gets in Your Eyes"—a song he had written thirty years earlier.

Sophisticated Lady
Lyrics and music by Duke Ellington, Irving Mills, and Mitchell Parish

When music publisher Irving Mills heard Duke Ellington's band, "The Washingtonians," in 1925, he realized that their complex jazz arrangements could become the basis of successful popular songs. Mills proposed a partnership to Ellington but insisted that his name appear on the credits for Ellington's songs, thus assuring himself not only the publisher's share of royalties but also a portion of the songwriter's. When people accused him of stealing from Ellington, Mills defended himself by saying, "I wrote 'Sophisticated Lady' with him and 'Mood Indigo,' 'Solitude,' 'In a Sentimental Mood.'" What Mills meant was that, as Ellington's publisher, he routinely suggested the composer write certain kinds of songs, offered

Duke Ellington. Courtesy of Photofest.

ideas about titles and themes, and simplified the music for popular consumption. "Whatever they did, I thinned out," Mills said. "His music was always too heavy."

If Mills profited from Ellington's creativity, it seems that Ellington did the same to his band members. Otto Hardwick and Lawrence Brown claimed to have worked out the melody for "Sophisticated Lady" and were supported by lyricist Barney Bigard, who said. "That's the only thing I didn't like about Duke. He never gave the boys in the band the credit they deserved."

Irving Mills could be just as niggardly about sharing credit with the lyricists he hired to put words to Ellington's compositions. However, when he commissioned Mitchell Parish to set words to "Sophisticated Lady," Parish insisted his name appear on the sheet music. Parish, who held a day job as a court reporter, was enjoying great success with the lyric he had set to Hoagy Carmichael's "Star Dust" and that may have given him the temerity to demand credit rather than a flat fee for his work.

Despite so many cooks, "Sophisticated Lady" has a unity of words and music. "The song is built on plaintive descending chromatics," observes James Lincoln Collier, "that do have something of the flavor of the decadent lady nursing her wounds in an expensive restaurant." In lines such as "Smoking, drinking, / Never thinking of tomorrow," however, Ellington's son heard his father's heartfelt concern for "my mother, her depressed state of mind and consequent drinking after their breakup."

We're in the Money
Lyrics by Al Dubin, music by Harry Warren

Rarely has a movie musical opened with such engaging deception. From the lie in the title to the inspired daffiness of having Ginger Rogers sing a chorus in Pig Latin, Harry Warren and Al Dubin's "We're in the Money" gives the Depression an unrelieved razzing right at the start of *Gold Diggers of 1933*. Melody and lyrics have the snappy rhythmic style of their best songs. Writing about money, Dubin sets a pulsating triple internal rhyme to Warren's emphatic tune, "Let's lend it, spend it, send it rolling along." However, there isn't any money; the song is nothing but fakery. The deception continues as Rogers sings at one end of a long line of chorines but, as the camera pans to the other end in a single shot, there she is again, still pert and sexy, still dressed in a shiny, scanty costume of oversized coins—thereby making the title line literal. She is, indeed, "in the money."

The audience is sure the song is a big production number in a Broadway musical until grumpy comedian Ned Sparks calls a halt to what turns out to be a rehearsal. In fact, he is calling a halt to the whole show because the finance men have just arrived to claim the sets and props. Of all the movies Warren and Dubin worked on together, *Gold Diggers of 1933* showed the effects of the Depression most directly, especially in the movie's final song, "Remember My Forgotten Man." Like Jay Gorney and Yip Harburg's 1932 classic, "Brother, Can You Spare a Dime?" this large-scale production number explored the shattered hopes of those who had fought in World War I. Harburg's lyric had let one man speak for all those who were reduced to begging while Dubin's invents a loyal woman who bemoans the fate of the man she loves. Dubin's lyric, set to Warren's dirge-like march, is a blunt and clumsy but powerful call to remember the "forgotten man": "You had him cultivate the land; he walked behind the plow, / The sweat fell from his brow, but look at him right now!"

1934

ANYTHING GOES
Lyrics and music by Cole Porter

As it went from being titled *Hard to Get* to *Bon Voyage*, the Cole Porter musical about a penniless playboy, an evangelist turned nightclub hostess, and a gangster disguised as a minister—all set aboard an ocean liner—went through more than the usual tryout tribulations. Only the first act was complete when rehearsals began, and it still lacked an ending on the eve of Boston tryouts. Ethel Merman remembered playwrights Howard Lindsay and Russel Crouse rushing "out of the men's room clutching wads of toilet tissue and announcing that they had just written the last sheet of the show." "It was during this period of panic and frustration that the show's ultimate title was bestowed on it," noted Charles Schwartz, "*Anything Goes*, a fitting title for a production born and nurtured in the line of fire."

Porter's title song takes the catchphrase "anything goes" and turns it to reflect the moral abandon of the age—"when good authors, too, who once knew better words now only use four-letter words"—but also to register the mutability of all material things in the Depression, when "Vanderbilts and Whitneys lack baby clothes."

From his trunk, Porter pulled a song he had written back in 1931; it suited the brassy character Merman typically played—in this case, Reno Sweeney, a world-weary dame "vainly fighting the old ennui." After complaining that she gets no "kick" from alcohol or cocaine, Merman pays her lover the back-handed compliment of wondering why "I get a kick out of you." Merman always got a laugh out of the line that "if" she took even a "sniff" of cocaine it would bore her "teriffic'ly." She would pretend to snort cocaine, then pause, seemingly tipsy, over the word "terrif—ic'ly."

In this song, too, Porter played with the ambivalence of his title phrase: on the one hand, the bored singer gets a surprising "high" from the man she loves; however, she says he "obviously" doesn't "adore me," so that the "kick" is also a cool rebuff that leaves her longing for more. The singer continues her catalog of things that fail to get her "high" by panning even the novelty of an airplane ride, but Porter altered his original lyric, which had a reference to "the fair Mrs. Lindbergh," out of respect for the Lindbergh family after the kidnapping and murder of their baby. The revised lyric contains one of his cleverest internal rhymes: "*Flyi*ng too *high* with some *guy* in the *sky* is my *i*dea of nothing to do."

The catalog song to end—or perhaps top—all catalog songs is "You're the Top." The pyrotechnical lyric juxtaposes images of high European art—the Louvre Museum, the Mona Lisa, a Shakespeare sonnet, a symphony by Strauss (who never wrote one)—with images drawn from American pop culture: cellophane, Ovaltine, Mickey Mouse, a "Berlin ballad." At times, however, these juxtapositions overlap: "You're Whistler's mama" slangily invokes a painting that hangs in the Louvre but is also a common cultural icon; "inferno's Dante" and "the nose on the great Durante" could be construed not only as a contrast between high European and low American culture but also (because Dante wrote *The Divine Comedy*) as a pairing of two Italian "comedians."

Audiences demanded encore after encore of "You're the Top," and Porter kept adding lyrics to satisfy them. At one performance, Ethel Merman signaled to the audience to stop applauding for another reprise: "There are no more lyrics," she yelled. Parodies of the song appeared in newspapers, and one ribald verse was long thought to have been written by Porter:

> You're the burning heat of a bridal suite in use,
> You're the breasts of Venus,
> You're King Kong's penis,
> You're self-abuse.

Historian Robert Kimball recently discovered the true author: Irving Berlin.

If "You're the Top" stopped the show with its witty lyrics, "Blow, Gabriel, Blow" gave Ethel Merman the opportunity to use her trumpet-like voice. Porter loved writing for Merman, whom he called "La Merman." When she had difficulty with "Blow, Gabriel, Blow," Porter took the unusual step of revising the song to suit her. Normally, he would throw a song out of a show rather than revise it. "Rewriting," he said, "ruins songs." When leading man William Gaxton complained about his song, "Easy to Love," saying he could not hit the high notes, Porter replaced it with "All Through the Night" and filed "Easy to Love" in his "trunk."

Blue Moon
Lyrics by Lorenz Hart, music by Richard Rodgers

In 1934, MGM told Richard Rodgers and Lorenz Hart to write a song for Jean Harlow to sing in *Hollywood Party*. Because the sultry sex goddess was playing an innocent young stenographer who longs to be a movie star, they wrote "Prayer": "Oh Lord, if you're not busy up there, / I ask for help with a prayer." The studio threw it out of the picture.

Rodgers liked the melody, however, so when MGM told them to write a title song for another movie, *Manhattan Melodrama*, Larry Hart supplied new words: "Act One: You gulp your coffee and run; / Into the subway you crowd. / Don't breathe—it isn't allowed." The studio cut the song again. Rodgers kept the same melody for yet another song, and Larry Hart came up with a *third* set of lyrics, "The Bad in Every Man": "Oh Lord, what is the matter with me? / I'm just permitted to see / The bad in ev'ry man." The song was ignored even when *Manhattan Melodrama* drew crowds because it was the movie John Dillinger watched before he was gunned down outside the Biograph Theatre in Chicago.

Rodgers was so disappointed that he took his song to a Tin Pan Alley publisher. The publisher said he thought it could be a hit if Larry Hart would just write a simple, down-to-earth set of words to it. Hart was offended. "You mean some junk about 'moon' and 'June'?" Nevertheless, he sat down and wrote a *fourth* set of lyrics: "Blue moon, you saw me standing alone, / Without a dream in my heart, without a love of my own." "Blue Moon" became Rodgers and Hart's most successful song—"the only success we ever had," Rodgers remarked, "that was not associated with a stage or screen musical."

I Like the Likes of You
Lyrics by E. Y. Harburg, music by Vernon Duke

Autumn in New York
Lyrics and music by Vernon Duke

Although the great Ziegfeld died in 1932, flattened financially by the Crash of 1929, his widow, Billie Burke, revived his lavish annual revues and even joined forces with the Shubert brothers, who had been Ziegfeld's archenemies. For their first production, the Shuberts asked Vernon Duke and Yip Harburg to contribute some songs to the score. One of the biggest hits from the show was "I Like the Likes of You," the "most relentlessly inarticulate of Yip's songs of love-struck inarticulation," note Harold Meyerson and Ernie Harburg. "The singer works and reworks his sentence to try to get it right, as he feels more and more deflated and unable to formulate his thought: "Oh dear, if I could only say what I mean / I mean, if I could mean what I say."

Although the song became a hit, Duke and Harburg, both volatile, temperamental men, never worked together again. Even though he wrote in popular and classical idioms, Duke, unlike George Gershwin, never achieved a singular musical style. While he was working on a ballet, he was also writing popular songs. At the time, he was living in Connecticut and one day was "seized with a longing to be back in New York, where things were always happening—particularly in late summer, producers' offices all a-buzz with new productions and orchestra conductors returning from their European jaunts with novelties hot off composers' griddles." Out of that longing, Duke wrote what he called "a paean to Manhattan," but because he was alone, he wrote a lyric as well, peppered with such urbane phrases as "glittering crowds and shimmering clouds in canyons of steel" and "jaded roués and gay divorcees who lunch at the Ritz." When he played it for friends in Connecticut, he found that the sophisticated music and lyrics had them "retreating to the bar in the middle of the verse."

Still, Duke regarded the song as "a genuine emotional outburst" and when Murray Anderson, the producer of a revue called *Thumbs Up*, said the show needed "a nostalgic evocation of Manhattan in the fall, red leaves falling in Central Park, young people coming home from vacations," Duke said "I may have what you want … only it's a crazy song; it moves from key to key and that makes it hard on a singer."

"Whose lyric?" Anderson asked.
"Mine."
"What do you call it?"
"Autumn in New York."

The producer "let out a refined whoop," ushered Duke into a cab to demonstrate the song, and immediately interpolated it into the score. "Autumn in New York" may be the closest Duke came to uniting his serious and popular compositions and in finding a collaborator—himself—with whom he could work.

I Only Have Eyes for You
Lyrics by Al Dubin, music by Harry Warren

By 1933, the Warner Bros. "backstager" musical formula was producing one hit movie after another, from *42nd Street* to *Footlight Parade*. The secret of their success was the way in which Busby Berkeley filmed production numbers based on the songs of Al Dubin and Harry Warren. Numbers like "Shadow Waltz," in which Berkley's chorines dance with violins, and "By a Waterfall," in which they swim in synchronized patterns, were presented as staged performances before a live audience, but no one in a theater audience could possibly have viewed them from such cinematic angles. As Berkley's production numbers became longer and increasingly elaborate, the songs had to be repeated over and over again.

No Warren and Dubin song was more durable than "I Only Have Eyes for You," whose chorus is heard eleven times while Dick Powell dreams that he sees Ruby Keeler's picture on billboards all over town. After dance routines performed on several revolving stages as well as a Ferris wheel, the number culminates with fragments of Keeler's face interlocking, jigsaw-puzzle fashion, to form an enormous image that underscores the assertion "I Only Have Eyes for You." What sustained the song through this elaborate sequence was Dubin's ability to match Warren's driving, insistent melody by subtly repeating rhymes, as in the *I / eye* rhyme in the title, "*Are* the *stars* out tonight" in the opening line of the chorus, the carryover from "*for you*" to "*or* on a crowded ave*nue*," and the way the *oo* sound in "ave*nue*" leads immediately to "*You* are here, so am I."

At the same time that he crafted these subtle sound effects, Dubin's ear was attuned to the Depression. His characters spend less time dreaming about trips to the stars than downing cups of coffee. Even when he devotes the first two choruses of a song to the stars and the moon, it's to say they don't matter. What he wrote almost always comes down to Earth in its outlook and in the feel of everyday talk that lends it conviction.

The pressure Warner Bros. put on the two men to crank out songs for movie after movie took its toll on Dubin. Always a gargantuan eater and drinker, he began taking drugs and would frequently escape to New York, Cuba, or Mexico. Once he called Harry Warren at two in the morning to say he had completed a new lyric but, more important, "I just ate some quail and they were delicious." Warren demanded to know where the lyricist was. "I'm in Juarez," Dubin answered, "I'm at the local cat house. I got my inspiration right here, Harry. I just finished the lyrics for that great tune of yours." He then sang into the phone, "Where Am I, Am I in Heaven?"

Let's Take a Walk Around the Block
Lyrics by Ira Gershwin and Yip Harburg, music by Harold Arlen

Lovers want nothing more than to be *alone together*. In the days of chaperones, that took a certain amount of ingenuity, so they would sneak off in canoes ("Paddlin' Madeline Home," lyrics and music by Harry Woods,

1925) or take long walks. "Walking songs" came into their own, though, during the Great Depression when almost everybody was broke. People could not afford to buy a car or even take in a movie but could always take a walk. In 1930, Harry Warren, Mort Dixon, and Billy Rose's jaunty "Would You Like to Take a Walk?" began with a beguiling invitation that quickly turned into a conversation as the lovers strolled along together, the lyric blending small talk with bigger ideas just hinted at: "Mm-Mm-Mm Are you tired of the talkies? / I prefer the walkies / Sump'n good'll come from that."

The same collaborators wrote an even better "walking song" a year later. "I Found a Million Dollar Baby" is about a man who ducks into a five-and-ten to get out of the rain and serendipitously finds the girl of his dreams. Even though it rained for only an hour, "I hung around for three or four / Around the million dollar baby in the five and ten cent store."

The cleverest and most expansive of the "walking songs" takes us back to the Depression: Harold Arlen, Ira Gershwin, and Yip Harburg's "Let's Take a Walk Around the Block," from the Broadway revue, *Life Begins at 8:40*. Arlen said of the lyricists' tight, witty wordplay, "Two very interesting guys, always experimenting with words. Using the language, twisting it, bending it," but the lyric's distinctive mix of comedy and fantasy suggests it is mainly Yip's song. In their biography of Harburg, Harold Meyerson and Ernie Harburg call it a "laid-back soft shoe" that "requires a slow-building lyric."

The singer can't afford to do anything but take a walk even though he's saving his nickels and imagining the future, so the comedy does not take off until the final stanza of the first chorus when references to "London and Maytime" and "Venice in playtime" turn into "Boston in bean-time." From here on, the play is unrestrained—"In winter at Christmas, we'll visit the isthmus / And see how they lock up a lock"—as the dream of travel becomes increasingly more inventive, unlikely, and funny.

Love in Bloom; June in January
Lyrics by Leo Robin, music by Ralph Rainger

Love Is Just Around the Corner
Lyrics by Leo Robin, music by Lewis Gensler

Listeners of a certain age have only to hear the opening measures of Ralph Rainger's "Love in Bloom" to imagine Don Wilson's familiar baritone intoning "It's the Jack Benny Program!" Though it was a hit song on its own in 1934, "Love in Bloom" survived for another forty years as the theme song for America's best-loved skinflint and as the tune most often massacred by Benny's mock-terrible fiddle-scraping.

The song was originally a major hit for Bing Crosby because it was the sort of overheated ballad that lent itself to crooning. Crosby's success inspired many dance bands to create special arrangements of the song. One night, Benny and his wife, Mary Livingstone, were in a supper club when the band asked him to join them for their next number. He borrowed a fiddle and played along on "Love in Bloom." He later explained that: "My spontaneous performance turned up being written about in some column, with the writer wisecracking that 'Jack Benny playing 'Love in Bloom' sounded like a breath of fresh air … if you liked fresh air ….'" The next week, as they entered another club, the orchestra leader started playing "Love in Bloom." "The thing just caught on," Benny said,

> … so I decided to adopt it as my theme song. Let's face it, it's also a pretty easy tune to play on the fiddle. I love it from that aspect, but actually "Love in Bloom" has nothing to do with a comedian. I mean, "Can it be the breeze that fills the trees with rare and magic perfume …" sounds more like it should be the theme song of a dog—not a comic!

In the same year, Robin and Rainger wrote "June in January" for another Crosby picture, *Here Is My Heart*. In a departure from the customary method of collaboration, Robin came up with the title before Rainger fashioned a lovely, sweeping melody for the phrase. Then Robin wrote a lyric about a lover who, despite the cold night and bare trees, feels spring in his heart. In one line, "The snow is just white blossoms that fall from above," Robin creates the kind of delicate seasonal image found in Japanese *haiku*.

It was precisely such literate sophistication that worried Hollywood studio heads, who found Robin and Rainger's songs "too high-class." When songs such as "Love in Bloom" and "June in January" became hits, the bosses calmed down. At Paramount, the most aristocratic of film studios, President Adolph Zukor called Robin over to tell him he liked his lyrics. "That's the first time I ever heard the word 'lyrics' in Hollywood," exclaimed Robin. "Nobody knew what the hell a lyric meant. They'd refer to 'the words.'"

Here Is My Heart reunited Robin with Lewis Gensler, his first important collaborator. Together they wrote "Love Is Just around the Corner," which gave a romantic twist to Herbert Hoover's promise about prosperity. Robin created comic effects with such feminine rhymes as "corner," "mourner," and "forlorner," but his wittiest touch came in the release, where he compared his beloved to Venus de Milo: "But strictly between us, you're cuter than Venus, / And what's more you got arms!" The learned allusion to classical Greece, the arch "strictly between us," and the thumping slang of "what's more you got arms" unite elegance and earthiness in the style of the greatest songs of the era.

Santa Claus Is Comin' to Town
Lyrics by Haven Gillespie, music by J. Fred Coots

Haven Gillespie was one of the few successful songwriters who chose to live among family and friends in his hometown—in his case, Covington, Kentucky—rather than in New York or Hollywood. Still, he would visit New York to peddle his latest numbers. On one trip, he learned that his brother, Irwin, had suddenly died of pneumonia; his last words had been to encourage Haven to push his songs.

When a music-publishing firm asked Gillespie to write their big Christmas song for that year, he doubted he could summon the spirit to write something cheerful. Nevertheless, he set to work with composer J. Fred Coots. On a cold and rainy autumn day, they boarded the subway, and Coots called out the names of New York streets on the subway-stop walls in the hope it would inspire his gloomy lyricist. Slowly, Gillespie's memories went back to his childhood in Covington with Irwin. He recalled how his mother would tell her boys to be sure to do things like wash behind their ears "or Santa Claus won't come." Reaching into his shoe, Gillespie pulled out a piece of paper he had put there to protect his feet from New York's wet streets. By the time they got to 49th Street, he had roughed out a lyric with clever admonitions, at once stern and affectionate: "You better not pout …. He's gonna find out who's naughty and nice."

Gillespie and Coots were kidded by other songwriters for the corniness of the song, but one person who loved it was Eddie Cantor's wife, who persuaded her husband to sing it on radio. Soon, "Santa Claus Is Comin' to Town" was selling twenty-five thousand copies a day—enough for Haven Gillespie to continue living and writing songs in his hometown. It vied with the more adult "Winter Wonderland," by Richard B. Smith and Felix Bernard, as the top Christmas song of 1934.

You and the Night and the Music
Lyrics by Howard Dietz, music by Arthur Schwartz

While Arthur Schwartz was leaning on the railing of a ship bound for England, a melody suddenly came to him. He rushed to the ballroom, but there he found Maurice Chevalier and other entertainers rehearsing a show they were going to give that night. "Please, gentlemen—ladies," Schwartz pleaded, "Could I just sit there and play one melody?" When they consented, Schwartz took down the tune, entitled it "Tonight," and filed it away in his trunk of unused songs.

When he returned to New York, Schwartz pleaded with Howard Dietz to collaborate on a book show rather than the little revues they had written with such success. The lyricist agreed to work on *Revenge with Music*, a musical based on a Spanish folk tale about a governor who tries to seduce a miller's wife, while the miller seduces the governor's wife with considerably more success. When Schwartz played Dietz the melody for "Tonight," the lyricist sensed that a longer title would capture the dark, swirling melody, and suggested "You and the Night and the Music." He also underscored the repetitive melody with bursts of alliteration ("fill me with flaming desire") and internal rhymes ("*thrill* me but *will* we be one?"). Although *Revenge with Music* flopped, "You and the Night and the Music" became a hit, as did another brooding song from the score, "If There Is Someone Lovelier Than You."

You Oughta Be in Pictures
Lyrics by Edward Heyman, music by Dana Suesse

The New Yorker dubbed composer Dana Suesse "The Girl Gershwin" because she wrote etudes and nocturnes as well as popular songs. Soon after she blew into town in 1934, Suesse and lyricist Edward Heyman bragged to a publisher they could write a hit in twenty minutes. They locked themselves in a cubicle with a piano and, eighteen minutes later, emerged with "You Oughta Be in Pictures," one of several classic songs about the movies. Suesse's bouncy melody is the setting for words that turn movie associations everybody knows into a 1930s anthem of praise: "Your voice would thrill a nation, / Your face would be adored."

Though there are hundreds of songs about the movies, some of which go back as far as silent films, most of them describe how beautiful a loved one is or figure out how a boy and a girl can spend some time together. Pete Wendling, Bert Kalmar, and Edgar Leslie wrote the clever, "Take Your Girlie to the Movies" (1919), in which Beatrice Fairfax, the original lovelorn columnist, dispenses some helpful advice to a frustrated lad who wants to be alone with his girl. In 1929, Bing Crosby crooned Ray Henderson, Lew Brown, and Buddy DeSylva's "If I Had a Talking Picture of You," in which a lonely lover yearns for a movie of his beloved so that he can "give ten shows a day and a midnight matinee."

1935

I'm in the Mood for Love
Lyrics by Dorothy Fields, music by Jimmy McHugh

After speculating that she had already used the word "love" in her lyrics "at least five thousand times," Dorothy Fields told a newspaper reporter in 1934, "I'm always looking for a new way to say 'I love you.'" In "I'm in the Mood for Love," she found it by creating a seduction scene in a lyric that simmers but never quite boils over. It lets an innocent word like "mood" suggest a young man's eagerness without frightening a young woman. He repeats it and "near you" to imply that she has aroused him by doing nothing more than being close.

He heaps on some conventional words of praise in the second chorus and takes a turn at empathy in the release ("Now we are one, I'm not afraid."), in which he also uses the euphemistic "heart" to take the place of something more bluntly sexual. He also has a way of dousing passion when it threatens to get too hot. Fields gives him slangy interjections to lower the temperature and give the line an effect of greater and thus more discursive length: "*simply* because you're near me / *Funny*, but when you're near me." Cocky and persistent to the end, he dismisses the rest of the world in an ardent but still quiet conclusion: "But for tonight, forget it, I'm in the mood for love."

Just One of Those Things; Begin the Beguine
Lyrics and music by Cole Porter

In August 1935, on a brief vacation before beginning rehearsals for his newest show, *Jubilee*, Cole Porter learned from playwright Moss Hart that the score needed another song for the second act. Porter did not usually welcome advice about his songs, but he took Hart at his word. The next morning, Hart found a nearly finished song on the piano. One word was missing because Porter had not been able to come up with anything that satisfied him. Typically, in such a bind, he turned to friends for advice. Architect Ed Tauch immediately suggested "gossamer" to complete the dazzling line, "A trip to the moon on gossamer wings," and "Just One of Those Things" was ready.

The song's portrayal of the end of a love affair captures its impermanence with all the breezy insouciance we expect from Porter. It may have been "one of those bells that now and then rings," but ultimately it was no more than "just one of those things." What remains is a cool, stylish parting with even a dash of grace under pressure during those years between the wars: "Goodbye dear and amen, here's hoping we'll meet now and then."

The story of "Begin the Beguine" is more complicated. It did not become a hit until a year after it first appeared (and was largely ignored) in *Jubilee*. It took Artie Shaw's swing arrangement minus the lyric to get the public to pay attention to it. (Porter liked Shaw's version and once greeted him at a party with "Happy to meet my collaborator.")

Porter, accompanied by Moss Hart, wrote the score for *Jubilee* while on a South Seas cruise. He originally said "Begin the Beguine" was inspired by a native dance at Kalabahai, a small village in the Dutch East Indies. Hart remembered Porter's singing it, "sitting at the upright piano in his cabin as the boat sailed toward the Fiji Islands." Later, however, Porter said he had "first discovered the beguine in Paris in 1933. There was a special dance hall on the left bank where French Negroes from Martinique used to dance every night and I went often to see them."

At 108 bars, "Begin the Beguine" is one of the longest popular songs ever written. Yet its long melodic lines feel torrid, its eroticism barely contained by its high-toned allusions to "moments divine" and "rapture serene." Unable to bear the loss of the one he loved, the singer finally bursts forth in a climax of denial, "So don't let them begin the beguine / Let the love that was once a fire remain an ember." Even though he has learned the bitterness of loss, the helpless lover begs for one more beguine that will last until "the stars that were there before return above you."

Porter, whose lyrics always pushed against the boundaries of popular taste, suggests that the dance is the equivalent of lovemaking, but to avoid censorship he changed the penultimate line from "And we suddenly know the sweetness of sin" to the benign "And we suddenly know what heaven we're in."

Lovely to Look At; I Won't Dance
Lyrics by Dorothy Fields, music by Jerome Kern

Not an easy man, Jerome Kern was used to getting his way, but lyricist Dorothy Fields put Kern's temperament to the test. RKO had bought the rights to Kern and Oscar Hammerstein's stage production, *Roberta,* because Pandro Berman, the studio's twenty-nine-year-old head of production, saw it as a vehicle for the team of Fred Astaire and Ginger Rogers. For the screen version of the musical, Kern wrote an unusually short sixteen-bar melody. Asked why it was so short, he replied with typical brusqueness, "That's all I had to say."

Berman asked Fields to supply a lyric. To complicate the assignment, Berman said it had to be a love song that could be used for a fashion show within the movie. *Roberta* tells the story of a young American whose aunt, a noted Paris designer, dies suddenly, leaving the fashion house to him

Jerome Kern and Dorothy Fields. Courtesy of Photofest.

even though he doesn't know a thing about *haute couture*. Fields came back the next day with the lyric to "Lovely to Look At," complete with opening lines that serve a lover's delight and a model's elegance: "Lovely to look at, delightful to know and heaven to kiss." Berman ordered the scene shot without Kern's knowledge or approval, even though Fields protested and Berman had to know there would be hell to pay when Kern found out. When he saw the rushes, however, the composer loved the scene and the lyric.

The year before, Astaire had seen Hammerstein and Kern's *Three Sisters* on stage in London and, despite its failure, wanted to use one of its songs in *Roberta*. Berman agreed but wanted some jazzy new words. Once again, he called on Fields. The character in Hammerstein's original lyric to "I Won't Dance" had refused to go out on the floor because he was not a very good dancer. In Fields' hands, the song moved effortlessly from the amusingly sexy ("But this feeling isn't purely mental for, heaven rest us, I'm not asbestos") to the slyly sensual ("I know that music leads the way to romance, so if I hold you in my arms I won't dance").

By then, Kern was sufficiently impressed to want to work with Fields even though she was fifteen years younger than he, a full head taller, and impishly called him "Junior." He allowed it.

Lullaby of Broadway
Lyrics by Al Dubin, music by Harry Warren

Between 1900 and 1930, America sang city songs, more specifically New York songs. Even in Warner Bros.' tough urban musicals from the 1930s, Ruby Keeler and the rest of the Gold Diggers were hoofing for stardom, not in the movies, but on Broadway. No songwriters better expressed that New York electricity than Harry Warren and Al Dubin. Despite his success in California, Warren, born Salvatore Guaranga in Brooklyn, never thought of himself as anything but a New Yorker. "I never liked Hollywood," he said, "but I got used to it."

One night in 1935, Dubin telephoned him, "I've written a song for you, Harry. I know how you still miss New York and this song is just for you. Come on down and I'll show it to you." Warren drove to Dubin's house in Malibu to hear the lyric to what became "Lullaby of Broadway." When they played it for studio boss Jack Warner, he told them the music was fine but they would have to write new words. Warren defended Dubin, saying the lyric fit too well with his offbeat melody to replace it. He said he would write a whole new song but there was no way he would separate that lyric from the driving melody he had written. Though Warren and Dubin were not close personal friends, Dubin's daughter wrote that they "were loyal to one another and … stood tight against the injustices and inequities of the studio."

The song was the movie's major production number and, in Russell Davies' words, "the noisiest lullaby in motion picture history." Busby Berkeley filmed it with hundreds of dancers en masse, tapping ferociously but impersonally on a huge, almost featureless set. As an image of the mid-1930s, it is oppressive and ominous. It isn't that long a reach from this spectacle of mass synchronization to the following year's Nazi Party rally in Nuremberg.

The dancers provide the background for an ambitious minimusical, which tells the story of a girl-about-town who eventually falls to her death from a skyscraper window. As with "Forty-Second Street," Dubin's lyric creates a series of witty images and vivid vignettes that typify this ironically blasé portrait of the high rollers and low-lifes who populate New York City: "The rumble of the subway train, the rattle of the taxis, / The daffydils who entertain at Angelo's and Maxie's." The point of view and the turn of phrase here, as throughout Warren and Dubin's songs, are very much in the spirit of New York. They feel as if they sprang from Harlem or Broadway or Grand Central Station. Concrete is their natural habitat.

My Romance; The Most Beautiful Girl in the World
Lyrics by Lorenz Hart, music by Richard Rodgers

Jumbo was producer Billy Rose's idea: an extravaganza that was half circus, half musical comedy, with songs by Richard Rodgers and Lorenz Hart, starring Jimmy Durante and featuring Paul Whiteman's Orchestra, mounted in the Hippodrome, for years the home of mammoth spectacles, and featuring an entire circus onstage. For this madhouse of a show, Rodgers and Hart wrote several lovely ballads. "My Romance" proved to be one of Rodgers' most difficult songs to write. He said it took him a day and a half to "get." Hart then wrote what Frederick Nolan calls "elegantly wistful lyrics," which work primarily through a series of denials, "My romance doesn't need …," leading eventually to the necessary reversal, "My romance doesn't need a thing but you."

The opposite of "My Romance," "The Most Beautiful Girl in the World" is a series of affirmations. To Rodgers' ecstatic waltz, Hart portrayed a love affair that soon reveals itself to be a marriage. The lyric sets the affirmation in the title against a chatty, apparently spontaneous list of the things about her that delight her husband, from the mundane picking out of ties to the good-humored familiarity of "Eats my candy, drinks my brandy." To underscore the lyric's conversational quality, Hart moves many of the emphatic words to the start of the line—"Social—not a bit, / Nat'ral kind of wit,"—until he explains her effect in a line whose suggestiveness makes it the most intimate, most touching moment in the song. It leads immediately to the incremental repetition of the final line: "When my slippers are next to the ones that belong to the one and only beautiful girl in the world!"

PORGY AND BESS
Lyrics by Dubose Heyward and Ira Gershwin, music by George Gershwin

In the middle of the night, George Gershwin picked up Dubose Heyward's best-selling novel *Porgy*, hoping it would help him fall asleep. Instead, Heyward's tale of the crippled Porgy, the sensuous Bess, and the violent Crown inspired Gershwin, and he wrote to Heyward proposing they do an operatic version of *Porgy*. Heyward was amenable, but he had already agreed to work with his wife, Dorothy, on a straight dramatic adaptation, which had a successful theatrical run in 1927.

After the Crash of 1929, it became difficult to find financial backing for any Broadway production, let alone an opera with the all-black cast Gershwin insisted upon. At one point, Heyward was so desperate he almost agreed to do *Porgy* as a musical starring Al Jolson—in blackface! In

1933, however, the Theatre Guild offered its support, and Gershwin traveled to Charleston to begin collaborating with Heyward. As they mingled among blacks in the city and on the offshore islands, Heyward marveled at Gershwin's ability to join in their spirituals and "shouting"—rhythmic chants "beaten out by the feet and hands … probably the only white man in America who could have done it."

After that initial meeting, Gershwin and Heyward had to collaborate by mail; because Heyward was a poet, rather than a lyricist, George agreed to alter his regular working methods by having Heyward write words first. Ira Gershwin marveled at his brother's ability to take Heyward's "fine and poetic lyrics" and set them to music "with scarcely a syllable being changed …. He takes two simple quatrains of DuBose's, studies the lines, and in a little while a lullaby called 'Summertime' emerges—delicate and wistful, yet destined to be sung over and over again."

As usual, Ira was being modest about his own contribution. The score took shape only when he blended Dubose's poetry with George's music. "This is no reflection on DuBose's abilities," Ira observed. "It takes years and years of experience to know that such a note cannot take such a syllable, that many a poetic line can be unsingable, that many an ordinary line fitted into the proper musical phrase can sound like a million."

On one of the rare times the three men worked side by side, George improvised a melody he thought would give Porgy "something lighter and gayer" to sing. For once, a title—the hardest part of a lyric to write— popped into Ira's mind: "'I got plenty o' nuthin', I said tentatively. And a moment later the obvious balance line, 'And nuthin's plenty for me.'" Dubose Heyward, noting that he had never fitted words to completed music, asked whether he could take the title and melody back to Charleston to work on a lyric. When he sent the completed song back, Ira still had to do some "polishing" to soften vowels, lengthen consonants, and make the song more "singable." "All in all," he said, "I'd consider this a 50–50 collaborative effort."

Both men worked together on such other songs as "I Loves You, Porgy," "Oh Bess, Oh Where's My Bess," and "Bess, You Is My Woman Now"; Ira was solely responsible for the lyrics to "A Red-Headed Woman," "I Can't Sit Down," "I Ain't Got No Shame," and two songs that greatly enhanced the role of Sportin' Life, who was a relatively minor character in the novel. "Ira's gift for the more sophisticated lyric," Heyward observed, "was exactly suited to the task of writing the songs for Sportin' Life." With a song such as "There's a Boat Dat's Leavin' Soon for New York," Sportin' Life, pimp and dope peddler, looms as a discordant urban intrusion into the pastoral world of *Porgy and Bess*.

The melody for Sportin's Life's other number, however, had Ira stumped. For days he had been using a dummy title phrase, then George suggested he try using the dummy title as the basis for the real lyric. Ira was thankful that the eight-syllable phrase, which could have been "an order of bacon and eggs" or "tomorrow's the Fourth of July," had been "it ain't necessarily so." Equally pleasing was the way the line fit the pattern of a limerick, the perfect irreverent form for a mock sermon filled with Sportin' Life's condescension toward his country cousins' religious beliefs. Mocking their faith, Sportin' Life retells such Bible stories as Pharaoh's daughter finding Moses in the bulrushes with leering skepticism: "she fished him—she *says*—from dat stream."

The opening night audience was stirred by a musical production that featured so many black performers, but critics were confused about the hybrid quality of *Porgy and Bess*. On the one hand, there were the kinds of wonderful songs that appeared in musical comedy, but the story was violent and dark, and the dialogue between songs was sung as operatic recitative. The initial production had only a short run and lost money, but *Porgy and Bess* has since become one of America's greatest operas.

TOP HAT
Lyrics and music by Irving Berlin

Top Hat was the first of five movie scores Irving Berlin would write for Fred Astaire. Berlin said, "You can't work with Fred without knowing you're working with him. He's a real inspiration for a writer." By the time he reached Hollywood, he had already written ten songs for the new picture. *Top Hat*'s producer, Pandro S. Berman, told one of Berlin's daughters,

> There wasn't anything I needed to do. We talked over the script. You could tell him this or that was needed. But you couldn't tell him how to do things. You wouldn't. My job was over when I engaged him …. Nothing more you had to do than hire him and let him alone.

The plot is romantic comedy fare, more than a little reminiscent of the story in *The Gay Divorcee* from the previous year. Fred and Ginger meet by accident. He annoys her; she enchants him. He spends the rest of the movie pursuing her, sometimes quite literally, as he uses Berlin's songs to woo and win her despite problems raised by her initial dislike and a case of mistaken identity.

When director Mark Sandrich insisted that the songs be integrated into the story, Berlin dumped everything he had written except "Cheek to Cheek" and holed up in his hotel for the next six weeks. He avoided everybody, living in his pajamas and writing music at night and lyrics during the day. Working at a kind of white heat, he emerged with a dozen songs, including "Get Thee behind Me, Satan" (used in *Follow the Fleet* the next year), "Top Hat, White Tie and Tails," and "No Strings."

Although Berlin could have returned to New York at that point, he remained in Hollywood to help with the filming of the songs. When they decided they needed an additional dance number, Berlin retreated to his penthouse a second time. The next day he invited dance director Hermes Pan to hear the new song, "Isn't This a Lovely Day?" Pan remembered the first eight bars and taught them to Astaire. "The next time Astaire and Berlin were playing gin, Fred began to sing this new song. Berlin was taken aback. 'Fred,' he asked, 'where did you hear that?' Astaire, ever nonchalant, replied, 'Oh, that, it's a tune from the Hit Parade.'" Berlin paled at the thought that he had inadvertently plagiarized a hit song. When he could no longer contain himself, Astaire burst out laughing and let the queasy composer in on the joke.

The songs demonstrate just how well, even as early as the mid-1930s, Berlin could write songs that developed character and advanced story. "No Strings," the opening number, introduces Fred as a dancer whose latest hit show has just closed. He revels in the sheer self-indulgence of having nothing to do: "No strings and no connections, no ties to my affections." Yet the very next line projects the quality that most humanizes the character he nearly always played and best explains the durability of our affection for him: his romantic readiness. No matter what, he was always ready to fall in love: "I'm fancy free and free for anything fancy." His pursuit of Ginger soon finds them together in a gazebo where a rainstorm keeps her from escaping. As he sings, "Isn't This a Lovely Day," he ignores her resistance but never notices the smile she gives the camera in response to his line: "Let the rain pitter patter but it really doesn't matter if the skies are gray / Long as I can be with you it's a lovely day."

"Cheek to Cheek" is one of Berlin's most remarkable songs. Every time you think you have him pinned down, he confounds you by doing something *apparently* beyond him—but *apparently* not. Who could predict that the great hustler of Tin Pan Alley tunes would write a song that went on for sixty-four bars rather than the usual thirty-two, and that he would tweak a conventional AABA structure so that it had an extra eight-bar section right before the end. AABA becomes AABBCA[1], and the penultimate eight bars feel like a little song all their own, characterized by a sense of heightened desire: "Dance with me, I want my arms about you."

Berlin had an uncanny ability to tune his melodies and inscribe his words to Astaire's particular sensibility. "Cheek to Cheek" begins with an ascending line whose final note reaches the upper limit of Astaire's vocal range. When he sings, "Heaven, I'm in heaven, and my heart beats so that I can hardly speak," in fact he can hardly speak. When the line, also characterized by a series of breathy "h" sounds, comes to an end, it's virtually mute, made only of breath, a suggestion of love as something ineffable, graspable only through dance.

Though the title song is strictly a performance number for Astaire, its genesis demonstrates Berlin's capacity to take the seed of an idea and transform it into a song with a distinctive identity. In 1930, for a Broadway flop called *Smiles*, Astaire had choreographed a dance for himself. Unable to sleep one night, he wrote that he got the idea for "a long line of boys in top hats and imagined myself using a cane like a gun." He leaped out of bed, grabbed a nearby umbrella, and "went through some motions while humming the tune." When he explained the idea to Berlin five years later, the songwriter wrote a new number that begins with an almost perfect first line. Though it's familiar and conversational, it also stirs your curiosity: "I just got an invitation through the mails." One of Astaire's most important signature songs, it embodies his—and Berlin's—naturalness, inventiveness, and capacity to delight.

When I Grow Too Old to Dream
Lyrics by Oscar Hammerstein, music by Sigmund Romberg

Soon after Jerome Kern and Oscar Hammerstein's *Three Sisters* flopped in London, both men signed on to work in Hollywood. One of Hammerstein's first assignments at MGM was a collaboration with Sigmund Romberg. Although the movie's title was *The Night Is Young*, the score's most important song was "When I Grow Too Old to Dream." Its composition reveals how hard Hammerstein often had to work to bring his lyrics to fruition.

Beginning with Romberg's eight-line refrain, he quickly hit upon the title line. He liked the way it sounded, the way it fit the music and was easy to sing. The next line came as easily: "I'll have you to remember." He thought he would have it finished in no time. Then he stopped. What did the line mean and when are you too old to dream? How did he ever come up with this nonsense? He tried different titles and wrote several choruses, but he didn't like any of it. He kept going back to his original opening line, but if it didn't mean anything, why did he like it so much?

He finally completed a chorus, but the song's reliance on the word "dream" bothered him for weeks. He finally decided what it meant: "When I grow too old to love you and to dream about loving you, I will be remembering our love in the past." Even though he hadn't quite convinced himself, he walked back and forth in his study singing it, wishing it weren't so obscure, but thinking if he liked it so much, maybe other people would, too. He finally showed it to Romberg, who loved it. Hammerstein kept his mouth shut about his doubts. After the movie's release, producer Max Dreyfus asked him exactly what the song meant. "I'm not quite sure," Hammerstein confessed.

1936

Easy to Love; I've Got You Under My Skin; It's Delovely
Lyrics and music by Cole Porter

"Rewriting ruins songs," Cole Porter said. When he was in Hollywood working on *Born to Dance*, Porter played "Easy to Love" for the producers. "The response was instantaneous," he said, "They all grabbed the lyric and began singing it, and even called in the stenographers to hear it." However, Hollywood had come under stricter censorship, and Porter's lines about a woman so "easy to love" that her boyfriend can imagine her "so sweet to awaken with" had to be bowdlerized to "So worth the yearning for, / So swell to keep ev'ry home fire burning for."

Porter suggested that Jimmy Stewart sing the song, but the producers doubted the actor could sing. The next day Stewart sang for Porter. "He sings far from well," Porter reported, "although he has nice notes in his voice, but he could play the part perfectly." Jimmy Stewart begged Porter to lower the notes of the melody, but again Porter refused. "His pipsqueak though earnest tenor did little justice to the song," observed Charles Schwartz, but Stewart later quipped, "The song was so good that not even I could spoil it."

The idea for "I've Got You under My Skin," Porter's other hit from *Born to Dance* came, as Stephen Citron points out, from "the opening lines of a French song Cole admired, a ballad so identified with Fanny Brice as to become her signature. The song, "My Man" ("Mon Homme") by Maurice Yvain, begins and is, in fact, subtitled "Je l'ai tellement dans le peau" ("I've got him so much in my skin"). Still, Porter makes the adaptation sound like an ordinary American catchphrase—"You're getting under my skin"—that makes love seem like an irritation, annoying yet erotic.

When his work on *Born to Dance* was over, Porter launched into another Broadway musical, *Jubilee*, and took playwright Moss Hart on a round-the-world cruise to work on the show. When their ship sailed into the harbor at Rio de Janeiro at sunrise, Porter looked at the spectacular view and exclaimed, "It's delightful." His wife Linda added, "It's delicious," and his friend Monty Woolley quipped, "It's delovely." In another version of the story, Porter claimed that the comments were inspired by his, Hart's, and Woolley's first taste of mangosteen melon in Java. Whatever the source of the song's inspiration, Porter did not use it for *Jubilee* but rather for another Broadway musical, *Red, Hot and Blue*, which he wrote in the same incredibly productive year.

"It's Delovely" celebrates nature's fertility in the spring with an equally fecund linguistic inventiveness. Cast in the classic mold of his catalogue songs, the number was tailor made for Ethel Merman, who longs to be wooed, not in "Berlitz French" but "plain Brooklynese," and who runs through a litany of adjectives: "delectable," "delirious," "delimit," "de voiks," and "deluxe" (which Porter stipulated should be pronounced "de-lukes"). Porter also wrote a bluesy torch song for Merman, "Down in the Depths," and a rousing upbeat number, "Ridin' High," in which she could trumpet joyously, "Life's great, life's grand .... How'm I ridin'? I'm ridin' high!"

I Can't Get Started
Lyrics by Ira Gershwin, music by Vernon Duke

After putting strenuous effort into *Porgy and Bess*, George Gershwin, for the first time in his life, admitted to creative exhaustion and went sailing in Mexico to recuperate. With his brother adrift, Ira Gershwin accepted an invitation to write songs with Vernon Duke for *The Ziegfeld Follies of 1936*. Although the cast included Fanny Brice, Judy Canova, Eve Arden, the Nicholas Brothers, and Josephine Baker, the hit of the show was a catalog song sung by a young comedian named Bob Hope.

Duke gave Ira Gershwin a melody called "Face the Music with Me," and Ira transformed it into "I Can't Get Started with You." He also wrote a sketch in which Hope plays a self-smitten egotist who encounters Eve Arden on the street. He begs her for a kiss, but when she spurns him, he plies her with song. He nonchalantly lists his phenomenal accomplishments—flying around the world, settling the Spanish Revolution, accepting nods from J. P. Morgan and FDR. Then, he expresses wonder that "I get no place with you." Finally, Arden relents. As she comes up "gasping for air," she exclaims, "Heavens! You're wonderful! Just marvelous!" "That's all I wanted to know," Hope coolly replies and strolls away.

I'm an Old Cowhand
Lyrics and music by Johnny Mercer

In the midst of the Great Depression, Johnny Mercer was out of a job and had no prospects. Once he finished songs for some movies at RKO, the studio did not renew his contract. He had already left a steady job with

Paul Whiteman's Orchestra to pursue his dream of becoming a singing movie star like Bing Crosby, but this had not panned out. With no place else to go, he drove back home to Savannah. During the three days it took to cross Texas, he was amused by the sight of cowboys with spurs and ten-gallon hats driving pick-up trucks instead of riding horses. He realized it was life imitating the movies because, in Hollywood, it was the era of western movies starring singing cowboys.

In only fifteen minutes, writing on the back of an envelope, Mercer worked his incongruous cowboy image into a song whose ironic underside expressed his own bitter frustration with Hollywood: "I'm a cowboy who never saw a cow, / Never roped a steer 'cause I don't know how." In the same fifteen minutes, he produced a rollicking melody that sharpened the satire with its clip-clopping imitation of horse's hooves. When Bing Crosby sang the song in *Rhythm on the Range*, it became a big hit and had studios clamoring for Mercer to return to Hollywood—but purely as a songwriter.

Pennies from Heaven
Lyrics by Johnny Burke, music by Arthur Johnston

Arthur Johnston had for years been Irving Berlin's "musical secretary," taking down Berlin's melodies in musical notation. However, Johnston had ambitions to be a composer, and in 1931 he and lyricist Sam Coslow collaborated on "Just One More Chance." The success of "Just One More Chance," as well as that of another song he wrote with Coslow in 1934, "Cocktails for Two," netted Arthur Johnston a job at Paramount, where he teamed with a young lyricist named Johnny Burke.

Burke had also worked for Irving Berlin Music, first in the company's Chicago office as a staff pianist and song plugger, then in New York where he also served as a vocal coach. It may have been the percussive, repeated notes of Johnston's melody that suggested the idea of a "rain" song to Burke, for he used short vowels and sharp consonants—"Ev'ry time it rains, it rains pennies from heaven"—to emphasize the repetitive, "raining" character of the melody. He also underscored that repetitiveness with internal rhymes: "You'll find your fortune *falling all* over *town* / Be *sure* that *your* umbrella is upside *down*."

"Pennies from Heaven" was used in a film starring Bing Crosby. The songwriters didn't know whether the crooner liked it, but at a screening of the movie, Burke learned that Crosby liked it so much that the title of the song had become the title of the film.

SWING TIME
Lyrics by Dorothy Fields, music by Jerome Kern

If *Top Hat* isn't the best of the Astaire–Rogers movies, then *Swing Time* is. Three of the score's seven songs are standards, two are surprisingly contemporary dance numbers, and one is a haunting original even more compelling than the others, especially in the context of the movie. Fred Astaire's strong desire for two up-to-date dance pieces made Jerome Kern uneasy. Although he thought Astaire's request was entirely reasonable, he was a musical traditionalist and a stubborn man. He didn't like jazz and he knew he didn't swing, but he agreed to work with arranger Richard Russell Bennett to see what they could manage. Eventually, Astaire helped as well by dancing around his living room for hours to teach Kern the kinds of rhythms he needed.

The always meticulous Kern acknowledged the help he got from Bennett on the "Waltz in Swing Time" by having the sheet music read, "Composed by Jerome Kern, Constructed and Arranged by R. Russell Bennett." Bennett told Gerald Bordman that Kern had given him basic themes and told him to link them in any way that would satisfy Astaire. At the same time, combining a waltz with swing was Kern's impish acknowledgment to Astaire for what he had put the dancer through in his struggle to write what Astaire wanted.

"The Way You Look Tonight" is the score's one oasis of romanticism; a limpid ballad sung by Astaire while Rogers washes her hair in the next room. Its dramatic setting gives it an amusing subtext and keeps it from soaring too high above the here and now. It is restrained yet infused with feeling. That combination helps to reveal how masterfully Dorothy Fields had learned to mix several voices in a single lyric. First, Astaire sings a line of romantic praise, "Keep that breathless charm," but follows with the wittily understated, "Won't you please arrange it" and the chatty, "'Cause I love you," before ending with a more matter of fact line of praise than the first, "Just the way you look tonight."

Just as Kern had written jazz-influenced dance melodies for the first time, so Fields departed from custom in her writing, too. For the only time in her career, she wrote two lyrics before she had melodies, "Pick Yourself Up" and "A Fine Romance." The second of them came from Kern's observation that they needed "a sarcastic love ballad." Fields went home, wrote the complete lyric, and presented it to him. What is most impressive about the song is her sureness of touch as she combines her honed ironic edge with a new emotional complexity. The song is as touching as it is sarcastic, with an undercurrent of confusion and looming loss bordering on helplessness. It's funny but it's also unsettling. Is there any wittier rhymed American talk than "I might as well play bridge with my old maid aunts," followed by the sharp but rueful, "I haven't got a chance," and then the equally sharp, sarcastic but also fearful title line, "This is a fine romance."

That fear of love's loss finds its most direct expression in the movie's final song. Astaire plays a gambler who has become a professional dancer and Rogers a dance teacher who has become his partner. Through a series of plot complications, Astaire's going home to get married and Rogers is going to wed a bandleader who has been pursuing her. In a moment of exquisite heartbreak, he sings "Never Gonna Dance," until, helpless not to, they dance for what they believe is a final time.

The melody is driven and insistent, with a lyric that mixes familiar slang with uncommon allusions to create a distinctive voice. Though he's penniless, the singer notes ironically that "The wolf was discreet. / He left me my feet." As a result, he can set them down on anything "But the la belle, / La perfectly swell romance," for the overwhelming reason that he's "never gonna dance." Within moments of the dance's conclusion, the plot rearranges itself for a happy ending. As Deborah Grace Winer observes, Kern and Fields' songs for *Swing Time* are "a culmination of their work together: sexy, sophisticated, shimmering."

There's a Small Hotel
Lyrics by Lorenz Hart, music by Richard Rodgers

Lorenz Hart despised a simple melody that Richard Rodgers gave him so much that he wrote a "dummy" lyric to it:

There's a girl next door
She's an awful bore
It really makes you sore
To see her.
She's got a forty waist, but she's got no taste,
I know I'm sure I'd hate to be her.
By and by perhaps she'll die—
Perhaps she'll croak next summer;
Her old man's a plumber,
She's much dumber.

But after Hart took a trip to a country inn in New Jersey, he turned back to Rodgers' "obnoxious" melody and wrote a beautiful pastoral lyric, "There's a Small Hotel."

"It was the melody—romantic, unsophisticated, youthful," said Rodgers, "that suggested the theme to Larry of an idealized country inn with its wishing well, one-room bridal suite and view of a nearby church steeple." Rodgers was amazed that Hart, who loved the hectic pace of New York City, "could write longingly about quiet pleasures far from the razzle-dazzle world .... When in 'There's a Small Hotel,' he wrote the lines 'Not a sign of people—Who wants people?' he made you believe that a rural retreat was his idea of heaven."

These Foolish Things (Remind Me of You)
Lyrics by Holt Marvell (Eric Maschwitz), music by Jack Strachey and Harry Link

Most of the great catalog songs of the 1930s, like Porter's "You're the Top" and Rodgers and Hart's "The Lady Is a Tramp," follow a longstanding comic tradition in which each successive image or allusion tries to "top" what came before. Even when the sentiment of the song is sad, as in Ira Gershwin and Vernon Duke's "I Can't Get Started" or Leo Robin and Ralph Rainger's "Thanks for the Memory," the catalog still leavens the sentiment with humor.

"These Foolish Things," however, is a list of haunting images of lost love—"a tinkling piano in the next apartment," "a cigarette that bears a lipstick's traces," "a telephone that rings but who's to answer." The fact that Eric Maschwitz, writing under the pen name Holt Marvell (probably because of fears of anti-German sentiment on the eve of World War II) was once married to Hermione Gingold has made Robert Gottlieb and Robert Kimball wonder, "Could all those 'foolish things' have reminded him of her?" Gingold, probably best known to American audiences as the proper aunt in *Gigi*, spent her later years appearing on late night talk shows as an unabashedly horny old woman, for whom the knowing leer and bawdy riposte were everything.

1937

BABES IN ARMS
Lyrics by Lorenz Hart, music by Richard Rodgers

One day Larry Hart and Richard Rodgers watched children playing in Central Park. "We began talking about kids," Rodgers recalled, "and what might happen if they were suddenly given adult responsibilities." They concocted a story about children whose vaudevillian parents are on tour. When the sheriff threatens to send them to a work farm, the kids decide to put on a show.

Babes in Arms produced more hits than any other musical by Rodgers and Hart. Taking an unused song from the score for the movie *Mississippi*,

"Pablo, You Are My Heart," Rodgers revised the melody by repeatedly pulling it down to middle C and then gave it to Hart, who enlivened this monotonous device with "Johnny One-Note," a lyric about a dazzling but limited vocalist who could sing only one note. The lyric bristles with such double and triple rhymes as *"gusto"* / *"just o*-verlorded the place" and "Got in *Aida indeed a* great chance to be brave."

The allusion to *Aida* may have inspired the staging of the song as an "Egyptian" number celebrating an opera singer who could sing louder than anything—trombones, drums, lions, thunder, train whistles, even the roar of Niagara Falls. "Instead of going in for exotic scenery and costumes," Rodgers recalled, "we emphasized the do-it-yourself nature of the show by having the cast come out wearing such household appliances as towels, bath mats, coat hooks and scrub mops."

For the pugnacious Mitzi Green, Rodgers and Hart created "The Lady Is a Tramp," one of their best catalog songs. In a single day, Hart created a lyric about a down-to-earth "lady" who scorns such affectations as arriving late at the theater, going to crap games with royalty, and wearing furs to Harlem nightclubs. Because the singer refuses to behave pretentiously, other women label her a "tramp," yet she relishes the charge, wittily affirming her love of all that is natural and unaffected—the wind, the rain, the green grass: "I'm not so hot, but my shape is my own."

Hart pushed romance to a masochistic extreme in "I Wish I Were in Love Again," where a jaded lover still longs for the "blackened eye," the "conversation with the flying plates," and the "self-deception that believes the lie" of romantic pledges of undying love: "When love congeals, / It soon reveals, / The faint aroma of performing seals, / The double-crossing of a pair of heels." Still to want to be in love—knowing how bad it feels, looks, and even smells—is Hart's backhanded tribute to its power.

Equally innovative was "Where or When," which took the hackneyed line, "Haven't we met before?" to introduce a sense of *déjà vu*. Using Rodgers' repeated notes, Hart had lovers who have just met experience the uncanny feeling that they have "laughed, and loved before"—but can't remember "where or when." "Larry was the first to use it in a lyric," Rodgers observed. "He and I even received letters from college psychology professors telling us they were using the song to help illustrate their lectures."

The best known song from *Babes in Arms* is "My Funny Valentine," yet it is one of the most unconventional of love songs. The singer admits her lover's looks are "laughable, unphotographable," that he's not very bright, and that his body is "less than Greek." Still, she finds him enthralling and celebrates him in mockingly archaic terms: "Thou knowest not, my dim-witted friend, / The picture thou hast made." Rodgers and Hart even changed the character's name to "Val" (short for "Valentine") so that the song fit more closely into the story.

By Myself
Lyrics by Howard Dietz, music by Arthur Schwartz

Although *Between the Devil* folded, one song from its score became a standard. "By Myself," like its ambivalent title phrase, suggests the sadness of being alone and also the satisfaction of accomplishing something "all by myself": "No one knows better than I myself / I'm by myself alone." In other lyrics, such as "Alone Together" and "Dancing in the Dark," Dietz could be melodramatic about facing the great "unknown," but here, given Schwartz's jaunty melody, his lyric says, "I'll face the unknown," with a casual shrug.

"The best lyric writers," Dietz said, "are the ones who write the most singable words. They need not be the fancy words … but words you can lean on …. A good lyric writer can put words to music and have it come out as though he'd put music to words." Dietz also prided himself on how quickly he could write, bragging that he could fashion a new lyric to any existing song in less than ten seconds. Taking him up on his boast, Arthur Schwartz's son, Jonathan, challenged Dietz to create new words for "Jealousy." Dietz thought for a second, then burst out with:

Cyd Charisse!
Get off that mantel piece!
You're quite a shock there,
But we need a clock there!

"That was Howard," Jonathan Schwartz recalled, "Ten seconds."

A Foggy Day; Let's Call the Whole Thing Off; Nice Work If You Can Get It; They All Laughed; Things Are Looking Up; They Can't Take That Away from Me
Lyrics by Ira Gershwin, music by George Gershwin

Irving Berlin said that the last songs George and Ira Gershwin wrote together were the greatest songs anyone had ever written in a single year. The fact that all of them were written for films starring Fred Astaire contributed to their wit and urbanity. Berlin had told the Gershwins that nothing could compare to writing songs for an Astaire picture, but RKO was wary. After all, the Gershwins had just done *Porgy and Bess*—an opera!—so George had to telegram the studio that he and Ira were coming out to "write hits."

Write hits they did. After nearly twenty years of working together, George's music and Ira's lyrics blended seamlessly together. As they worked on a song for *Shall We Dance?* George's melody was typically irregular and rhythmically abrupt, but Ira had learned to follow his every step. George started off with a ten-note phrase,

They all laughed at Christopher Columbus,

followed by a seven note phrase,

When he said the world was round.

When he repeated the initial ten-note phrase, any other composer would have also repeated the subsequent seven-note phrase—but not George Gershwin. After the second ten-note phrase, he stopped short on one note. Nevertheless, Ira fitted that one note with as much creativity as the inventors his lyric celebrated:

They all laughed when Edison recorded
Sound.

The inspiration for his title, Ira explained, came from a 1930s self-improvement advertisement: "They All Laughed When I Sat Down to Play the Piano."

Another of George's melodies started out with a brief, four-note phrase, but Ira pleaded, "George, can you just give me two more notes?" George did and gave Ira the chance to craft a catalog of understated, even back-handed compliments: "The way you wear your hat … The way you sing off key … The way you hold your knife …" Such wry sentiments imply much deeper affection than any soaring flattery. Although George resented the fact that "They Can't Take That Away from Me" was not pre-sented in a full dance number, Astaire sang it tenderly as he and Rogers stood motionless on a ferryboat.

Knowing that every Astaire–Rogers movie had to have a "quarrel" song, the Gershwins created "Let's Call the Whole Thing Off," in which Ira played off his wife's upper-class and his own lower-class pronunciations of such words as "either" and "neither" and "potato" and "tomato." The verbal sparring goes on through such other words as "banana" and "oysters" and registers the combative affection that characterized Astaire and Rogers on screen. With the movies' new microphone prerecording and playback system of filming songs, Ira and George could revel in staccato notes and crisp consonants, ending the song in a sharp "Let's call the calling off *off*." Similarly, they could create songs around such percussive title phrases as "I've Got Beginner's Luck" and "Stiff Upper Lip."

After *Shall We Dance?*, the public began to tire of Fred and Ginger's magic. The couple parted ways, and for Astaire's next picture, set in England, RKO told the Gershwins to write British-sounding songs. With their deepened symbiosis, Ira could simply ask George to play a "fog" song for a working title he had in mind, "A Foggy Day in London." However, when George immediately came up with a melody, it had an extra note, so Ira added an extra syllable: "A Foggy Day in London *Town*," which both of them thought gave the song a quaint touch. When they added a verse, Ira asked George to play something "Irish" for contrast, and he said his brother "sensed instantly the degree of wistful loneliness I meant."

As Astaire's leading lady, RKO cast Joan Fontaine, who could neither sing nor dance. In the verse to "Things Are Looking Up," Ira created one of the cleverest "excuses" for a character to break into song. Astaire smoothly passes from straight dialogue into the verse, where he announces, "If I should suddenly start to sing / Or stand on my head or anything, / Please don't think that I've lost my senses." With that up-front apology, he can then burst into song at the chorus.

Yet another song from the Gershwins' *annus mirabilis*, "Nice Work If You Can Get It," demonstrates their thoroughgoing collaboration. When George wrote a flowing melodic phrase, Ira matched it with ardent romantic lyrics: "Holding hands at midnight / 'Neath a starry sky." When George took a syncopated, jazzy turn, Ira followed with punchy, vernacular shards: "Nice work if you can get it—and you can get it if you try." Although the title phrase sounds as if it were newly minted during the Depression, Ira Gershwin said he took it from a cartoon in the British humor magazine *Punch* in which two London charwomen discuss the daughter of a mutual friend who, as the first charwoman confides, "has become an 'ore." "Nice work if you can get it," the second replies.

In the Still of the Night; Rosalie
Lyrics and music by Cole Porter

Cole Porter returned to Hollywood after the tepid Broadway success of *Jubilee* and *Red, Hot and Blue*, determined to write simple songs "with wider appeal to the common people and less of the brittle, bright poesy with which I've been associated."

MGM assigned Porter to write the score for the film version of the successful Broadway show *Rosalie*. In typical Hollywood fashion, the studio discarded the show's original score, even though it had been created by Sigmund Romberg, P. G. Wodehouse, and the Gershwin brothers. By commissioning Porter to write a new score, MGM knew it would reap more profits on royalties from sheet-music and record sales.

Porter pulled out all the stops with "In the Still of the Night," an inordinately long, seventy-two measure melody with a sixteen-bar stretch marked "Appassionato": "Are you my life to be / My dream come true?" The song was so overblown even Nelson Eddy refused to sing it. Porter took the song to studio head Louis B. Mayer, who was so moved by it that he wept. "Imagine making Louis B. Mayer cry," Porter told friends, "What could possibly top that?" Nelson Eddy sang the song.

Porter struggled as he had never before with the title song for the picture. Louis B. Mayer had wept over "In the Still of the Night," but the tough-nosed studio head rejected version after version of Porter's "Rosalie" as "too high-brow." "Forget you're writing for Nelson Eddy," he told Porter, "and simply give us a good, popular song."

Porter resented being forced to rewrite but dutifully "took 'Rosalie No. 6' home and in haste wrote 'Rosalie No. 7.'" Invoking the standard "night when stars danced above," Porter penned, "Won't you make my life thrilling, / And tell me that you're willing / To be mine, Rosalie, mine." Charles Schwartz has suggested that Porter "deliberately set out to write the worst song he could … with insipid lyrics and an uninspired melody." Whatever Porter did, it finally placated Mayer, and "Rosalie" became a hit. The experience may have tempered Porter's decision to write down to the general public, however, for he disparaged "Rosalie" to his friends. Irving Berlin, nonetheless, cautioned, "Never hate a song that has sold half a million copies."

September in the Rain
Lyrics by Al Dubin, music by Harry Warren

As in most songwriting collaborations, lyricist Al Dubin usually put words to Harry Warren's notes. "September in the Rain" was the exception. Dubin came up with the title and was very fond of it, and Warren wrote a swinging melody to fit what Dubin had written. Although tenor James Melton sang it in *Melody for Two*, they had actually written it two years earlier for another movie, *Stars over Broadway*, where it appeared as a background instrumental. Perhaps they went into their trunk because the studio was keeping them so busy turning out songs.

By 1937, Dubin was exhausted. Even though he was still writing hits, he was beginning the downward spiral that would eventually destroy him. He had earned a lot of money, but his daughter wrote that "he had the house, the pool, the servants, the girlfriends, the respect of his colleagues—and he was miserable." The pressure to produce, and to top what he had previously written, took an emotional toll. He was too frightened to drive, even on a quiet residential street. He kept a gun in the glove compartment of his car, and he would grab the steering wheel from his driver and scream at imaginary roadblocks. When he had surgery for a fistula later that same year, his doctors prescribed morphine for the pain. When he left the hospital, he took home a nurse who knew a less than fastidious physician, and he was soon on his way to a morphine addiction. Yet in the midst of this turmoil, Dubin wrote one of his most affecting ballads.

The lyric and melody of "September in the Rain" combine to create a vivid memory of driving rain tumbling the leaves from the trees. For such a remembrance, the lyric's rhythm is suitably interruptive—"remember / In September—in the rain"—as the conversational tone points to what's particular about the memory: "The sun went out *just* like a dying ember, *that* September in the rain." Looking back, the song concludes that the memory of autumn remains more vivid than the current spring: "Though spring is here, to me it's still September." The claim is hyperbolic, the language offhanded, the effect arresting.

"September in the Rain" was Dubin's last great song with Harry Warren. In 1938, Warner Bros. assigned the younger lyricist Johnny Mercer to work with Dubin and Warren and, although Dubin liked Mercer personally, he was humiliated by having to work with another lyricist and demanded that Warner Bros. let him out of his contract. Desperately traveling between New York and Hollywood to try to re-establish himself as a songwriter, he collapsed on a New York street and died two days later. An autopsy found barbiturates in his bloodstream. He was fifty-three.

Thanks for the Memory
Lyrics by Leo Robin, music by Ralph Rainger

"Thanks for the Memory" was the featured song in Bob Hope's first movie, *The Big Broadcast of 1938*, where he sang it with costar Shirley Ross. The movie was dreadful but the song settled into a long life as Hope's signature song on radio and television—an unlikely success story for a song about divorce. Almost from the start of his movie career, Hope was a wise guy with a quick smirk and a cool demeanor. He kept his distance from us, and he always had more hormones than heart. In those early years, however, before he became an icon safely encased in punch lines and platitudes, he was capable of projecting genuine emotion and of light, musical singing that radiated sincerity.

Hope and Ross' rendition of "Thanks for the Memory" set a new movie standard for sophisticated romanticism performed with warmth and grace. Its initial success came from Ralph Rainger's gentle melody, Leo Robin's sad yet witty lyric, and the two singers' debonair yet poignant performance. Hope plays an emcee on an ocean liner who stands to lose

Sheet music for "Thanks for the Memory." Courtesy of David A. Jasen.

everything if the ship loses a trans-Atlantic race. Ross is the only one of his three ex-wives who still loves him more than the alimony he owes her.

You don't hear a lot of songs about divorce, especially one that combines loss with a sense of humor. Suggesting less than perfect confidence in Rainger and Robin, director Mitchell Leisen asked them to fix a problem. "I want to show they are still in love but they dare not say it," he told the songwriters. "Now if you guys can write a song like that, fine." Then he told them Bob Hope would sing it and added, "While it's a serious song, a guy like that has got to get laughs."

When Rainger and Robin first played their new song for the studio moguls, they were amazed to find these tough businessmen listening with tears in their eyes. A catalog song written as a duet, it portrays two people still half in love with each other. He's down in the dumps; she tries to cheer him up. They toast one another and, as she sips, he begins to sing. To create the tension of two people who always stop short of admitting how they feel, the song's first A-section rises through a series of repeated musical phrases to which the lyric mixes elegant images of castles along the Rhine and the Parthenon with such ordinary American images as the Hudson River Line. Rather than rising to something even more majestic to end the section, it turns instead to common experience. Similarly, the second A-section builds from "motor trips" to "burning lips" but drops off to the comic, "burning toast and prunes." The lyric parallels what is hidden within the two characters: their pulling back from their strongest emotions.

The list of what they remember from their marriage provides a lesson in how lyricists create a new song that is familiar and fresh at the same time. Hope is pensive and wry through much of the song; Ross is jolly but soon finds herself close to tears. They laugh together and remember the hidden sadness of their parting in Robin's touchingly ironic lyric: "No tears, no fuss. Hooray for us."

"Oh, Buzz," Ross says as the song ends.

"I know. I know, dear," Hope answers.

She leaves him sitting at the bar. In about ten minutes the movie ends with their embrace—a terrible film with a saving grace.

Too Marvelous for Words; Hooray for Hollywood
Lyrics by Johnny Mercer, music by Richard Whiting

As Al Dubin turned increasingly to alcohol and drugs to escape the pressures of writing songs for Warner Bros., composer Harry Warren told the skinflint studio it needed to hire more songwriters. Warner Bros. hired Richard Whiting, whose string of hit melodies went back to "Till We Meet Again" (1918) and "Ain't We Got Fun?" (1921), and lyricist Johnny Mercer, who had redeemed his initial failure in Hollywood with the hit "I'm an Old Cowhand" (1936). Whiting's long experience at Paramount and Twentieth Century-Fox made him a father figure to Mercer, guiding the young lyricist through the labyrinth of studio life.

They were assigned to write songs for *Ready, Willing and Able*, a typical Warner "backstager" featuring Ruby Keeler. For the lavish finale, the producer told them the melody would be repeated more than a dozen times, so Mercer would have to write a different set of lyrics for each reprise—as well as rhymed dialogue. Mercer stormed off the lot shouting, "I'll never find the words." Whiting, whose weak heart had disciplined him into maintaining a calm demeanor, bought the biggest dictionary he could find, took it to Mercer's house, and handed it to the lyricist with a note: "Onward!"

Mercer turned his problem into his solution. Taking the catchphrase, "too marvelous for words," he created a lyric for a singer who cannot find the words to describe his beloved. Even Whiting's dictionary made it into the song: "You're much too much and oh so very very / To ever be in Webster's dictionary." The number was staged with Ruby Keeler tap dancing her way down the keys of a gigantic typewriter while behind her chorus girls lay on their backs and kicked their legs as the typewriter's keystrokes. Above it all was a huge sheet of paper with Mercer's lyric, replete with such staggering rhymes as "possible" and "collosable" and "Keats and Shelley's lyrics" and "panegyrics."

Mercer was able to work side by side at the piano with Whiting in a way he could not with most of his other collaborators. Normally he would take a composer's melody and go off by himself to work on the lyric;even if they were in the same room, Mercer would lie down on the couch and drift off into a creative trance so deep he would be oblivious to his collaborator's presence. Such rapport between Mercer and Whiting was critical when the studio told them to write a march for *Hollywood Hotel*, which featured Benny Goodman's band in parade. At first, Mercer matched Whiting's tricky opening phrase with a dummy title, "*Piece* of ma-*ter*-i-*al!*" but then he struck upon another phrase for those percussive six notes: "Hooray for Hollywood."

The song has become a show business anthem, but an anthem with its tongue planted firmly in its cheek. Drawing on his bitter experiences trying to establish himself in pictures, Mercer said, "Hollywood seemed to me like a big put-on and I just tried to make a little fun of it." The target of the lyric's ironic bite is the hype that says, "you're terrific if you're even good." Mercer's jivey, staccato rhyming fits perfectly with Whiting's driving tune: "Where any office boy or young mechanic can be a panic with just a good-looking pan." With its unlikely rhymes ("Paducahs" and "bazookas" and "from Shirley Temple / To Aimee Semple") and its use of slang ("screwy, ballyhooey Hollywood"), "Hooray for Hollywood" sends up flickerdom in its own argot.

Although Mercer and Whiting could laugh at Hollywood in song, Whiting especially found it trying when they had to demonstrate their songs to producers. He would fortify himself with heart pills but still cringed when a stone-faced producer suddenly leapt up, grabbed his sheet music, and hurled it to the floor. Mercer too was stung when one of his lyrics elicited the comment "Phooey!" Warner Bros., the roughest of all Hollywood studios, was hardly the place for a man of Whiting's sensitivity; as he and Mercer were working on the song "Ride, Tenderfoot, Ride" for *Cowboy from Brooklyn*, the composer had a heart attack and died at the age of forty-six. Johnny Mercer once more found himself alone and adrift in the bewildering and sometimes brutal world of Hollywood.

1938

At Long Last Love; My Heart Belongs to Daddy
Lyrics and music by Cole Porter

Accepting an invitation to weekend at a friend's home on Long Island, Cole Porter organized a riding party and chose a horse the groom warned him was skittish. In the course of the ride, the horse threw him and then rolled over his legs, crushing them. As he lay there waiting for help, Porter claimed, he wrote "At Long Last Love" with its insouciant musings about falling in love even though his wife was planning to divorce him: "Is it an earthquake or simply a shock? / Is it the good turtle soup or merely the mock? / Is it a cocktail—this feeling of joy, / Or is what I feel the real McCoy?"

In truth, Porter went into shock on the way to the hospital and was unconscious for two days. When he did regain consciousness, however, he again evinced his cavalier aplomb, remarking, "I know now that fifty million Frenchmen can't be wrong; they eat their horses instead of riding them." When she heard of the accident, his wife rushed to his side and refused to allow doctors to amputate his legs, certain that such maiming would break his spirit. Instead, she brought in a prominent surgeon, who began a series of excruciating operations that left Porter in continual pain but at least enabled him to hobble along on crutches.

At the doctor's suggestion that he keep working, Porter launched into another Broadway musical, *Leave It to Me*. The show featured Mary Martin in her Broadway debut, though when she auditioned for the role Porter thought her a "dreary little girl who appeared to be the last word in scared dowdiness." Once she began singing, however, Porter said, "It was the finest audition I had ever heard." "Dress her up," he ordered, and she got the part. Porter maintained that Martin "is probably the most basically naïve person I've ever met. I'm convinced she never had any idea about the many meanings of 'My Heart Belongs to Daddy,'" a suggestive song whose risqué lyrics took on more pungency from Martin's innocent, wide-eyed delivery: "If I invite a boy some night / To dine on my fine finnan haddie, / I just adore his asking for more / But my heart belongs to daddy." When Martin coyly did a mock striptease as she sang, she stopped the show.

For the first time in his career, however, Porter missed the opening night—because he did not want people to see him in his crippled condition.

Falling in Love with Love; This Can't Be Love
Lyrics by Lorenz Hart, music by Richard Rodgers

After their bitter experience in Hollywood, Rodgers and Hart re-established themselves on Broadway with *Jumbo* (1935), *On Your Toes* (1936), and *Babes in Arms* (1937). Taking the train to Atlantic City in the hope that the fresh sea air would inspire them with an idea for a new show, they struck upon something that had never been done on Broadway—a musical based on a Shakespearean play. Hart pointed out that his actor brother, Teddy, bore a striking resemblance to the great comic Jimmy Savo. "Why don't we do *The Comedy of Errors*?" Rodgers recalled Hart suggesting, "rubbing his hands together as he always did when a good idea hit him. 'Teddy and Jimmy would be a natural for the twin Dromios.'" With a swipe at upstate cities with Mediterranean names, they called it *The Boys from Syracuse*.

As they started to work with George Abbott as producer, director, and librettist, Hart's alcoholism and homosexual partying began to take its toll. Until then, his family had given him some stability. He lived at home with his mother and, despite the fact he was in his forties, still shared a room with his brother. However, in 1938, Teddy married and moved out of the house, and Hart's life began to veer out of control. He would disappear from rehearsals and sometimes could not be found when changes were needed in the lyrics.

"When he was there," Rodgers said, "he worked rapidly; all we had to say was that we wanted a new line or two or a complete new verse and it wouldn't take him long to come up with exactly what was needed." On one occasion, while Rodgers and Abbott were discussing the show at a restaurant, Hart scribbled away on a piece of paper and wrote the verse to "Falling in Love with Love" amid the din. Supposedly his personal favorite among his songs, "Falling in Love with Love" is the perfect example of what Rodgers once described as the secret to their songs: the "sweet and sour" clash of music and lyrics. To Rodgers' sumptuously beautiful waltz, Hart set lyrics that turn romantic conventions upside down: falling in love is "falling for make believe," "playing the fool," and a "juvenile fancy." Only at the end of the song does the singer explain her bitterness when she confesses that once she fell in love "with love everlasting, / But love fell out with me."

In "This Can't Be Love," the other major hit from *The Boys from Syracuse*, Hart was even more unconventionally romantic. Like Shakespeare, he was intrigued by the formulas of courtly love: falling in love at first sight, being in love as the source of fever and chills, and the association of love with hearts and flowers (an association born of the fact that in Provençal, the language of the medieval troubadours who invented this thing called love, *cor* and *flor* were convenient rhymes for *amor*). Hart turns such conventions upside down, saying "this can't be love" because there are "no sobs, no sorrows, no sighs," no "dizzy spells," and, in an allusion to his lyric for "My Heart Stood Still," "my heart does not stand still—just hear it beat!"

With such songs, *The Boys from Syracuse* was a hit, but in an ominous foreshadowing of deeper problems to come, Larry Hart missed the first opening night of his career because he was forced into convalescence from pneumonia brought on by drinking and partying. Friends even wondered whether he had begun to lose interest in the theater. "Larry was always a sweet and lovely guy," one told Hart biographer Frederick Nolan. "But by the time he was doing *The Boys from Syracuse*, he was sweet, lovely, and screwed up."

1938 (1918)

God Bless America
Lyrics and music by Irving Berlin

The adoption of "God Bless America" as an unofficial new national anthem began long before 9/11. On July 4, 1939, before a doubleheader at Brooklyn's Ebbets Field and eight months after Kate Smith had introduced it on her radio show the previous Armistice Day, the organ played it and the fans stood to sing. On February 3, 1945, when American forces liberated Manila's Santo Tomas Internment Camp, the prisoners (including seventy-seven U.S. Army nurses) were afraid to come out until a G.I. climbed up on a tank and yelled, "Hi folks." As everyone gathered around to celebrate, a single voice from the rear began to sing "God Bless America."

What is there about this brief, simple song that makes it stand for all we choose to believe about ourselves, especially in times of adversity? Ironically, it began with its composer uncertain about its originality or suitability. Irving Berlin first wrote it in 1918 as the finale for his all-soldier revue, *Yip, Yip, Yaphank*, in which the cast seemed to be leaving for France. One story, denied by Berlin, claimed that when his musical secretary Harry

Ruby first heard it and reacted, "Geez, Irvy, another patriotic song," that was enough for Berlin to drop it. He later said that having soldiers perform it in wartime would have been "painting the lily," and added that it was a little sticky and solemn to ring true for the irreverent doughboys.

Twenty years later, Berlin was crossing the Atlantic after having been in England during the signing of the Munich Pact. Convinced that war was inevitable, he determined to write a peace song. Then he remembered his unused patriotic song from World War I. It took his staff a full week to find it before he set to work. He would need to change the words to turn it into a peace song and that meant he would probably need to revise the melody as well. In 1918, he had written, "Stand beside her and guide her to the right with a light from above." By the 1930s, a reference to the "right" could be read as a political statement. He changed it to the familiar, "through the night with a light from above." He also changed the bellicose, "Make her victorious on land and foam," to the all-embracing "from the mountains, to the prairies, to the oceans white with foam" and then linked his embrace of America to a prayerful but familiar domestic image at the heart of America's view of itself: "God bless America, my home sweet home."

When Kate Smith sensed the country's changing mood in the late 1930s, she sought out Berlin for a new patriotic song. She wanted something that would stir as well as reassure her audience. As she sang it repeatedly during the War, her hearty optimistic manner and her clarion voice seemed to embody the nation. Berlin's song, as sung by Kate Smith, became a stirring image of our oneness as a people during a terrible war. As FDR said when he presented her to the King and Queen of England in 1938, "Your majesties, this is Kate Smith. This is America."

I'll Be Seeing You
Lyrics by Irving Kahal, music by Sammy Fain

In 1938, longtime collaborators Sammy Fain and Irving Kahal wrote their most important song, "I'll Be Seeing You," for a short-lived revue called *Right This Way*. That should have been that, except that the song re-emerged in 1943 when both Bing Crosby and Tommy Dorsey's Orchestra with Frank Sinatra had hit recordings.

How do you explain a song's great success after initial obscurity? In the 1930s, "I'll Be Seeing You" was merely a romantic ballad of separation characterized by references to the places where lovers meet: a "small cafe" or a "park across the way." During the war, however, this recollection of "familiar places" plus the breezily reassuring title took on new resonance as an image of true love, just as being apart had a particular poignancy when it might be forever. It is a song not merely about "familiar places," but also "familiar places that this heart of mine embraces." A lyric of memory, loneliness, hope, and fidelity—"I'll be looking at the moon but I'll be seeing you"—rests believably on a hushed, melancholy tune.

Jeepers Creepers; You Must Have Been a Beautiful Baby
Lyrics by Johnny Mercer, music by Harry Warren

After Richard Whiting's death and Al Dubin's dissipation, Warner Bros. teamed Harry Warren with Johnny Mercer. Mercer quickly proved he was as skilled as Dubin in finding vernacular phrases to match Warren's jazzy melodies. When Mercer heard Henry Fonda exclaim "Jeepers creepers" in his Midwestern twang, it struck him as a euphemistic way of saying "Jesus Christ!" Around the title phrase Mercer wove a variation on one of the oldest of romantic themes—a lover's praise for his beloved's eyes—but laced the lyric with such colloquial expressions as "Where'd you get those peepers?" "Gosh all git up / How'd they get so lit up" and "When you turn those heaters on ... got to put my cheaters on." Sung in *Going Places* by Louis Armstrong portraying a farmer serenading his favorite cow, "Jeepers Creepers" garnered an Academy Award nomination—Mercer's first, Warren's second.

When Warren played another of his driving melodies, Mercer's memory went back to a recent visit to his family in Savannah. As they were going through an old photo album, his wife, Ginger, saw a picture of Johnny as a baby on a bearskin rug and exclaimed, "You must have been a beautiful baby." Johnny's mother then produced a blue ribbon Johnny had actually won in a baby contest. The ribbon and the contest found their way into the song: "And when it came to winning blue ribbons, / You must have shown the other kids how / I can see the judges' eyes as they handed you the prize / I bet you made the cutest bow."

Love Is Here to Stay
Lyrics by Ira Gershwin, music by George Gershwin

Like many Broadway songwriters, George Gershwin hated writing for Hollywood films. Among other reasons, studio heads could be dismissive of his and Ira's work. When the Gershwins demonstrated "Love Walked In," a melody George considered "Brahmsian," to Sam Goldwyn, the producer advised George Gershwin to try to write more like Irving Berlin. "Imagine that," George lamented to his brother, "After all I've done—to be told to try to write more like Irving Berlin!"

Shortly after arriving in Hollywood, George complained of excruciating headaches that were accompanied by an odor of burning rubber. Because he had always been a hypochondriac, however, nobody paid much attention, not even Ira. After George collapsed on the street, he was rushed to a hospital, where doctors found he had a malignant brain tumor. They operated, but on July 9, 1937, George Gershwin was dead at the age of thirty-eight.

Despite his grief, Ira Gershwin still had to complete the songs for *The Goldwyn Follies*. With the help of composer Vernon Duke, he managed to write the remaining songs, but completed music and lyrics for the last song he and George had been working on by himself. The song, ironically, was about undying love. When George had first played the melody, Ira asked for a few extra notes so that he could insert the simplest of words—"and"—but that word did the trick: "The radio *and* the telephone *and* the movies that we know / May just be passing fancies *and* in time may go." When it was finished, Ira made one last revision that reflected his grief: He crossed out the word "our" from the title, so the song was published as "Love Is Here to Stay."

For years, Ira Gershwin was devastated by the death of his brother. He revered George as the genius in the family and, as older brother, had always made it his duty to take care of him. Doctors tried to reassure him that there was nothing that could have saved George, friends such as Jerome Kern and Harold Arlen tried to get him to write lyrics again, and his wife Leonore told him that he must now step into the spotlight and assume the Gershwin mantle. Nothing worked.

Then, one afternoon, Ira put on a recording of Fred Astaire singing the songs he and George had written during their year in Hollywood. "In a few moments," he said, "the room was filled with gaiety and rhythm, and I felt that George, smiling and approving, was there listening with me—and grief vanished."

September Song
Lyrics by Maxwell Anderson, music by Kurt Weill

One night after dinner, playwright Maxwell Anderson asked his friend, composer Kurt Weill, if he thought they could turn Washington Irving's early nineteenth-century burlesque, *Diedrich Knickerbocker's History of New York*, into a musical comedy. From that curious question came *Knickerbocker Holiday*, a show that gave the Broadway theatre one of its greatest songs. As they reworked the plot, their emphasis shifted from an indirect satire of Franklin Roosevelt to a more conventional story about young lovers and the tyrannical governor of seventeenth-century Nieuw Amsterdam, Peter Stuyvesant. Director Joshua Logan immediately sensed that the show needed a great star because, he wrote, "It wasn't until peg-legged

Peter Stuyvesant entered, flashing his silver-encrusted stump of a leg, that things began to crackle."

The old man's entrance was to come near the end of the first act when he proposes to Tina Tienhoven, who is young enough to be his daughter. She asks him to wait a few years, and he sings the heartbreakingly bittersweet "September Song" in response. A man accustomed to exercising power heartlessly suddenly reveals something from his deepest heart: "The autumn weather turns the leaves to flame and I haven't got time for the waiting game."

Weill suggested Walter Huston for the part of Stuyvesant, but the veteran actor was leery. He thought the part was "skimpy," though he was intrigued by the prospect of wearing a peg leg. Logan flew to California to court him. Huston eventually told Logan that Stuyvesant was

> ... such an old sonofabitch .... I can't stand him, but I'll play him if I have one chance to be charming and I can make love to the young girl. Not win her, just give her a squeeze or a tickle under the chin, and she could even consider him for a fraction of a second when she hears his song.

"What song?" Logan asked.

"Something nice I can sing to her, a moment for the old scoundrel to be charming."

"I'll get you a song," Logan promised.

"No, no, I'm smarter than that," the shrewd Huston replied, "I want to *hear* the song. Over the phone if necessary."

Weill soon called Huston to ask the range of his voice. "I have no range," the actor said, but he told Weill to listen to him sing on the radio that night. Weill said, "I heard this odd, almost tuneless but appealing voice ... and it came to me, all at once, that that voice singing a sentimental song would be unique." The next morning, Anderson wrote the words in about an hour and gave them to Weill, who wrote the music that afternoon. The composer then called Huston to sing him the song, but Huston could not understand it through Weill's thick German accent. Logan sang it next and then repeated it at Huston's request. What happened after that, neither Logan nor Weill could believe. Huston sang it back to them—perfectly. The dumbfounded Logan wrote, "In my entire professional career, I have never seen anything to equal the dexterity, the professional ease of Walter Huston."

Perhaps the most touching part of this autumnal reflection on the passing of time is the seven-bar release, in which, struggling to move beyond memory, Stuyvesant expresses his personal sense of what has gone and what remains, the passing of time and the passing of his time. Huston performs the elliptical lines with a rare combination of common sense and pathos, what he has been and what, in this moment, he has become: "Oh, the days dwindle down to a precious few; September, November." All that remains is his fondest hope, requiring nothing more than direct utterance and simple repetition: "And these few precious days I'll spend with you. These precious days I'll spend with you."

Two Sleepy People
Lyrics by Frank Loesser, music by Hoagy Carmichael

Hoagy Carmichael was an established songwriter from Indiana with a cool, deceptively low-key manner. Frank Loesser was, in Broadway producer Ernest Martin's words, "strictly a city boy. Loved to quote Nunnally Johnson, who said if he had a place with green grass, he'd pave it." Loesser was also notorious for his violent temper. Carmichael commented in that laconic way of his, "It was a good thing that he worked with me for awhile. I had a sobering Indiana effect on him." They wrote together successfully for a few years at Paramount and, in 1938, had three songs on the Hit Parade at the same time: "Small Fry"; "Heart and Soul," that favorite of piano-thumping adolescents; and, most important, "Two Sleepy People."

After Bob Hope and Shirley Ross' success with "Thanks for the Memory" in *Big Broadcast of 1938*, Paramount cast them in a new movie and assigned Carmichael and Loesser to write them a song. There are two stories about how they did it. According to Loesser's daughter, very late one night, the Loessers were leaving the Carmichael's after Frank and Hoagy had tried unsuccessfully to come up with an idea. On her way out, Loesser's wife, singer Lynn Garland, remarked, "Look at us, four sleepy people." Loesser and Carmichael said, as if on cue, "That's it," and went back into the house to write. The sheet music reads, "Title suggested by Lynn Garland."

Carmichael told an interviewer in 1973:

> I sat at the old upright piano Loesser had in the rented cottage, just fiddling around, Frank with a beer in his hand. The girls yelled, "Write something, you bums." At that moment Frank was trying to find a cigarette and I was too …. So Frank's first reaction to writing a song was his line, "here we are, out of cigarettes," and I followed with my next melody line to match his words … and he sang "holding hands and yawning." By that time we could both see that here was the song situation.

In "Two Sleepy People," Loesser wrote a lyric that combined unlikely emotions in perfect conversational English. The song is loving, sexy, intimate, and amusing: "Here we are, in the cozy chair / Picking on a wishbone from the Frigidaire." The unlikely mix focuses the emotion rather than diffusing it. A seductive, bantering conversation between married lovers, "Two Sleepy People" was a gentler, less ambiguous song than "Thanks for the Memory" but a worthy successor.

You Go to My Head
Lyrics by Haven Gillespie, music by J. Fred Coots

As Haven Gillespie was sitting in Aylward's, his favorite saloon in his home town of Covington, Kentucky, he stared at a row of bourbon bottles and noticed that one label proclaimed "Can Get You as Crazy as the Girl You Can't Get." Lyrical phrases started to come to him about a lover who "goes to your head" and "spins around in your brain" like the "bubbles in a glass of champagne." Another metaphor, "like a sip of sparkling burgundy brew," confused the brewing of beer with the aging of wine, but a third, "like the kicker in a julep or two," was on the relatively more solid ground of distilled spirits. Gillespie closed out the lyric with a clever twist on one of the oldest of romantic clichés about the power of a beautiful woman's eyes: "You intoxicate my soul with your eyes."

When he sent the lyric to J. Fred Coots, the composer found a melody in his trunk that, with some adjustments, fit the words. The problem, however, was that, even though Prohibition had been abolished three years earlier, radio stations still refused to play songs that mentioned alcohol. Once that ban was lifted, however, "You Go to My Head" became as big a hit as Gillespie and Coots' 1934 success, "Santa Claus Is Comin' to Town."

By then, however, alcohol was taking its toll on Gillespie. "I always thought I had to be drunk to write," he said. "I thought I couldn't write sober." Yet one morning, as he was drying out from a binge, he watched the sunrise hit the bell tower of a church near his backyard. Possessed by demons that drove him to drink, Gillespie could only envy the sun, which had "nothing to do but roll around heaven all day." "That Lucky Old Sun" (1949) was his last enduring hit.

1939

All the Things You Are
Lyrics by Oscar Hammerstein, music by Jerome Kern

The musical theater graveyard is filled with shows whose cause of death was a weak book. Jerome Kern and Oscar Hammerstein's *Very Warm for May* is one of the classic examples. Even though Hammerstein had written a charming book for the most lighthearted show he and Kern had ever done together, producer Max Gordon took an instant dislike to it and forced a rewrite before it opened on Broadway. With its wit and verve left behind in Boston, the show closed after fifty-nine performances. The word got around quickly. On the second night, only twenty-two people showed up to see it.

What is amazing is that Kern and Hammerstein's score was so good it survived the debacle: "All in Fun," "Heaven in My Arms," "In the Heart of the Dark," and, most important, "All the Things You Are," a soaring melody Alec Wilder calls ingenious and daring. Even though the song has at least the suggestion of an AABA structure, it also has a sense of continuous surprise because each of the A sections is just different enough from each of the others. What makes the release distinctive is its relative simplicity. Hammerstein properly called the song "the most surprising hit Jerry and I ever had. We never thought the public would take it; it had three changes of key in the middle of the refrain, which is a very risky thing to do."

In a 1964 poll in *Saturday Review*, more composers called it their favorite song than any other. Yet Hammerstein was never completely satisfied with the lyric. He disliked using the word "divine" in the penultimate line. He felt it had become hackneyed, but he could not find anything else. He knew Kern would dislike it, too, and he was right. He worked for days to find a replacement, but he was trapped by his satisfaction with the final line: "Some day I'll know that moment divine, when all the things you are, are mine." That last line was just what he wanted and the rest of the song pleased him, but he never liked the word he had to use to rhyme with "mine." Even so, "divine" fits the song better than any substitute he might have found. The imagery is convincing, even though its formal rhetoric and almost purple language links it, not to musical comedy, but rather to the operettas Hammerstein had written earlier in his career: "Touching your hand, my heart beats the faster, / All that I want in all of this world is you."

And the Angels Sing
Lyrics by Johnny Mercer, music by Ziggy Elman

Ziggy Elman, the lead trumpeter when Benny Goodman's orchestra appeared on radio's *Camel Caravan*, dazzled listeners with his brassy rendition of an old klezmer melody he called "Frälich in Swing." Johnny Mercer, who was also on the show as singer and emcee, suggested to Goodman that if Elman's melody was slowed down it could be "kind of a Gershwin tune." The producer decided to create an on-the-air event by having Goodman assign Mercer the task of setting a lyric to "Fṙålich in Swing" by the following week's show. Mercer agreed to the assignment but meekly asked if he could change the song's title.

It all sounds like a prearranged plug for a completed song, but on the following week's show Mercer had to confess he did not have a lyric and Elman muttered that he was going to take his melody to Irving Berlin. Given a week's extension by Goodman, Mercer came up with two different lyrics: one called "And It All Came True" and the other, which more people preferred, "And the Angels Sing." The melody was unusually intricate, with sudden twists and turns of phrases that brought out Elman's virtuosity, but Mercer matched those sinuous, soaring phrases with extended images: "silver waves break on some undiscovered shore" and "long winter nights with the candles gleaming." Bing Crosby wrote to Mercer that he thought it was the lyricist's best song to date, adding "You're getting practically poetic."

I Didn't Know What Time It Was
Lyrics by Lorenz Hart, music by Richard Rodgers

"Not knowing what time it was" was a catchphrase for someone completely unaware of what was going on around him. Unfortunately, it was an apt description of Larry Hart in the late 1930s. His alcoholism led to frequent blackouts when he could not remember where he had been and protracted absences when Richard Rodgers had to write lyrics as well as music to their songs.

When he was sober, however, Hart continued to work his lyrical magic. *Too Many Girls* was a collegiate musical about football players with academic difficulties, so he crafted "I Didn't Know What Time It Was" to fit the educational and romantic themes. In the verses for the male and female leads, Hart has them wryly comment on their youthfulness: the girl saying "I thought I had a trick or two / Up my imaginary sleeve, / And now I know I was naïve" and the boy calling himself old at "Twenty years or so" but "Rather well preserved / The wrinkles didn't show." However, in the chorus, Hart puts aside cleverness and gives himself over to Rodgers' sumptuous melody with such soaring lines as "Grand to be alive, to be young, / To be mad, to be yours alone."

Desi Arnaz, who made his Broadway debut in *Too Many Girls*, told Frederick Nolan that after the out-of-town opening performance, director George Abbott asked Hart to write some extra choruses to one of the show-stopping numbers. "Larry looked in his coat pocket and took out an envelope, put it on top of the rehearsal piano onstage, borrowed a pencil and started to write." The rest of the cast left him there and went to a party across the street. "In about a half-hour Larry came in, went to Mr. Abbott and Dick Rodgers and said, 'What do you think of this?' as he handed them the envelope. He had written three more choruses as good as, if not better than, the ones he had written before."

Too Many Girls had a successful run; however, Rodgers and Hart's next show, *Higher and Higher* (1940), did not. The only song that has endured from it also has a title that eerily resonates with Hart's deteriorating alcoholic condition: "It Never Entered My Mind."

I Thought about You
Lyrics by Johnny Mercer, music by Jimmy Van Heusen

In Hollywood in the late 1930s, Johnny Mercer hit one of several dead ends as a songwriter, but after he and Bing Crosby had a surprise hit with their recording of "Mr. Crosby and Mr. Mercer" in the summer of 1938, CBS invited him to New York to join its popular radio program, *Camel Caravan*, as a singer. The revival of his prospects as a performer spurred his efforts as a songwriter. He soon wrote a number of hits, including "I Thought about You," with Jimmy Van Heusen. Mercer liked working with Van Heusen because "he seems to have a series of chords waiting at his command to which he can fashion a melody the moment his lyricist springs any idea on him." "I Thought about You" was also the first of Mercer's important "train songs"; he would follow it with "Blues in the Night" in 1941 and "On the Atchison, Topeka and the Santa Fe" in 1946.

The song was one of the few instances in which Mercer wrote the words first. The idea came to him as he rode the train from California to New York. What he described as "all these little towns with the lights and cars parked and the glow worms in the dark" became a setting for longing whose wistful quiet only deepens the pain of separation. Set in a Pullman sleeper, it begins with the unadorned title statement, "I took a trip on a train." There is something nearly desperate in the separation as the lyric, set to the rhythms of the train, contrasts the changing rural scene the character sees as the train rolls past—a shadowy lane, parked cars, the stars and moon, and a stream—with the unadorned statement of what remains constant: "I thought about you." The song is as much about fidelity as loneliness, but with an undertone of implied eroticism. She is at her loneliest when she pulls down the shade of her berth and lies in her bed alone. As the train speeds through the night, she even envies the train track, "The one goin' back to you."

I'll Never Smile Again
Lyrics and music by Ruth Lowe

On the road as a piano player with Ina Ray Hutton's All-Girl Orchestra, Ruth Lowe met and married a music publicist named Harold Cohen when she was twenty-four. A year later, Cohen died during surgery, and the distraught Lowe returned to her family in Toronto. After telling her sister that she would never smile again without him, Lowe poured her grief into a song that she wrote in a single evening.

Though the song's emotional outlook is intensely personal, Lowe knew the conventions of the time well enough to transform her personal loss into something broadly familiar: "For tears would fill my eyes, my heart would realize / That our romance is through." Lowe was able to get it to Tommy Dorsey, who recorded it in 1940 with a vocal by his new singer, Frank Sinatra. Sinatra remembered the recording session years later:

> We were rehearsing on a Saturday afternoon, up at the roof of the Astor Hotel, and Tommy asked pianist Joe Bushkin to play the song. I noticed that everybody suddenly was very quiet, the whole orchestra sat quietly when he played it. There was a feeling of a kind of eeriness that took place, as though we all knew that this would be a big, big hit, and that it was a lovely song.

The recording was Sinatra's first hit with Dorsey and launched his career.

The lyric's defining word is "smile," rhymed internally with "I'll" in the very first line and repeated in the second line and again at the end, helped along by the rhyming of "eyes" and "realize" in the release. Rather than following a typical AABA pattern, the song is ABAC, with the release following the first chorus and with another variation concluding it. Typical of the lush romantic ballads of the time, the song speaks in unvarying absolutes that, in turn, articulate its unrelieved sadness.

Lydia, the Tattooed Lady
Lyrics by Yip Harburg, music by Harold Arlen

Yip Harburg loved Gilbert and Sullivan. He had grown up in the wretched poverty of New York's Lower East Side, but in school he learned to love poetry, particularly the witty light verse of Don Marquis, Carolyn Wells, and others whose work appeared in New York newspapers. One day, he found that a classmate seated near to him alphabetically, Ira Gershwin, shared his love of light verse, and Yip confided to Ira that his favorite poet was William Schwenck Gilbert. Ira gently asked if Yip knew that Gilbert's poems were also song lyrics. When Harburg asked, "There's music to it?" Ira invited him home, where he put a recording of H.M.S. *Pinafore* on the

Victrola. "There were all the lines I knew by heart, put to music!" Harburg recalled. "I was dumbfounded, staggered."

Harburg dated his aspiration to become a lyricist from that day, so when he and composer Harold Arlen wrote a song for Groucho Marx in *At the Circus*, Harburg was determined "to get as near to Gilbert and Sullivan as possible." He and Arlen created a song about a circus sideshow denizen, "Lydia, the Tattooed Lady," but Harburg's lyric about Lydia, the "encyclopidia"—with her adorable and educational torso ("You can learn a lot from Lydia"), her "view of Niag'ra that nobody has," and her depiction of Andrew Jackson, who, "when her muscles start relaxin'," appears riding up a hill—was banned by the Hollywood censors.

To get around the censors, Harburg added another verse that described how Lydia's tattoos so beguiled an admiral that he married her, and that happy marital ending persuaded the censors to let the song stay in the film, even with Groucho's leering, arched-brow delivery. Not even the censors, however, could be fooled into allowing this particularly risqué verse about Lydia's storied anatomy: "When she stands, the world grows littler, / When she sits, she sits on Hitler."

Over the Rainbow
Lyrics by E. Y. "Yip" Harburg, music by Harold Arlen

MGM originally planned to have Jerome Kern write the musical score for *The Wizard of Oz*, but when Kern suffered a mild stroke, the studio turned to Harold Arlen and E. Y. "Yip" Harburg. They produced a series of brilliant songs that carried the story for extensive stretches, from "Ding Dong! The Witch Is Dead" through the Gilbert and Sullivan patter of "If I Only Had a Brain" to the infectious "We're Off to See the Wizard." All that remained was for them to write a ballad of "yearning" for Dorothy to sing early in the film.

Harold Arlen and Yip Harburg wanted to write an extraordinary ballad for Judy Garland, but the composer was stymied. "I can't tell you the misery that a composer goes through when the whole score is written, but he hasn't got that big theme song that Louis B. Mayer is waiting for," said Harburg. "The contract was for fourteen weeks, and we were on our fourteenth week. We didn't get paid after the fourteenth. He surely sweated it out, but he couldn't get a tune." Then one night Arlen drove by Schwab's Drug Store on Sunset Boulevard, where so many famous stars had been discovered. Suddenly, a broad, sweeping melody popped into his mind. He later recalled, "It was as if the Lord had said, 'Well, here it is. Now stop worrying.'"

Arlen drove to Harburg's house even though it was after midnight. However, when Harburg heard the melody, he said, "My heart fell. He played it with such symphonic sweep and bravura that my first reaction

Sheet music for "Over the Rainbow." Courtesy of David A. Jasen.

was: 'Oh no, not for little Dorothy. That's for Nelson Eddy.'" So they took the melody to their friend, Ira Gershwin. When Arlen again played it with same sweeping harmonies, Ira asked him to drop the grandeur and just pick the tune out with one finger. Suddenly, the simple beauty of the melody shone through. "I confess with my head bowed," Harburg said, "the song almost suffered extinction by me while it was still aborning."

Back cover of sheet music for *The Wizard of Oz.* Courtesy of David A. Jasen.

Frank Baum's *Oz* books never mentioned a rainbow, but Harburg thought that a little girl in barren Kansas would find color in her life only by looking to a rainbow. His inspiration, in turn, gave the director the idea of filming the Kansas sequences in brown and sepia tones, then switching to Technicolor when Dorothy enters the Land of Oz.

Once the film was shot, the director, the producers, and practically everybody else thought the song should be cut because it slowed down the film. After each preview, they dropped it, but after each cut the songwriters, backed by a young assistant producer named Arthur Freed, who was also a songwriter, stormed into Louis B. Mayer's office to fight for it. Mayer, who could be a tyrant, had a soft spot for songwriters. Finally, he told Freed, "Let the boys have the damned song. Get it back in the picture; it can't hurt."

What's New?
Lyrics by Johnny Burke, music by Bob Haggart

Bob Haggart, bass player for Bob Crosby's orchestra, created a beautiful melody, "I'm Free," that Crosby presented with a dazzling trumpet solo by Billy Butterfield. Hoping to repeat the success of "And the Angels Sing," in which Johnny Mercer set lyrics to an instrumental by Benny Goodman's trumpeter Ziggy Elman, Crosby asked Mercer to create lyrics for the instrumental. This time Mercer was stumped. "He worked on it for two months," Bob Haggart recalled, "but he said, 'I keep coming up with the same thing—I'm free, free as the birds in the trees, dad dad a da.'"

The tune was then given to Johnny Burke, who took the advice of Crosby that he write in a less "poetic," more conversational style—"like 'What's new?' 'How's things?' something like that." Burke crafted a dramatic monologue, one side of a conversation between two ex-lovers who meet by chance on the street. Burke shrewdly used the soaring, wide-ranging melody as a counterpoint to the lovers' low-keyed but strained small talk. The tension between passionate music and chatty lyric reveals the singer's unspoken ardor, right down to his nervously cheery "adieu." Only the prosaic "I haven't changed a bit" releases his suppressed (but barely whispered) "I still love you so" as the melody plunges downward.

At the time Johnny Mercer and Johnny Burke had been vying to be the lyricist for Bing Crosby, and with the success of "What's New?" Burke got the nod and, teamed with composer Jimmy Van Heusen, went on to write the scores for the Bing Crosby–Bob Hope "Road" pictures. Johnny Mercer always carried a chip on his shoulder about the loss. When his son-in-law, a jazz pianist, tried his hand at writing popular songs, Mercer looked at his lyric and scoffed, "Sounds like Johnny Burke!"

1940 – 1949

1940

How High the Moon
Lyrics by Nancy Hamilton, music by Morgan Lewis

Nancy Hamilton and Morgan Lewis specialized in witty patter songs for sophisticated Broadway revues. When their songs were criticized for lacking "social significance," Hamilton quipped, "I seen my ditty and I done it." When the revue *Two for the Show* needed a romantic ballad, however, Lewis created an unusual and enchanting tune. Hamilton put aside her witty patter and wrote a straightforward, soaring lyric that shifts its long vowels as intricately as Lewis' music changes chords: "Somewhere there's music / How faint the tune! / Somewhere there's heaven, / How high the moon!" Alec Wilder called "How High the Moon" "the 'bop' hymn" because for years, it was the most played tune in jazz with recordings by artists such as Ella Fitzgerald, the Nat King Cole Trio, and Charlie Parker. Benny Goodman's Orchestra had the initial hit recording, but the most famous was by Les Paul and Mary Ford, a multi-tracked rendering of guitar and vocal, which made the song a hit again ten years after it was written.

The Last Time I Saw Paris
Lyrics by Oscar Hammerstein, music by Jerome Kern

When Oscar Hammerstein learned about the fall of Paris to the Nazis in the spring of 1940, he was so despondent he could not work. He found his mind filled with memories of the city he had visited so often over the years, including the time when, at seventeen, he had run from a sidewalk cafe because a pretty girl had flirted with him. He pictured the city as it had been and began to write: "The last time I saw Paris, her heart was

165

Buddy Lewis and Nancy Hamilton. (Photo by John Erwin). Courtesy of Photofest.

warm and gay," a love song that was also a lament for something lost, perhaps irretrievably. It was the only lyric he ever wrote without a scene in which to place it.

About to leave for California, Hammerstein called Kern to read him the words, telling him he did not know what he wanted to do with them but insisting they were something he had had to write. He urged Kern to break his rule against writing music after the lyrics. Hammerstein said that Kern "nearly fell dead" at the request, but when Hammerstein returned, Kern met him with the melody. He had chosen to emphasize the happiness of Hammerstein's memories rather than his sadness at the city's fall. The delighted Hammerstein noticed Kern's note on the sheet music: a reminder to himself to "phone Ira about George's taxi horns." Kern wanted to see if he could borrow the notes Gershwin had used for the sound of taxis in *An American in Paris*.

Producer–songwriter Arthur Freed bought the song for MGM's adaptation of the Gershwins' 1924 musical, *Lady Be Good*. It won the Oscar for best song—Oscar's first Oscar—but Kern did not attend the ceremony because he did not think they had a chance to win.

PAL JOEY
Lyrics by Lorenz Hart, music by Richard Rodgers

John O'Hara, who had been writing short stories for *The New Yorker* about an amoral emcee working in a Chicago dive, wrote to Richard Rodgers, "I got the idea that the pieces, or at least the character and the life in general, could be made into a book show, and I wonder if you and Larry would be interested in working on it with me." The upshot was *Pal Joey*, a landmark musical on the road from *Show Boat* to *Oklahoma!*.

Like Kern and Hammerstein, Rodgers was increasingly interested in writing integrated musicals that told believable stories about psychologically complex characters. Hart, on the other hand, "needed laughter the way some men need praise," wrote David Ewen, "A carefully timed wisecrack, a well-told joke, a neatly turned pun, a skillfully perpetrated prank—these were the meat and drink of his soul." During the writing of *Pal Joey*, he would call Josh Logan in the middle of the night to read him his latest double entendres, most notably for "Bewitched." He loved nothing better than putting one over on the censors.

Joey is an unlovable, not very bright heel, who will do just about anything to get what he wants. He drops his innocent girlfriend Linda and starts an affair with Vera, a wealthy older woman, who sets him up in his own nightclub. When some of his less savory friends try to blackmail her, she winds up throwing him out. The loutish Joey saunters off without a regret. The trick in writing the score was to retain the cynicism in the original stories yet draw audiences to a musical. "Larry and I were scrupulous in making every song adhere to the hard-edged nature of the story," Rodgers said. Nonetheless, they wrote the score's fifteen songs in just three weeks.

The show's first important plot song, "I Could Write a Book," was also its only love ballad; however, Joey, who probably never read a book in his life, sings it to impress a girl he has just picked up. He begins by reciting the alphabet from A to G and counting from one to seven, as Rodgers repeats the same note twenty-six times. He and Hart are suggesting that this is a bad song by a pretty dumb guy to a woman not smart enough to recognize just how bad it is or how dumb he is. It's as if Joey wrote the song. Still, Hart said it was his favorite song in the score, not for its sentiment but its irony.

On the other hand, Hart wasn't especially impressed with "Bewitched," even though it emerged as the show's most important song. According to Vivienne Segal, who played Vera, "None of us really knew what we had in 'Bewitched.'" When the show opened in New York, however, Hart had to write additional couplets because audiences demanded encores, including, "Vexed again, perplexed again, / Thank God, I can be oversexed again." The song is Vera's soliloquy as she reflects on Joey's limits, his bravura sexual performances, and her erotic appetites that worship "the trousers that cling to him." Gerald Mast suggests that to underscore a middle-aged woman's knowing ways with sex, Hart builds the song around the frequent repetition of "again," as Vera revels in her delight with Joey, despite his loutishness. She is using him as much as he is using her, except that she knows it.

In writing the song, Rodgers said he tried something particularly effective in comedy numbers: "the contrast of a flowing, sentimental melody with words that are unsentimental and self-mocking." After hearing the song, director George Abbott took Rodgers aside and said, "Dick, don't you think that melody is too sweet for the kind of lyrics Larry has written?" "If it is," Rodgers retorted, "it'll be the first time."

Polka Dots and Moon Beams; Imagination; Moonlight Becomes You
Lyrics by Johnny Burke, music by Jimmy Van Heusen

Jimmy Van Heusen was surprised one day when lyricist Johnny Burke came into his office at Warner Bros. Burke had been collaborating with composer Arthur Johnston on such Bing Crosby hits as "Pennies from Heaven" (1936) and then with Jimmy Monaco on songs for *The Road to Singapore* (1940), the first of the crooner's "road" pictures with Dorothy Lamour and Bob Hope.

Van Heusen was even more surprised when Burke asked, "Got any tunes?" but he managed a casual "Sure!" and together the new collaborators wrote "Oh, You Crazy Moon." "The next time he was in," Van Heusen recalled, "We did 'Polka Dots and Moonbeams,'" which typifies what fellow lyricist Sammy Cahn described as the "lacier, more fragile" character of Burke's lyrics, whom he dubbed "the Irish poet." Burke's more down-to-earth explanation of his success was that he would simply listen to Bing Crosby talk "and either take my phrases directly from him or pattern some after his way of putting phrases together."

Burke's lyrics were woven of poetic imagery, but he kept them down to earth with vernacular expressions. In "Polka Dots and Moonbeams," amid the astral imagery he inserts an Irish-sounding phrase:"pug-nosed dream." In another song he wrote with Van Heusen, "Imagination," Burke began by saying that "imagination is funny" and then followed with, "Imagination is crazy, your whole perspective gets hazy."

Burke and Van Heusen wrote the songs for most of the road pictures featuring Bing Crosby, Bob Hope, and Dorothy Lamour. The best song from these formulaic pictures about two wise-cracking picaresque heroes was "Moonlight Becomes You" from *Road to Morocco*. Its casually passionate tone suited Crosby's style, with Johnny Burke following up the guarded compliment of the title with the understated, "It goes with your hair." The song and the film were enormously successful, prompting Crosby to dub Burke and Van Heusen his "Gold Dust Twins" and see that they were paid $150,000 a year at Paramount—more than any other songwriting team in Hollywood.

Taking a Chance on Love
Lyrics by John LaTouche and Ted Fetter, music by Vernon Duke

When the Russian Revolution forced Vladimir Dukelsky's family to flee to Constantinople, he encountered the jazz- and blues-based songs of Irving Berlin and George Gershwin. Soon he was writing his songs under the pen name of Ivan Ivin. Eventually, Gershwin encouraged him to change it to Vernon Duke.

After he emigrated to America, his most successful popular numbers were such sophisticated, elegant melodies as "April in Paris" and "Autumn in New York." Then, in 1940, his Russian compatriot, choreographer George Balanchine, asked him to write the score for a black musical called *Little Joe.* "On reading the script," Duke said, "my first impulse was to turn it down because much as I admired the Negro race and its musical gifts, I didn't think myself sufficiently attuned to Negro folklore." Nevertheless, he asked his black maid if she thought he could compose a "colored" score. "You sure could, Misst' Duke," he reports her response, "Why, you is the music-writingest gemmun I ever see."

He took off for Virginia with lyricist John LaTouche to absorb "southern talk and Negro spirituals ... fried chicken, and Smithfield ham." They came up with a score that was good enough to induce Ethel Waters to accept the lead in the musical whose title had changed to *Cabin in the Sky.* Duke recalled that he charmed the notoriously difficult star by greeting her with a dashing European kiss of the hand. Such chivalry, however, could not assuage Waters' complaints about the plaintive lullaby Duke and LaTouche had written for her to close the first act. She told Duke she wanted a song with more "meat and potatoes" *sock,* so he rummaged about in his trunk for a song he had written for an unproduced show with lyricist Ted Fetter, "Fooling Around with Love." John LaTouche liked the melody but felt it needed a new lyric, more "on the nose." An afternoon's work produced "Taking a Chance on Love." LaTouche's lyric equated love with gambling and had such punchy vernacular lines as "I thought the cards were a frame up ... But now I'm taking the game up / And the ace of hearts is high."

When Duke played "Taking a Chance on Love" for Ethel Waters, she stopped him after the first eight bars. "Mister, our troubles are over," she exclaimed, "That's it!"

When You Wish Upon a Star
Lyric by Ned Washington, music by Leigh Harline

Though Leigh Harline and Ned Washington wrote it for an animated cricket to sing in *Pinocchio*, "When You Wish upon a Star" has lasted long enough to become a universal paean to dreaming of something better: "When you wish upon a star, your dreams come true." Although Walt Disney's films produced such enduring songs as "Someday My Prince Will Come," "Whistle While You Work," and "Zip-a Dee-Doo-Dah," it was "When You Wish upon a Star" that became the theme song of the Disney television program. Surprisingly, the success of the song rests on Cliff "Ukulele Ike" Edwards' very brief performance at the start of the movie. Although Edwards was a star in the 1920s, his career had faded when Disney hired him. His sweet falsetto seemed perfect for the eager, energetic Jiminy Cricket and, although he sang only the final eight bars of the song, that was enough to turn "When You Wish upon a Star" into a classic.

1941

Blues in the Night
Lyrics by Johnny Mercer, music by Harold Arlen

After successful collaborations with Ted Koehler and Yip Harburg, Harold Arlen teamed with Johnny Mercer to write songs for a Paramount film called *Hot Nocturne*. On the surface, the collaborators were diametric opposites: Arlen the son of a cantor from Buffalo and Mercer the scion of a prominent Savannah family that could trace its ancestry back to the Revolutionary War. However, both men had a deep love of jazz and the blues. Arlen believed the blues had parallels in Middle Eastern music, and Mercer grew up listening to the music that emanated from black churches. As a teenager, he hung out in record stores in Savannah's black district listening to the songs of Ma Rainey and Bessie Smith.

Despite Arlen and Mercer's affinity for the blues, their collaboration got off to a rocky start. Arlen had worked for days on a melody to be sung by a black man in jail. Although he did not follow traditional twelve-bar blues, Arlen stretched the standard thirty-two bar pop song format to fifty-two bars. "I couldn't wait to get over to Johnny's house to play it for him," Arlen recalled. "He's not much of a reactor so we fussed around with it for quite a while. I remember he had lots of phrases and lines written down but none of them seemed to fit that opening phrase right."

Mercer's original opening line was the lugubrious, "I'm heavy in my heart, I'm heavy in my heart." Rather than express disapproval, Arlen looked over some of Mercer's other phrases. "Then I saw those words, 'My momma done tol' me,' way down in the pile and I said, 'Why don't we move them up to the top?' It sure worked." With that change, the lyric took off in a vernacular wail that bristled with such slang phrases as, "Give ya the big eye" and "I've heard me some big talk." Even Southern place names sounded like earthy poetry: "From Natchez to Mobile, / From Memphis to Saint Jo," and Mercer crafted a haunting bit of onomatopoeia for the sound of a train whistle: "A whoo-ee-duh-whoo-ee."

When Arlen suggested that they change the title of the song to "My Momma Done Tol' Me," however, Mercer balked, and the two men took the song to Irving Berlin. Berlin listened carefully then concluded that the song should remain "Blues in the Night." When the studio executives heard the song, however, they were so impressed that they even changed the movie's title from *Hot Nocturne* to *Blues in the Night*.

I Got It Bad (and That Ain't Good)
Lyrics by Paul Francis Webster, music by Duke Ellington

During the 1930s, when Duke Ellington was under contract to Mills Music, the company would assign lyricists to turn his jazz instrumentals into popular songs. Such lyricists, more inspired by titles such as "Solitude" (1934), "In a Sentimental Mood" (1935), and "Caravan" (1937) than by Ellington's intricate melodies, would lace their lyrics with such strained poeticisms as "reveries of days gone by" and "the wings of ev'ry kiss."

When Ellington ended his association with Mills Music, his lyricists got more down to earth. One of the first was Paul Francis Webster, a young man from Long Island who disappointed his well-to-do parents by not taking his place in the family's clothing business. Paul had published poems in campus literary magazines at Cornell and New York University. Soon, musical classmates sought him out to write lyrics.

Invited to set several Ellington melodies for the revue *Jump for Joy*, Webster dropped his poetic aspirations to write colloquial, racially tinged lyrics for "The Chocolate Shake," "The Brown-Skin Gal in the Calico Gown," and, his first major success, "I Got It Bad." The title phrase had a subtle assonance: "I got it *bad* (and *that* ain't good)." Other lines, such as "I end up like I start out / Just cryin' my heart out" and "He don't love me like I love him—nobody could," had a gritty tenderness.

"It was an odd creation from the man whose name later became synonymous with formal, flowery lyrics," notes Tony Hill, who adds that "the lyric was well suited to the vocal style of the Ellington band, and it was a marked improvement over some of the lyrics the band had been creating in-house."

1942

As Time Goes By
Lyrics and music by Herman Hupfeld

Popular songs don't often get a second chance, especially when they fail the first time around. Its inclusion in one of America's best loved movies transformed "As Time Goes By" into one of our most popular songs twelve years after it initially flopped. It was in *Casablanca* because playwright Murray Burnett had fallen in love with it as a Cornell undergraduate in 1931. In 1940, when he and Joan Allison collaborated on a play called *Everybody Comes to Rick's*, he used it as the ballad Rick and Ilsa had listened to as lovers in Paris. When Warner Bros. turned the play into a movie, they kept the song because Warner's music division owned the publishing rights to it. Producer Hal Wallis got its rights for—as they say—a song. Composer Max Steiner, hired to write the movie's score, thought "As Time Goes By" was weak and convinced Wallis to let him write a replacement, but director Michael Curtiz had finished shooting by then and Ingrid Bergman had cut her hair short to begin filming *For Whom the Bell Tolls*. Wallis decided a wig was not worth the time and money. "As Time Goes By" survived—by the timing of a haircut.

Another oddity emerged from the song's new popularity. Although Dooley Wilson was under contract to Paramount, the Warner Bros.' executives decided he had to be in the movie. Only after Wilson signed for the part of Sam did they learn he could neither play piano nor sing. They considered giving him lessons but eventually decided to dub his piano playing and let him sing the number in his scratchy tenor.

Aside from its association with a great tragic love story played out against World War II, "As Time Goes By" is worthy of our affection, especially in its opening chorus. The first 'A' section of this conventional AABA song ascends through the first three lines before descending quietly and anticlimactically in the final two. The lines are short and the language is simple—largely monosyllabic except for the key words "remember" and "fundamental." Both are instrumental in shaping the song's point of view.

The speaker may be someone older and wiser, certainly someone knowing about love and what it means, someone with memories to pass on to someone else. The song's second word, "must," insists on the listener's attention. The next two lines are parallel, characterized by their use of "just," as if to downplay their importance. It's a nice touch; through the repetition of "just" used first conversationally, then ironically, and as a rhyme with "must," its meaning is enhanced. Then comes the surprising line, "The fundamental things apply," that makes this a love song for adults. The brilliance of the line lies in its focus

Sheet music for "As Time Goes By." Courtesy of David A. Jasen.

on "fundamental," its directness and brevity, the contrasting practicality of "apply," and the sense of understanding raised here and completed in the title line that follows: what matters most plays out against a background of time passing. The song possesses a sense of urgency whose understatement does nothing to diminish its intensity.

Don't Get Around Much Anymore
Lyrics by Bob Russell, music by Duke Ellington

As America changed during World War II, its love songs became more introspective and reflective, perhaps because the characters who sang in them were almost always alone. The ballads of those years were a direct reflection of what the women left behind were living through. Few songs caught that mood with greater poignancy than "Don't Get Around Much Anymore." Duke Ellington was well known for long, abstract jazz instrumentals, though he sometimes used the forms of popular songs for his compositions. "Don't Get Around Much Anymore" began as an instrumental entitled "Never No Lament," but Bob Russell added a lyric and turned it into one of Ellington's biggest hits.

The song's melody has a smoky but sad quality that sustains Russell's tense, cryptic lyric. It is a song for the shadows. While others go on dates or dance on crowded floors, the singer prefers solitude. As bad as it is, it's better than a night of solicitude and companionship without her lover. Even though the song's sentiments are intensely personal, it almost never uses "I," as if she denies her identity during these dark days of separation. Finally, she makes herself go to a club, though she only gets "as far as the door." What stops her is the thought that old friends will ask about him: "They'd have asked me about you / Don't get around much anymore." The elliptical lyric is filled with gaps and suggestions that make the song more poignant and must have brought its original listeners even closer to their own stark emotions.

I Don't Want to Walk Without You
Lyrics by Frank Loesser, music by Jule Styne

In the hierarchy of Hollywood studios, Paramount and MGM were at the top, and Republic Pictures, which specialized in making westerns, was at the very bottom. Occasionally, though, Republic mounted a big-budget picture, and in 1941 it lent its star, John Wayne, to Paramount, in return for Bing Crosby to star in *Sis Hopkins*. Republic's main composer, vocal coach, piano accompanist, and musical jack-of-all-trades was a young songwriter named Jule Styne. Styne begged Republic to get him a top-notch lyric writer, so the studio brought over Frank Loesser from Paramount as well.

Loesser resented being rented out to lowly Republic, and when he found he was to collaborate with Jule Styne, the short-tempered lyricist exploded at being teamed with what he termed a "half-ass piano player." At Paramount, songwriters had elegant bungalows in which to work, but at Republic Styne's quarters doubled as a western-movie set, with a "Hay &

Feed" sign over the door. As Loesser picked his way across a lot bestrewn with horse manure, he screamed at Styne, "You've demeaned me by asking for me …. You have no respect for my talent … this pile of shit, Republic. You've ruined me forever."

"The reason I wanted you," Styne explained, mustering his courage, "is because I want to do something very good. I've watched horses whinny in sync. I've written arrangements for coyotes. I've written songs about watermelons and grits and gravy."

"I don't want your history," Loesser fumed. "Play me something …. I hate your guts right now."

Styne then launched into a melody, but after five bars Loesser raced across the room and slammed the door shut. "Ssssh. Stop!" he said. "Don't play that here. Never play that here again. Don't you ever play that for anyone else. We'll write that song at Paramount."

A month later, Loesser had Paramount borrow Styne to write songs for *Sweater Girl.* Styne was astonished at how relaxed and elegant working conditions were at the upper-echelon studio. For five weeks, all he had to do was play his melody over and over as Loesser walked around the piano, working the lyric out in his head. Just when Styne was about to go stir crazy, Loesser recited the entire lyric in one extraordinary sweep. Styne was astounded at the grace and polish of the lyric, in which every syllable matched his notes and the sentiment was flippant yet forceful.

"I Don't Want to Walk Without You," gave Styne a new appreciation of how a brilliant lyricist could enhance his melodies. "Don't ever write with smart-ass rhymers," Loesser told him. "Write with people who have something to say with their words. Fellows who are thoughtful and literate, and have wit."

I Had the Craziest Dream; There Will Never Be Another You
Lyrics by Mack Gordon, music by Harry Warren

After the death of his son from pneumonia, Harry Warren, who had never liked Hollywood, negotiated an end to his contract with Warner Bros. and planned to move back to New York. Instead, Darryl F. Zanuck persuaded him to work for Twentieth Century-Fox, where he teamed him with lyricist Mack Gordon. When Twentieth-Century Fox was not contributing to World War II morale by making "period musicals" set at the turn of the century, it was releasing movies that may have looked contemporary but usually omitted any reference to the war. It was as if the war were the dream and snow-covered slopes and sun-drenched Caribbean cruises in vivid Technicolor the reality. No matter what the location, the heroine would always find true love—and make friends with Carmen Miranda.

Although Twentieth Century-Fox was not as much a pressure cooker for songwriters as Warner Bros. had been, Warren recalled, "They used you. It was always, 'C'mon, fells, help us out, we're in a spot here with the picture, put in a little extra time for us, you're part of the family.'" More than ever, he longed to return to New York, but the pressure to produce hits kept him working. "Hell, sometimes we were working on two pictures at a time," he recalled. "You get a script and you read it, and then your subconscious mind goes to work. When I do a picture, I must write reams of melodies. I might write maybe fifteen, twenty tunes before I get the right one, the one I like."

For *Iceland*, a vehicle for skater Sonja Henie, Warren and Gordon had only one hit song, "There Will Never Be Another You," but it was one of their finest. Warren's melody has a beautifully symmetrical pattern of rising and falling phrases, and Gordon's lyric matches them with a series of parallel phrases that contrast the singer's vision of his future loves with his present one. Speculating that there will be "many other nights like this" with other lovers, the singer affirms, "but there will never be another you." Taken with his romantic future, the singer goes on to say "there will be other lips that I may kiss," then relegates the present to a past memory: "but they won't thrill me like yours used to do." The beloved so addressed may well wonder if she is more arresting as a sensuous presence or a ghostly recollection.

In *Springtime in the Rockies*, one of the most successful Warren–Gordon songs was performed, not by stars Betty Grable or John Payne, but by a dance band and a girl singer. "I Had the Craziest Dream" began with band leader Harry James' sweet trumpet solo and continued with Helen Forrest's vocal as dancers fox-trotted outdoors with the Rocky Mountains as backdrop. Forrest and James had been lovers even though both were married, but the relationship soured during the filming of the movie because, Forrest wrote, "He met Betty Grable and how could I compete with the pin-up girl of the world?"

Her breakup with James may help explain the film's strange treatment of "I Had the Craziest Dream." Rather than standing at the front of the band where she belongs, Forrest first appears in the distance behind the dancers. After close-ups of James playing the trumpet, she enters as a disembodied voice. The people dancing must turn around and make room for her to reach the bandstand halfway through her chorus. She finishes standing next to James and then turns and walks out of the picture while the band winds up the arrangement.

The oddest aspect of the lyric is the almost total lack of imagery and rhyme. Instead, Gordon relies on internal rhyme ("When I'm *awake* such a *break* never happens"), internal half rhyme ("I found your lips close to *mine* so I kissed you / And you didn't *mind* it at all"), and a pattern of language beginning with "craziest" in the title and continuing through "strangest," "oddest," and "insane and silly," playing off against the vivid, clear desire to turn a dream about a kiss into the real thing: "Say it and make my craziest dream come true."

I'll Be Around
Lyrics and music by Alec Wilder

Alec Wilder was a composer of serious music who also loved jazz and wrote popular songs. His biographer, Desmond Stone, observes that he was impossible to categorize; his melodies were "leaping and lovely, sinuous and sequestered, elusive and wistful." When David Dempsey recorded an album of his music, including classic pieces for saxophone and popular songs:

> Retail chains didn't know where to put it. They didn't feel comfortable putting it in the jazz bins with Sonny Rollins, Duke Ellington, etc., and they didn't feel right about putting it in the classical bins next to all of the Yo-Yo Ma … discs. It often ended up in the dreaded "instrumental" bin along with Lawrence Welk, Percy Faith, and The 101 Strings …. Alec's music is a classic example of a music marketing impossibility.

When the Mills Brothers recorded "I'll Be Around," they made changes in what Wilder had written. The composer went into a record store and, according to Milford Fargo, "listened to the record, broke it over his knees, threw it out on to the floor, paid for it and walked out, because, he said, those awful men changed his chord progressions and changed the melody, and he just hated the record." Ironically, the song had become a hit for the Mills Brothers even though they recorded it as the B side to their hit song, "Paper Doll." When "Paper Doll" wore out, the jukebox operators saved money by turning the record over. Thus, the B side became a hit as well.

"I'll Be Around" began as an inexplicable impulse. Wilder was in a cab when the song's title "literally popped out of nowhere." He scribbled it on the back of an envelope and forgot about it. "Quite by accident," he remembered, "I spotted it as I was crumpling up the envelope some days later. Since I was near a piano, I wrote a tune, using the title as the first phrase of the melody. I remember it only took about twenty minutes. The lyric took much longer to write." His lyric about a jilted lover—"I'll be around, no matter how you treat me now"—in other hands might have invited something bitter or self-pitying, but Wilder sets his brief, tightly written lines to a melody that resists despair and shows, in Mark Tucker's words, "the philosophical calm that may follow emotional turmoil." Not all hope is lost: "Perhaps you'll see you're meant for me / So I'll be around when he's gone."

I'm Old Fashioned
Lyrics by Johnny Mercer, music by Jerome Kern

As a boy growing up in Savannah, Johnny Mercer loved listening to popular songs and adored the great songwriters such as Irving Berlin and Jerome Kern. When he had his success on Tin Pan Alley in 1933 with "Lazybones," Berlin called on him to offer congratulations. However, when Mercer met his other idol, Jerome Kern, he found the composer "irascible, and rather conceited." Ten years later, when Mercer was teamed with Kern to write songs for the film *You Were Never Lovelier*, he found that what he had thought was brusque conceit was a cover for Kern's painful shyness.

Kern's sumptuous, soaring melodies could sometimes lead even seasoned lyricists into purple prose, but Mercer managed to stay down to earth in the title song and such others as "Dearly Beloved" and "I'm Old Fashioned." For "I'm Old Fashioned," Mercer created a wry, understated affirmation of his love for traditional things: moonlight, rain drops on a window pane, the coming of spring. When he brought the lyric to Kern's house, the normally taciturn composer was so taken with it that he jumped up from the piano and kissed his lyricist on the cheek. He then called his wife in to hear the song and proclaimed Mercer a genius.

I've Heard That Song Before
Lyrics by Sammy Cahn, music by Jule Styne

Sammy Cahn says, "I don't write a song as much as the song writes me. What I do is sort of trigger it with the title and then follow wherever it leads." He and his first collaborator, composer Saul Chaplin, parted amicably in 1942 because their songs were not doing well, and Cahn found himself at one of the lowest points in his career. When Cy Feuer of Republic Pictures called to ask whether he would like to write with Jule Styne, Cahn drove out to meet him. Styne played a melody. Cahn said, "I've heard that song before."

Styne bristled, "What are you, a tune detective?"

"That wasn't a criticism. It was a title."

A dramatic monologue, the lyric plays off the power of a song to conjure up a distant but deeply felt memory. How funny, the singer says, that something as simple as a musical phrase "recalls a favorite dream, a dream that brought you so close to me." There is no sense of the love affair's ending but rather of its having lost its intensity over time. Yet he needs only to hear the music to recall that somehow unforgettable moment when he "heard that lovely song before."

Unlike Cahn, Styne was in demand when they wrote the song. As soon as they finished it, he moved on to work with several other lyricists, including Kim Gannon and Harold Adamson. One day, Cahn and Gannon ran into one another.

Gannon asked, "Did you write a song about a song?"

Cahn said he had and called it "one of the best lyrics I've ever written."

"Maybe you think it's the best lyric you've ever written; Styne thinks it's the wor-r-rst lyric he ever heard."

When it became a hit, Styne called out of the blue to say, "Hey, Sammy, I think we ought to write some songs." Even though they became friends, there was always an undercurrent of tension between them.

Skylark
Lyrics by Johnny Mercer, music by Hoagy Carmichael

Hoagy Carmichael wanted to write a musical about his friend Bix Beiderbecke, the legendary cornetist who drank himself to death at the age of twenty-eight. One of the songs Carmichael wrote was "Bix Licks," a soaring melody that wound around itself like one of Beiderbecke's musical "hot licks." Although the show was never produced, Carmichael kept the melody and played it for Johnny Mercer. "I didn't hear from him for six months," Carmichael said of Mercer. "He is the original 'Don't call me, I'll call you' guy." By the time Mercer finished the lyric, the composer had forgotten his melody, but when Mercer sang it to him over the phone, Carmichael said, "Quite some kick to sit back comfy like that at the telephone and listen."

Although Mercer insisted his lyrics did not derive from Shelley's "To a Skylark," he expressed a similar poetic yearning that may reflect his effort to recapture, amid his frenzied career in New York and Hollywood, the simple rural peace of his boyhood in Savannah. "He was really a man who liked simple pleasures and nature's beauty," a friend said of Mercer's life in "the fast lane with fame and fortune. I just don't think he was ever happy with it .... I just felt like he didn't have a home. I guess his heart didn't have a home." That sense of wandering homelessness is expressed in appeals to the skylark to lead him to a valley "green with spring" where "my heart can go a-journeying."

Mercer came closest to finding such a place when he found words to music as enchanting as Carmichael's. He once compared the struggle to find a lyric as a quest for

> ... something you never heard of, the Golden Fleece. You don't know where it is, it's just up there somewhere and you can tune in on it, and you get a little glimmer and you say, ah—you don't even know if it's a word, and then it begins to—it's like you're tuning into a musical instrument that's miles away, and you say, oh, there's something there if I just dig hard enough.

When he dug hard enough to create such a lyric that asks the skylark if he can hear the "music in the night" that is "faint as a 'will o' the wisp,' crazy as a loon, sad as a gypsy serenading the moon," Johnny Mercer found his home in a song.

That Old Black Magic
Lyrics by Johnny Mercer, music by Harold Arlen

When Harold Arlen came up with a sinuous, sensuous melody that stretched to seventy-two bars, he was amazed that Johnny Mercer listened to it only once before he left to start work on the lyric. Mercer took his inspiration from Cole Porter's 1929 hit, "You Do Something to Me," with its archly witty line, "Do do that voodoo that you do so well." He thought an entire song could be built around the idea of the bewitching power of love.

Johnny Mercer and Nat King Cole. Courtesy of Photofest.

Mercer's other source of inspiration came from his tempestuous love affair with Judy Garland. Garland, who resented her typecasting in movies and in life as "little Dorothy" from *The Wizard of Oz*, was notorious in Hollywood for her profligacy, and she clearly enflamed Mercer. "He was really ga-ga," a friend said, "Oh, she was, too—it was just like young love."

In "That Old Black Magic" Mercer matched Arlen's passionate music with images of burning lips, icy fingers, and plunging elevators to describe how "down and down I go, 'round and 'round I go." "That Old Black Magic" came as close as a song of its day could to celebrating the rapture of sex. Because of his love affair with Garland and his timely collaboration with Harold Arlen, Mercer's lyric registers romantic agony and ecstasy as powerfully as any song in the history of American popular music.

Wait Till You See Her
Lyrics by Lorenz Hart, music by Richard Rodgers

The first in many years that did not see a new Rodgers and Hart musical on Broadway was 1941. "The reason, I'm afraid," said Richard Rodgers, "was Larry." Hart's drinking grew worse and, although he agreed to "drying out" periods in New York's luxurious Doctors Hospital, he refused any psychiatric help. Rodgers realized that he would have to consider breaking up their long partnership and approached Oscar Hammerstein. "I think you should keep working with Larry just so long as he is able to work with you," Hammerstein said. "It would kill him if you walked away while he was still able to function. But if the time ever comes when he cannot function, call me. I'll be there."

Hart was able to perform for one more original musical, *By Jupiter*, though only because Rodgers checked him into the hospital and had a piano brought in. The score included two of their most plangent songs, "Nobody's Heart" and "Wait Till You See Her." The more important of the two, "Wait Till You See Her," celebrates love as a hushed, ecstatic hymn of innocent adoration: "Wait till you see her, / See how she looks, / Wait till you hear her laugh." Alec Wilder called it "one of the loveliest of all Rodgers and Hart waltzes," pointing out how Rodgers characteristically built his melody on a rising scale and how, at the extended climax of the song, Hart perfectly matched that musical contour with the "lovely word 'free'": "All of it lovely, / All of it thrilling, / I'll never be willing to free her / When you see her / you won't believe your eyes."

By Jupiter turned out to be Rodgers and Hart's most successful musical ever, running for 427 performances, but already by the tryouts in Boston, Rodgers said, "Larry was up to his old tricks and disappeared for three days." When Rodgers proposed that for their next show, they do a musical adaptation of

Green Grow the Lilacs, Hart demurred, saying he needed to take a vacation in Mexico and adding that he did not think New York audiences would be interested in a show about cowboys and farmers in the Oklahoma territory.

"This show means a lot to me," Rodgers said. "If you walk out on me now, I'm going to do it with someone else."

"Anyone in mind?" Hart snapped.

"Yes, Oscar Hammerstein."

"Well, you couldn't pick a better man," Hart said. Then, in what Rodgers said was the first time in his life, Hart looked directly into his collaborator's eyes. "You know, Dick," he said, "I've never really understood why you've put up with me all these years. It's been crazy. The best thing for you to do is forget about me."

When Hart walked out of the room, Rodgers, usually a stoically self-controlled man, broke down in tears.

Within a year, Lorenz Milton Hart was dead from pneumonia at the age of forty-eight. Eleanor Roosevelt ordered a dosage of penicillin, then in short supply, to be flown to save him but to no avail. His dying words, according to a nurse who attended him, were "What have I lived for?" Perhaps his musical collaborator had the answer: "He didn't care where he lived, how much he earned, what the social or financial standing of his friends was, or what row he sat in on opening night," Rodgers recalled. "He did care tremendously, however, about the turn of a phrase or the mathematical exactness of an interior rhyme."

White Christmas
Lyrics and music by Irving Berlin

Although Irving Berlin had been brought up in an orthodox Jewish home amid the wretched poverty of New York's Lower East Side, he learned to love Christmas. "I bounded across the street to my friendly neighbors, the O'Hara's," he recalled, only later realizing that, because the O'Haras were as poor as his family, their annual Christmas tree was short and had broken branches. "But to me," he said, "seemed to tower to heaven."

When Berlin married the Catholic socialite Ellin MacKay, Christmas became an important part of their family life; therefore, in 1937, when he was compelled to stay in Hollywood to work on his film, *Alexander's Ragtime Band*, while his family celebrated back in New York, he was despondent. He decided to work on a Christmas song for a Broadway show he had been thinking about called *Holiday Revue*, which would be based on the annual sequence of holidays. Starting with a verse about the balmy weather of Beverly Hills in December, he envisioned a mournful carol

Sheet music for "White Christmas." Courtesy of David A. Jasen.

sung by a group of sophisticates who, with cocktails and cigarette holders in hand, reminisce about the Christmases of their youth. In contrast to the days, weeks, and even years it took him to complete other songs, Berlin wrote "White Christmas" in one of his classic all-night marathons. "Maybe because it was so easy to write, comparatively," he admitted later, "I didn't realize its potential."

From the haunting opening of its chorus to the final note on the nebulous, evocative word "white," the song reflects Berlin's utter mastery of his art beneath its apparent simplicity. Another songwriter, for example, would have made the emphatic words of the first line "dreaming" and "Christmas," the verb and noun, but on the first whole note Berlin places the relatively unimportant pronoun "I'm," then on the next whole note he puts the adjective "white," the sustained notes underscoring the long *i* in each word. Although written in the key of C, the melody wanders chromatically, climbing above the octave in lines such as "just like the *ones* I used to know," but steadily progressing downward in a melancholy descent to the almost unpronounceable "all your Christ-mases." This rootlessnesss of lyric and music reflects the plight of the singer who can only dream of memories of home, family, and landscape—not share in them again. If Berlin's brooding Russian heritage ever came to bear on the perfect subject, it was in this secular carol of nostalgic loneliness

He was able to sell his idea of a "holiday" show to Paramount, which saw it as a vehicle for its current musical star, Bing Crosby. With his remarkably attentive ear to shifts in the national sensibility, Irving Berlin realized that World War II had turned Americans away from the glamorous world of New York sophistication that had dominated the 1930s. What Americans wanted now was not Fred Astaire and Ginger Rogers dancing in an elegant ballroom, but rather a homespun tale of simple characters in a rural setting. Berlin thought a movie about an entertainer who gives up Broadway to run a pastoral inn could be a vehicle for the songs on which he had been working. Crosby portrayed such a wholesome character; opposite him, Fred Astaire was cast as the dark embodiment of big-city showbiz. What *Holiday Inn* needed, Berlin knew, would be what in his early songwriting days on Tin Pan Alley during World War I were termed "home songs."

Berlin went to Crosby's dressing room to demonstrate his songs. "I was nervous as a rabbit smelling stew," he said. "I sang several melodies and Bing nodded quiet approval. But when I did 'White Christmas,' he came to life and said, 'Irving, you won't have to worry about that one.'" Still, Berlin did not expect "White Christmas" to become a classic. In writing a score of songs tied to holidays, he thought that few of them would become hits. The one song he thought might become independently successful was the Valentine's Day song, "Be Careful, It's My Heart." However, "White Christmas" and the general holiday song, "Happy Holiday" (which many people incorrectly call "Happy Holidays") have become standards. "White Christmas" first caught on with servicemen, particularly those in the South Pacific. "It became a peace song in wartime," Berlin said, "nothing

I'd ever intended. It was nostalgic for a lot of boys who weren't home for Christmas."

1943

MEET ME IN ST. LOUIS
Lyrics by Hugh Martin, music by Ralph Blane

Meet Me in St. Louis was the very best of MGM's "period musicals" of the 1940s and the earliest of the truly great movie musicals. Typical of a "period musical," it had a score that combined nostalgia with the up to date. Hugh Martin and Ralph Blane wrote new songs that became hits, like "The Boy Next Door," "Have Yourself a Merry Little Christmas," and "The Trolley Song," but the movie also revived two classic American songs: the 1904 title number by Kerry Mills and Andrew Stirling and "Under the Bamboo Tree," a 1902 "coon song" by black songwriters Bob Cole, James Weldon Johnson, and J. Rosamond Johnson, to which Judy Garland and child star Margaret O'Brien do a jaunty but innocent cakewalk. When O'Brien won a special Oscar for her performance, actor Lionel Barrymore grumbled, "Two hundred years ago, she would have been burned at the stake!"

The movie tells the story of the Smith family, their domestic crises, the eventual happy ending, and their delight as the fair opens and they visit it, dressed in white and borne in horse-drawn carriages. Its songs are an essential part of the storytelling. Although the three older children pursue romance and the two younger ones pursue mischief, the father announces his intention to move the family to New York City right after Christmas because he has been offered a promotion.

The crisis nearly shatters everything, from budding love to family affection, and produces the movie's most touching song, "Have Yourself a Merry Little Christmas." With its catch-in-the-throat use of "little" in the title, it's one of three important Christmas songs from World War II (along with the equally melancholy "White Christmas" and the more hopeful "I'll Be Home for Christmas"). Although it is set in 1904, Martin and Blane's song is really about 1943. Devastated by the impending move, Totie, the youngest Smith child, destroys her backyard snowmen and weeps inconsolably. Her sister Esther (Judy Garland) tries to comfort her with a song that expresses her melancholy as well.

Blane and Martin thought they had written the perfect song for the scene, but Garland demanded something more optimistic. Their initial version began, "Have yourself a merry little Christmas, it may be your last / Next year we will all be living in the past." Garland's insistence reflected the time she had spent entertaining the troops and the sense she had developed of their need to believe that they would eventually return home. Martin and Blane's revision made the lyric a delicate balance of longing and affirmation: "Here we are as in olden days, happy golden days of yore. / Faithful friends who are dear to us, will be near to us once more."

"The Boy Next Door," the movie's major love ballad, also joins past and present in a mix of formality and slang—"Doesn't try to please me, doesn't even tease me"—that sounds very much like the musings of an adolescent. The verse melts from talk into song in something very much like recitative—"Though I live at fifty-one-thirty-five Kensington Avenue and he lives at fifty-one-thirty-three"— that leads in turn to a lyric that plays his apparent aloofness against her deepest feelings: "And though I'm heart-sore, the boy next door / Affection for me won't display."

Where "The Boy Next Door," is gentle, "The Trolley Song" is boisterous. Blane said that he and Martin "thought it was too corny to be on the nose in writing a song about a trolley. Instead we went home and wrote a marvelous song that would be great to sing on a trolley—not *about* it." When they showed it to Arthur Freed, he told them he loved it and then told them to write a song about the trolley. Finally, Blane said, "in desperation, and a bit of anger too, we went home and just said, 'Oh, hell! Let's just write something about the trolley, and to hell with it.'" When he went to the library to find some books about old St. Louis, he found a photograph of a double-decker trolley from 1903, with the caption, "Clang, clang, clang, went the trolley." "Well, I dashed back, told Hugh the title and we wrote it in about ten minutes." Martin's lyric wittily links the sounds of a speeding trolley to Garland's onomatopoetic expressions, from "Clang, clang, clang went the trolley" to "Zing, zing, zing went my heartstrings."

OKLAHOMA!
Lyrics by Oscar Hammerstein, music by Richard Rodgers

Because Oscar Hammerstein was one of the few lyricists of his era who also wrote the books for his musicals, he could tailor a lyric to character and dramatic situation, building a scene to the moment when dialogue flowers into song. When he began working with Richard Rodgers, Hammerstein adopted another technique that made his lyrics even more integral to his book. Most lyricists usually wrote *to* music. Hammerstein had worked the same way in his earlier collaborations with Jerome Kern, but with Rodgers, he started with a melody—either an existing song or a "dummy" melody that he made up. However, he would never tell Rodgers what the melody was. Rodgers would then take Hammerstein's lyric, sit down at the piano, and write *to* words. By working in this fashion, Rodgers

Stage still from the original production of *Oklahoma!* with Joan Roberts (Laurey) and Alfred Drake (Curly) seated in the "surrey with the fringe on top," with Celeste Holm (Ado Annie) and Lee Dixon (Will Parker) at far right. Courtesy of Photofest.

and Hammerstein wrote songs that were even more integrally wedded to story and character.

Hammerstein spent three weeks on the opening song, "Oh, What a Beautiful Mornin'," before he even showed the lyric to Rodgers. He devoted an entire week to placing the word "Oh" at the beginning of the song, to give it a rural innocence. He changed another line, "The corn is as high as a cow pony's eye," to "elephant's eye" when he saw that the corn in his neighbor's field was much higher than a pony.

Rodgers recalled:

> When Oscar handed me the words of our first song together, I was a little sick with joy because it was so lovely and so right ....
> I had a feeling that I must say something very important musically. It isn't often a composer gets a chance at lyrics as perfect as "Oh, what a beautiful morning."

Hammerstein was astounded that, after his three weeks of labor, his new collaborator fitted a melody in ten minutes. Rodgers, however, credited the lyric with being so polished that it practically dictated a melody to him. Musically, Rodgers gave the song an old-fashioned strophic structure, in which verses alternate with a brief chorus, to resonate with the show's turn-of-the-century setting. The song was so moving that Rodgers and Hammerstein decided that the curtain would rise, not on the usual bevy of chorus girls, but on an old woman churning butter to the strains of "Oh, What a Beautiful Mornin'" sung, *a capella*, offstage by Curley, the cowboy hero.

The next song Hammerstein worked on was "The Surrey with the Fringe on Top," in which Curley describes an imaginary surrey to persuade the heroine Laurey to accompany him to the box-supper social. Again, Rodgers took the lyric and set it to a clip-clop melody that imitated the horse's trotting before suddenly veering upward when chicks and ducks and geese "scurry" out of the way.

Hammerstein also transformed the play's original character of Ado Annie from a shy, backward girl to one with a very primitive urge to indulge her natural impulses. "I'm Just a Girl Who Cain't Say No" registers her dilemma when her boyfriend Will insists that Annie bridle her instincts. Yet, in "Kansas City," Will relishes his visit to a burlesque house where a girl he thought was "padded from her shoulder to her heel" proved, "when she begun to peel," that "everything she had was absolutely real."

The only song from *Oklahoma!* written music-first was "People Will Say We're in Love." This time it was Rodgers' turn to slave over his composition for days before he was satisfied with even the first eight bars. Initially, it was planned for the second act as the show's big romantic ballad, but it was so good they moved it to Act One. At that point in the story, the lovers were still quarrelsome, so Hammerstein created a coyly bickering "list" song, in which Laurey warns Curley about all the things he must not do lest people think them in love. The lyric shows Hammerstein at his theatrical best as he provides lines that inspire the performers to act the song out: "Don't start collecting things / Give me my rose and my glove."

With this new musical by Rodgers and Hammerstein, originally entitled *Away We Go*, producer Theresa Helburn felt "this was the moment for the fulfillment of my dream, the production of a totally new kind of play with music." As she rode in a cab with Rodgers and Hammerstein to audition the show for potential backers ("angels," as they are called in Broadway parlance), a sudden inspiration prompted her to suggest that they conclude the show with a song that celebrated the earth. When Hammerstein asked her what she meant, she could only reply, "I don't know. Just a song about the land."

Hammerstein later said he thought it was "one of the silliest and vaguest suggestions I had ever heard." Strangely, however, he said, "Two days later I wrote a lyric I never intended to write." It described a western territory emerging into statehood, clinging to its roots in the earth but joining the modern world by supplying the rest of the country with wheat and cattle. "I spoke of wind sweeping down the plain and how sweet the wheat smelled when the wind came behind the rain."

When he gave the lyric to Rodgers, the composer cast it in the modern song structure of AABA, signaling the territory's passage into statehood and the twentieth century, thus counterbalancing, as Graham Wood points out, the old-fashioned ABA structure he had used for the opening number, "Oh, What a Beautiful Morning." Hammerstein was so taken with "Oklahoma" he wanted to use it as the title for the show, but others thought such an allusion would evoke memories of the Oklahoma dustbowl, which had recently been underscored in America's collective imagination by John Steinbeck's *The Grapes of Wrath*.

The show had a rocky time in out-of-town tryouts. When producer Mike Todd saw it in Boston, he quipped, "No gags, no girls, no chance." At the last minute, just before the show opened in New York, the title was changed to *Oklahoma!*. Although opening night was not a sell-out, the audience realized this was a distinctly new kind of musical *drama*, and *Oklahoma!* ran for a record-breaking 2,212 performances.

One for My Baby; My Shining Hour
Lyrics by Johnny Mercer, music by Harold Arlen

The love affair between Judy Garland and Johnny Mercer was doomed from the start. After years of being ignored at MGM, Garland's success in the 1939 film *The Wizard of Oz* had finally made her a star, but she would have quickly lost that status if word had gotten out that she was having an affair with an older married man when she was engaged to composer David Rose. Mercer had recently adopted a little girl, written a song for her ("Mandy Is Two"), and, as a patrician southerner, disparaged divorce. Just as he had overcome his genteel antipathy and asked his wife, Ginger, for a divorce, Walter Winchell's voice came over the radio to announce that Garland had eloped with Rose to Las Vegas.

During the course of the affair, Mercer had written several lyrics that reflected his love for Garland, but the song that came closest to expressing his romantic loss was "One for My Baby." Mercer's main collaborator at the time was Harold Arlen, whose feel for blues melodies spoke directly to Mercer's heartache, and the lyricist created a song that conjures up a time: "It's quarter to three"; a scene: "There's no one in the place except you and me"; and a character to whom the song is addressed: "So set 'em up, Joe." Yet in the course of the song, the singer never tells the bartender the "little story you ought to know."

Mercer had intuitively learned Ernest Hemingway's technique of the "iceberg effect"—leaving the bulk of emotion "below the surface" so that the small portion that does appear suggests enormous depths of feeling: "Could tell you a lot, but you've got to be true to your code, / Make it one for my baby and one more for the road." Arlen called "One for My Baby" another of his "tapeworms"—songwriter slang for any song that exceeded the standard length of thirty-two bars. "Johnny took it and wrote it exactly the way it fell. Not only is it long—forty-eight bars—but it also changes keys. Johnny made it work."

Arlen also did an about-face and wrote a simple, moving hymn. For *The Sky's the Limit*, he needed to come up with a song that reflected wartime solemnity for Fred Astaire, who played a World War II fighter pilot. Mercer took Arlen's bone-simple melody and crafted a lyric that reminded him of songs such as "Keep the Home Fires Burning" that he remembered from his boyhood during World War I. "My Shining Hour," in which nearly every word is a monosyllable, expresses the yearning of lovers, separated by the war, for the hour when "I'm with you again."

You'd Be So Nice To Come Home To
Lyrics and music by Cole Porter

When Cole Porter submitted his score for the film *Something to Shout About*, the director praised it as the songwriter's best work since *Anything Goes*, but when the film evoked only a tepid response from the public, Porter referred to it as "Something to Cry About." The only song to survive the picture was "You'd Be So Nice to Come Home to," a ballad that Porter had variously titled "You Would Be So Wonderful to Come Home to," "Someone to Come Home to," and "Something to Keep Me Warm."

His struggles may reflect his awareness that his decade of the 1930s, with its insouciant wit and flippant sophistication, had been replaced by wartime simplicity and unadorned, emotional directness. In one of the drafts of his lyrics, he even included a line "you reek of the old prewar chic" and in the finished verse he plied his cleverness by saying "you're rarer than asparagus out of season." In the chorus, however, he wrote passionately and unaffectedly of longing "under stars chilled by the winter" and "under an August moon burning above." Although *Something to Shout About* was quickly forgotten, "You'd Be So Nice to Come Home to" touched the hearts of lovers separated by the war.

You'll Never Know
Lyrics by Mack Gordon, music by Harry Warren

Many movie musicals of World War II were exercises in nostalgia. Set at the turn of the century, they touched a public chord with their uncomplicated recreations of a safer, more innocent time. In stories about sentimental family life or eager young performers trying to succeed in vaudeville, they gave us an America worth fighting for, even if it had not existed in nearly half a century. *Hello, Frisco, Hello*, one of the most successful of these backstage musicals, combined new and period songs in its opening number. A vaudeville foursome, working in a Barbary Coast joint, springs a new number on the boss, a combination of the title song from 1915 and one of the most popular love songs of World War II.

Incongruously, Warren found the source for his melody in a military sound. He told a friend:

> You know my big Academy Award song, "You'll Never Know"? Well, it wasn't entirely original—I did a little steal on that one. Songwriters always borrow a few bars here and there. I don't know how the hell it came to me but I was thinking about the notes in a bugle call and dammit if it wasn't just what I wanted to get "You'll Never Know" started.

Even so, "You'll Never Know" is sentimental and convincing despite the abstraction of the lyric. Because it has little imagery and tells almost no story, it relies largely on a sustained tone of private longing made persuasive through a combination of hushed romanticism in the melody and whispered passion in the words: "If there is some other way to prove that I love you, / I swear I don't know how." Yet even though most people first heard "You'll Never Know" in a movie set fifty years earlier, it is important to remember that its appeal to a largely female audience reflects its contemporary point of view. Like so many of the good songs of the war years, it finds ways to deepen and intensify the emotions of loneliness and longing central to America's emotional life. Millions of couples were separated, and those remaining at home to pray for their loved ones' safe return, take jobs in war plants, and buy the recordings were women. "You'll Never Know" spoke what they felt: "You went away and my heart went with you."

1944

Ac-cent-tchu-ate the Positive
Lyrics by Johnny Mercer, music by Harold Arlen

As a boy growing up in Savannah, Johnny Mercer loved to visit black churches, not only to hear the singing but also to listen to the sermons, particularly when they were delivered by Savannah's premier evangelist, Daddy Grace. Although he lived in New York and Hollywood for most of his adult life, Mercer regularly returned to Savannah, and on one of these visits he heard Daddy Grace preach upon the theme "Accentuate the Positive." Back in Hollywood, he and composer Harold Arlen were driving along the freeway to work at Paramount when Arlen began whistling what Mercer called an "offbeat little rhythm tune" and Mercer suddenly remembered Daddy Grace's sermon. "With a beginning like that," he said, "the rest of it practically wrote itself." Mercer cast the lyric in the form of a sermon—"listen while I preach some"—and laced the chorus with Biblical allusions to "Jonah in the whale / Noah in the ark." "It was like getting an elusive crossword clue," he said. "By the time we finished our drive, the song was more or less complete."

Don't Fence Me In
Lyrics and music by Cole Porter

"Don't Fence Me In" is so uncharacteristic of the urbane Cole Porter that many thought he had written it as a parody of "singing cowboy" movies. In fact, Porter had written the song back in 1934 for just such a film, the unreleased *Adios Argentina*. As historian Robert Kimball has shown, Porter based the lyric on a poem by a Montana writer named Robert Fletcher, a friend of Lou Brock, the movie's producer. Brock had hoped that Porter would collaborate with Fletcher, but Porter, insisting on maintaining his reputation as his own lyricist, bought the rights to Fletcher's poem for $250 and reworked the lines to fit his clip-clop melody.

Fletcher's opening lines, "Give me land, lots of land, / Stretching miles across the West" became "Oh, give me land, lots of land under starry skies above." Porter also kept most of Fletcher's images—cottonwood trees, western skies, hobbles—and catchy phrases such as "on my cayuse," "straddle my old saddle," and "where the West commences." When *Adios, Argentina* was shelved, "Don't Fence Me In" was not published but kept for possible use in a film biography of humorist Will Rogers. As for Porter, he forgot about it.

With the onset of World War II, the era of suave sophistication passed, and Americans responded to simpler sentiments and regional themes. Warner Bros. producer Walter Gottlieb remembered "Don't Fence Me In" and thought it would be perfect for cowboy star Roy Rogers to sing in *Hollywood Canteen*, one of many loosely structured musical revues designed to showcase stars and boost wartime morale by presenting songs as if they were being performed before servicemen at the famed canteen. The song's laconic celebration of western independence and natural beauty struck a chord with Americans, and it became one of Porter's most successful songs. The published sheet music sold more than a million copies but did not mention Robert Fletcher, an omission Porter said occurred without his knowledge. Even though he was under no legal obligation to compensate Fletcher, Porter assigned him a portion of the royalties.

"Don't Fence Me In" was so unlike the rest of Porter's output that he always referred to it, dismissively, as "that old thing."

I Should Care; Day by Day
Lyrics by Sammy Cahn, music by Paul Weston and Axel Stordahl

The knock on Sammy Cahn was that he wrote too fast. Ideas for titles or opening lines suddenly came to him. He said he went where they took him and, he often added, "We got that song in less than an hour." During the war, he and arrangers Paul Weston and Axel Stordahl were sharing an apartment in Los Angeles. Cahn walked in one day to find them sitting at a table heaped high with their arrangements for Cahn and Jule Styne's "I've Heard That Song Before." They indulged in some mock complaining about the drudgery of arranging: "Fifteen minutes for him to write it and hours for us to arrange it." Cahn replied, "Why don't you fellows write a song with me? . . . . They played a melody and the moment I heard the first three notes, I also heard in my head, 'I Should Care.'"

Somehow, when Cahn heard a musical phrase, a title or a lyrical line popped into his head. He rarely questioned or revised it, but he knew intuitively how to follow its logic. "I should care" led him almost immediately to "I should go around weeping" and then "I should go without sleeping." Both lines are really questions: "Do you expect me to go around weeping? Do you expect me to give up sleep?" Transforming the verbal equivalent of common ironic Yiddishisms into romantic confessions was not necessary to the song, but it was the start of a set of associations everyone would recognize. Soon, though, the lyric switched to the language of conventional songwriting, with a reliance on assonance and internal rhyme: "Funny how sheep can lull you to sleep," and, ultimately, to the tidy reversal in the final line: "But I should care and I do."

Soon after "I Should Care," Cahn, Weston, and Stordahl set out to write a second hit together. As they played the melody, Cahn said, "I listened—and sorry if it sounds made up but it's true—a title came into my mind and I said, "How do you like 'Day by Day'?" As usual with Cahn, the lyric developed logically: "Day by day, I'm falling more in love with you." Cahn valued the integrity of the craft. In "Day by Day," he carried forth the alliteration in the title through his use of "d" words through most of the lyric. He repeated the title line four times and also included "devotion," "deeper," and "dear." In a song about the meaning of the passing days, Cahn played off the measured time in the title phrase against a promise of endless devotion, "As we go through the years day by day."

I'll Walk Alone
Lyrics by Sammy Cahn, music by Jule Styne

The hit songs about walking from the 1930s and 1940s suggest how we saw things during the Great Depression and then during World War II. In 1930, young lovers sang, "Would You Like to Take a Walk?" and in 1934, they sang, "Let's Take a Walk Around the Block" because they were broke and wanted to be together. During the war, though, songs about walking underscored the poignancy of lovers separated. Jule Styne and Sammy Cahn charted the way American attitudes changed after Pearl Harbor. During the darkest days of 1942, "I Don't Want to Walk Without You" was a cry of despair from a woman who could not even rouse herself to take a walk. In "I'll Walk Alone," the single most popular love ballad of World War II, she has made her peace with the loneliness and dread. She takes walks even though she must walk "alone." She accepts things as they are but finds them bearable only because "my heart tells me you are lonely too."

Cahn's lyric is an act of extended imagining as each night the woman brings herself close to her beloved through a prayer for his safety and a promise to hear his call no matter where he is. That may reassure her, but it still isn't enough to. She has her moment of doubt as she calls on him in turn to be faithful—"Please walk alone"—and to send his love and his kisses "to guide me" until "you're walking beside me." Imagining his return helps to keep her going as she walks alone.

I'm Beginning to See the Light
Lyrics and music by Don George, Johnny Hodges, Duke Ellington, and Harry James

Whenever Johnny Hodges, saxophonist with Duke Ellington's orchestra, would segue between solos, he played a musical transition that intrigued lyricist Don George. "That's a hell of a phrase," George said to Ellington. "It sounds to me like it could be a hit."

"Really?" said Ellington. "If you like it that much, let's get with Johnny and finish the thing."

After Hodges and Ellington had worked out the melody, they asked George what his title was.

"Don't worry," he said, "I'll get a title," but he later admitted, "I kept racking my brain but came up empty."

Killing time one afternoon, he walked down Broadway to the Paramount Theatre. Before the feature, there was a short film about a "Holy Roller" revival meeting in the Deep South, in a tent church with an all-black congregation." George was awestruck at the preacher who ranted and raved at his parishioners until a huge woman, shaking all over and her eyes rolling, raised herself from her pew, screamed "I'm beginning to see the light!" and then fell to the floor in a dead faint: "I got up and ran out of the theater." He found Ellington rehearsing the band and shouted, "Hey, fellows, we've got a title!"

George then developed the catchphrase through a series of images of light and darkness: stars in the eyes, a lamp turned down low, "shadow-boxing in the dark," winking back at fireflies, and a spark "that's a four-alarm fire now." He concluded with a clever twist on his title phrase: "Now that your lips are burning mine / I'm beginning to see the light." However, George could not get any bandleaders or music publishers interested in the song, and even Ellington advised him to stop devoting all of his efforts to promoting it. "Of all the songs we had written," George said, "this one kept walking back and forth through my mind, talking to me, saying, 'Me, me, I'm the one. Do something about me.'"

In desperation, he borrowed money to take a train to California—a difficult journey during wartime. With only a few dollars left in his pocket, he began making the rounds, first approaching Johnny Mercer. Mercer was not only a songwriter and singer, but also a founder of Capitol Records, the first major recording company on the West Coast. Mercer told George that "I'm Beginning to See the Light" was a cute title with a monotonous melody and then said condescendingly, "C'mon, Don. How about that lyric?"

He got the same cold shoulder from everyone else he approached. "Here I am," he thought, "with a song I bet my shirt on, written with a great and well-known writer like Duke Ellington, and after all these months I still can't get arrested with it." Finally, Harry James agreed to record the song (with him listed as one of its creators). "I'm Beginning to See the Light" sold more than a million records. Although he would have an even bigger commercial success with his lyric to an old minstrel tune called "The Yellow Rose of Texas" (1955), Don George always cherished "I'm Beginning to See the Light."

When he later ran into Johnny Mercer at a bar, Mercer demanded to know why George had never shown him the song.

Long Ago and Far Away
Lyrics by Ira Gershwin, music by Jerome Kern

Ira Gershwin's collaboration with Jerome Kern for the movie, *Cover Girl*, was the most difficult of his career. George Gershwin's melodies had been abrupt and jazzy, but Kern's melodic lines were long and flowing. Kern, moreover, was known as a "provoking" composer who adamantly refused to change a note to accommodate a lyricist. The two men could not even agree on a place to work, even though they lived within a few blocks of each other in Beverly Hills. Ira liked to work in his study, where he was surrounded by his books, but Kern insisted they work at his home on his piano. Ira agreed but only until he had jotted down a dummy lyric; then he would dash home to complete it.

Nowhere was their antipathy more evident than in the score's big ballad. Kern was famous for his sumptuous romantic melodies, but Ira always found writing a straightforward love song his most difficult task. When Kern wrote a melody based on a long, seven-note phrase repeated over and over at higher and lower intervals, Ira was stumped. Finding a title was always difficult for him and, no matter how hard he tried, he could not come up with anything to fit the phrase. Annoyed at the delay, Kern sarcastically suggested a seven-syllable title: "Watching Little Alice Pee."

Finally, the producer called to say he needed the lyric immediately because they were filming the song later that day. Ira tried to stall for more time, but the producer was adamant, so Ira read his current version of a lyric over the phone, even though it seemed to the "mentally pooped" lyricist "just a collection of words adding up to very little." "I heaved an enormous sigh of relief," he said, "at not having to go down to the studio to face anyone with this lyric."

Phil Silvers, the movie's second banana, said that on the day the song was shot everyone was nervous because Kern would be there and no one knew how he would respond to Gene Kelly's singing. Somebody had once described the dancer's voice as "gargling with pebbles." Silvers continued:

> The great man arrived ... sat himself down, and Gene began to sing. When he was through, Kern was silent. Not a single word did he utter. We all thought the worst—that he had hated what had been done to his beautiful song. Then very quietly he said to Gene, "If you want to make an old man happy, please sing it again."

When he saw the song in the film, Ira Gershwin was pleasantly surprised. Although the words were simple, they brought out Kern's beautiful melody. "Long Ago and Far Away" proved to be the most popular song Ira Gershwin ever wrote.

Moonlight in Vermont
Lyrics by John Blackburn, music by Karl Suessdorf

The moon is one of the most familiar images in popular music. It also rhymes with June, to suggest that spooning may lead eventually to marriage. The first important moon song recorded in the twentieth century was Nora Bayes and Jack Norworth's "Shine on, Harvest Moon" (1908). However, there is no end to these songs, especially after lyricists started to link them to specific places. Most often, as in "Moon over Miami," the songs were love ballads that combined heavenly imagery with an alluring place. There are also songs in which the location feels incidental, as in "Stars Fell on Alabama" or is everything with not even a trace of a love story, as in "Moonlight in Vermont."

"Moonlight in Vermont" takes us through a year of "falling leaves," "ski trails down a mountain side," and the "warbling of a meadowlark"; the sharpness of its observation and the wistfulness of its melody suggest something fondly remembered. Only a few generalized lines suggest what might have happened long ago: "When people meet, in this romantic setting / They're so hypnotized by the lovely evening summer breeze." Margaret Whiting was raised in Beverly Hills and resisted Johnny Mercer's efforts to get her to record the song.

"How can I sing a song about a place I've never been to?" she asked. Mercer answered, "Neither have I, but we'll use your imagination." Whiting described what happened next:

> So he had me imagine the four seasons, and what each season would be like there, the warmth, the chill, what it was like to ski there, the smell of maple syrup. All these things conjured up a place with great memories that helped me sing the song …. After it became a hit for me, he would come and hear me sing and say, "Do the song that hasn't got a rhyme in it." I think it's the only hit song ever written without a rhyme in the entire lyric.

New York, New York
Lyrics by Betty Comden and Adolph Green, music by Leonard Bernstein

Leonard Bernstein wrote this joyfully gritty song about New York as a "helluva town" where the "Bronx is up," "the Battery's down," and people ride "in a hole in the ground," while he was riding a train across the plains of Nebraska. Said a fellow traveler:

> I noticed Lenny take a pad of staved paper from his briefcase, then draw notes …. I pretended not to watch, but was amazed at the speed with which he covered sheet after sheet, rarely pausing or making an erasure. He looked up for a moment, smiled handsomely as he caught my peeping eye, and said, "You have no idea how exciting it is to hear in one's head the music that comes out in these black dots."

Bernstein was traveling to California to conduct his ballet, *Fancy Free*, but he was already working with choreographer Jerome Robbins and lyricists–librettists Betty Comden and Adolph Green to transform the ballet into *On the Town*, a musical about three sailors on leave for a day in New York City. Bernstein brought the same energy to the Broadway musical as he did to his classical works. "New York, New York" incorporates a complex overlapping of phrases in canonic style as it registers the exuberant response of three American sailors on their first trip to New York. In Betty Comden and Adolph Green, Bernstein found lyricists–librettists committed to the principle of dramatic integration: "that music and song and book must be all of one piece and never stop telling the story."

However, because none of the creators had had experience with a Broadway musical, they had difficulty finding "angels" to back the show. Only when they presented the idea to George Abbott, Broadway's consummate director and "play-doctor," did they get backers. "I like the smell of this," said Abbot, "let's do it tomorrow." Abbott cut many songs; however, although he kidded Bernstein about all of the "Prokofiev stuff" in the score, he preserved its classical base. *On the Town* was the first American musical composed by a primarily classical musician, and it was the first to have black and white dancers perform side by side—even holding hands. Everyone thought the hit song from the show would be the mournful ballad, "Lonely Town," about the alienation one feels in a large city; however, it was the rousing "New York, New York" that proved to be the show's enduring standard.

Spring Will Be a Little Late This Year
Lyrics and music by Frank Loesser

For years, lyricist Frank Loesser wrote dummy tunes so he could hear his lyrics until a composer wedded them to music, but he never felt confident enough to use any of them. In 1942, he wrote his wife, "I have a title—'Praise the Lord and Pass the Ammunition'—which is a quotation from a news story a few months ago—a sentence supposedly spoken by a brave army chaplain." Loesser wrote a lyric and a dummy tune, and then sang the result for his friends. At their urging, he agreed to make it a song, and it became a wartime hit. He continued to work with collaborators but also wrote more and more songs on his own, including "Spring Will Be a Little Late This Year."

Loesser rarely wrote sad ballads, not even during the war when most songs were drenched in longing. Yet "Spring Will Be a Little Late This Year" is so perfectly defined by its melancholy hush that one wonders why he did not write in this vein more often. Despite the expansive imagery of delaying the seasons, Loesser reduces it to human scale—"a little late"—to ponder the absence of "our April of old." Though spring is late because the lovers are apart, the lyric eventually suggests that the separation is temporary. Although "you have left me, and winter continues cold," the song asserts that he "needn't cling to this fear" because "it's merely that spring will be a little late this year." Susan Loesser suggests that the idea of the season's slow start "doesn't make the mood less sad, but it makes it clever at the same time." Rather than mere cleverness, though, the shift in attitude transforms the song into an anthem of hope.

1945

CAROUSEL
Lyrics by Oscar Hammerstein, music by Richard Rodgers

Although Ferenc Molnar had rejected overtures from Puccini and George Gershwin, once he saw *Oklahoma!* he agreed to let Rodgers and Hammerstein turn his classic 1921 play *Liliom* into a musical. They renamed it *Carousel* and moved its setting from Budapest to New England. They also tried to soften its bitter ending in which a rough carnival barker kills himself after a robbery, to avoid capture by the police, and then returns to Earth for a day only to be rebuffed by his daughter. Rodgers and

Jan Clayton (Julie Jordan) and John Raitt (Billy Bigelow) in the original production of *Carousel.* Courtesy of Photofest.

Hammerstein rewrote the ending to show that Liliom, now named Billy Bigelow, does manage to reach his daughter and help her live free of fear.

Rodgers thought they should end the first act with a soliloquy that would reveal Billy's emotions as he approaches fatherhood. "How would this be for the music," he asked Hammerstein and played a theme at the piano, "not the actual melody, but the general tone, color, and emotion I thought would be appropriate." Two weeks later, when Hammerstein finally gave him the lyrics for the eight-minute song, Rodgers set them to music in two hours. "Soliloquy" is the score's most important song because it explains why Billy commits the robbery that leads to his death. Although his manner is blunt, he also reveals a more loving side as he anticipates fatherhood and what it will mean to him: "You can have fun with a son but you've gotta be a father to a girl."

In the process of creating *Carousel*'s innovative weave of dialogue and lyrics, Hammerstein wrote "If I Loved You," a long and emotionally convincing "falling in love" song that springs directly from Molnar's dialogue and the inarticulateness of the characters' speech. Hugh Fordin notes that Hammerstein's revisions made the song simpler and clearer, "pared to the essence of the meaning that it carries": "If I loved you, words wouldn't come in an easy way— / 'Round in circles I'd go!" The sexually experienced Billy and the innocent but quick-witted Julie think about their deepening feelings for one another. Facing an uncertain future, she wins his heart by insisting she does not love him.

Hammerstein hated inaccuracy in his lyrics. Sometimes, though, he said his research "poisoned" him. For "June Is Bustin' Out All Over," he wrote "All the rams that chase ewe-sheep are determined there'll be new sheep," but then he found out that sheep do not mate in June. He kept the stanza anyway, explaining to purists with his tongue in his cheek, "What you say about sheep may all be true for most years, but not in 1873. 1873 is my year and that year, curiously enough, the sheep mated in the spring."

Rodgers and Hammerstein ended the show with "You'll Never Walk Alone," an anthem-like hymn for Billy's return to Earth and his implied reconciliation with his daughter. Some theatergoers find it deeply stirring; others consider it banal. On the day of the show's first full run-through, Rodgers and Hammerstein were sitting next to one another in the middle of the orchestra. For some reason, Rodgers turned around. There, with his coat over his shoulders and a monocle in one eye, was the great Molnar. The two songwriters sat through the rehearsal in a nervous sweat. They were convinced he hated their work, especially the new ending with "You'll Never Walk Alone," in which another child puts her arm around Billy and Julie's daughter, a gesture designed to tell the audience that the girl will no longer be afraid. "This so completely changed the spirit of the original," Rodgers wrote, "that we awaited a humiliating dressing down from the playwright." When they met Molnar after the play, his monocle popped out of his eye as he said, "What you have done is so beautiful. And you know what I like best? The ending!"

It Might As Well Be Spring
Lyrics by Oscar Hammerstein, music by Richard Rodgers

After Darryl F. Zanuck, the head of Twentieth Century-Fox, saw *Oklahoma!* on Broadway, he asked Rodgers and Hammerstein to help him turn *State Fair*, Phil Strong's popular novel about a farm family's annual visit to the Iowa State Fair, into a film musical. Rodgers and Hammerstein signed the contract, but, after their bitter experiences in Hollywood, insisted on writing the score in the East. Hammerstein much preferred writing for the stage where, in Hugh Fordin's words, "he could see the whole thing unfold before him. Writing a picture felt like navigating without a compass. 'I don't know where the hell I'm going,' he declared.'" He persisted, though, completing the book and lyrics for six songs.

The most important of them, "It Might As Well Be Spring," comes near the start of the movie. Daughter Margy isn't looking forward to this year's

Richard Rodgers and Oscar Hammerstein II. Courtesy of Photofest.

fair but doesn't know why. Her enervated state felt like spring fever to Hammerstein—not because she's in love but because she's not. Hammerstein's problem was that state fairs were usually held at harvest time, but he halfheartedly suggested to Rodgers that he write a lyric in which Margy says she has spring fever even though it's autumn, so "it might as well be spring." Rodgers leaped to his feet and cried, "That's it!"

Within a week, Hammerstein had finished a lyric that possessed the sort of innocent romanticism at which he excelled. What is especially effective is the way his skill with sound serves the song's emotional development. It begins, "I'm as restless as a willow in a windstorm, I'm as jumpy as a puppet on a string." The short vowels suggest her unease, as does Rodgers' equally restless, jumpy melody. Later, in the bridge, as the character becomes more reflective, the song's line becomes longer and more melodic: "I keep wishing I were somewhere else, walking down a strange, new street." Rodgers had written the melody at what he called "a bright, medium tempo," but the studio's musical director wanted it done as a slow ballad. Rodgers, recalling his former hassles with Hollywood studios, stipulated that they would reshoot if it did not go over well at a preview. "They telephoned us to say the song had been enthusiastically received," he later wrote, "so we reluctantly agreed. Later, when we saw the picture, we had to admit that they were right and we were wrong."

Laura
Lyrics by Johnny Mercer, music by David Raksin

Although composer David Raksin wrote hundreds of scores for movies and television, we remember him for one haunting melody. After he finished the score for a Twentieth Century-Fox movie called *Laura*, director Otto Preminger told him he wanted to use Duke Ellington's "Sophisticated Lady" as the theme. Raksin protested. "What?" said Preminger, "You don't like it?" "Of course I like it. Everybody likes it. But it has nothing to do with your movie." Preminger gave him the weekend: "Come in Monday with something you like better, or else we use 'Sophisticated Lady.'"

On Saturday, Raksin got a letter from his wife saying she was leaving him. "I felt the last of my strength go, and then—without willing it—I was playing the first phrase of what you know as 'Laura.' I knew it was the real thing and stumbled through it again and again in a sweat of catharsis and self-indulgence."

An instrumental recording of the theme was so popular that moviegoers pleaded with Twentieth Century-Fox to turn it into a song. The studio first approached Oscar Hammerstein to write a lyric but balked at his insistence that the song be published by his company. They next turned to Irving

Caesar, who had written such 1920s classics as "Tea for Two" and "Crazy Rhythm," but the best Caesar could come up with was a lyric called "Two Dreams," which did not even cash in on the title of the movie. At that point, Raksin said, "Well, there's a guy I don't know, but he's such a wonderful lyricist I would love to have him." He was thinking of Johnny Mercer.

The studio telegrammed Mercer that there had been "tremendous calls for this tune from all over the country" and asked him to "hop on it right away." Typically, Mercer took the lyric and went off to work by himself. Although he wished he could use the title "Footsteps in the Dark," he immersed himself in Raksin's complex melody, determined to craft a lyric that would blend Southern Gothic ("footsteps that you hear down the hall") and bittersweet nostalgia ("she gave your very first kiss to you"). The result was doubly amazing because Mercer had not seen the movie. He told an interviewer, "I simply absorbed the tune and let it create an atmosphere for me."

In just sixty-two words, Johnny Mercer had matched the implicit emotions of Raksin's seventy-two note melody. "I thought Johnny's achievement was amazing," Raksin said, "that he should get that feeling into the lyric. And I know that Johnny worked hard, sweated blood sometimes, but you would never have known it. He would show up without a hair out of place—with this thing he had written on the tip of his little finger." Mercer's genteel upbringing forbade his revealing that he had slaved over a song, even one of such artistry. Another patrician songwriter, Cole Porter, paid Mercer the ultimate compliment of saying "Laura" was his favorite song—among those he did not write. Whenever Mercer was asked how he knew his words had brought out the emotional meaning of a melody, he always cited "Laura" as his *locus classicus*.

Sentimental Journey
Lyrics by Bud Green, music by Les Brown and Ben Homer

In 1940, a song plugger told bandleader Les Brown about Doris Day, the girl singer with Bob Crosby and the Bobcats. "I went and saw the show," Brown said, "went backstage and hired her .... The band started cooking, you might say." Before long, though, Day left to get married. The marriage soon soured when her husband began to abuse her. At the same time, Brown had his first hit recording, a novelty by Ben Homer and Alan Courtney called "Joltin' Joe DiMaggio," based on DiMaggio's record fifty-six game hitting streak in 1941. In 1943, Day had finally had enough; she divorced her husband and rejoined the band.

A year later, Homer took Brown another song on which he was working. Within a half hour, the band leader changed the rhythm of the verse and added a bridge to complete the song. He gave the melody to his publisher, Buddy Morris, who had three different lyricists try their hands. Brown described what happened next: "Buddy was reading a travel book written by an Englishman and it was called *Sentimental Journey*, about this guy going all over Europe. He mentioned the inns he was staying in." Morris thought it would make a good title for a song and mentioned it to Bud Green, who had added the nonsense words to the jive classic, "Flat Foot Floogie with the Floy Floy." Brown said, "Bud Green wrote a nice lyric. He even had to make up a word to rhyme with 'journey': 'Never thought my heart would be so *yearny* …'"

Doris Day's recording of "Sentimental Journey" became one of the defining anthems of return for soldiers taking a "sentimental journey home." Like other train songs from the Swing Era, the 2/4 rhythm and strong beat fit the clickety-clack of a train, here punctuated by a line that echoes the whistle's wail: "Seven … that's the time we leave at seven."

1946

ANNIE GET YOUR GUN
Lyrics and music by Irving Berlin

When Dorothy Fields heard about a sharp-shooting serviceman who had won all of the prizes at a Coney Island shooting gallery, she immediately thought of a musical about Annie Oakley. She called Ethel Merman, who had just given birth, and, from her bed in the maternity ward, the singer agreed to do the role. Fields then got Rodgers and Hammerstein to produce the show. Fields would write the book and lyrics, and Jerome Kern would write the music.

Just as he was starting to work on the score, however, Kern died of a heart attack. "That was the worst week of my life," Fields said, "the worst week of everybody's life." After the funeral, she and Rodgers and Hammerstein realized that "the show must go on" and discussed other possible composers. Finally, Rodgers said, "Well, I know somebody, but it means that Dorothy can't do the lyrics." Always the trouper, Fields said, "Well, I have enough to do with the book. I don't care. Who is it?" "Irving," Rodgers said.

When they approached Irving Berlin, he was skeptical. Nearing sixty, he was wary of the new "integrated" musicals that had been ushered in on Broadway with *Oklahoma!*. He was also skeptical about his ability to write in the "country" idiom called for by Annie Oakley's story, but Hammerstein assured Berlin that all he had to do to create countrified lyrics was to drop final consonants, as in "singin'" for "singing."

Berlin agreed to take Dorothy Fields' book home to see if it gave him any ideas. In twelve days, he wrote "Doin' What Comes Natur'lly," "You Can't Get a Man with a Gun," and "They Say It's Wonderful," and then went on to write such other superbly "integrated" songs as "I Got Lost in His Arms" and "I Got the Sun in the Mornin'." These songs redefined Ethel Merman's theatrical image. Until then, she had played a brassy big-city dame, wise to all guys, but as Annie she displayed a folksy, disarming innocence. On meeting the handsome sharpshooter, Frank Butler, she sang "You Can't Get a Man with a Gun" as an expression of her secret longing for the traditional feminine role she outwardly scorns. Even as she bemoaned her romantic plight, however, Annie's—and Ethel's—thoroughgoing pugnacity asserted itself in an outraged comic complaint that "You can't shoot a male in the tail like a quail."

"They Say It's Wonderful" gave Annie a hesitant foray into the unfamiliar territory of romance. The vernacular catchphrase "so they say" provided her with a defensive retreat from the exuberance of "They say that falling in love is wonderful." Merman heightened that tension by booming out the word "wonderful" then quickly added the qualifying "so they say" with almost legal detachment. Only the Annie who had mocked "book larnin'"

Performing "There's No Business like Show Business" in the 1946 production of *Annie Get Your Gun* are William O'Neal, Marty May, Ethel Merman, and Ray Middleton. Courtesy of Photofest.

in "Doin' What Comes Natur'lly" would confess that she can't recall where she had heard about the wonders of love: "I know I never read it."

Berlin's songs also defined the character of Frank Butler, from "A Bad, Bad Man," where he portrays himself as a womanizer who leaves broken hearts (and shotgun-toting fathers) behind in every town, to "The Girl That I Marry," where he reveals how he staves off marriage by insisting upon an impossible ideal of womanhood: "The girl that I marry will have to be / As soft and as pink as a nursery." Not only did these songs fit the story and characters of *Annie Get Your Gun*, many became popular hits—the greatest number of independently popular songs to emerge from any Broadway musical.

For all his success, however, Berlin was terribly insecure. When he demonstrated a new song to anyone, he watched their eyes for a reaction. "Only by fixing his eyes on the listener could he sense if the song worked," noted biographer Laurence Bergreen. "If one blinked too often or one's eyes glazed for a second, Irving was apt to put the song away." When he first sang "There's No Business like Show Business" to his secretary, she seemed unimpressed. When he demonstrated it to Josh Logan, Rodgers and Hammerstein, and Dorothy Fields, they too seemed unmoved. In fact, they were dumbstruck at its brilliance, from Berlin's use of such showbiz slang as "turkey that you know will fold" and "angels come from ev'rywhere with lots of jack" to such clever rhymes as "There's *no* business like *show* business like *no* business I *know*."

Taking their stunned silence as criticism, Berlin set the song aside. Later, when he played through the score, they all asked what happened to "There's No Business like Show Business."

"I didn't like the way you all reacted this morning," Berlin said. "It didn't register."

"It wasn't petulance," Logan recalled. "He meant it. I was astounded. I asked him what he'd done with the lead sheet, and he shrugged and said he'd put it away in his files somewhere, and I said, 'Irving! Get it out of those files.'" When everyone went rummaging through Berlin's office, they finally found it under a telephone book.

Logan also recalled a discussion about the need for a strong duet to punch up the second act. When Berlin realized the song would be tied to a shooting match between Annie Oakley and Frank Butler, he shouted, "Challenge song!" and left the meeting. Fifteen minutes later, Berlin called Logan to sing him the first chorus of "Anything You Can Do" over the phone. In it, Annie and Frank boast about their superiority in marksmanship, drinking, and a host of other feats, even as they confess,

"Can you bake a pie?"

"No."

"Neither can I."

Logan was astounded that Berlin could write such a brilliant and dramatically integrated song in the time it had taken him to get back to his hotel.

The Christmas Song
Lyrics by Bob Wells, music by Mel Tormé

On a blistering hot July day, Mel Tormé dropped by the home of Bob Wells. The two men were under contract to write songs for a music-publishing firm headed by songwriters Johnny Burke and Jimmy Van Heusen. Tormé noticed a spiral notebook sitting on the piano with several lines jotted down, beginning with "Chestnuts roasting on an open fire." When he asked his collaborator about them, Wells said, "I am so hot today. I jumped in the pool, took a cold shower, and tried everything I could think of to cool off. Nothing worked. So I sat down and wrote these few lines as an experiment to see if thinking about winter scenes would do the job." Tormé suggested they turn it into a song and in forty-five minutes they had completed "The Christmas Song."

When they showed it to Burke and Van Heusen, however, they got the cold shoulder. "No fellas, no good," Burke growled. "The minute you say 'They know that Santa's on his way' you make it a 'one-day' song–Christmas Eve. No one's going to buy a tune that's only good one day of the year."

Dejected but undaunted, Wells and Tormé took the song to Nat King Cole. Cole listened to it twice then said, "That song is mine. Nobody gets that song except me." The songwriters took it back to Burke and Van Heusen with the news that Cole wanted to record it, so "The Christmas Song" was accepted with great reluctance. It became Nat King Cole's biggest-selling recording, thanks to a hot day in July.

Come Rain or Come Shine
Lyrics by Johnny Mercer, music by Harold Arlen

Johnny Mercer and Harold Arlen were great *song* writers, but they were not great *show* writers. At a time when the Broadway musical followed the lead of Rodgers and Hammerstein's *Oklahoma!*, Mercer and Arlen still thought more in terms of the song rather than its dramatic context. Moreover, they were not very good judges of musical books. Their greatest score, for *St. Louis Woman*, was saddled to a weak book by Arna Bontemps and Countee Cullen. However, the prospect of having Lena Horne as the show's star—bolstered by the dazzling dancing of the Nicholas Brothers and the singing of sultry newcomer Pearl Bailey—promised to make *St. Louis Woman* a winner. The show quickly became embroiled in politics, however, because the NAACP objected to the demeaning racial caricatures in the book (even though Cullen and Bontemps were black) and pressured Horne into withdrawing. When *St. Louis Woman* flopped, among the losses were such great songs as "Any Place I Hang My Hat Is Home," "Legalize My Name," and "It's a Woman's Prerogative."

Only one song survived to become an independent hit. When Arlen played its melody to Mercer, the lyricist immediately came up with "I'm gonna love you like nobody's loved you," but then he was stumped. Arlen suggested "Come hell or high water?" "Of course," Mercer said. "Why didn't I think of that?" What he thought of, however, was "come rain or come shine."

Mercer and Arlen asked singer Margaret Whiting to make a recording of "Come Rain or Come Shine" that would be released immediately after *St. Louis Woman* opened. Both songwriters were in the studio that day, and Whiting thought of them as

> ... the most unlikely, wonderful team. Johnny was a true son of the South, and Harold Arlen a true son of a cantor from Buffalo. But these two disparate heritages meshed. Harold wrote songs with a marvelous blues chord structure that was sensuous and sophisticated and also primitive. Johnny's lyrics blazed with orig-inality and an American earthiness.

Such reflections inspired Whiting to take an unusual liberty with her rendition of "Come Rain or Come Shine." Her father, composer Richard Whiting, had always told her, "Sing the song the way the writers wrote it. They worked hard to get it just right." However, Margaret said that

> Something happened in my mind. I started thinking about Harold, the cantor's son. On that last note, I just let it wail: "I'm gonna love you, come ra-in or sh-i-i-i — ne." Well, Johnny just burst through the door, mad as hell: "What in God's name are you doing?" He was followed by Harold, who shouted, "No, leave it, leave it. That's the way I should have written it."

Let It Snow, Let It Snow, Let It Snow
Lyrics by Sammy Cahn, music by Jule Styne

One very hot day in August 1945, waiting at a red light at the corner of Hollywood and Vine, Sammy Cahn said, "Why don't we go to the beach?" Jule Styne replied, "Why don't we write a winter song?" They drove the few blocks to the Morris Music Company where Cahn used a spare typewriter to write a dummy lyric and Styne sat at a nearby desk jotting notes on paper. Later, at Styne's house, they polished up what would be their newest hit.

"Let It Snow, Let It Snow, Let It Snow" belongs in the same company as Irving Berlin's "I've Got My Love to Keep Me Warm" from 1937, and Frank Loesser's "Baby, It's Cold Outside" from 1949. It's an intimate conversational duet that listens in on an amusing skirmish in the battle of the sexes. The storm is outside and it is cozy inside, but it is not long before coziness turns seductive. The title phrase appears three times, each time with a different meaning to reflect the state of the goings-on. In the first stanza, it describes the couple's feelings about the weather as they settle down and get comfy. In the second stanza, the line is suggestive and euphemistic. He may have brought "some corn for popping," but "the lights are turned way down low." The title becomes a case of erotic indirection. The next thing you know, they are kissing goodnight and the fire is dying. All she needs before she leaves is his pledge of love and then it can snow as long as it wants: "But as long as you love me so, / Let it snow, let it snow, let it snow."

The following year, Cahn said, "Remember how lucky we got with that winter song last year? Let's do something for summer." They wrote "The Things We Did Last Summer," which did almost as well.

On the Atchison, Topeka and the Santa Fe
Lyrics by Johnny Mercer, music by Harry Warren

When Harry Warren and Johnny Mercer worked on *The Harvey Girls*, an MGM musical about the upright young women who worked in the Harvey restaurant chain along the major stops of the transcontinental railroad, the composer was amazed at the intensity of his collaborator. Mercer would lie on the couch for hours, concentrating on finding the words to fit Warren's melody. At times, Warren would greet Mercer, whom he dubbed "Cloud Boy," with an innocuous question such as "How's your wife?" Hours later, Mercer would come out of his creative trance to answer nonchalantly, "Oh, Ginger's fine."

The big production scene for *The Harvey Girls* had Judy Garland singing alongside a train as she and the other waitresses arrived in the western town they would help to tame. Mercer mentioned that he had once noticed a railroad boxcar with the emblem "The Atchison, Topeka, and the Santa Fe." "I thought it had a nice, lyrical quality to it," Mercer said, and Warren told him, "Fine. I've just the right tune for it." "On the Atchison, Topeka and the Santa Fe" was, Mercer said, "an easy one to write. As I recall, it took me about an hour."

However, the producer and director of *The Harvey Girls* knew how slowly and painstakingly Mercer and Warren worked, so when they decided the song needed a series of verses in which each "Harvey girl" introduces herself, they turned the task over to associate director Roger Edens and vocal arranger Kay Thompson, but did not tell Mercer and Warren. When Mercer heard the interpolated lyrics, such as "I'm from Paris—Paris, Texas," he was furious. "They're going to make me look like an idiot," he said, "Everybody's going to think I wrote that junk."

Warren was equally incensed, but over a different matter. Johnny Mercer had made a recording of the song for Capitol Records, and Warren walked into a record store one day to see an ad extolling "Johnny Mercer's 'On the Atchison, Topeka and the Santa Fe.'" Although the ad referred only to Mercer's recording of the song, Warren felt that his role as composer had been slighted, and he refused to speak to Mercer for years. Warren, whose real name was Salvatore Guaranga, "was Italian and everything that goes with it," Mercer said. "He is quick-tempered, he is suspicious, and he is clannish."

When "On the Atchison, Topeka and the Santa Fe" won the Academy Award for best song, neither Mercer nor Warren was present at the ceremonies, each man nursing his wounded pride.

Stella by Starlight
Lyrics by Ned Washington, music by Victor Young

After writing the lyrics for songs such as "Whistle While You Work" and "When You Wish upon a Star," Ned Washington left Disney Studios to freelance as a lyricist for individual theme songs in movie dramas. He worked very quickly, usually finishing a song in less than a day, but he had a habit of holding onto a finished song until his contract was nearly up. That way, he could bargain for a new contract to write a new song for a new movie. He never wanted the studios to know how fast he wrote.

The most important of these individual songs was "Stella by Starlight," derived from the theme music Victor Young wrote for a 1944 haunted house movie, *The Uninvited*. The theme was part of the title sequence and then reappeared when the movie's hero composed a song for the young woman whose mother haunts the seaside house he and his sister have recently bought. As with David Raksin and Johnny Mercer's "Laura," audiences liked the theme so much that Young reworked it as a song and Washington added words.

Royal S. Brown calls Young "one of the most natural melodists ever to work inside or outside Hollywood." For "Stella by Starlight," he wrote a melody that was unusually tight yet flowing. Typically, musical phrases in popular songs run seven or eight notes. In "Stella by Starlight," they are between two and four notes long. As a result, Washington was limited to very few words, and the lyric had to be suggestive and allusive. It has no narrative line but only a few apparently random natural associations—"the song a robin sings" and "the murmur of a brook"—until the music swells as would be expected in a movie's moment of grand passion. Washington follows its rise to the lyric's climax: "A great / symphonic theme, / That's Stella by starlight."

1947

BRIGADOON
Lyrics by Alan Jay Lerner, music by Frederick Loewe

When Fritz Loewe casually remarked to Alan Jay Lerner that "Faith can move mountains," the lyricist began thinking about "all sorts of miracles occurring and eventually faith moved a town." The town became Brigadoon, a Scottish village that comes alive for only one day in each century. When two Americans stumble upon it during a hunting expedition, it

Alan Jay Lerner and Frederick Loewe on a day when the songs were not coming easily. Courtesy of Photofest.

takes the love of one of them to bring the village back to life so that he can be part of its eternal cycle.

Loewe's score was steeped in Scottish dance music and ballads, and Lerner's lyrics for "Come to Me, Bend to Me" and "The Heather on the Hill" had a romantic plangency that appealed to audiences looking for escapism after World War II. The hit of the show was "Almost like Being in Love," a hesitant, guarded affirmation of love between two people separated by centuries and culture: "I would swear I was fallin', / I could swear I was fallin', / It's almost like being in love."

Virtually every Broadway producer turned *Brigadoon* down, however, and even when Cheryl Crawford, who had produced *One Touch of Venus*, agreed to take the show on, Lerner and Loewe had to play their score to backers more than sixty times—sometimes two or three times a day— to raise the $175,000 to mount the production. Once they had the money, Lerner, Loewe, and Crawford approached Agnes DeMille, hoping she would choreograph *Brigadoon* as brilliantly as she had *Oklahoma!* and *Carousel*. DeMille loved the score, but she objected to "Almost like Being in Love," saying "Don't use that song, throw that one out." Ironically, she had made similar objections to "People Will Say We're in Love" when she was working on *Oklahoma!* "Well, of course," DeMille later admitted, "it was the hit of the show."

FINIAN'S RAINBOW
Lyrics by E. Y. "Yip" Harburg, music by Burton Lane

The most politically radical lyricist of his day, Yip Harburg conceived of a musical in which a Southern congressman was turned into a black man. For the magical transformation, Harburg invoked the Irish legend of stolen leprechaun's gold from the end of the rainbow. Working with librettist Fred Saidy and composer Burton Lane, he created his greatest Broadway show. It opened with the haunting, incantatory "How Are Things in Glocca Morra?" a fictitious place whose etymology sounds more Yiddish than Celtic. It "became the signature song of the show—indeed a universal cry of all immigrants," Ernie Harburg and Harold Meyerson point out, "a ballad not of worlds to come but of worlds that have been lost."

Finian's Rainbow bristled with songs of political protest, satire, and hope: "Look to the Rainbow," "Necessity," and "When the Idle Poor Become the Idle Rich." It also included such brilliantly witty songs as "Something Sort of Grandish," written for the leprechaun Og. Lane's minuet-like melody inspired Harburg to revel in suffixes and create such rhymes as "Thou'rt so adorish / Toujour l'amourish" and "It's so terrifish, magnifish, delish, / To have such an amorish, glamorish dish."

Og's other song, "When I'm Not Near the Girl I Love," began with Harburg's idea for the turnaround title ("I Love the Girl I'm Near"). "I was tickled with the title," Burton Lane said. "It was just wonderful coming out the way it did with the leprechaun beginning to turn mortal, and all I could think of was Yip. Yip was the only leprechaun I had ever met." That night a melody came to Lane in his sleep, and as the collaborators were conferring the next morning, Lane began to play it. "Yip perked up his ears and said, 'What is that?'" Lane explained it was just a melody that had come to him in his sleep:

> I had been subconsciously working with "When I'm Not Near the Girl I Love," but even then I did not associate that tune with that title. Yip said, "Play it again." I did and he started to sing these little slurs on "nee-ar the girrr-l"—and that made the title fit.

The lyric captures Og's emerging libido as he confesses, "Always I can't refuse 'em / Always my feet pursues 'em / Long as they've got a 'boo-som' / I woos 'em."

The most enduring standard to emerge from *Finian's Rainbow* was one that had its musical origin as "This Is Where I Came In," a song Lane had written for Lena Horne to sing in an unproduced movie. He asked Harburg to set a new lyric to it and replace a song for *Finian's Rainbow* called "We Only Pass This Way One Time." When Harburg demurred, Lane went to Harold Arlen and said, "You know, I've been trying to get Yip to rewrite for this other melody because I think it would make a better song." Arlen backed Lane, and Harburg dutifully went to work on the lyric that became "Old Devil Moon."

He sensed in Lane's melody "more of a Negro feeling" and looked for "an idea, something that had to do with witchcraft, something eerie, with overtones of voodoo." He concocted a lyric that blended such catchphrases as "too hot to handle," "can't hold a candle," and "razzle dazzle," with such slangy cries as "wanna cry, wanna croon, / wanna laugh like a loon." "Old Devil Moon" was Yip Harburg's last great standard.

1948

Baby, It's Cold Outside
Lyrics and music by Frank Loesser

At show business parties, everybody performed. When Frank and Lynn Loesser threw a housewarming party after they moved into the swank Navarro Hotel, they sat down at the piano and sang "Baby, It's Cold Outside." Lynn was the "mouse" who kept protesting "I really must go ...."

"My mother will start to worry ...." "The neighbors might think—"; Frank was the "wolf" who persisted, "I'll hold your hands, they're just like ice ...." "please don't hurry ...." Baby, it's bad out there." It was Loesser's first contrapuntal duet, and the guests ate it up. "The room just fell apart," Lynn Loesser recalled. "We had to do it over and over again and we became instant parlor room stars. We got invited to all the best parties for years on the basis of 'Baby.'" The Loessers carried their party song to Hollywood, where Frank sold it to MGM for Esther Williams to sing it with Ricardo Montalban in *Neptune's Daughter*. Lynn Loesser said,

> I felt as betrayed as if I'd caught him in bed with another woman. I kept saying "Esther Williams and Ricardo Montalban!!!" He finally sat me down and said, "If I don't let go of 'Baby' I'll begin to think I can never write another song as good as I think this one is."

Be a Clown
Lyrics and music by Cole Porter

Peru, Indiana, was headquarters for the Hagenback and Wallace Circus, and as a boy Cole Porter loved seeing elephants barge into the local drugstores, watching the bareback riders train, and talking to the Wild Man of Borneo, who spent winters shining shoes in the town barbershop. "The lure and lore of the circus filled our thoughts," a friend recalled, adding that Cole aspired to be a circus performer and treasured his own clown suit. Thus, when Gene Kelly asked Porter to write a knockabout clown song for Kelly and Judy Garland to sing in *The Pirate*, the composer produced a paean to buffoonery overnight: "Why be a great composer with your rent in arrears, / Why be a major poet and you'll owe it for years, / When crowds'll pay to giggle if you wiggle your ears?"

When Porter played "Be a Clown" for Kelly, George Eels says, "the actor detected a certain melancholy quality which he related to the sadness of all great clowns." Producer Arthur Freed proclaimed it "the best number Cole had ever written." (Within five years Freed would "borrow" the melody, note for note, for his song "Make 'Em Laugh" in *Singin' in the Rain*.) Only Judy Garland demurred. "She pointed out that there were hardly any laughs where I had attempted to provide an infinite number," Porter lamented. Because Garland did not want to sing "Be a Clown," Kelly and the dynamic Nicholas Brothers introduced it instead. Harold and Fayard Nicholas were an extraordinary black dance team who had climaxed the all-black film musical *Stormy Weather* by tap-dancing up a huge pair of spiraling stair-cases and then descending the steps in bounding and what must have been agonizing splits. In *The Pirate*, they did an energetic knockabout dance to

"Be a Clown" with Kelly that marked the first time blacks and whites had danced together, as equals, on the screen.

KISS ME, KATE
Lyrics and music by Cole Porter

When Arnold Saint Subber, the young stage manager for a production of Shakespeare's *The Taming of the Shrew*, overheard stars Alfred Lunt and Lynn Fontanne arguing in the wings, he thought of doing a musical play-within-a-play about a production of *The Taming of the Shrew* that starred a quarrelsome divorced couple (who, of course, secretly still love each other). Together with Lemuel Ayers, an equally young stage designer, he approached the noted playwright Bella Spewack only to find that Spewack thought that *The Taming of the Shrew* was the worst of Shakespeare's plays. "It's a lousy play," she said. "I read it in high school."

She did, however, agree to think about their idea as long as they commissioned Cole Porter to do the score. "He hasn't had a hit in three years," Subber and Ayers cried, "The last show he did was a flop." When Spewack presented the idea to Porter, she met more opposition. Unlike Oscar Hammerstein, Porter had never written his own book, and he considered one of his greatest handicaps his inability to judge a good libretto. Spewack

Stage still from *Kiss Me, Kate*: Alfred Drake (as Petruchio) spanks Patricia Morrison (as Kate). Courtesy of Photofest.

also saw that Porter's insecurity was augmented by physical pain from the riding accident that had crippled him ten years earlier. Knowing that he believed that the way to succeed in a popular music industry dominated by Jews was to "write Jewish," Spewack finally won him over by explaining that the premise of *The Taming of the Shrew*—the plight of a father who cannot marry off a younger daughter until he has found a husband for her older sister—was a Jewish custom that had been the basis of several successful plays in New York's Yiddish theater.

Despite his misgivings, Cole Porter agreed to read the libretto, which Spewack completed with her husband, Sam. Porter immediately wired the couple, who would soon divorce: "The best musical comedy book I ever read arrived this morning. Congratulations." The book, and Shakespeare's play, launched Porter into an incredibly fertile burst of creativity, as he wrote "I've Come to Wive It Wealthily in Padua," "Where Is the Life That Late I Led?," and "Were Thine That Special Face," all based on lines from *The Taming of the Shrew*. The inspiration was so powerful that Bella Spewack insisted he stop writing songs because they already had too many.

However, the songwriter worried that a scene between two gangsters lacked a strong ending, so he created yet another song to fill the gap. "Brush Up Your Shakespeare" was a witty contemporary version of the Bard's bawdiness in which the vaudevillian gangsters wrench risqué rhymes from Shakespeare's titles: "her clothes you are mussing, / What are clothes? 'Much ado about nussing,'" "Kick her right in her 'Coriolanus,'" and "When your baby is pleading for pleasure / Let her sample your 'Measure for Measure.'" When he sent the song to the producers, Porter added a note that "Madame Spewack," as he called her, would probably cut her throat at the sight of yet another song.

Even the show's big ballad, "So in Love," with its masochistic plea, "So taunt me and hurt me, / Deceive me, desert me," had its Shakespearean roots in *A Midsummer Night's Dream*, in which the heroine begs her estranged lover to beat her: "Use me but as your spaniel—spurn me, strike me, neglect me." Other songs resonated with the Shakespearean theme that had so deeply stirred Porter's creativity. As a musical about a theatrical production, *Kiss Me, Kate* called for not one but two curtain-raising songs. For the play-within-a-play, the troupers sing, "We Open in Venice," but for the opening of the musical, Porter wrote, "Another Op'nin', Another Show," which evokes such American locales as "Philly, Boston, or Baltimo'."

Porter again and again found in Shakespeare's bawdiness a license for "Tom, Dick or Harry," in which a "maid mad to marry" longs to take "double-quick" any "Tom, Harry or Dick"; "Too Darn Hot," in which a man laments that, although he would like to "blow my top with my baby tonight," the summer heat would make him "a flop with my baby tonight"; and "Always True to You in My Fashion," in which a girl explains to her boyfriend that, because an "oil man known as Tex" gives her "checks," it means "sex is here to stay."

Equally contemporary, yet still resonant with *The Taming of the Shrew*, was "Why Can't You Behave?" which Porter completed at 2:30 in the morning and immediately called Bella Spewack to sing it to her over the phone. "Bella was not happy to hear 'his lovely, velvety small voice' singing the new number at that hour," reported George Eels. "She let him know it, saying that the song was a 'lay-me-down' piece which would make it difficult for her to get the book moving following it." Another show stopper was the uproarious "I Hate Men," in which the shrewish Kate exults in her misanthropy: "I hate the most the athlete with his manner bold and brassy, / He may have hair upon his chest but, sister, so has Lassie."

The only song Porter did not write expressly for *Kiss Me, Kate* turned out to be one of its biggest hits. He had originally written "Waltz Down the Aisle" for an unproduced show. He liked it and inserted it into *Anything Goes* and *Jubilee*, but it was cut from both. For *Kiss Me, Kate*, he changed the title to "Wunderbar" and made it a comic oom-pah waltz in which the feuding lovers recall their supposedly blissful past.

Kiss Me, Kate struggled to find backers who would invest in a show produced by two neophytes, but Bella Spewack was undaunted: "I knew Cole had come through brilliantly," she said. "We had nothing to change. I knew it so I didn't have to be superstitious. In the history of American musicals this is the only one where they didn't have to touch a scene or a song." When Cole Porter arrived at the party after the opening night performance, Subber stood at the top of a grand staircase and shouted that the show would get a rave review in *The New York Times*. Porter, who had been painfully climbing the staircase, suddenly straightened up, tossed his canes aside, and strode up the stairs.

Once in Love with Amy
Lyrics and music by Frank Loesser

"I don't write for posterity," Frank Loesser snarled," I write for the here and now." Occasionally, he turned out a standard like "On a Slow Boat to China" by taking a poker player's catchphrase when he found himself in a card game with an inept but well-heeled opponent—"I'd like to get you on a slow boat to China"—and turning it to romantic ends: "all to myself alone."

Nevertheless, he soon realized the surest way to guarantee his songs' survival was to write for Broadway. When Cy Feuer and Ernest H. Martin approached him about turning a classic English stage farce into a musical, Loesser was ready to listen. At first the producers planned to have Harold Arlen write music and Loesser do lyrics, but when Arlen withdrew from the project, Loesser begged to write both.

Where's Charley? had a shaky opening, including the failure of audiences to warm to what was supposed to be its show-stopping number, "Once in Love with Amy"—even though Loesser's lyric had seamlessly mixed Victorian-like locutions ("ever and ever fascinated by her") with up-to-date hyperbole ("tear up your list, it's Amy") and the likeable eccentric dancer Ray Bolger performed it "in one" in front of a closed curtain during a scene change. One night, Bolger asked the orchestra leader for a cue when he forgot the words. Feuer's seven-year-old son, who had sat in on rehearsals, called out the line from his seat. At first Bolger was annoyed, but the audience loved it, and Bolger invited everyone to sing along. The routine soon evolved into a show-stopping, soft-shoe routine that ran nearly half an hour and made a hit of *Where's Charley?*

1949

Rudolph, the Red-Nosed Reindeer
Lyrics and music by Johnny Marks

When advertising copywriter Robert May learned that his wife was dying of cancer, he wrote a story called "Rollo, the Reindeer" to help his daughter through her mother's impending death. Hired by Montgomery Ward to write a booklet that Father Christmas could give to children who visited the main Chicago store, May went to the Lincoln Park Zoo with the company's illustrator. Noticing how cute the reindeer looked, they changed May's character to "Rudolph" and gave him a red nose. The booklet was a success and in 1949, May's brother-in-law, Johnny Marks, based a song on the story. Every singer Marks approached rejected "Rudolph, the Red-Nosed Reindeer," except the singing cowboy Gene Autry, who recorded it because his wife, Ina, liked it.

The song became the second-biggest-selling record of the first half of the twentieth century, surpassed only by Bing Crosby's recording of Irving Berlin's "White Christmas." Although "Rudolph, the Red-Nosed Reindeer" spawned many imitation holiday novelty songs, only a few, such as "Frosty, the Snow Man," (Steve Nelson and Jack Rollins, 1950) have endured.

SOUTH PACIFIC
Lyrics by Oscar Hammerstein, music by Richard Rodgers

The disappointing run of Rodgers and Hammerstein's *Allegro*, after their enormous success with *Oklahoma!* and *Carousel*, had Richard Rodgers combing his little black notebook of ideas for new shows and songs. Finding a cryptic entry that read "Fo' Dolla," he wondered what it meant. A few days later, Josh Logan called to ask if Rodgers had taken the director's suggestion to read the story, "Fo' Dolla'," by a young writer named James Michener. It told the story of a South Seas virago named Bloody Mary, whose daughter has an affair with a socially prominent American naval lieutenant. Logan thought it could be the basis of a musical; bedridden with a bad back, Rodgers read not only "Fo' Dolla'" but also Michener's entire collection of stories, *Tales of the South Pacific*. Then he had Oscar Hammerstein do the same.

Rodgers and Hammerstein thought that "Fo' Dolla'" could be combined with another story in the collection, "Our Heroine," about Nellie Forbush, a nurse from Little Rock who falls in love with Emile de Becque, a French plantation owner, only to find he has fathered Polynesian children. The two serious tales revolved around the theme of racial prejudice, so for

Mary Martin as Ensign Nellie Forbush sings "I'm Gonna Wash That Man Right Outa My Hair" in *South Pacific*. Courtesy of Photofest.

comic relief they went to stories that detailed the shenanigans of a naval con man named Luther Billis.

As they were blocking out the libretto, they got a call from a producer who had Metropolitan Opera star Ezio Pinza under contract to do a musical. The musical had fallen through, and the producer would have to pay Pinza $25,000 unless he could find another show for the star. Did Rodgers have a production that could use the aging but still virile bass singer? "I think I do," Rodgers said, "I think I do." To play opposite Pinza, Rodgers said, "We needed someone young, pretty, and lively, who could sing well but not necessarily with an operatic range and who could project the quality of believable innocence. Oh, yes, and it wouldn't hurt if she had a slight Southern accent."

The logical choice was Mary Martin, but the Texas-born singer was wary of singing opposite the Met's "Don Giovanni." Rodgers reassured her that she would not have to sing a duet with Pinza and then played some of the songs he and Hammerstein had written for her. Promising to call with her decision in the morning, Martin left Rodgers' house, but within hours the phone rang and she accepted, saying she was afraid that he would offer the part to someone else.

The first lyric Hammerstein completed was "A Wonderful Guy," a love song for Martin's simple, down-to-earth character, "corny as Kansas in August" and "normal as blueberry pie." When Rodgers and Hammerstein demonstrated it for her, Martin could not restrain herself. Meryle Secrest notes:

> She decided she had to sing it at once, so she sat down on the piano bench, getting more and more excited and making ever wider gestures. When she reached the final words, "I'm in love with a wonderful guy," she flung back her arms and threw herself off the bench. Rodgers peered down at her and said solemnly, "Never sing it any other way."

Martin had the lion's share of songs in *South Pacific*, including "A Cock-Eyed Optimist," "Honey Bun," and "I'm Gonna Wash That Man Right Outa My Hair." Hammerstein was embarrassed by his prosaic lyric to "Honey Bun," but when Martin donned an oversized sailor's suit to sing it, burlesque style, in the "amateur-night" troop show, the audience loved it. For "I'm Gonna Wash That Man Right Outa My Hair," Martin came up with the idea of washing her hair each night on stage.

As promised, Rodgers and Hammerstein did not write any duets for Martin to sing with Pinza. The closest they came was "Twin Soliloquies," in which Martin's character inwardly wonders why a cultured Frenchman would be interested in "a little hick" and Pinza, in turn, fears that "younger men than I, officers and doctors," have already locked up her affections. Those soliloquies lead up to, not a duet, but a rapturous solo for Pinza, "Some Enchanted Evening" (though Martin joined him in one of the choruses). Pinza's English, never a problem in opera, was so weak that his dialogue could barely be understood, and in rehearsals he sang "Some Enchanted Evening" as "Some Enchanged Evening."

Pinza's other solo, "This Nearly Was Mine," was a substitute for an earlier song, "Now Is the Time." Accustomed to the "hallowed traditions of opera," Pinza was "bewildered by the constant changes in dialogue and songs." His difficulties in adapting to show "doctoring" along with his problematic English led to calls that he be replaced, but Rodgers and Hammerstein held firm. Rodgers' melody for "This Nearly Was Mine" started out on subtly repeated notes but then climbed more than an octave to display Pinza's vocal range. Hammerstein was not pleased with his lyric, which relied on such hackneyed poetic terms as "divine" and "paradise." However, as Rodgers observed, the words fit the musical notes and "did convey exactly the way the character felt; he *was* close to paradise, whether Oscar liked it or not."

Some of the best songs from *South Pacific* were written for secondary characters. For the patrician naval lieutenant impossibly in love with a Polynesian girl, Rodgers went back to a melody he had written for *Allegro* but forgotten. His wife and daughters, however, had not, and they insisted he play it for Hammerstein. "Sure enough, Oscar agreed that it had exactly the qualities of romantic innocence for the song Lieutenant Cable sings to Liat. He took the music home, and in place of his trite lyric for "My Wife"—"You are so lovely, my wife, / You are the light of my life"—Hammerstein's new lyric soared: "Younger than springtime are you, / Softer than star-light are you."

The other song for Lieutenant Cable, "Carefully Taught," was a diatribe against the racial prejudice that prevented his union with Liat and that clouded Nelly Forbush's love of a man who had sired Polynesian children. Confronted by backers who feared the song would bar bookings in the South, Rodgers and Hammerstein, who were the controlling producers, insisted that it remain. "That's what the play is about," Hammerstein said.

South Pacific abandoned customary Broadway dance routines. In place of the traditional chorus line of girls, it used an ensemble of sailors in such rousing numbers as "Bloody Mary" and "There Is Nothing like a Dame." The first song celebrates the island madam, though Hammerstein's line, "Her skin is tender as Dimaggio's glove" was wonderfully in character but too hard to sing and comprehend, and had to be changed to "a leather glove." "There Is Nothin' like a Dame" is a lusty catalog song that extols the virtues and vices of women through a lonely sailor's eyes: "There are no books like a dame / And nothin' looks like a dame, / There are no drinks like a dame / And nothin' thinks like a dame." With its alternating verses and choruses, "There Is Nothin' like a Dame" was yet another Rodgers and Hammerstein song that pushed far beyond the confines of the standard format of the thirty-two bar popular song.

When the overture began for *South Pacific*, the opening notes were those of "Bali Ha'i." This song typifies the unusual collaborative methods of Rodgers and Hammerstein, as opposed to most songwriting teams, for whom songs began with the music. With Rodgers and Hammerstein, the words came first but only after considerable discussion about where the song would come, who would sing it, and what character it would have. As Hammerstein worked on the lyric, he went back to Michener's book to study the author's description of an island: "green, like something ever youthful, and it seemed to curve itself like a woman into the rough shadows formed by the volcanoes." Hammerstein spent a week crafting the lyric, always singing it to his made-up melody, then gave it to Rodgers over lunch. With his fresh memory of Juanita Hall's rich voice, Rodgers knew it was

> … a song for Bloody Mary which would evoke the exotic, mystical powers of a South Sea island. I knew the melody would have to possess an Oriental, languorous quality, that it would have to be suitable for a contralto voice, and even that the title was going to be "Bali Ha'i." I spent a minute or so studying the words, turned the paper over and scribbled some notes, then went into the next room, where there was a piano, and played the song. The whole thing couldn't have taken more than five minutes.

When he negotiated with Rodgers and Hammerstein for the rights to his short-story collection, Michener, a novice writer, settled for a mere 1 percent of the gross profits from the show. "The supposedly hard-hearted business team of Rodgers and Hammerstein turned soft at the last minute," notes William Hyland. Before *South Pacific* opened, they offered Michener the opportunity to buy another percentage for $4,500. When Michener declined, saying he did not even have $1,000, they lent him the money. "This generous gesture gave Michener lifelong financial independence, enabling him to work full-time as a writer."

1950 – 1959

1950

Autumn Leaves
English lyrics by Johnny Mercer, French lyrics by Jacques Prévert, music by Joseph Kosma

Mickey Goldsen, head of Capitol Record's music publishing division, loved French popular songs, so he asked the company's French representative to send him songs that were popular there. As he listened to a stack of records, one, "Les Feuilles Mortes," stood out with its mournful melody and a lyric about falling leaves so abundant "they can be collected in shovelfuls." "Oh, man," Goldsen exclaimed, "this is the greatest song I ever heard." He cut a deal with the French songwriters, Jacques Prévert and Joseph Kosma that gave him four months to produce an American version.

Goldsen then went to Johnny Mercer, president of Capitol, and beseeched him to write an English lyric, but Mercer was a notoriously slow worker. Goldsen waited for three months, then called and reminded Mercer of the deadline. Mercer said he had to catch a train to New York the next day, but if Goldsen would drive him to the station, he would work on the lyric and send it back in the mail.

When Goldsen got to Mercer's house ten minutes late, the songwriter said he had used the time to draft a lyric. "And as I'm driving," Goldsen recalled, "he read it to me, and tears came to my eyes." Although Mercer did not speak French, he instinctively knew that although French was a rhyme-rich language (with fifty-one rhymes for *amour*), English is a relatively rhyme-poor language (with only five rhymes—*dove, glove, above, shove,* and *of* for *love*). The poetic strength of the English language lies in alliteration rather than rhyme. Mercer used only three rhymes in "Autumn

223

Leaves," but he laced his lyric with subtle alliteration: "*d*rift by my win*d*ow," "*r*e*d* and gol*d*," "sunburne*d* han*d*s I use*d* to hol*d*."

Mercer seems to have poured into the lyric his foreboding that the world of popular music was leaving him behind. As he found less and less success, he cherished the enduring popularity of "Autumn Leaves." "You know something, Mickey," he told Goldsen, "'Autumn Leaves' is the biggest income song I have ever had."

From This Moment On
Lyrics and music by Cole Porter

Despite the success of *Kiss Me, Kate* (1948), Cole Porter feared that he could not write for the new kind of integrated "book musicals" that had come to dominate Broadway after *South Pacific* (1949) and *Guys and Dolls* (1950). "Suffering constant pain, insomnia, and blinding headaches" from his crippled condition, notes Frederick Nolan, Porter pinned his hopes on a new show called *Amphitryon*, a story based on the Greek myth of Zeus' affair with a mortal woman. The best number in the show, "From This Moment On," was a simple song of abrupt, driving phrases ("No more blue songs / Only whoop-de-doo songs"), but it bore little relation to the story or characters. During out-of-town tryouts, Porter agreed to cut "From This Moment On," as he put it, "to help the book along." Still, *Out of This World* had a disappointing run of only 157 performances.

Porter's depression deepened and, although he scorned psychiatric help as an invasion of his privacy, he consented to electric shock treatments. Still, he maintained his faith in "From This Moment On." When Hollywood made a film version of *Kiss Me, Kate*, he insisted on the song's interpolation into the score. The movie made "From This Moment On" into one of his biggest hits. Porter could still recognize a great song, but by this point he considered the success of *Kiss Me, Kate* as a fluke in his efforts to write an integrated "book" show.

GUYS AND DOLLS
Lyrics and music by Frank Loesser

"I took one little section of New York," Damon Runyon once said, "and made half a million dollars writing about it." Notes William R. Taylor:

> For journalists like Runyon, Times Square was a crossroad where special languages—dialects, cants, argots—hitherto confined to ethnic or occupational groups, converged in a kind of linguistic funnel to create a new national slang with a pronouncedly New York accent. The sporting world, the underworld, the worlds

Composer–lyricist Frank Loesser and librettist Abe Burrows. Courtesy of Photofest.

of vaudeville, theater, and carnival, had all developed rich and expressive argots by the beginning of the twenties.

Runyon, a Midwesterner (born in Manhattan, but Manhattan, *Kansas*), had absorbed this New York lingo and woven it into stories about gamblers, petty hoods, and their "dolls." Translating this "Runyonese" into song would produce one of the greatest American musicals.

Appropriately subtitled "A Musical Fable of Broadway," *Guys and Dolls* is probably the greatest of all musicals about New York. No other show is like it: *On the Town* is more star struck, *Gypsy* tawdrier, *West Side Story* more ominous. By the time librettist Jo Swerling finished writing an adaptation of Runyon's "The Idyll of Miss Sarah Brown," Loesser had finished the score as well. When Swerling's book proved unusable, producers Cy Feuer and Ernest Martin hired Abe Burrows on Loesser's recommendation. Burrows, a writer for the popular radio show *Duffy's Tavern*, was well known as a wit and raconteur, and as a quintessential New Yorker. He and Loesser had first met at a party at which Burrows improvised two of his classic party songs, "The Girl with the Three Blue Eyes" and "Memory Lane" ("I am strolling down Memory Lane without a single thing to remember").

Burrows' rewrite kept the story of an innocent Salvation Army sister who wins the heart of big-time gambler Sky Masterson, but also borrowed some of the shady but lovable gamblers, tinhorns, and touts from other stories by Runyon, including Nicely–Nicely Johnson, Harry the Horse, Benny Southstreet, and, most notably, Nathan Detroit, lover of Miss Adelaide, the adorable floozy with the incurable head cold. Nathan is also the sole proprietor of "the oldest established permanent floating crap game in New York."

Loesser's score combines comedy and skepticism, advances plot, and creates atmosphere and character. Isabel Bigley as Miss Sarah sings the bouncy romantic ballad, "If I Were a Bell," when she is drunk, and in "I'll Know," she and Masterson (Robert Alda) have an argument in song as they are falling in love. Paralleling "I'll Know" is the comic argument between Nathan and Miss Adelaide, "Sue Me." Just as "I'll Know" is serious with a comic undertone, so "Sue Me" is comic with a serious undertone.

The songs are as diverse as any Broadway score's yet they serve the play's needs perfectly. The opening number, "Fugue for Tinhorns," makes affectionately ironic use of a classical form to introduce the characters and establish their world. In "Adelaide's Lament," Miss Adelaide (Vivian Blaine) attempts to understand why an "unmarried female, just in the legal sense" is unable to get over what appears to be no more than a common cold. One of the wittiest of all theater songs, it demonstrates Loesser's ability to create character while writing a funny song with heart.

The rest of the score demonstrates Loesser's range: "Marry the Man Today," a cynical complaint about men; "Luck Be a Lady," a rousing production number as Sky appeals for help in a crap game; "More I Cannot Wish You," a father's loving wish for his daughter's happiness; "A Bushel and a Peck" and "Take Back Your Mink," two parodies of lousy nightclub acts; "Sit Down, You're Rocking the Boat," a comic revival number that reforms the sinners at the end of the show; and the title song, the gamblers' boisterous explanation of what a doll can do to a happily independent guy.

Unfortunately, the rehearsals for *Guys and Dolls* were not as happy as the outcome. Loesser was a taskmaster with a notoriously short fuse. He expected stars and chorus members alike to perform his songs exactly as written, without embellishment. He once wrote that "singers love to vocalize beyond the sense of a lyric. They're always so sure you want to hear their goddamned tones." He also wanted it loud, especially in the days before shows used microphones. Once, he interrupted a rehearsal to scream four-letter words at the chorus for saving their voices. Then he strode out of the theater, went next door to buy a huge ice cream cone, and strolled peacefully back to his hotel room. During one tantrum, he actually leaped to the stage and slapped Isabel Bigley in the face when she failed to sing the way he wanted her to. Overcome with remorse, he fell to his knees and begged forgiveness. When Feuer recounted the story years later, he said the incident cost Loesser a very expensive piece of jewelry but that it was "the only time I ever saw a guy punch a soprano in the nose."

Paramount Studio, which had the right of first refusal, chose not to make the movie version because Burrows had been blacklisted. Instead, Sam Goldwyn produced it in 1955. Despite Loesser's attempts to control the production, Goldwyn insisted on casting Frank Sinatra as Nathan and two nonsingers, Marlon Brando and Jean Simmons, as Sky and Miss Sarah. Loesser disliked Sinatra's silky crooning; he believed Nathan's character required a brassy singing style. As gently as he could, he offered to help Sinatra with "Sue Me," to explain what he had in mind when he wrote the song. He said, "Why don't we meet in my bungalow and rehearse it?" Sinatra replied, "If you want to see me, you can come to my dressing room." Loesser walked outside, literally jumped up and down, swore profusely, and then calmed himself. When he went to Sinatra's dressing room, he encountered a dozen flunkies and a loud radio. That led to a blow-up between them. Sinatra sang the song his way, and the two men never spoke again.

Mona Lisa
Lyrics and music by Ray Evans and Jay Livingston

"Mona Lisa" started out as a melodic phrase that occurred to Jay Livingston on his way to the studio to work on *Captain Carey, U.S.A.*, a film about an American soldier who collaborated with Italian partisans during World War II. The melody was originally called "Prima Donna" and was sung in brief snatches in Italian by a blind accordionist on a street corner to warn Carey that Nazi troops were approaching.

Evans and Livingston reworked the fragmentary melody into a full song, retitled it "Mona Lisa," and took it to Johnny Mercer, then President of Capitol Records, in the hope that Nat King Cole, Capitol's biggest star, would record it. However, neither Mercer nor Cole liked the song. "It's pretty," Mercer told the songwriters, "Just not very good." Nevertheless, Mercer and Cole agreed to record it on the "flip side" of what they considered a more important song, but it was "Mona Lisa" that became popular. It sold more than three million records and held the Number One song spot for eight weeks.

What may have put off Mercer and Cole initially is that "Mona Lisa" is very operatic. As Graham Wood observes, "The bold leaps and wide span of the melody are more characteristic of nineteenth-century Italian bel canto than of Tin Pan Alley songs." The lyric, too, reaches an emotional pitch as the singer asks a woman as enigmatic as the subject of Leonardo Da Vinci's painting, "Are you warm, are you real?" but then wonders if she is "just a cold and lonely, lovely work of art."

Nat King Cole's recording, however, contained all of this impassioned sentiment in the cool, detached quality of his singing style, which embodied the austere, impervious character of a work of art.

You're Just in Love
Lyrics and music by Irving Berlin

"You're Just in Love," Irving Berlin's last great song, was the most important number in *Call Me Madam*, his last Broadway hit. Librettist Howard Lindsay was the first to have the idea of starring Ethel Merman in a show based on Perle Mesta, the Washington "Hostess with the Mostes' on the Ball," appointed by Harry Truman as ambassador to Luxembourg. Lindsay and fellow librettist Russel Crouse had wanted to write another show for Merman ever since they had done the book for Cole Porter's *Anything Goes* in 1934. Vacationing at a Colorado resort where Merman was also staying, Lindsay sent a letter to his partner to say he had the perfect vehicle for her:

> I've been watching her …. She seems so *American*—raucously, good naturedly, almost vulgarly American. I got to wondering how we could spot her in a foreign setting. And then I thought of Perle Mesta. How about making her Madame Ambassadress? She would be very funny …. The title would be "Call Me Madame" or is that terrible?

Merman loved the idea but she did not want to sing. "I want a good solid dramatic role," she insisted. Only when Lindsay refused to outline the plot unless she agreed to sing did she cave in: "All right—a few songs if they could be worked in." Crouse asked about possible songwriters and Merman replied, "Why not Irving?" Once he agreed, Berlin wrote six songs very quickly and then, in his own words, "I just went blank for two months." Then, perhaps because Lindsay and Crouse had such faith in him, "suddenly, everything was all right again, and I wrote two or three songs in one week." By the time they took the show for tryouts in New Haven and Boston, Berlin had written a score notable for such charming songs as "It's a Lovely Day Today," "Marrying for Love," and "The Best Thing for You."

However, they were having a major problem, what Berlin called a "big hole" in the second act. He tried to fix it with a moody song called, "Mr. Monotony," which he had previously cut from *Easter Parade* and *Miss Liberty*. When New Haven audiences responded coolly, Merman let Berlin know what she thought: "I've gone along. I've cooperated, I've sung the song and it doesn't fit. It's out." Realizing it would be foolish to force Merman to sing a song she hated, Berlin cut it. Then he wrote two replacements, neither of which was good enough.

At that point, audiences were especially interested, not in Merman, but in Russell Nype, the young actor who played her press attaché, whose "crew-cut" set a new hair-styling trend. His first act number, "It's a Lovely Day Today," was going so well he was hoping Merman would not have him fired. However, Berlin liked him and, as Laurence Bergreen points out, anyone singing a Berlin song successfully was not going to be fired from a Berlin show. Thus, Merman did the next best thing. She told Berlin, "I want a number with the kid."

Abbott suggested that Berlin write one of his patented counterpoint songs, especially because Bing and Gary Crosby's recording had revived his first one, "Play a Simple Melody," from 1914. The insomniac songwriter took to his hotel suite and went to work. Crouse had the room above, and Berlin's playing kept him up all night. Two mornings later, however, George Abbott wrote that Crouse "hurried into the theater with a big grin and said gleefully, 'I think he's got something. I keep hearing the same tune over and over.'"

Ironically, it was not Abbott, Crouse, or even Merman who first heard the song. Nype was in his hotel room when the phone rang. Berlin said, "Would you come down to the suite? I've written a song for you." When Nype arrived, Berlin, dressed in pajamas and a bathrobe, sang Merman's part in his distinctively croaky voice. Then he handed Nype the other part and they sang together. When they finished, Berlin cautioned him, "Don't tell Ethel you heard this number before her." The first time Nype and Merman sang it in Boston, they had to do seven encores.

Aside from the two engaging melodies and the musical magic trick of their perfect fit, the song opposes experience and innocence. A young man sings a sweet melody about his confusion when it comes to love, and an older woman replies with guidance in a syncopated tune that offers sympathy and a touch of humor: "You're not sick, you're just in love." Instead of a generation gap, there are a trusting youth and a more experienced guide. Innocent wonder encounters worldly wise know-how in one of the musical theater's most engaging songs.

1951

In the Cool, Cool, Cool of the Evening
Lyrics by Johnny Mercer, music by Hoagy Carmichael

As television invaded American homes in the 1950s, people went to the movies less often, and Hollywood studios cut back on their film output, particularly of musicals. Even films that were slated for production got cancelled, including *Keystone Girl*, for which Johnny Mercer and Hoagy Carmichael had written several songs. One song had been inspired by an off-color joke Carmichael told Mercer as they were driving to work. The joke involved a lion and a jackass, and its punch-line was the jackass' response to the lion's invitation to a party: "Tell the King of the Jungle that in the cool, cool, cool of the evening I'll be there." Mercer pounced on the phrase and as Carmichael's complex melody subtly changed key every few bars, the lyricist kept pace with such homegrown expressions as "slickum on my hair," "in the shank of the night," and "If I ain't in the clink and there's sumpin' to drink, / You can tell 'em I'll be there."

Although *Keystone Girl* was shelved, Paramount went ahead with *Here Comes the Groom*, a musical assigned to director Frank Capra, who was on the verge of retiring. After such classic films as *It Happened One Night* and *It's a Wonderful Life*, Capra had come to feel that the "spiritual meat" had gone out of his work. People had come to his films hungering for "soul food," as he put it, but recently all he had been giving them was "blue-plate specials."

However, the story of a reporter who returns from World War II with two French orphans that he must give up for adoption unless he can find a wife in five days appealed to the director's sense of what some critics labeled "Capracorn." Bing Crosby was to play the reporter and Jane Wyman the woman who gives up her engagement to a stuffy socialite to marry Crosby in the nick of time. When filming started, Capra made a wonderful discovery: "Jane Wyman—short nose, long legs, big heart, and all talent—had a rarely used flair for singing and dancing .... I *had* to have a song for Jane to do with Bing. But you don't just find great songs lying around on shelves."

However, that's just what he did. At a Hollywood party, Mercer and Carmichael performed "In the Cool, Cool, Cool of the Evening." According to Frank Capra, Jr., "My father heard the song and loved it. He asked Mercer and Carmichael if he could use it." When he filmed the number, Capra had Crosby and Wyman wired with shortwave radio receivers in their ears so they could hear their accompaniment played by an orchestra on a sound stage a few blocks away. *Here Comes the Groom* was hailed by critics as "Capra at his best," and the director stayed in the movie-making business.

Not only did "In the Cool, Cool, Cool of the Evening" work well in *Here Comes the Groom*, but it also went on to win the Academy Award for best song. The award created a controversy, however, because the song had not originally been written for *Here Comes the Groom*. However, because it had not been published or recorded prior to its appearance in the film, the songwriters were permitted to keep their Oscars, thus enabling Mercer to make good on his promise of an Oscar for Carmichael after "On the Atchison, Topeka and the Santa Fe," which Mercer had written with Harry Warren, beat out Carmichael and Jack Brooks' "Ole Buttermilk Sky" for the award in 1946.

THE KING AND I
Lyrics by Oscar Hammerstein, music by Richard Rodgers

Although she previously had played brassy, sophisticated roles on Broadway, British musical star Gertrude Lawrence asked Rodgers and Hammerstein to write a show for her based on *Anna and the King of Siam,* Margaret Landon's best-selling novel about the English governess of the children of a despotic Eastern ruler. Rodgers and Hammerstein were wary. They had already rebuffed the same suggestion from their wives, who had urged the songwriters to do a show based on Landon's book. Furthermore, they did not like to write for "stars," preferring instead to work with talented unknowns who made no demands about how they were featured. They also were concerned about Lawrence's singing; "her vocal range was minimal," Rodgers said, "and she had never been able to overcome an unfortunate tendency to sing flat." Still, they agreed to watch the movie version of the story starring Rex Harrison and Irene Dunne, and that sold them. The thought of writing songs for Lawrence in a new kind of role was tempting, and it would give Rodgers and Hammerstein another chance to deal with class and racial conflicts.

Knowing Lawrence's vocal limitations, they wrote songs that stayed within her range even as they delineated her character. "I Whistle a Happy Tune" covers only a single octave but dramatizes Anna's trepidation as she and her son arrive in Bangkok. "Hello, Young Lovers," which registers Anna's passionate memory of her dead husband and her sympathy with lovers everywhere, shifts between occidental waltz time and more exotic 6/8 time to reflect Anna's presence in Siam. Hammerstein agonized over this lyric for five weeks and was bitterly disappointed when Rodgers merely said, "It works fine." "Shall We Dance?" is a rousing polka in which Anna teaches the king to dance and both dimly realize they are sexually attracted to one another.

Rodgers and Hammerstein reserved their more soaring operatic numbers, such as "We Kiss in a Shadow" and "I Have Dreamed," for the stronger voices of the singers in the romantic subplot about one of the king's concubines who falls in love with a court ambassador. In these songs, Rodgers sought to create the atmosphere of oriental music, but

Yul Brynner as the king and Gertrude Lawrence in her final role as Anna Leonowens face off in *The King and I.* Courtesy of Photofest.

no more than that. "Western audiences are not attuned to the sounds of tinkling bells, high nasal strings and percussive gongs," he said, justifying his refusal to try to recreate authentic Siamese music. "If a composer is to reach his audience emotionally—and surely that's what theatre music is all about—he must reach the people through sounds they can relate to." He compared these songs to the way in which an American artist such as Grant Wood would paint his impressions of Bangkok: "It would look like Siam, but like Siam seen through the eyes of an American artist."

After failing to secure Rex Harrison, Noël Coward, or Alfred Drake for the male lead, Rodgers and Hammerstein cast an unknown actor, Yul Brynner, on the recommendation of Mary Martin. Although Brynner could sing, he chose to talk his way through songs, in a manner Rex Harrison would imitate four years later in *My Fair Lady*. This technique lent a dramatic, thoughtful character to such songs as "A Puzzlement," in which the king ponders the doubts his English governess has raised in his royal mind about his omniscience.

As *The King and I* began its Boston tryout, Rodgers and Hammerstein realized the show needed a lighter touch in the first act. Lawrence suggested she sing a song with the king's children, so Rodgers took "Suddenly Lucky," an unused melody from *South Pacific*, gave it to Hammerstein, and the lyricist set the same notes with "Getting to Know You." The song suited Lawrence's vocal range and that of the children, and it proved to be the biggest hit of the show.

The King and I opened on Broadway on March 29, 1951, and ran for three years. Gertrude Lawrence was a sensation. "Though I had known all along that her singing would be a problem," Rodgers said, "she had a radiance that could light up the entire stage." After starring in the show for more than a year, however, Lawrence complained of severe pains from her heavy costumes and was found to be suffering from a rare form of stomach cancer that led to her sudden death. Other actresses played the role and "each was more vocally secure than Gertrude Lawrence," Rodgers observed. "Just the same, when I think of Anna I think of Gertie."

Silver Bells
Lyrics and music by Ray Evans and Jay Livingston

Jay Livingston called "Silver Bells" "the annuity." It has sold more than 150 million copies since he and Ray Evans wrote it for *The Lemon Drop Kid*, a Bob Hope vehicle about a racetrack tout who needs to pay off a gambling debt by Christmas Eve—or else. He gets his friends to collect money by standing on street corners with bells. Of all the Christmas songs, this is one of the few set in a city. The snow falls on sidewalks rather than open fields as shoppers rush by, Salvation Army Santas jingle their bells in front of decorated store windows, and colored lights blink at every corner. If you were raised in a Northern city, it is a Christmas you will immediately recognize. Yet Evans and Livingston set their elliptical impressionistic view to a simple waltz, not as a contrast but to underscore the familiar emotional responses to the season, in the city as well as the country: "Children laughing, people passing, meeting smile after smile."

At first, the songwriters resisted the assignment. "It's impossible to write a Christmas song," they said. "Every year everybody sings the same old Christmas songs, and new ones never make it." However, Paramount was insistent, so they acceded reluctantly and soon found their inspiration in a small silver bell Evans kept on his desk. "We set our attention," they explained, "to Christmas in the city—in contrast to 'White Christmas' and other standards, with lots of snow and country and small-town images." They first wrote a song called "Tinkle Bell," about the people who stand on the corners tinkling their bells. When Livingston told his wife what they had written, she replied incredulously, "Are you out of your mind? Do you know what the word 'tinkle' means to most people?" Evans said later, "We never thought that 'tinkle' had a double meaning until Jay went home."

The two men started to write a new song, but they liked what they had written. They simply changed "tinkle" to "silver," and the money began pouring in.

1952

Glow Worm
English lyrics by Johnny Mercer, music by Paul Lincke

The melody for "Glow Worm" was based on "Glühwürmchen," a 1902 German song by Paul Lincke. When it was interpolated into the 1907 musical *The Girl Behind the Counter*, Lilla Cayley Robinson added English words. Robinson's lyric is characteristic of most turn-of-the-century songs with its tremulous apostrophe to the glow worm to "Lead us, lest too far we wander, / Love's sweet voice is calling yonder." Johnny Mercer probably knew the song as a boy, but when he added a new lyric in 1952, it bristled with clever puns and hipster slang: "Light up, you li'l ol' bug of lightnin,'" "Turn on the A-C and the D-C," and "When you gotta glow, you gotta glow."

The lyric is one of Mercer's most fertile and inventive, going on for verse after verse as Mercer urges "Thou aer-o-nau-tic-al boll weevil" to "Illuminate yon woods primeval" and observes, "You got a cute vest pocket Mazda / Which you can make both slow or 'Fazda.'" "One can only imagine," wrote Mercer's friend Bob Bach, "how stunned the original lyricist, Lilla Cayley Robinson, might have been could she have heard Mercer's hepcat update."

SINGIN' IN THE RAIN
Lyrics by Arthur Freed, music by Nacio Herb Brown

Arthur Freed, head of musical production at MGM, had made *An American in Paris* (1951) by taking old songs by George and Ira Gershwin, and putting them in a contemporary story about Gene Kelly as a painter in Paris after World War II. Freed thought a similar film could be made using songs he had written with composer Nacio Herb Brown. When he assigned Betty Comden and Adolph Green to write a screenplay, they listened to Freed and Brown's songs from the 1920s and 1930s and decided that, rather than to try to fit these old songs into a contemporary story, they would write a period script about the early days of the "talkies."

They consulted Freed and Douglas Shearer, head of MGM's sound department, who remembered the convulsive effect of the coming of sound to film: how the whirr of the camera had to be muffled by putting camera and cameraman in an immobile, sound-proof box; stationary microphones had to be concealed in props such as flower vases, while actors huddled nearby to make sure the microphone picked up their voices. These immobile cameras, stationary microphones, and rigid actors made the movies stop *moving*.

Singin' in the Rain, however, is one of the most dynamic films ever made. It bubbles over with songs, with 60 of its 103 minutes of running time given over to music. Much of that on-screen dynamism radiated from Gene Kelly, who, although he was busy choreographing *An American in Paris* when he read Comden and Green's script, agreed to do the role. He also supported the screenwriters in their insistence that his sidekick role go to a dancer, Donald O'Connor, rather than Freed's choice for the part, Oscar Levant.

Debbie Reynolds, who had played only a bit part in an earlier MGM movie, was cast as Kelly's romantic costar. Her first song was "All I Do Is Dream of You," which Freed and Brown had written for a 1934 film called *Sadie McKee*. When Reynolds' character has a chance encounter with famous movie star Don Lockwood, played by Kelly, she affects disdain for movies and expresses her ambition to become a dramatic actress. In the next scene, at a Hollywood party, she pops out of a huge cake followed by a bevy of chorines. As Kelly watches with amusement, she and her fellow flappers sing "All I Do Is Dream of You" in a 1920s "boop-boop-a-doop" style. "All I Do Is Dream of You" is one of the few songs in the movie that Reynolds actually sang. In most of her other songs,

Gene Kelly in *Singin' in the Rain.* Courtesy of Photofest.

A scene from *Hollywood Revue of 1929*, in which Cliff Edwards, who performed as Ukulele Ike, originally sang "Singin' in the Rain" in a downpour. Courtesy of Photofest.

including those in which she appears to be dubbing for star Lina Lamont (played by Jean Hagen), Reynolds' voice was dubbed by Betty Royce. To compound the irony, at one point, when Reynolds appears to be dubbing the speaking voice of Jean Hagen, Hagen actually dubbed for *her*. "Jean's voice is quite remarkable, and it was supposed to be cultured speech," director Stanley Donen explained, "and Debbie had this terrible western noise." For a movie about the "smoke and mirrors" of filmmaking, these ironies should not be surprising.

The only new song Freed and Brown wrote for *Singin' in the Rain* was "Make 'Em Laugh." None of their old songs worked as a dance number for Donald O'Connor, so Stanley Donen asked Freed to write something new and suggested a number like Cole Porter's "Be a Clown" from the 1947 MGM film *The Pirate*. To Donen's amazement, Freed simply took the melody from "Be a Clown" and wrote a similar lyric, "Make 'Em Laugh." Because Freed was head of production, nobody had the nerve to tell him it was a plagiarism. Only Irving Berlin, who was on the set the day the number was filmed, gasped in astonishment and demanded to know why his friend Cole Porter's song was being copied. Freed laughed it off, however, and Porter never registered a complaint. "Make 'Em Laugh" is one of the most stunning comic dances ever filmed, with O'Connor bouncing off floors and walls, but because of the many injuries he sustained, it took several weeks to film.

The production number for the title song, "Singin' in the Rain," is equally stunning and has become one of the most memorable moments in the history of film. The song was originally written for *The Hollywood Revue of 1929*, in which it was filmed with all the visual and sound limitations of early talkies. Singer Cliff "Ukulele Ike" Edwards appears in static shots as he huddles next to a microphone hidden behind a nearby tree. To his side, dancers cavort and climb staircases, all amid pouring stage rain, but they never utter a sound.

In *Singin' in the Rain*, though, Kelly and the camera move dynamically across the set, the camera zooming, tracking, almost dancing with him. As Kelly choreographed the number, he struggled with the problem posed by every song in a movie that is done, not as a "performance" by an actor playing a singer or dancer, but as an emotional expression of what a character feels — in this case love for Debby Reynolds. Roger Edens suggested that Kelly start with a vamp, "doodedoo do," to ease the transition from talking to singing and from walking to dancing. Kelly asked that holes be dug at certain key points in the street so that water could accumulate in puddles and he could splash in them as part of the dance. The effect was one of childish abandon in joy so overwhelming it could even find cause for singing in the midst of a downpour.

Other songs from *Singin' in the Rain* included "Would You?" from *San Francisco* (1936), "You Are My Lucky Star," from *Broadway Melody of 1936*, and "You Were Meant for Me," from *Broadway Melody* (1929). This last song epitomizes the stunning way song can be used in a film. Kelly introduces the neophyte Reynolds to the illusions Hollywood can create with film. On an empty sound stage, he shows her that 500 kilowatts of electricity imitate the sunset, machines create breezes, and then, just when we think that nothing genuinely moving can come out of such artificiality, he sings "You Were Meant for Me," and we realize that, hardened Hollywood pro that he is, it is his way of expressing his love for her innocence.

1953

CAN–CAN
Lyrics and music by Cole Porter

Although Cy Feuer and Ernest Martin had produced *Guys and Dolls*, Feuer thought of Cole Porter rather than Frank Loesser to write the score for a musical he had had in mind since he returned from Paris after World War II. He did not know Porter, so he looked him up in the phone book and told him that he and Martin had produced *Guys and Dolls*; Porter invited them over. He liked Feuer's idea of a musical about censorship that centered upon the can-can and the Puritanical opposition it aroused. This show would also return him to his beloved setting of Paris. He asked, however, that he not be included in any of the production meetings with director–librettist Abe Burrows and choreographer Michael Kidd, where the "integration" of story and songs would be hammered out. "I don't want to go," Porter would say, "I have nothing to contribute to that. I don't want to be uncomfortable. Just tell me what you want written, and I'll write it."

Although Martin told Porter he did not want any hackneyed "Paris" songs in the show, Porter quietly defied him. Reverting to his long-held belief that songwriting success came from "writing Jewish," he crafted a chromatic, minor-key melody called "I Love Paris" that Alec Wilder suggested could easily have been called "I Love Russia." In the song's release, though, Porter shifted to a major key. He demonstrated "I Love Paris" to Feuer rather than Martin. Feuer, a graduate of the Juilliard School of Music, was so taken by it that he played the melody for his wife, who, equally enraptured, exclaimed, "For God's sake, it's a Jewish song." "Not in the middle," Feuer said, noting the major-key release.

"I Love Paris" helped make *Can-Can*, with its run of 892 performances, the second most successful of Porter's Broadway shows. The song went on to independent popularity, along with five other numbers from the score, including "C'est Magnifique" and "It's All Right with Me." The latter is one of Porter's most intricate twists to the theme of falling in love, in which he catalogs all the reasons why the singer should not fall in love at the "wrong time," in the "wrong place," and with the "wrong face." Yet under these urbane negations, the singer reveals heartache— "It's not *her* face"—sensuous attraction—"but such a charming face"—and the casual seductiveness of an ordinary catchphrase—"that it's all right with me."

While Porter was writing the score during the summer of 1952, his ninety-year-old mother suffered a cerebral hemorrhage and never regained consciousness. Porter hurried to Indiana and remained with her until her death. During those weeks, he sat on her porch writing some of the score's funniest songs while his mother lay dying inside: "If the Louvre custodian can, / If the Guard Republican can, / If Van Gogh and Matisse and Cézanne can, / Baby, you can can-can, too."

Here's That Rainy Day
Lyrics by Johnny Burke, music by Jimmy Van Heusen

When it became clear that the Broadway musical was enjoying its greatest era during the 1950s, several Hollywood songwriters tried their hand at stage musicals. Frank Loesser succeeded on Broadway with *Guys and Dolls* and Jule Styne and Leo Robin with *Gentleman Prefer Blondes*; Johnny Mercer and Sammy Cahn usually found only disappointment. Unfortunately, the same fate held true for Johnny Burke and Jimmy Van Heusen when they wrote a score for *Carnival in Flanders*.

Yet the failed show produced Burke and Van Heusen's greatest "torch song," a genre that takes its name from Greek mythology, in which Orpheus "carried a torch" into the underworld in search of his beloved Eurydice. Van Heusen's melody, with its sudden changes of key, is harmonically complex and much more challenging to sing than most popular songs. "It is a great illustration of absolute honesty," notes composer Alec Wilder, "quite irrespective of its extremely inventive character as a melody."

Lyrically, Burke matches that complexity with an emotionally understated, almost bemused reflection on lost love that makes the loss all the more wrenching because it is implied rather than directly stated: "Maybe, I should have saved those leftover dreams," the singer speculates, then, in a casual afterthought, notes, "Funny—but here's that rainy day." Sammy Cahn considered "Here's That Rainy Day" one of the ten greatest songs ever written.

KISMET
Lyrics and music by George Forrest and Robert Wright

One of the closest collaborations in American popular song was between George Forrest and Robert Wright. They became friends in high school, wrote songs and special material for radio and cabaret performers in New York, and then moved to Hollywood in 1936 and lived together. At MGM they regularly showed up for work at 9:00 in the morning. "We were told," Wright recalled, "that we were embarrassing other people because nobody comes in until 11 A.M."

Although Wright and Forrest wrote some original songs in Hollywood, they found greater success by writing songs based on classical music. When Herbert Stothart gave them a melody he had adapted from Rudolf Friml, Wright and Forrest set a lyric to it as "The Donkey Serenade" (1937). When they returned to New York to write Broadway musicals, they continued to borrow from the classics. *Song of Norway* (1944) portrayed the life of Edvard Grieg with a score based on the Norwegian composer's music.

Kismet adapted the music of Russian composer Alexander Borodin into the kind of lavish extravaganza Broadway had not seen for decades. Billed as "a musical Arabian night," *Kismet* (the Turkish word for "fate") wedded Borodin's haunting Oriental music to the lush imagery of *The Rubáiyát of Omar Khayyám*. "Stranger in Paradise," based on Borodin's *Polovetsian Dances*, dominated the Hit Parade for weeks, but "Baubles, Bangles, and Beads" has proved more enduring in its ability to lend itself to jazz interpretations. Based upon Borodin's *Second String Quartet*, it bristles with such onomatopoeic phrases as "glitter and gleam so" and "jing-jing-a-ling-a."

Another melodic adaptation from Borodin's quartet, "And This Is My Beloved," was the most dramatically intriguing song in the show. Sung by a quartet rather than the traditional duet between two lovers, "And This Is My Beloved" belies its title phrase by having the two romantic leads sing the song to someone else, unaware, in the darkness, that their true love is only steps away.

That's Entertainment
Lyrics by Howard Dietz, music by Arthur Schwartz

When MGM decided to do *The Band Wagon*, a musical built around the standards of Howard Dietz and Arthur Schwartz, the brilliance of the film only underscored how regrettable it was that the collaborators had not written more songs together. Dietz and Schwartz wrote several new songs for the film and, although only one was used, it has proven to be one of their greatest. "That's Entertainment" rattles off a catalogue of show business clichés with trenchant verve—"the bride with the guy on the side," a "gay divorcee who is after her ex," "the boss who is thrown for a loss by the skirt who is doing him dirt"—then boils down the plot of *Hamlet* to a pithy summary: "a ghost and a prince meet / And everyone ends in mincemeat." Perhaps it was Dietz's devotion to public relations, press agentry, and advertising that made him regard songwriting as a "sideline" and inspired the quick-witted colloquial phrases he set to Schwartz's rousing melody.

Not long after *The Band Wagon*, Dietz contracted Parkinson's disease, and his lyrical brilliance as well as business acumen quickly deteriorated. Yet "That's Entertainment" has taken its place beside Irving Berlin's "There's No Business like Show Business" and Cole Porter's "Another Op'nin', Another Show" as one of the classic anthems of show business.

WONDERFUL TOWN
Lyrics by Betty Comden and Adolph Green, music by Leonard Bernstein

Wonderful Town began with a phone call. Rosalind Russell had agreed to star in a musical adaptation of her 1942 movie, *My Sister Eileen*, and Joseph Fields and Jerome Chodorov had already adapted their screenplay into a libretto. Leroy Anderson and Arnold Horwitt had also written a score, but everybody gave it a crashing thumbs down. That's when director George Abbott called lyricist Betty Comden to ask whether she and Adolph Green could find a composer and finish a new score in less than five weeks; otherwise, they would lose Russell to other obligations.

Comden and Green sought out Leonard Bernstein. They did not think he would do it because he had promised his mentor, Serge Koussevitsky, that he would never write another musical. Green reported:

> We had no sooner entered Lenny's apartment and were blurting out the facts about the show when the phone rang. It was George, never one to waste time, barking at us impatiently, "Well, is it yes or no?!!" To our surprise, with no hesitation Lenny said, "Yes." He always liked deadlines, and four weeks to write a score was an irresistible challenge.

By the time Comden and Green wrote *Wonderful Town*, they had their own way of working. A friend watched them some years later:

> Adolph Green might have been the only writer in all of history who never wrote. Betty's the one who jotted everything down. Adolph jotted absolutely nothing down. I never saw him use a pen or pencil, let alone a typewriter .... The form and structure came from Betty, so did style and sensibility. Then what, you might ask, did Adolph do? The answer is: the madness. The sheer, outlandish, surreal, weird, goofy, uniquely Adolphian madness.

Like Ruth McKenney's original stories in *The New Yorker*, the musical is set in 1935 and follows the lives of two sisters, an aspiring writer named Ruth Sherwood and an aspiring actress, her sister Eileen. They move from Columbus, Ohio, to Greenwich Village, where they find eccentric neighbors and try to find work and romance. Despite pressure to update the show to the 1950s, the lyricists knew they were right to stick with the 1930s when Bernstein "exuberantly banged out on the piano the Eddie Duchin vamp, a characteristic musical sound of the 1930s by the great orchestra leader and pianist of the 1930s. As soon as Lenny started playing that, we felt inspired." The overture to *Wonderful Town* starts with that vamp, and the score includes characteristic song styles of the time: a conga and swing, among others, handled with the lightly satiric touch typical of Comden and Green. Yet the score also marked a change in their style. "For a long time," Comden said, "we were known as 'those kids without any heart, who write all this brittle stuff.'" However, this score also had two touching ballads, "A Quiet Girl" and "It's Love," and a wistful mock ballad, "Ohio." Sung by the two sisters on their first night in New York, "Ohio" expresses their homesickness in comic terms, especially when a sudden thunderstorm terrifies them. Comden and Green's lyric is a series of questions beginning with the repetition of "why-oh-why-oh" to anticipate the title word. the "w" of the question, and the long vowels "i" and "o" echo through the song until they become a lonely, but funny, wail.

Young at Heart
Lyrics by Carolyn Leigh, music by Johnny Richards

Carolyn Leigh started out in advertising, moved up to writing sketches for television's *The Phil Silvers Show*, and finally landed a job as a lyricist with a music publisher who routinely gave her completed melodies to work on. After she had written some 200 unsuccessful lyrics, the publisher gave her a melody by Johnny Richards, and Leigh added a lyric to it within three hours. The lyric was unusually mature for a twenty-five-year-old woman, taking, as it does, a knowing point of view on life and love. At the time, Leigh's father had suffered a heart attack and was in the hospital, so it was understandable that she could observe that being young at heart was worth "every treasure on Earth."

"Young at Heart" was recorded by Frank Sinatra and helped the singer make his dramatic comeback by giving him his first number-one song since 1947. The song also garnered Leigh the opportunity to write lyrics for the Broadway musical *Peter Pan*, starring Mary Martin. When Martin's husband, Richard Halliday, the producer of *Peter Pan*, heard "Young at Heart" on the radio, he knew he had found his lyricist, but when he called Leigh to offer her the job, she thought he was playing a practical joke and nearly hung up on him. Once he convinced her it was a serious offer, she accepted. Then, in abject terror of the prospect of writing for Mary Martin, Leigh recalled, "I threw up."

However, with composer Moose Charlap, she created such delightful songs as "I'm Flying," "I Gotta Crow," and "I Won't Grow Up," establishing herself as a Broadway lyricist.

1954

Fly Me to the Moon
Lyrics and music by Bart Howard

Bart Howard told an interviewer in 1988, "It took me twenty years to find out how to write a song in twenty minutes." He had learned the lesson well by the time he wrote "Fly Me to the Moon." As he explained, "The song just fell out of me. One publisher wanted me to change the lyric to 'Take Me to the Moon.' Had I done that I don't know where I'd be today." Yet he initially called the song "In Other Words" until Peggy Lee suggested the name change. Howard also thought of it as an intimate ballad until Frank Sinatra recorded it as an uptempo number. Howard never had to work again and, with very few exceptions, he did not. The most important exception was "Man in the Looking Glass," written for Sinatra in the mid-1960s.

All these changes somehow fit the man, who was born Howard Joseph Gustafson in Burlington, Iowa. He left home at sixteen to play piano in a touring dance band that featured Siamese twins, and, when he got to Hollywood, he was the accompanist for a female impersonator. He soon fled to New York, where he changed his name. After World War II, he played for the great cabaret singer Mabel Mercer and was the house accompanist at the well-known nightclub, The Blue Angel. However, he was not earning a lot of money. Then came "Fly Me to the Moon."

The song's lyric is mainly an invitation, but its tone is confident. It lists a series of hyperbolic possibilities from flying to the moon to singing forevermore, although they all come down to the same recognizable desire: to escape with the one you love. This is what the lyric's about, even though it has several ways of saying it, from holding "my hand" to the culminating profession of love: "In other words, please be true / In other words, I love you."

The Man That Got Away
Lyrics by Ira Gershwin, music by Harold Arlen

A Star Is Born was to be Judy Garland's big comeback after drug addiction had nearly ended her movie career. Warner Bros. thought Harold Arlen would be the perfect composer to do the score because he had given Garland her first film triumph with "Over the Rainbow." However, Yip Harburg, the lyricist for *The Wizard of Oz*, had long been blacklisted in Hollywood for his left-wing politics, so Arlen was teamed with Ira Gershwin.

As they were working on a song for Garland to sing with jazz musicians in a late-night jam session, Arlen played a long, intricately structured "tapeworm" melody he had written years before when he was collaborating with lyricist Johnny Mercer. Mercer had set a lyric to it that began "I've seen Sequoia / It's really very pretty / The art of Goya / And Rockefeller City / But since I saw you I can't believe my eyes." Arlen felt that Mercer's lyric made his melody sound "puny" and put the song away in his trunk."

When he played the same melody for Gershwin, however, the lyricist leaned over the piano. Although he always found the title the hardest part of a lyric to write, Ira whispered "The Man That Got Away." "I like," Arlen quietly replied. The lyric Gershwin set to Arlen's melody was far more mournful and searing than Mercer's: "The night is bitter, the stars have lost their glitter / The wind grows colder, and suddenly you're older, / And all because of the man that got away." Gershwin's lyric, Arlen said, "made that melody sound like the Rock of Gibraltar."

Everyone was sure that *A Star Is Born* would win several Academy Awards, including Best Actress for Garland and Best Song for Gershwin and Arlen. Surprisingly, however, the film won none. Judy Garland lost out to Grace Kelly, and the film that was to have marked her comeback virtually ended her movie career. Sammy Cahn and Jule Styne's "Three Coins in the Fountain" won the Oscar for Best Song. Arlen scornfully tacked his Oscar nomination letter on his bathroom wall. Ira Gershwin took the loss more philosophically; noting that his two other Oscar nominations, for "They Can't Take That Away from Me" and "Long Ago and Far Away," had also lost, he speculated that it must have been the word "away" in the title of all three songs and wryly advised himself to do "away with 'away'."

Midnight Sun
Lyrics by Johnny Mercer, music by Sonny Burke and Lionel Hampton

One day as Johnny Mercer was driving along a California freeway, he heard a jazz instrumental called "Midnight Sun," written nine years earlier by Sonny Burke and Lionel Hampton. Mercer pulled into a filling station, called the radio station, and said, "This is Johnny Mercer. Would you mind playing that again? I love it." On hearing it a second time, Mercer committed the melody to his uncanny memory and set to work on a lyric.

The melody posed one of the most difficult challenges to a lyricist: coming up with a triple set of "feminine rhymes," two-syllable rhymes where the accent falls on the first syllable. Yet Mercer said these were the first rhymes to pop into his mind: "Your lips were like a red and ruby *chalice* .... The clouds were like an alabaster *palace* .... Each star its own aurora bore*alis*." Despite the haphazard manner of collaboration, words and music form a seamless whole. "I know of no lyric in the world of popular music," Ken Barnes observed, "in which so many unwieldy and seemingly alien elements have been so cleverly fused to form a natural union."

THE PAJAMA GAME
Lyrics and music by Richard Adler and Jerry Ross

The Pajama Game was the breakthrough musical for two young song-writers who seemed destined to carry on the tradition of Rodgers and Hammerstein. Richard Adler had grown up in a Manhattan home filled with music by a mother who was a noted classical pianist and a father who was a music teacher. However, it was only after college, service in the Navy during World War II, and a stint as an advertising copywriter during which he was fired for writing songs on company time that Adler decided to pursue a career as a songwriter.

Jerry Ross, born Jerold Rosenberg to a poor family in the Bronx, was blessed with singing and acting talent that garnered him a place in the synagogue choir and roles in Yiddish theater. He wrote his first songs when he worked at summer camps in the Catskills, where he was encouraged by singer Eddie Fisher.

Adler and Ross met in 1951 and decided to collaborate. Unlike most songwriting teams, however, they sat down at the piano and worked on music and lyrics together. "It's impossible to say who does what and when," Adler said. "But we've set rules. If I come in with what I think is a beautiful idea, and he says, 'I don't like it,' I can scream, I can rave, but it's out." They first wrote songs for radio, and these caught the ear of Frank Loesser, who, flush with the success of *Guys and Dolls*, had created his own music company. Loesser signed them to an exclusive contract, and in 1953 Loesser's faith was rewarded when one of their songs, "Rags to Riches," became a huge success through a recording by Tony Bennett.

That song got Adler and Ross their big break on Broadway. When Loesser could not spare the time to accept George Abbott's invitation to write the score for a new musical, Abbott turned to Adler and Ross. The story about labor–management conflicts in a garment factory was called *The Pajama Game*, and the young songwriters created a superb score that generated several hit songs. The biggest was the romantic ballad "Hey There," whose melody was taken—at Frank Loesser's suggestion—from a Mozart sonata. The lyric is an innovative departure from most romantic songs in that it is not sung from lover to beloved but by an older, wiser friend ("take this advice I hand you like a brother") to someone who has just fallen hopelessly in love. In *The Pajama Game*, "Hey There" was presented even more cleverly: John Raitt first sang it into a Dictaphone and then, as he replayed the recording, sang a duet with himself.

The Pajama Game was also choreographer Bob Fosse's first Broadway show. Adler and Ross wrote several songs that played to his aggressive, sexy dance stylings. "Hernando's Hideaway" was a percussive tango, and

Damn Yankees meets *The Pajama Game*: Richard Adler (left) and Jerry Ross (right) with director George Abbott; Gwen Verdon (star of *Damn Yankees*) and John Raitt (star of *The Pajama Game*) look on from the far left. Courtesy of Photofest.

"Steam Heat" a sensual number underscored by substituting the sound of escaping steam for lyrics to create the effect of "steamy" syncopation. Both songs also went on to independent popularity, and *The Pajama Game* ran for more than a thousand performances. Leonard Bernstein was so impressed with the score that he dubbed Richard Adler and Jerry Ross "two young Loessers."

This Could Be the Start of Something Big
Lyrics and music by Steve Allen

Steve Allen was a polymath. Known mainly as an innovative TV comedian, he was also a prolific author, musician, recording artist, and songwriter. Depending on the source, he wrote more songs than anyone, anywhere from four to eight thousand of them. Once, in front of 200 people in a hotel lobby in Kalamazoo, he wrote 400 songs in a single day. Though he wrote songs in the conventional way, seated at the piano, he also wrote while he was driving, taking a shower, even sleeping. Yet of all his songs, only one became a standard.

In 1954, struggling to finish a song for a TV production called *The Bach-elor*, "I wakened from my sleep," he said, "having just dreamed the catchy melody and four or five lines of lyrics …. I went to the piano and played the tune. The basic idea of it was all there in my dream, and when I awoke, I just wrote it down and finished it off." The song was, "This Could Be the Start of Something Big," a hip treatment of love that soon became his signature song: "Or else you're alone and then you suddenly dig, / You're looking in someone's eyes, you suddenly realize that this could be the start of something big." The song is an irreverent look at the way in which love surprises even the chic and sophisticated and, when it does, links them to the rest of us: "You're lunching at Twenty-One and watching your diet, / Declining a charlotte russe, accepting a fig / When out of clear blue sky, it's suddenly gal and guy …"

Allen's lyric is less interested in evocative imagery than it is in telling a series of brief stories through familiar associations, quick moving yet easy rhythms, and an undertone of irony that sometimes breaks through: "You're watchin' the sun come up and countin' your money." However, the song is mainly notable for its effortless swinging and the understated plea-sure it takes in what it observes—not unlike Allen's humor.

1955

DAMN YANKEES
Lyrics and music by Richard Adler and Jerry Ross

After their enormous success with *The Pajama Game*, Richard Adler and Jerry Ross scored another triumph with *Damn Yankees*, a musical about an aging fan of the baseball team then known as the Washington Senators, who sells his soul to the devil to be transformed into a young player and lead the Senators to the pennant by defeating the seemingly indomitable Yankees. Gwen Verdon played the devil's seductive assistant in her first leading role on Broadway and stole the show with such steamy numbers as "Whatever Lola Wants (Lola Gets)."

Just before *Damn Yankees* opened, Adler and Ross added "A Little Brains—a Little Talent," but Gwen Verdon was thrown by the lyric. It had few end-line rhymes but subtle internal rhymes such as, "I took the *zing* out of the *King* of Siam" and "no great *art* getting the *heart* of a man." When Adler and Ross did give her end rhymes, they were bizarre, such as "Lola" and "boffola," or near-rhymes, such as "Alaska" and "Madagascar." During the first performances, the stage manager had to prompt Verdon, but once she had mastered its language, it became a showstopper.

For Verdon's duet with lead Stephen Douglass, Adler and Ross wrote a blues lament, "Two Lost Souls," in which two characters who have sold their souls to the devil pledge to stand by one another. The rhymes here are also cleverly distorted: "no rudder" / "got each udder." These grim numbers were counterbalanced by "(You Gotta Have) Heart," in which the coaches and players of the hapless Washington Senators do an old-fashioned barber-shop quartet to muster rugged optimism in the face of defeat.

With two smash musical hits on Broadway, Adler and Ross seemed destined to carry on the tradition of Rodgers and Hammerstein, but six months after the opening of *Damn Yankees,* Jerry Ross died. In an eerie portent, one newspaper mistakenly used Adler's photograph with Ross' obituary. Adler would go on to write occasional hits, such as "Everybody Loves a Lover" (1958) and even advertising jingles such as "Let Hertz Put You in the Driver's Seat," but he would never fulfill the promise he and Ross had generated with *Pajama Game* and *Damn Yankees*. Even though each man could write music and lyrics, they clearly, as "Two Lost Souls" said, needed "each udder."

Misty
Lyrics by Johnny Burke, music by Erroll Garner

Just as the collaboration between Johnny Burke and Jimmy Van Heusen was falling apart because of Burke's heavy drinking, the equally successful team of Sammy Cahn and Jule Styne dissolved when Styne left Hollywood to try his luck on Broadway. While Cahn was looking for a new partner, he received a phone call from Frank Sinatra, asking him to collaborate on a song with Van Heusen. "I said, 'No, no, he's a team with Burke.' They were joined at the hip."

Then Van Heusen called. Just as the men started working on a song at Van Heusen's home, Cahn recalled, "Suddenly the doorbell rang and Johnny Burke came in. For a lyric writer that's like being caught with somebody else's wife." After some small talk, however, it was clear to everybody that from then on Sammy Cahn and Jimmy Van Heusen would be Sinatra's "in-house" songwriters as Burke and Van Heusen had been Bing Crosby's.

Adrift on his own, Johnny Burke set lyrics to "Misty," a jazz instrumental by Erroll Garner. Burke's lyric was one of his most evocative, shifting from the extravagant "Walk my way—and a thousand violins begin to play" to the casually understated "And I find I can't tell my right foot from my left, / My hat from my glove, / I'm too misty and too much in love." Although Sammy Cahn confessed to disliking Johnny Burke personally, he felt empathy for his decline and, "personal feelings aside," could say "Johnny Burke was a real Irish poet, a real talent."

Something's Gotta Give
Lyrics and music by Johnny Mercer

When Fred Astaire came out of his brief retirement in the mid-1940s, he was paired in a string of musicals with younger and younger costars: Judy Garland in *Easter Parade* (1948); Jane Powell in *Royal Wedding* (1951); and Cyd Charisse in *The Band Wagon* (1954). In each film, the screenwriters struggled with the problem of the age discrepancy between Astaire and his leading lady. With *Daddy Long Legs*, however, in which Astaire was paired with the girlish Leslie Caron, the screenwriters threw up their hands. A script conference dissolved without a solution, and Johnny Mercer was asked if he could resolve the age disparity with a song.

That night, Mercer suddenly awoke. "I don't know what woke me up," he said. "I went to the piano in the front room, out of bed, and quietly picked it out with one finger. And I wrote it down in my little hieroglyphics, which is my way of writing music. And then finished it the next day." Whatever the inspiration, Mercer produced an extraordinary song, musically and lyrically: a romantic combat between Caron's "irresistible force" and Astaire as "an old immovable object," her "irresistible smile" and his "old implacable heart." Then, after these erudite oppositions, Mercer shifted to such vernacular phrases as "you can bet as sure as you live" and "something's gotta give." The song then returns to Astaire's debonair *"en garde,"* which is offset by the punchy colloquial idiom: "Fight, fight, fight, fight, fight it with all of your might." These shifts of tone registered Astaire's inner struggle as he succumbed to Caron's youthful charm; as he lost that dramatic battle, he won over the movie audience's misgivings.

"Something's Gotta Give" not only worked wonderfully in *Daddy Long Legs*, but it also became an enormous popular hit at a time when rock and roll was shoving songwriters like Mercer to the sidelines. The song's success prompted a note from Frank Loesser, congratulating Mercer on the song's success and adding, "It's a real pleasure to see carriage trade writers getting the hits."

1956

BELLS ARE RINGING
Lyrics by Betty Comden and Adolph Green, music by Jule Styne

In a career that lasted a half-century, lyricists Betty Comden and Adolph Green wrote only three standards, two of them in a single score.

They envisioned *Bells Are Ringing* as a vehicle for their old friend Judy Holliday. "We were in Adolph's apartment, looking in the phone book," Comden remembers, "and suddenly we saw this ad for an answering service." Holliday would play Emma Peterson, an operator for a New York City answering service who likes to meddle in people's lives. Even though she has never met him, she falls in love with one of her clients, a playwright named Jeff Moss, but decides to keep her identity from him by pretending to be a solicitous old lady. For this now dated fairy tale, Comden and Green concocted another of their affectionately satiric depictions of New York as tough and demanding but never grotesque or ugly.

Green told an interviewer they wrote the entire score in a week, with the exception of one of their major songs. Actually, they were struggling over it and, with rehearsals approaching, the score was only a third finished. Director Jerome Robbins said to Comder, Green, and composer Jule Styne, "I'm locking you in my house, then I'll know you're writing. I'll serve you lunch and you can go home at the end of each day."

Composers and lyricists for the theater often begin a song with a sense of where it comes in the story and which character will be singing it, but often their talk is about technique and content. One day, Comden and Green suggested to Styne that it would "be nice to have something in the show like an old Youmans tune, where there's two notes, but the bass keeps changing and moving under the notes, making the different harmonies and moving a melody." In response, "Jule went to the piano and started playing a simple thing—*da, dee, dah*. He asked if that was what we meant, and we said, 'Absolutely!'" They loved it but did not know what to do with it. Comden said, "It had no name, no place in the show, no words. Jule used to sing it at parties—*da da da*, over and over again."

As they worked on the book, Comden and Green wrote a scene in which the playwright realizes the telephone operator has saved his life:

> So there was a place for him to express that to her. Suddenly it came to one of us—don't ask which one—the right words for that situation and that character. And we fitted the melody Jule had been playing at parties—*da da da*—"Just in time, / I found you just in time."

Though "Just in Time" has an ebullience that suits Comden and Green, the score's other standard, "The Party's Over," is unusually poignant for them. It comes after Emma has left a party because she fears she cannot fit into Jeff's more sophisticated world. The lyricists gave Styne the title:

> He sat right down at the piano and set it. Sometimes you give a composer a lyric and he goes away with it and you hear from him

much later. But with Jule we very often work on a spontaneous combustion principle. We stand around Jule, singing it while he's writing.

Styne said, "I figured Holliday, a great star, had a Charlie Chaplinesque quality, one who could make you cry." He told Comden and Green, "Let's play on that. She'll handle the rest." The song is an exercise in truth telling. Someone whose love affair rests on deception moves from the bursting of a "pretty balloon" to the flickering of once bright candles to waking up at the end of a dream. "It's time," she says, "to wind up / The masquerade" because "the party's over."

MOST HAPPY FELLA
Lyrics and music by Frank Loesser

Despite the richness and variety of his score and the sheer quantity of his music, Frank Loesser insisted that *Most Happy Fella* was not an opera, just "a musical—with lots of music." He adapted classical forms for Broadway and, for the first time, also wrote the book for a show. Uncertain about how to proceed, he took advice from his friend, playwright Samuel Taylor: "Any time you have doubts about what you're doing, write a song." To showstoppers like "Standing on the Corner" and "Big D," he added arias, duets, trios, quartets, choral passages, even recitative, but only a mug who wrote for Broadway would have hung a sign backstage to remind the singers, "Loud is good."

Richard Rodgers once said that in opera, you sing the music, but in musicals, you sing the words. Musicals sing American English. Their joyful razzmatazz is antithetical to song so pure the language barely matters. Grand opera embraces romantic tragedy with all its heart to lift us out of this world. Musicals willingly give up heaven to embrace the world's rambunctious comedy. Their impossible trick is to make the romantic and the antic live under the same roof, with enough lyricism and laughter to keep us from noticing the occasional bit of masking tape holding it all together. It's the mongrel mix that gives a musical vitality and makes it American.

Yet on occasion, songwriters attempt a kind of opera unique to Broadway. *Most Happy Fella* keeps company, not with *La Bohème* or *La Traviata*, but rather with *Porgy and Bess* before it and *Sweeney Todd* after it. What keeps it at home in the theater rather than the opera house is the innate sense of jazz it carries in its inner ear, its reliance on the lyrics to propel the action, and its use of singing styles more committed to conveying the words than making beautiful sounds for their own sake—just the sort of aestheticism Loesser detested.

Adapted from Sidney Howard's 1924 play, *They Knew What They Wanted, Most Happy Fella* tells the story of a wealthy, middle-aged Napa Valley wine grower named Tony, who falls in love with Amy, a pretty young San Francisco waitress whom he calls Rosabella. He writes to propose marriage to his "mail-order bride," but, fearing she will reject him, he encloses a photograph of his foreman, Joe. After a passionate liaison with Joe, Amy finds herself pregnant, but Tony overcomes his hurt and anger to embrace her and the unborn child.

Set against this nearly tragic story is the comic love affair between Cleo, an irreverent waitress, and a meek hired hand named Herman. Before Cleo arrives, Herman and three of his pals hang out in town on a Saturday night. Somebody says that Tony should be happy now that he has Rosabella. They, on the other hand, have nothing to do but watch the pretty girls walk by. Soon they begin to sing, "Standing on the corner, watching all the girls go by."

Like so many of Loesser's lyrics, it demonstrates his mastery of colloquial English set to the not-quite-heard rhythms of American forms like ragtime, jazz, and country. The American vernacular swings and shucks, and even a white guy like Loesser had learned to make it look easy: "Brother, you can't go to jail for what you're thinking or for the 'Woo!' look in your eye." To a melody that bounces along like a jazzy barbershop quartet, Loesser writes a lyric that feels like especially clever, inventive talk that reflects the young men's combination of braggadocio and regret: "I'm the cat that got the cream, haven't got a girl but I can dream." The way in which the lines' crisp wit and alliterative snap immediately create character ensures that *Most Happy Fella* will always have a place on Broadway.

MY FAIR LADY
Lyrics by Alan Jay Lerner, music by Frederick Loewe

A musical that celebrates the glories of the English language was initiated by a man who could barely speak it. Romanian-born film producer Gabriel Pascal invited Alan Jay Lerner to lunch one day in Hollywood and said, in a dialect Lerner described as bereft of "any known place of national origin," "I want to make musical of *Pygmalion*." Lerner wondered how anyone could imagine making a musical out of George Bernard Shaw's play about a misogynistic linguist who transforms a Cockney flower girl into a fashionable society lady simply by teaching her to speak with an upper-class accent. He was also curious about how Pascal had gotten the rights to the play because it was well known how stubborn Shaw was about releasing his works.

From left to right, Robert Coote as Col. Pickering, Julie Andrews as Eliza Doolittle, and Rex Harrison as Henry Higgins celebrate when Eliza finally manages to say "the rain in Spain" in *My Fair Lady*. Courtesy of Photofest.

Pascal told Lerner he had gone to Shaw's home and when the maid asked who had sent him, he replied, "Fate sent me." Shaw overheard the remark and asked Pascal who he was. When Pascal said he was a motion picture producer, Shaw asked him how much money he had. "Twelve shillings," answered Pascal, pulling the coins from his pocket. Shaw invited him in, saying "You're the first honest film producer I have met." When Pascal left, he had exclusive rights to three of Shaw's plays.

What Pascal did not tell Lerner was that he had unsuccessfully tried to get several other songwriters, including Rodgers and Hammerstein and Cole Porter, to undertake the project. When Lerner and Loewe read the play, they saw the same insurmountable problems that had led others to turn it down: no love interest; no subplot built around a secondary comic couple; no group of characters who could serve as a chorus—it was *all* talk, talk, talk. Lerner and Loewe, like all the other songwriters Pascal had approached, said no.

Lerner's mind returned to *Pygmalion* when news came of Gabriel Pascal's death. Admittedly feeling ghoulish, he proposed to Loewe that they pursue it. Traveling to London, they visited Covent Garden in the early morning hours when the flower and vegetable sellers were setting up shop. "Fritz absorbed some of the sounds of the vendors," notes Stephen Citron, "while

Alan expanded his feeling for their special language. He was fascinated by the Cockney way of inserting expletives within words—'unbloodyl-ikely' was eventually transformed into 'absobloomin'-lutely.'" Observing costermongers huddled around a fire, Lerner came up with "Wouldn't It Be Loverly?" and Loewe wrote the melody that afternoon. Loewe also went to the races at Ascot, where he captured the sense of upper-crust propriety in "The Ascot Gavotte." Before leaving London, they cast Stanley Hollo-way as Eliza's father to give the show some much needed comic relief in such numbers as "With a Little Bit of Luck" and "Get Me to the Church on Time."

During their stay, Lerner and Loewe approached several British actors, from Noël Coward to John Gielgud, finally settling on Rex Harrison. Because Harrison could not sing, Loewe explained, "an entire new way of presenting numbers had to be invented. It is what is called in German *sprechtgesang*." When Harrison talk–sang his way through such witty pat-ter songs as "Why Can't the English (Learn to Speak)?" "I'm an Ordinary Man," "You Did It," and "A Hymn to Him," it defined a new kind of male lead in a musical.

Lerner's initial lyric for the first song threw Harrison because he felt it made him sound like "an inferior Noël Coward" to sing such patter as "Why can't the English teach their children how to speak? / In Nor-way there are legions of literate Norwegians." Lerner wisely changed it to the simpler, "Norwegians learn Norwegian / The Greeks are taught their Greek." The inspiration for "A Hymn to Him" (originally entitled "Why Can't a Woman Be More like a Man?") came as Lerner and Harrison were walking down New York's Fifth Avenue commiserating with each other about how many women they had married and then divorced. Suddenly, Harrison stopped and in a loud voice said, "Alan! Wouldn't it be wonderful if we were homosexuals?"

For Eliza Doolite, Lerner and Loewe first wanted Mary Martin, even though she was forty-two years old. After listening in silence to their songs, Martin declined the part, and her husband later told Lerner and Loewe that she had said, "Those dear boys have lost their talent." Lerner and Loewe then auditioned a young British singer named Julie Andrews, whose voice covered four octaves. Her songs had an equally extensive emotional range, from the ecstatic "I Could Have Danced All Night" through the vengeful "Just You Wait, ('Enry 'Iggins)" to the sarcastic "Without You." Director Moss Hart found that "she was charming, but it seemed to me she didn't have a clue about playing Eliza." Dismissing the company, he sat with her on the stage for long hours over several days, going over every line in her script, determined, as he put it, to "*paste* the part on her." "He bullied and pleaded, coaxed and cajoled," Andrews recalled. "He made me *be* Eliza …. Talk about Pygmalion and Galatea; Moss was my Svengali!"

The biggest hit to emerge from *My Fair Lady*, however, was not one of the songs written for Harrison or Andrews; it was "On the Street Where You Live," sung by Eliza's upper-class suitor Freddy and nearly cut from the show several times by Loewe, who always thought it a poor song.

The Edwardian setting of the show provided Loewe with the chance to write in a variety of musical styles, and Shaw's theme that dialects enforce class barriers gave Lerner the opportunity to write about a subject every lyricist loves: language. The witty playfulness of such lines as "I'd prefer a new edition of the Spanish Inquisition / Than to ever let a woman in my life" and Eliza's "Words—words—words—I'm so sick of words" grow out of the characters' preoccupation with language.

In Shaw's play, there is a brief scene in which Higgins helps Eliza with her pronunciation of the alphabet. Lerner and Loewe agreed this should be expanded into a climactic moment when, after weeks of coaching, Eliza finally masters the upper-class dialect. Lerner suggested the title, "The Rain in Spain," because Eliza has the greatest difficulty with the vowel "A." "Good," Loewe said, "I'll write a tango." The two men put the song together in ten minutes. The inane title led to one of the most moving moments in musical theater. "It is brought about," as Stephen Citron observes, "not by Higgins' slave-driving pigheadedness, but by his kindness. At last Eliza sees he has a heart, and she wants to please him." Inspired by that first show of kindness and Higgins' love of "the majesty and grandeur of the English language," Eliza finally succeeds.

The climax of the second act comes with "I've Grown Accustomed to Her Face," Higgins' belated and understated realization that he has fallen in love with Eliza. Loewe wrote an abbreviated twenty-bar chorus that followed none of the standard popular song formats but instead flowed along more like talk than song. "He speaks while the music just attempts to underpaint the scene," said Loewe, "and then drifts back to the rhythm with the lyrics." Lerner's lyrics are subtly moving as Higgins, the master of language, bursts out with "Damn! Damn! Damn! Damn!" and then haltingly admits that Eliza's "smiles, her frowns, her ups, her downs / Are second nature to me now, / Like breathing out and breathing in."

My Fair Lady overwhelmed its opening night audience, but Lerner was always haunted by his mother's question after the curtain rang down, "What, my son, can you ever do to top this?"

1957

THE MUSIC MAN
Lyrics and music by Meredith Willson

Meredith Willson was an entertaining raconteur with a great supply of stories about growing up in Mason City, Iowa, in the early years of the twentieth century. He had never thought about writing a Broadway musical until one day in 1949 when Frank Loesser reacted to one of his reminiscences, "Why don't you write a musical about it!" The voluble Loesser was soon pacing back and forth as he envisioned a new show somewhere between *Oklahoma!* and *Our Town*:

> Maybe you can start with the fire chief. Let's make him the leader of the town band. Maybe *you* can play the fire chief. And maybe instead of a pit orchestra, you can have a real brass band in the pit. And you're the leader of the band. You could also be sort of a narrator and talk directly to the people in the audience. That way you could tell everybody about your town. It would be real Americana!

The musical that Willson finally completed eight years later bore little resemblance to Loesser's spontaneous outburst, although certainly the idea of combining Willson's boyhood memories with a celebration of "real Americana" came from Loesser. Unlike the musical comedies of the 1920s and 1930s, the more recent musicals of Rodgers and Hammerstein usually preferred remembrance to the up-to-date, sincerity to wit, and innocence to worldliness.

Willson did not think the show would be all that hard to write. He knew from the start that he wanted to capture the small Midwestern town of his boyhood: "Innocent, that was the adjective for Iowa. I didn't have to make anything up for *The Music Man*. All I had to do was remember." Only after many different versions, however, did he finally hit upon Harold Hill, the lovable scoundrel reminiscent of the traveling salesmen who had passed through Mason City long ago. Just before the show opened, Willson wrote that "Hill … is so many people that I remember different ones every time I see the show."

Willson also thought he could build the score from songs he had already written but never published. Before he finished, though, he had written thirty-two drafts, replaced all the songs he had previously written, and, in an admission of his inability to get the book right, hired playwright Franklin Lacey to help shape it. Then he had trouble finding a producer. Few were interested in a Broadway show about sweet nostalgia. Once Kermit Bloomgarten agreed to produce it (writing Willson,

Barbara Cook as Marion Paroo and Robert Preston as Harold Hill in *The Music Man.* Courtesy of Photofest.

"Meredith, may I have the privilege of producing your beautiful play?"), they had the same problem finding a leading man. Danny Kaye, Phil Harris, Dan Dailey, and Gene Kelly all turned them down. Finally, the director and music director urged them to hire Robert Preston, who had spent most of his career playing bad guys in Westerns.

The Music Man's eclectic score includes ragtime, barbershop quartets, ballads, vaudeville turns, and, of course, marches: the song types that characterized American popular music before World War I. What is distinctive about it is Willson's reliance on unusual rhythms to take the place of rhyming, as in much of "Rock Island," "Iowa Stubborn," and "Ya Got Trouble." Even the score's major love ballad, "Till There Was You," relies primarily on repetition. Its only significant rhyme spaces its three appearances through the three 'A' choruses: "ringing" in the first rhymes with "winging" in the second and "singing" in the last.

"Rock Island," the opening number performed within the confines of a single railroad car filled with traveling salesmen, sets their alliterative, repetitive conversation to the rhythms of the train: "Cash for the noggins and the piggins and the frickins / Cash for the hogshead cask and demijohn …." Because Preston had a small voice with a narrow range, his great secular sermon, "Ya Got Trouble," exploited his uniquely dynamic approach to patter and used an occasional rhyme only to underscore the problem the song identifies ("Ya got trouble, right here in River City! With a capital 'T' / And that rhymes with 'P' and that stands for Pool!").

Willson also plays off songs against one another. He borrows the barbershop classic, "Goodnight Ladies" (originally entitled "Farewell Ladies," 1843) for a Loesser-like contrapuntal duet with the comic "Pick a Little, Talk a Little." In "Piano Lesson," he uses the musical scale to accompany an unrhymed conversation in song between Marian Paroo and her mother as Marian gives a lesson to a young girl. Finally, "Goodnight, My Someone" and "Seventy-Six Trombones," Paroo and Hill's respective signature songs, have the identical melody, changed by tempo and rhythm from a wistful song of longing into a rousing Sousaesque march.

WEST SIDE STORY
Lyrics by Stephen Sondheim, music by Leonard Bernstein

In 1949, Montgomery Clift asked choreographer Jerome Robbins' advice about acting in a production of Shakespeare's *Romeo and Juliet* with a contemporary setting. The question spurred the choreographer to sketch an idea for a musical called *East Side Story*, which translated Shakespeare's feuding Montagues and Capulets into a star-crossed romance between Jewish and Catholic lovers on New York's Lower East Side. He took the idea to Leonard Bernstein, who was hoping to compose a genuinely American opera, and Bernstein, in turn, roughed out several songs, then presented them to playwright Arthur Laurents. At first, Laurents dismissed *East Side Story* as an attempt to set *Abie's Irish Rose*, the mawkish 1920s drama of romance between a Jewish boy and an Irish girl, to music. Because Robbins, Bernstein, and Laurents were all busy with other projects, they put *East Side Story* on hold.

A few years later, talking with Laurents in Los Angeles, Bernstein noticed a newspaper headline about gang warfare between Hispanics and whites. The two men wondered if the musical could be set in Los Angeles and shifted from a religious to a racial conflict; after more reflection, they decided to set it back in New York but on the West Side, where Puerto Ricans and Italians were in combat. It was the era of rock 'n' roll and juvenile delinquency, and a musical about gang warfare promised to catch the public's attention. After first changing the show's title to *Gangway*, the collaborators finally settled on *West Side Story*.

Bernstein wanted to write music and lyrics, but as he worked on the score, he found that its aggressive, violent rhythms called for more and more dancing—more than in any previous Broadway musical. For help

Stephen Sondheim and Leonard Bernstein, Courtesy of Photofest.

with the lyrics, Bernstein turned to young Stephen Sondheim, a protégé of Oscar Hammerstein. Sondheim had grown up as Hammerstein's neighbor and, after taking a musical he had written for his high school to the older lyricist (clearly expecting Hammerstein to offer to produce it on Broadway), the fifteen-year-old received a rigorous and sobering lesson in writing for the theater.

When he was offered the chance to help Bernstein write lyrics for *West Side Story*, Sondheim at first demurred. He regarded himself primarily as a composer, but Bernstein only offered him the job of "co-lyricist." Sondheim, moreover, doubted his ability to write about gangs and slum life. "I can't do this show," he told Hammerstein. "I've never been that poor and I've never even *known* a Puerto Rican." However, Hammerstein persuaded him that he should not pass up the chance to work with such talents as Robbins, Laurents, and Bernstein.

Bernstein and Sondheim understood music as well as lyrics, which, in Bernstein's words, "made the collaboration a joy. It was like writing with an alter ego. We also found we shared a love for words and word games and puzzles, to say nothing of anagrams." Despite their verbal camaraderie, Sondheim felt that his job was to "bring the language down to the level of real simplicity. The whole piece trembles on the brink of self-conscious pretentiousness," he said, "and Lenny's idea of poetry was much more purple than mine."

When Bernstein gave Sondheim the song "Maria," which the composer had drafted back in 1949, Sondheim objected to its soaring sentiments and such clichéd rhymes as "Lips like mine" and "divine." Sondheim reasoned that because the song was the hero's effusion over a girl he has just met, it should be a simple celebration of the sound of her name: "the most beautiful sound I ever heard." When Sondheim demonstrated "Maria" for the Hammersteins, Dorothy Hammerstein said, "He sat down at a piano in our living room and sang, 'Maria, I just met a girl named Maria / And suddenly that name will never be the same to me.' I stood in the doorway listening and I started to cry. I thought, 'He's grown up. He's growing up.'"

For the musical's version of the great balcony scene from *Romeo and Juliet*, which was staged on a dreary tenement fire escape, Bernstein had originally planned to use the song, "Somewhere." When Oscar Hammerstein dropped in on a rehearsal, however, he suggested that they needed an entirely new song that would capture the emotion of the young urban lovers. Bernstein's music for the new song soared, Sondheim still kept the lyric in character, having the lovers revel in their romantic union with the straightforward exultation of "Tonight, Tonight."

Sondheim's emphasis on realism and character in lyrics ran up against 1950s mores in songs written for the gangs to sing, as in "Jet Song," where gang members pledge their support for each other even when "the spit hits the fan." In "Gee, Officer Krupke," Sondheim originally had the youths taunt the local cop with "Gee, Officer Krupke, fuck you." When one of the show's producers blanched, Bernstein suggested "Krup you!" As Sondheim pushed his colloquial vocabulary into the language of the streets, however, even Hammerstein became critical. "This show changed his attitude toward me," Sondheim said. "It was like seeing a bird fly for the first time. He was no longer protective."

Sondheim's only lapse into the poetical came in "I Feel Pretty," where he wanted to show that he could create clever internal rhymes: "It's a*larming* how c*harming* I feel." Sheldon Harnick pointed out that such clever patter might suit a drawing room musical by Noël Coward, but it did not fit the character of a Puerto Rican girl from the tenements. Sondheim revised the lyric to make it simpler, but Bernstein, Laurents, and Robbins refused to let him change it. "So there it is," Sondheim said, "embarrassing me every time it is sung."

After *West Side Story* proved to be a smashing success, Bernstein told Sondheim, "Look, the lyrics are yours" and generously offered to give Sondheim sole credit as lyricist. The composer even went so far as to say he would readjust the royalty arrangement whereby Bernstein, as composer and co-lyricist, received 3 percent of the royalties, and Sondheim, as co-lyricist, received only 1 percent. "Oh, don't bother about that," the young Sondheim responded. "After all, it's only the credit that matters." In later years, Sondheim would ruefully reflect, "I'm sorry I opened my mouth."

1958

GIGI
Lyrics by Alan Jay Lerner, music by Frederick Loewe

After the astounding success of *My Fair Lady* in 1956, composer Fritz Loewe, as biographer Stephen Citron put it, "wanted to sit back and enjoy *dolce far niente*." However, lyricist Alan Jay Lerner wanted to plunge into another project and cabled Loewe, who was gambling at Cannes, that they should do a movie musical based on *Gone with the Wind*. Loewe, who scorned films and insisted upon writing only for the stage, dictated a cable back in his Viennese accent: "*Vind* not funny. Love, Fritz."

When MGM offered to mount a lavish film musical based on *Gigi*, Colette's 1944 novel about a young girl who is trained to be a courtesan, Lerner again proposed a collaboration with Loewe and again was rebuffed, but when Loewe later read Lerner's script, he overcame his antipathy to writing for film—particularly because Lerner said they would write the score in Paris. The film featured an aging but still dashing Maurice Chevalier, who, at seventy-two, agreed to do the role, saying, "I'm too old for women, too old for that extra glass of wine, too old for sports. All I have left is the audience."

For Chevalier, they wrote "I'm Glad I'm Not Young Anymore," in which a man of the world reflects upon the advantages of growing old; "Thank Heaven for Little Girls," in which he rides the fine line between enchantment and lechery as he contemplates nubile young ladies; and "I Remember It Well," an utterly charming duet in which his former lover, Hermione Gingold, has to correct his memories until, his confidence collapsing, he abjectly asks, "Am I growing old?" and she replies, "Oh, no. Not you!"

Lerner, who was meticulous about his lyrics, at one point held up production for nine days until he came up with the rhyme "She's so oo-lah-lah / So *untrue* lah-la" to complete "She's Not Thinking of Me." Producer Arthur Freed, who had put his job at MGM on the line by agreeing to shoot much of the film on location in Paris, was so frustrated by the delay that he ordered musical director Andre Previn to break into Lerner's hotel room and filch the lyric. Previn refused but told Lerner about Freed's stratagem, and the song was expeditiously completed.

Loewe, by contrast, always forgave Lerner's dilatory efforts to fit syllables to the notes he had written. "The poor little boy," he would say, "I have knocked him up," meaning that his music had impregnated the lyricist with verbal ideas that would take time to give birth, while the composer could spend more time cavorting and gambling in Paris. After a full evening of partying, he would sometimes look in on Lerner who, in the wee small hours of the morning, would still be struggling with lyrics. The sight always pleased the composer because he knew he could continue to dally while his collaborator slaved away.

Lerner always said his favorite of all his lyrics was the title song for *Gigi*. He and Loewe wrote it for Louis Jordan as a wealthy but bored young Parisian who thinks of Gigi, played by Leslie Caron, as a charming child. "Gigi" portrays his dramatic realization that this matured child has become so attractive that he wants her not as the courtesan she has been groomed to be but for his wife. From denouncing his infatuation for "a child! A silly child," he comes to question, "When did your sparkle turn to fire" and "your warmth become desire?" then confesses that he has been "too blind" to realize that Gigi has "been growing up before my eyes."

GYPSY
Lyrics by Stephen Sondheim, music by Jule Styne

After producer David Merrick read Gypsy Rose Lee's best-selling memoir, he approached playwright Arthur Laurents and director–choreographer Jerome Robbins, who had had such success with *West Side Story*. Laurents was reluctant at first to write a musical about a burlesque star, but eventually saw that a story could focus on the character of Rose, Lee's domineering and indomitable stage mother. After Irving Berlin and Cole Porter turned down the chance to write the score, Robbins and Laurents agreed that Stephen Sondheim, who had written lyrics for *West Side Story*, should be given his long-sought chance to write both lyrics and music.

When they offered the lead to Ethel Merman, however, she demanded that Sondheim, who had never written music for a Broadway show, be teamed with a more seasoned composer. "After Ethel put the kibosh on my doing it," Sondheim recalled, "I decided to bow out as lyricist." However, he first sought the advice of Oscar Hammerstein. "I said, 'If I do this, I'm going to be trapped as a lyricist,' and Oscar said, 'It's only six months out of your life.' And, you know, he was right."

Robbins suggested they get Jule Styne, but Laurents was skeptical. "To my mind," he said, "musicals were beginning to take a different turn in the fifties. I knew Jule wrote great 'tunes' but this was a dramatic piece and I didn't know that he was capable of turning out a dramatic score."

However, Styne had left a flourishing career in Hollywood turning out hits with Sammy Cahn because he wanted to write dramatic scores on Broadway. "When you can give characterization," Styne said, "you are a dramatist."

As Laurents listened to Styne play songs from *Bells Are Ringing*, he was deeply moved. "The music had more guts than I thought possible. Listening to it, I realized that this man had a far greater range than I had thought. I also believe that when you work with better people, you become better. So I then readily accepted Jule as the composer." Styne regarded *Gypsy* as

> ... the biggest kind of landmark that ever was for me. I became the superb dramatist out of that because, God, I mean, to me that was like *Traviata*—that first act, writing a thing like "Everything's Coming Up Roses," which was so macabre, with this child thing, and the woman crying, and all that. It was just unbelievable.

For Ethel Merman, too, *Gypsy* offered an opportunity to give a truly dramatic performance. When Laurents offered her the role of Rose, he said, "I want to do a show, but I don't want it to be the usual Ethel Merman show."

"Neither do I," she said. "I want to act."

"How far are you willing to go?" he asked.

"As far as you want me," she told him. "Nobody's ever given me the chance before."

When Merman heard Sondheim and Styne play their score, she burst into tears: "Jule had written some big hits, but these were dramatic songs with dimension. He was reaching out, stretching himself just as I wanted to do. I had eight songs. Not one was included to give me a show-stopper. Not one was intended to have a sock ending."

She urged Sondheim and Styne to play their score for Cole Porter, who, after suffering from a crippling horseback riding accident twenty years earlier, had finally had to have one of his legs amputated. It was Sondheim's first meeting with a man he had considered a pioneer in writing complex songs that eschewed the traditional pop format of a thirty-two-bar chorus and a lyric that tells a simple, straightforward story. As he and Styne entered Porter's apartment at the Waldorf Towers, however, Sondheim was appalled to see the songwriter "carried in like a sack of potatoes by a burly manservant." However, when Sondheim and Styne played their score, Porter rallied, tapping a spoon as his way of applause. In particular, Sondheim recalled how Porter relished "Together": "No fits, no fights, no feuds and no egos / *Amigos!*":

> He chortled, and I knew I got him. He didn't see the last rhyme coming. It was a real Cole Porter rhyme—he inserts foreign words

into lyrics—an homage to Cole Porter without meaning to be. He got such a moan of pleasure, it was absolutely sexual. It was great! It was such a great moment!

Still, there were conflicts between Sondheim and Styne over the old and the new ways of writing musicals. Styne was appalled when Sondheim wrote the line, "Funny, I'm a woman with children" in "Small World." "Well!" he shouted, "that means Sinatra can't sing the song." Sondheim argued that the line had to suit the scene: "Here's this lady, she's trying to con the guy into handling her vaudeville act—it's a con song. It's got to be terribly personalized." Although Sondheim agreed to generalize the lyric for the printed sheet music so male and female singers could record it, he was adamant about keeping the line in the show.

Even Ethel Merman, proud as she was of her dramatic songs in *Gypsy*, relied on her old show business instincts for her final number, "Rose's Turn," in which, after she thinks her successful daughter and the rest of the cast have left the theater, she takes the bare stage to herself and wrenchingly demands to know why she never had the limelight. The number was to be dramatically ironic by letting the audience see that her daughter was still in the theater, witnessing her mother's powerful yet pathetic outpouring. "Look, I have to have a finish for this," Merman demanded. "I've worked too hard. I demand I have a finish—for me, for me, for MEEEE! Vooom! Then let her come in." As Martin Gottfried notes:

> When Hammerstein saw the show in Philadelphia, he advised Sondheim and Laurents that they had to put a "button" on the number, a rousing ending to let the audience stand up and cheer. The writers were appalled by the suggestion that they make their distraught character's enraged soliloquy into a musical comedy "star turn." Sondheim told Hammerstein, "That seems dishonest to me." "Yes, it's dishonest," Hammerstein replied, "but there's also *theatrical* honesty and an audience out there."

Satin Doll
Lyrics by Johnny Mercer, music by Billy Strayhorn and Duke Ellington

According to Mercer Ellington, his father wrote "Satin Doll" for Bea "Evie" Ellis, his longtime mistress, whom he was always addressing as "'Dearest Doll,' 'Darling Doll,' and so on." Although Evie may have been the inspiration for the song, a lot of the composing was done by Billy Strayhorn, as was often the case in Ellington's popular songs. They wrote the music in 1953, when Ellington signed with Capitol Records, and in 1958, Capitol asked Johnny Mercer to set lyrics to "Satin Doll."

Mercer had long since stepped down as cofounder and first president, but he still maintained his affiliation with the company. For "Satin Doll," he wrote one of his cleverest lyrics, celebrating the charms of a Latin-speaking beauty who "digs me" "over her shoulder" and sports a "cigarette holder" that "wigs me." The portrait is a far cry from Ellington's Evie, who was gullible enough to fall for his rebuff of her demands that they marry by pointing out that if he divorced his first wife, alimony payments would severely reduce their income.

Ellington also relied upon Evie when his numerous affairs proved unmanageable; he was sometimes juggling three or four women at a time. As the women called demanding his attentions, he would put Evie on the phone, and "Thunderbird," as he called her, would set the callers straight. Just as he used Evie to extricate himself from affairs, Ellington would use "Satin Doll" to initiate or maintain them. Before his orchestra performed it, Ellington would say, "The next song is dedicated to the most beautiful lady here. We will not point her out because we do not want her to feel conspicuous. We will just let her sit there and continue to feel guilty."

According to lyricist Don George, only one time was Ellington so taken with a beautiful woman in the audience that he dedicated "Satin Doll" directly to her. George recalled:

> She took his breath away. He tried all his ploys, but she ignored it. He sent champagne to her table, but she didn't drink it. He asked the management who she was, but no one knew. They had never seen her before. Duke couldn't get to first base with her, yet she appeared every night, sitting alone at the same table, listening to the band, watching him.

Then on his closing night, the lady stopped him before he took the stage and asked him what hotel he was staying at, offering to meet him there later. It was at that point that Ellington turned to an old friend named Rubberlegs. Rubberlegs stood over six-feet tall, had rugged good looks, and boasted a deep bass voice; however, he was gay, so Ellington gave him a key to his hotel room and said, "Rub, take this lady to my hotel … order some champagne and caviar … keep her company till I get there."

After playing what George recalls was a "short show," Ellington rushed back to his hotel room only to find Rubberlegs and the lady of his illusions in *flagrante delictu*. "The champagne bottle was empty, the caviar was gone. Dismayed, Duke looked at Rubberlegs and exclaimed, 'My God, and all these years I've respected you as a woman. Why, you're nothing but a counterfeit.'"

Witchcraft
Lyrics by Carolyn Leigh, music by Cy Coleman

During the days when early rock 'n' roll was unmaking careers among songwriters and performers over the age of thirty, lyricist Carolyn Leigh bumped into composer Cy Coleman. They knew each other slightly and, as they chatted, Coleman asked if she would be interested in writing with him sometime. She said, "What about right now?" Two days later, they had finished their first song, "Witchcraft," and began an often fractious collaboration that produced two Broadway musicals and some of the biggest nonrock hits of the late 1950s and early 1960s: "Firefly," "Rules of the Road," and "The Best Is Yet to Come," among others. Coleman told an interviewer, "Carolyn and I were the Gilbert and Sullivan of the day. We fought constantly." Much of the friction came from Coleman's insistence on playing jazz in clubs around the country; Leigh wanted him to remain in New York to work on scores for Broadway musicals. "When you can play piano, and I say this unabashedly, as well as I do," Coleman told an interviewer shortly before his death in 2004, "you don't like for people not to be able to hear you."

Whatever is edgy and insinuating about Coleman's music finds a tangy, suggestive match in Leigh's words, from the "fingers in my hair" and the "sly come-hither stare that strips my conscience bare" in "Witchcraft," to the knowingly sexy pun that alludes to the Garden of Eden—"Out of the tree of life I just picked me a plum"—in "The Best Is Yet to Come." Both songs end with erotic promises kept. In "Witchcraft," the tight, contained short "i" sound runs through the song like a nibbled earlobe, culminating in, "My heart says 'Yes, indeed' in me / Proceed with what you're leadin' me to." Similarly, "The Best Is Yet to Come" offers a promise in the form of a warning: "Wait till the warm-up's underway / Wait till our lips have met." In these two songs, Coleman and Leigh were unmistakably and unabashedly writing about sex.

1959

High Hopes
Lyrics by Sammy Cahn, music by Jimmy Van Heusen

Sammy Cahn and Jimmy Van Heusen wrote songs for Frank Sinatra and then partied with him around the clock. "I hung around Frank in the

Jimmy Van Heusen and Sammy Cahn. Courtesy of Photofest.

afternoon," Cahn said, "Van Heusen was the night shift!" When they were working on the film *A Hole in the Head*, Van Heusen told Cahn, "Frank thinks we ought to have a song for the young boy, the kid in the picture who plays his son." Cahn said he had been thinking about a title phrase, "High Hopes," and already had come up with the line "high apple-pie-in-the-sky hopes."

The first melody Van Heusen concocted was very martial. "I didn't like it," Cahn said, "and he knew right away it wasn't good, so he said, 'Let me try again,' and he came back the next day with a spiritual." Cahn did not like that melody either, but he had learned that in artistic collaboration, "You never say 'I don't like that.' There's a gentler, kinder, more graceful way." Cahn took the diplomatic approach of blaming himself as the lyricist. "We're writing this song from the wrong angle," he said. "Instead of writing the song from the angle of human beings, why don't we try it from the angle of animals?" As soon as he made that suggestion, Cahn said, "I wanted to tear out my tongue," because he realized that Van Heusen, with lyricist Johnny Burke, had written one of the greatest "animal" songs of all time in "Swinging on a Star," with its allusions to mules and pigs and monkeys.

Before Van Heusen could take offense, Cahn said, "Forget that—not animals" and looking down at the studio floor he noticed ants crawling around. "'Insects!' I said." Improvising before the befuddled composer, Cahn said, "Just what makes the little old ant think he'll move a rubber tree plant?" The line made no sense because, as Cahn admitted, an ant *can't* move a rubber tree plant, but it suggested that "an ant has a sense of fulfillment when it moves from one place to another" and the syllables of the phrase perfectly suited the cadence of Van Heusen's melody. "The minute you say that, it writes itself," Cahn marveled. "The song is home and free, and you just happen to be lucky to be there getting it written."

THE SOUND OF MUSIC
Lyrics by Oscar Hammerstein, music by Richard Rodgers

Mary Martin, who had played the lead in *South Pacific* in 1949, resented the fact that in 1958 Rodgers and Hammerstein chose the younger Mitzi Gaynor for the film version of the show. Close-ups make movies a much crueler medium for aging performers than the stage is, but that fact worked in Martin's favor a few years later when she saw a role for herself in a stage version of a German movie about the Trapp family of folk singers who fled Austria after the Nazi invasion. She thought a musical could be created with her in the role of Maria, the young, rebellious nun hired to tutor the children, who then falls in love with their autocratic father. The play would feature folk songs the Trapps had sung, but she asked Rodgers and Hammerstein if they could write one additional song for the production.

Rodgers and Hammerstein were concerned that, after all they had done to create a genuinely American form of musical drama, they were considering a sentimental story set smack in the heart of operetta land. "But the truth is that almost everything in it was based on fact," Rodgers said. "No incidents were dragged in to tug at the heart strings." "No one is comfortable with an excess of hearts and flowers, but there is no valid reason for hiding valid emotion," they reasoned. "Anyone who can't, on occasion, be sentimental about children, home or nature is sadly maladjusted." After such reflections, they offered to write a full score if Martin would wait until the collaborators had completed their current show, *Flower Drum Song*.

"We'll wait," Martin said.

Martin had already commissioned playwrights Howard Lindsay and Russel Crouse to write the libretto; Hammerstein, aged sixty-four and in failing health, was not up to his usual duties as lyricist and librettist. Just before rehearsals began, he underwent an operation for an ulcer, but doctors discovered he had terminal cancer. They told his family and Rodgers, but withheld the knowledge from Hammerstein.

Rodgers and Hammerstein had completed most of what would be their last score: the rousing title song; "Do-Re-Mi," in which Martin teaches music to the children by rhyming the notes of the scale with such homophones as "Doe—a deer, a female deer" (except for "La," which Hammerstein simply dubbed "A note to follow Sol"); a catalogue song of childhood images ("raindrops on roses and whiskers on kittens") in "My Favorite Things"; the folksy "Lonely Goatherd"; and "Climb Ev'ry Mountain," which the family sings as they cross the Alps to escape the Nazis (even though the real Trapp family left Austria by train).

Hammerstein was not well enough to travel to New Haven for the first tryout performance, but he got as far as Boston, where he completed "Edelweiss," Baron Von Trapp's nostalgic farewell to his homeland. It was the last song he would ever write. Theodore Bikel, who played the baron, recounted the tale of an autograph seeker who stopped him at the stage door to say, "I love that 'Edelweiss'" and then added, with sublime assurance, "of course, I have known it a long time, but only in German."

As his condition worsened, Hammerstein confronted his doctors and demanded to know the truth. When he was told he could undergo another excruciating operation, try equally painful radiation treatments, or simply retire to his Pennsylvania farm and wait for death to come, he made a lunch date with Rodgers. As he broke what he thought was news to his longtime collaborator, he said he had decided to take the third option and advised Rodgers to seek out a younger partner. As the two men were deep in discussion, another autograph seeker came to their table. "He could not help observing," Meryl Secrest notes, "that here were two men at the top of their profession who should not have a care in the world. 'I was just wondering what could possibly make you both look so sad.'"

1960 – 1969

1960

CAMELOT

Lyrics by Alan Jay Lerner, music by Frederick Loewe

Like many great songwriting teams, Alan Jay Lerner and Frederick Loewe complemented one another artistically but were ill matched personally. "Fritz" Loewe was a hedonist who loved wine, women, and gambling. Lerner polished his lyrics obsessively, insisted upon writing the books for his musicals, and, once his current show was complete, wanted to launch a new venture immediately.

During *My Fair Lady*, Lerner and director Moss Hart, who was as driven as Lerner, put such pressure on Loewe that the composer suffered a massive heart attack. A heart attack, Loewe observed, can be a salutary event if you survive it, and afterward he gave up his all-night bouts of drinking. Nevertheless, Loewe succumbed to Lerner and Hart's plea that they take on a new project, even though he thought a musical based on T. H. White's sprawling novels about King Arthur was doomed. "Who wants to see a musical about a cuckold?" he snapped, alluding to Guinevere's affair with Lancelot and Arthur's forgiveness of his wife and friend as he dies on the battlefield. When Lerner and Hart argued that the English and Americans had loved the story of King Arthur for centuries, Loewe sniffed, with Viennese hauteur, "That's because you are all such children."

Nevertheless, Loewe relished the chance to write quasimedieval music for *Camelot* and crafted what Stephen Citron considers his most "ambitious" score, "almost operatic in its introduction of *leitmotifs*." Lerner matched those melodies with lyrics that sparkled with wordplay. In "I Wonder What the King Is Doing Tonight," Arthur confesses his nervousness about marrying a bride he has never met. Asking whether a king "who fought a dragon, / Whacked him in half and fixed his wagon" faces marriage in "terror and stress," he answers, "Yes!" Guinevere charmingly displays her sexual energy in "The Lusty Month of May," as she celebrates the season when "every maiden prays that her lad / Will be a cad!" In Lancelot's "If Ever I Would Leave You," he implies—but never states—his romantic ardor for the wife of his friend. The title song is first presented by Arthur as he charms his bride-to-be by extolling the virtues of a kingdom where "The rain may never fall till after sundown, / By eight the morning fog must disappear." At the end of the show, the dying king reprises it as he beseeches a page to flee the battle and spread the story that "once there was a spot / For one brief shining moment that was known / As Camelot."

Problems plagued the book, though. Initially, Lerner had asked Moss Hart to be his coauthor but then, to Hart's dismay, decided he wanted to write it himself. Kitty Carlisle Hart consoled her husband by saying, "You're well out of that. There's no way *Camelot* can ever be as good as *My Fair Lady* and you'll be the one who gets the blame. Just do what you did on *Fair Lady*, direct it, and help as much as you can." Despite Hart's efforts, the show dragged on for nearly four hours in tryouts, although dynamic performances by Richard Burton, a matured Julie Andrews, and newcomer Robert Goulet as Lancelot held the wobbly work together. The pressure landed Lerner in the hospital with a bleeding ulcer; when he was finally released, he noticed another patient being wheeled in on a gurney. The nurse told him it was Moss Hart, who had suffered a heart attack.

Lerner now assumed the role of director—over Loewe's objections that they needed a true professional to "fix" the show. By the time *Camelot* limped into New York, it had been dubbed "Costalot" because of its lavish sets and costumes and staggering production investment of half a million dollars. As everyone feared, reviews were terrible, and it looked as if *Camelot* would close in a few months. Then, what Lerner called several "miracles" occurred. Moss Hart was released from the hospital and, even though *Camelot* was already running on Broadway, he cut the show to a reasonable length. Then columnist Ed Sullivan featured Lerner and Loewe on his hugely popular Sunday evening television show, the second half of which consisted of scenes from *Camelot*. The next morning, when Lerner went to the theater, the line at the box office stretched halfway down the block. Then, after the assassination of John F. Kennedy, Jacqueline Kennedy mentioned in an interview that the President had enjoyed listening to records before he went to bed, especially the cast album of *Camelot*. A grieving nation seized upon the score, which seemed to epitomize the glorious era of the Kennedy presidency before it, too, ended in tragedy.

Hey, Look Me over
Lyrics by Carolyn Leigh, music by Cy Coleman

At the heart of Cy Coleman's music was his passion for jazz and his affection for Broadway razzmatazz, and at the heart of Carolyn Leigh's lyrics was her gift for innuendo and an ability to write words that could strut. Michael Kidd called to ask Coleman and Leigh to write the score for *Wildcat*, a new show starring Lucille Ball in her stage debut. Ball was going to play Wildcat Johnson, a tough prospector looking for oil.

Coleman and Leigh had the most difficulty with the show's opening number. For some reason, everything came out sounding as if they had written it for Ethel Merman. Finally, Leigh said, "Cy, if you didn't care at all, if it wasn't the opening number, and it wasn't for Ball making her stage debut, and it was just a simple little number for the scene and the character, what would you write?" Coleman replied, "If this number weren't so important, I'd write something as corny and as simple as this." He played a few measures of something, and the two of them laughed over it, but Leigh could not get it out of her head. Two days later, she showed up with a lyric that began, "Hey, look me over, lend me an ear / Fresh out of clover, mortgaged up to here."

This is a song about refusing to give in to your troubles, as if singing about them becomes the way to get over them. Ultimately, though, it's an affirmation of independence, as Wildcat admonishes whoever might be listening, "Don't pass the plate" and "Don't thumb your nose." It's better to stand on your own two feet, especially if you have Leigh's jaunty wordplay to carry the message along: "I'm a little bit short of the elbow room but let me get me some / And look out, world, here I come."

Make Someone Happy
Lyrics by Betty Comden and Adolph Green, music by Jule Styne

Betty Comden and Adolph Green worked together every afternoon for sixty years. People were always asking if they were married. Comden had an answer: "We never thought we were. That's the important part." She wrote of Green that he "must have sprung full-blown from his own head. There is no other head quite capable of having done the job. Only his head has the antic, manic imagination and offbeat creative erudite-plus-childlike originality to conceive of such a person. I can just hear his head making him up." Surprisingly, though, most of their love songs have an unvarnished, unadorned quality. They set aside the wild wordplay for the simplest, most direct expression of emotion. They make up in honest affirmation and clarity what they lack in ardor. Of the sixteen lines in "Make Someone Happy," six are variations on the title.

Jule Styne had the idea to turn a novella about crooked goings-on in the music business into a musical. One day, he ran into comedian Phil Silvers. They had not seen each another in several years. "You interested in doing a show?" Styne asked. "Yeah," Silvers replied. "It's a story of how the Mafia comes out of retirement. Garson Kanin wrote the book. Betty and Adolph are doing the lyrics." Silvers interrupted. "I'll do it."

For *Do, Re, Mi,* Styne, Comden, and Green wrote one of their few standards. In the course of writing the music, Styne, as always, tried to slip in a melody that would become a hit. When he heard Comden and Green's lyrics to "Make Someone Happy," he called the song "gold record material." A duet for the middle of the second act, Comden explained,

> It stopped the show and, believe me, very seldom do you have a ballad that does that in that spot. Jule wrote a very big climax to the song. It actually has two of them. The end starts coming, and then you think it's almost over, and then he goes on to a slightly bigger ending.

During those years, Styne was writing two shows a year: "I was practicing, I was acquiring, because out of every show, good or not good, comes a song." Comden responded, "Whenever I say in Jule's presence that all the songs and words come out of situation and character, Jule says, 'But we want to look for a hit song, too.'"

Try to Remember
Lyrics by Tom Jones, music by Harvey Schmidt

The miracle is not that a musical runs for a decade but that it gets written and actually opens in the first place. After serving during the Korean War, two unknowns named Tom Jones and Harvey Schmidt moved to New York to establish themselves as songwriters for the theater. Jones survived by teaching while Schmidt worked as a commercial artist and freelance illustrator. At the same time, they were struggling to adapt *Les Romanesques,* a little known one-act spoof of *Romeo and Juliet* by Edmond Rostand. Initially, they envisioned what eventually became *The Fantasticks* as a big brassy musical set on two ranches in the Southwest, one Anglo and one Latino. Jones said they spent several years "trying to take the story and force it into a Rodgers and Hammerstein mold, which is what everybody did in those days. Eventually, the whole project just collapsed, our treatment was too heavy, too inflated for the simple little Rostand piece. It seemed hopeless."

In the summer of 1959, a friend from college days, director Word Baker, told them he needed a one-act version of their musical in three weeks. They threw out everything except one song and wrote what became the basis for *The Fantasticks* in less than the time Baker had given them. The song they kept was the opening number, "Try to Remember." Just under a year later, on May 3, 1960, *The Fantasticks*, now a full-length musical, opened to mixed reviews at the tiny Sullivan Street Playhouse in Greenwich Village. Schmidt said he was hoping for a second night and then a third: "We'd only have three people in the audience on some nights, but you'd look out and it'd be Tallulah Bankhead, Richard Rodgers, and Vivien Leigh." By the time it closed forty-two years later, each of its 17,162 performances began with the character of El Gallo appearing to sing the show's touchstone, an invitation to "remember" and "if you remember, then follow." *The Fantasticks* remains the longest running musical in American theater history.

Schmidt liked "Try to Remember" so much when he wrote it that he thought he had stolen it unintentionally from something he knew: "I thought, 'Oh that's pretty, it must be 'Streets of Laredo' or something.'" He said he composed its melody in a single burst and never changed a note. Jones' lyric for Schmidt's gentle waltz establishes the story's tone and point of view rather than introducing its characters or starting the plot. Because *The Fantasticks* tells a story of young love thwarted and abetted by the lovers' fathers, it relies on a combination of affection for the youngsters' innocence and mockery for their folly. Jones' lyric invites an adult audience to watch sympathetically by persuading us to remember the joy and folly of our first love. The song asks us to remember "When you were a tender and callow fellow," but also when "love was an ember about to billow." Even more importantly, it anticipates what is to come as it introduces the play's central theme: "Without a hurt the heart is hollow." Looking back on their song, Schmidt commented, "I'd like for people to remember 'Try to Remember.' I'm going to put that on my tombstone."

1961

I Believe in You
Lyrics and music by Frank Loesser

Wit and romance thrive in the Broadway musical, but satire's combination of moral outrage and corrosive irony has not often lent itself to song and dance. *How to Succeed in Business Without Really Trying* is one of the few exceptions. It succeeded in substituting breezy disdain for rage in one of the funniest musicals ever written, as the show's cartoon-like send up of corporate life transforms charming antihero J. Pierpont Finch from window washer and mailroom nebbish to business executive. From the start, librettist Abe Burrows and composer–lyricist Frank Loesser tailored the show to their star, Robert Morse, a small, brash, compulsively energetic song-and-dance man with a gap-toothed smile that conveyed the innocence of childhood and concealed a thousand connivances.

Although the show became only the fourth of seven musicals to win the Pulitzer Prize for drama, neither Loesser nor Burrows had any initial interest in it. They thought the Shepherd Mead book on which it would be based lacked drama as well as romance. Loesser believed he had already written his "wise guy" musical in *Guys and Dolls*, and he had moved on to the operatic *Most Happy Fella*. Yet once Burrows agreed to do it, he talked Loesser into it as well. Loesser was soon at work on a score attuned to the show's cynical comedy. It doesn't even have a love ballad.

Actually, there is one number that could pass for a love song, but, like Richard Rodgers and Lorenz Hart's "I Could Write a Book" from *Pal Joey*, "I Believe in You" works differently within the show than popular recordings made it sound to the general public. Finch sings it, not to the secretary who has fallen for him, but to himself in his bathroom mirror, accompanied by six kazoos approximating the sound of an electric razor. Loesser had initially written it for a female character to sing, but Burrows approached him to say, "Frankie, you're going to kill me for saying this, but how would it be if our young, ambitious, climbing hero sang 'I Believe in You' to himself?" Typically, the suggestion infuriated Loesser, but, once he calmed down, he realized Burrows's suggestion would improve the show.

"I Believe in You" is an ingratiatingly sharp-witted, egotistical song. Finch sings, "You have the cool clear eyes of a seeker of wisdom and truth," when what he is seeking has nothing to do with wisdom or truth. Only at the end does he reveal the truth about himself to himself: "Yet there's that slam-bang tang reminiscent of gin and vermouth, / Oh, I believe in you."

Moon River
Lyrics by Johnny Mercer, music by Henry Mancini

At a time when most songwriters were New Yorkers, the children of Jewish immigrants, Johnny Mercer stemmed from a prominent Savannah family. John Herndon Mercer spent his boyhood summers in a house on the coastal waterway where he and his friends swam, fished, and went "huckleberrying" to gather fruit for homemade ice cream. That rural upbringing gave Mercer's lyrics a pastoral quality, a feel for nature that is absent from such urban and urbane lyricists as Lorenz Hart and Ira Gershwin. During the 1940s, Mercer's songs dominated the airwaves and the pop charts. During one stretch, he had a song in the Top Ten for 221 weeks (the songwriting equivalent of DiMaggio's hitting streak); at another point, four of the Top Ten songs of the week had a lyric by Johnny Mercer.

However, by the late 1950s, rock 'n' roll had shoved songwriters like Mercer to the sidelines, and Hollywood, after the advent of television, made fewer and fewer of the kinds of film musicals that had been the primary outlet for his songs. About all Hollywood offered was the occasional "theme" songs for dramatic pictures. In an attempt to pull himself out of personal and professional depression, Mercer approached the young composer Henry Mancini. They managed to get the assignment to write the theme song for a film based on Truman Capote's *Breakfast at Tiffany's*.

Like Holly Golightly, the heroine of the story, Mercer had left the South to try for success in New York City. He loved Capote's book, and when he heard Mancini's melody for the theme song, it evoked his rural childhood. As usual, Mercer took the melody and worked on it by himself until he had several possible sets of lyrics to present to his composer. The first matched the first three notes of the melody to "I'm Hol-ly" and presented a winsome portrait of the main character. However, the second set of lyrics caught Mancini's fancy. Though he originally entitled it, "Blue River," when Mercer learned there was already a song with that title, he changed it to "Moon River."

Into the lyric Mercer poured his memories of lying alongside rivulets with his childhood friends, dreaming of going out in the world, and coming back home to flaunt their success: "I'm crossing you in style some day." The line that troubled people was the one that alluded to his cousin and best friend from those summers: "my huckleberry friend." When a preview audience in Pasadena gave the film a cool reception, the producer threatened, "That damn song can go." The song stayed, though, and won the Academy Award for Best Song.

"Moon River" revived Johnny Mercer's career and, as Irving Berlin predicted, has become a folk song. The line "my huckleberry friend" conjures up the traditional American image of Tom Sawyer and Huckleberry Finn on a raft, drifting "off to see the world." Little wonder that another great New York songwriter, Oscar Hammerstein, dubbed Johnny Mercer "the most perfect American lyricist alive—American—pure American," and still another, Yip Harburg, called Mercer "one of our great folk poets."

1962

Days of Wine and Roses
Lyrics by Johnny Mercer, music by Henry Mancini

After their Academy Award for "Moon River," Johnny Mercer and Henry Mancini were in demand. Their next assignment was to write a theme song for a movie that took a brutal look at how alcoholism destroys a marriage. Despite the harsh subject, director Blake Edwards thought the film should include a song. He told Mancini he thought "days of wine and roses," a phrase from a poem by Ernest Dowson (one of the "decadent" poets of the 1890s), himself a victim of alcoholism, would make a good title. "Get together with Johnny," he said, "and see what you can come up with."

"The title determined the melody," Mancini recalled. "I went to the piano and started on middle C and went up to A, 'The days ....' The first phrase fell right into place. That theme was written in about half an hour. It just came, it rolled out." When he played it for Mercer, the lyricist taped it and drove home to work on the lyric, worrying all the way about how he would create a lyric for such a lengthy title phrase. He poured himself a drink, leaned against the wall, and stared at the bar. Suddenly an image came to him of days that "run away / Like a child at play." Five minutes later the rest of the image followed: "toward a closing door, / A door marked 'nevermore' / That wasn't there before."

"I couldn't write it down fast enough," Mercer said. "It just poured out of me. I have no idea. I labored over it later, but the song came to me first, the words came to me, leaning against that wall, looking at the bar." For a lyricist who normally labored for days, weeks, even months over a lyric, "Days of Wine and Roses" was an unusually sudden inspiration. "I can't take credit for that one," he said, "God wrote that lyric. All I did was take it down."

Mancini had learned the hard way never to call to ask whether Mercer was finished with a lyric. "I made the mistake of calling him once," Mancini recalled, "and he let me know he wasn't ready." So the composer was amazed when the telephone rang so soon after Mercer left: "Hank, I've got it, I've got the lyric." Mancini and his wife went to Mercer's house, where Johnny sang the lyric with what Mancini described as "his best bullfrog voice." When Ginny Mancini heard it, she remembers saying, "'My goodness, that undoubtedly is going to win an Academy Award.' And it did."

When the songwriters went to demonstrate the song to Blake Edwards, he asked whether Jack Lemmon, the star of the movie, could come along. Edwards and Lemmon had just finished a grueling scene that had left the actor, as he put it, "an emotional mess." They entered a huge, empty soundstage, "nothing except this enormous empty stage—one work light way over in the corner—one tiny light and the rest in total blackness. And beside it an old, beat-up, upright piano. And not a stool—just a little broken-backed chair." Lemmon remembered Mancini sitting at the piano and Mercer taking a folded piece of paper out of his pocket:

> He started to sing this song and I have never been through any-thing like it in my life …. When I heard this, I was wiped out, I was gone. And I'll never forget the circumstances. It was one of the most thrilling moments that I've ever had in my thirty-five years of being in this business.

1964

FIDDLER ON THE ROOF
Lyrics by Sheldon Harnick, music by Jerry Bock

In *Fiddler on the Roof*, Jerry Bock and Sheldon Harnick's most impor-tant show, only two songs received any commercial play, "Matchmaker, Matchmaker" and "Sunrise, Sunset," even though the score included such great theater pieces as the opening number, "Tradition"; the insight-ful but funny soliloquy, "If I Were a Rich Man"; and the poignant finale, "Anatevka." *Fiddler's* plot, based on stories by the Yiddish writer Sholem Aleichem, concerned Tevye, a poor Russian Jew at the turn of the twenti-eth century, his nagging wife, their five daughters, and the anti-Semitism they faced. Thematically, it was also about the breakdown of tradition and the family's struggle to adapt to drastic change.

At one point, Bock and Harnick went to a benefit for a Hebrew actors' union to find some actors for the cast. Harnick said,

> Two women came out … and they did a Hasidic chant with no words, all syllables. All these very interesting sounds. Bock was enchanted by what he heard, and wrote the music to "If I Were a Rich Man" while inventing different sounds. So we thought wouldn't it be fun to preserve some the Hasidic chant sounds. The problem was that I could not duplicate the authentic sound. I looked for syllables to represent the sounds. "Daidle" kind of sounded like it. I played it for Zero Mostel, and he said I can do the authentic chanting. So I said do that.

Although such early songs of Harnick's as "Merry Little Minuet" and "Boston Beguine" are bitingly funny, he says his later lyrics reflect his attempts to empathize with the characters. "Through a combination of living and therapy," he says, "little by little I got to be able to deal with those simple emotions." Harnick also believes that his most direct lyrics

Carol Channing as Dolly Levi returns to the Harmonia Gardens in *Hello, Dolly.* Courtesy of Photofest.

come unintentionally from his experiences. Out of town, watching a performance of the charm song, "Do You Love Me?" soon after he and Bock added it to the score, he began to weep. He ran out of the theater as he recognized that the song's subject reminded him of his parents' marriage, defined by friction but loving beneath the surface.

The simplicity of language to express elemental emotions and complex relationships is central to a song like "Sunrise, Sunset." Tevye and Golde find themselves lost in their own thoughts as their oldest daughter marries. Harnick's lyric expresses their mutual emotions by linking their memories of their daughter's growing up with their recognition of their aging. Their personal emotions emerge in a series of questions: "Is this the little girl I carried? Is this the little boy at play?" The universal application of the question lies in the natural imagery that emerges in the bridge and the final chorus as seedlings become sunflowers, apparently overnight. The imagery then expands from sunflowers to the rising and setting of the sun, and to the passing of the seasons "laden with happiness and tears." Despite its universal implications, the song never forsakes the personal. Harnick avoids banality by adding a poignant undercurrent of gentle irony: "I can't remember growing older, / When did they?"

HELLO, DOLLY
Lyrics and music by Jerry Herman

Not long after *Hello, Dolly* won ten Tony Awards, Jerry Herman's lawyer called with bad news. Another songwriter had claimed that the opening notes to the show's title song were similar to something he had written. The incident troubled Herman although he later wrote about it dismissively: "This was some hillbilly tune, and of course I had never heard it in my life. It was a published song and it had been recorded, but it was hardly being sung in nightclubs in Manhattan." Though no one ever filed suit, Herman had to sit through a deposition in which he said, "The only notes that stay in my brain are from songs that I love and admire, and I would never, ever fall in love with a song about the joys of being born and raised in Kansas."

However, writing a song about being from New York and returning to the Harmonia Gardens on 14th Street after a long absence was obviously the real McCoy for Herman, at one time a theater-struck kid from Jersey City. By the mid 1960s, Herman had written a couple of off-Broadway musicals, and had had moderate success with *Milk & Honey*, his first Broadway effort. Then came *Dolly*. An adaptation of Thornton Wilder's *The Matchmaker*, the musical retells the story of the irrepressible Dolly Levi, a middle-aged widow who is, in her words, "a woman who arranges things … like furniture and daffodils and lives." Dolly makes matches for everyone else until she finally casts her eye on Yonkers merchant Horace Vandergelder for herself. Because she has been out of circulation for so long, her arrival at the Harmonia Gardens, a restaurant she had frequented with her late husband, is a sign of her return to the world and a cause for celebration.

Herman was surprised when the title song became a hit because he had written it as a production number that began as his boyhood memory of seeing Alice Faye singing with a group of waiters in the movie musical,

Lillian Russell. He also felt the song had too much of an 1890s feel and was too much a theater piece to have a separate life as a popular recording. The show was originally called, *Dolly (A Damned Exasperating Woman)*, and Herman admitted later:

> I know this sounds very dumb—but I never thought about calling the show *Hello, Dolly* because in the show the song really starts with Dolly singing to the waiters, "Hello, Harry / Well, hello Louis / It's so nice to be back home where I belong." Only when the waiters answer Dolly do we ever hear the words, "Hello, Dolly."

From that point on, the song thumps along agreeably, its simple repetitive lyric, short musical line, and close internal rhymes welcoming Dolly back and providing plenty of opportunity for increasingly acrobatic staging until it finally became a showstopper. It became a title song only after Herman heard Louis Armstrong's recording, released while the show was still in tryouts in Detroit. Herman could not believe that even as great a jazz singer as Armstrong could do much with it. He and his music publisher listened to the recording and, Herman wrote, "It just took our breath away …. Our song had taken on a life of its own." The publisher began to jump up and down, "That's it! That's the title of your show!"

Finding a title was not the only problem for *Hello Dolly* as it approached its Broadway opening. David Merrick, the show's temperamental bully of a producer, was living in a state of rage because the first act finale was weak. "He sent not one but two different composer–lyricist teams to frighten me," Herman later said in an interview, so he "bought two candy bars and locked myself in my hotel room." Dressed in a bathrobe he found in the closet, he wrote "Before the Parade Passes By" in a few hours. Then he called Carol Channing to come down to hear it. She knocked on his door dressed in *her* hotel bathrobe. The song so excited her, she called Gower Champion who came down (as you've already guessed) also wearing the same bathrobe. Herman remembers the three of them, dressed identically, "marching around the hotel room to this new song at two or three in the morning."

1965

It Was a Very Good Year
Lyrics and music by Ervin Drake

Ervin Drake was one of several Tin Pan Alley songwriters trying to survive in the era of Bob Dylan and the Beatles. The last big hit in which he had a hand was "I Believe" (1952), but he thought he also had a promising "folkie" song that perhaps a group like The Weavers could record. Like

Composer Jerry Bock and lyricist Sheldon Harnick. Courtesy of Photofest.

most folk ballads it told a story—in this case, the reflections of an aging man-about-town looking back on the many women in his life. Drake also included a brief refrain between each verse in which the singer could sing such nonsense phrases as "Hey, nonny, nonny, non."

Frank Sinatra heard about the song and was so taken by it that he recorded it and then made the recording session the basis of a television special. Sinatra turned fifty in 1965 and the romantic nostalgia of Drake's song resonated with the singer's much publicized love life. Instead of singing the "hey nonny, nonny" refrain, however, Sinatra's arrangement gave that part of the melody over to violins. When Drake protested to Sinatra about the omission of the lyric, the singer told him, "Just be glad I didn't sing 'do-be-do-be-do' at that point." In a year dominated by rock and folk music, Sinatra's recording of "It Was a Very Good Year" won the Grammy for best male vocal performance.

The Shadow of Your Smile
Lyrics by Paul Francis Webster, music by Johnny Mandel

One of the more cynical practices of Hollywood studios was to assign several different songwriters to a song but not tell them. Johnny Mercer thought he was the lyricist for a Johnny Mandel melody that was to be the theme song for *The Sandpiper.* Mercer wrote a lyric that took its inspiration from the script: "Today I saw a bird that broke its wing, / Which isn't in itself a tragic thing." Another lyricist, Paul Francis Webster, crafted a more generalized lyric called "The Shadow of Your Smile." "They didn't tell him that they were making a sweepstakes out of this," a songwriter friend of Mercer's said, "They were submitting it to other lyric writers."

The producers chose Webster's lyric over Mercer's. Webster's lyric sounds simple but, Tony Hill observes, is quite intricate in the way it puts "every rhyme (but one) on a one-syllable word" and "deftly manages to turn the song into a circle by both starting and ending the lyric with the title."

When "The Shadow of Your Smile" won the Academy Award for Best Song, beating out Johnny Mercer and Henry Mancini's "The Sweetheart Tree," Mercer's disappointment was even more acute. Friends recalled that he pinned his original lyric on the wall near his piano with the caption "You can't win them all." Friends also recalled how Mercer "got even" by saying, "By the way, 'The Shadow of Your Smile'—doesn't that kind of suggest the faint mustache on a lady's lip?"

1966

CABARET
Lyrics by Fred Ebb, music by John Kander

What struck Hal Prince about Christopher Isherwood's *Berlin Stories* was the parallel between "the spiritual bankruptcy of Germany in the 1920s and our country in the 1960s." After commissioning Fred Ebb and John Kander to write the score, Prince assembled the cast on the first day of rehearsal and held up a photograph of

> … a group of Aryan blonds in their late teens, stripped to the waist, wearing religious medals, snarling at the camera like a pack of hounds. I asked the identity, the time and place of the picture. It seemed obvious I'd lifted it from Munich in 1928. In fact, it was a photograph of a group of students in residential Chicago fighting the integration of a school.

A musical about the rise of Nazism would seem inconceivable to some producers; however, Prince realized that by setting it in a sleazy Berlin cabaret and presenting numbers as part of a nightclub show, he could make "an important statement" that still "provide entertainment"—a musical that would be "more than a musical."

Composer John Kander plays while lyricist Fred Ebb and Jan Clayton, star of the Broadway production of *Cabaret*, sing along. Courtesy of Photofest.

Kander and Ebb were the perfect songwriters for this musical. Instead of writing a dark score full of brooding songs, they gave many of their numbers a gay, glitzy patina. From the opening "Willkommen," sung by Joel Grey as the Kit Kat Club's smarmy emcee, the songs have a joyous verve. Grey's character was based upon Prince's memory of his days as a soldier in Stuttgart. A dwarf hosted a nightclub carved out of the rubble of a bombed church: "hair parted in the middle and lacquered down with brilliantine, his mouth made into a bright-red cupid's bow," he "wore heavy false eyelashes and sang, danced, goosed, tickled, and pawed four lumpen Valkyries waving diaphanous butterfly wings."

The biggest hit from the show was the title song, in which free spirit Sally Bowles celebrated the joys of nightlife—"What good is sitting alone in your room? / Come hear the music play; / Life is a cabaret, old chum"—that by the end of the play underscores her and much of Germany's obliviousness to the rise of Nazism. Kander and Ebb also wrote the kind of "story" songs that, ever since *Oklahoma!*, had become obligatory in the "integrated" musical, in which characters sing expressive songs that arise out of the dramatic action. Thus, Sally and the leading man sing romantic solos and duets, as do their comic counterparts, Sally's landlady and her Jewish boyfriend. Unlike traditional musicals, however, the hero, Cliff, leaves Sally out of disgust at her blindness to the political realities of Berlin, and Frau Schneider breaks off her romance out of fear of the growing anti-Semitism.

When director–choreographer Bob Fosse brought *Cabaret* to the screen, he presented it as a "performance" musical, cutting many of the "story" songs (though some of the missing songs were alluded to in the dialogue or heard as background music). Every song in the film was done as a "number" in true Hollywood "backstager" tradition; most were performed on the stage of the Kit Kat Klub. The story unfolded in scenes shot away from the club so that the songs functioned as they did in the new kind of "concept" musical that was developing at the time: They comment on the story metaphorically rather than advance it in dramatically expressive songs.

Even "Maybe This Time," a new song Kander and Ebb wrote for the film, is sung by Sally onstage. As she sings, the camera cuts to shots of her in bed with Cliff (whose homosexuality is treated more directly in the film than in the stage production), to underscore the ardor and futility of Sally's romantic dreams. The only song in the film not rendered in the Kit Kat Klub is "Tomorrow Belongs to Me," but it, too, is a performance number sung by a cherubic Boy Scout at an outdoor tavern scene oozing Gemütlichkeit. It is only as the song progresses that we realize this is a Hitler Youth expressing his growing confidence that the future belongs to the Nazis—not the jaded sophisticates of the Kit Kat Klub.

SWEET CHARITY
Lyrics by Dorothy Fields, music by Cy Coleman

The late 1950s and early 1960s were a tough time for Dorothy Fields. Her brother and husband died, she suffered from depression, and she still needed to look after her two children. She had begun to feel that time and musical styles had passed her by. Things changed dramatically when she met Cy Coleman at a party. He had written all of two Broadway shows and was nearly twenty-five years her junior, but he got up his nerve to say, "I'd like to write a song or two with you." She answered, "Thank God somebody asked." Their ease of collaboration soon led to *Sweet Charity*, a loose adaptation of Federico Fellini's *Nights of Cabiria*. Director–choreographer Bob Fosse had the original idea for turning the movie into a musical set in a sleazy Manhattan dancehall rather than an Italian bordello, and he had already hired Coleman for the music. Neil Simon's book is a series of sketches about taxi dancer Charity Hope Valentine and the rotten men she keeps hooking up with. Her life is a torch ballad waiting to happen.

Coleman, Fosse, and librettist Neil Simon were in their thirties, but Fields had just turned sixty. Nonetheless, Ethan Mordden wrote, "This wonderful talent may be the only lyricist in musical theater history who sounded more youthful as time ran on." Deborah Grace Winer wrote that Coleman's "energy sharpened her contemporary focus, and her experience lent their work mastery and polish." Fields retained her gift for sassy American speech with no unnecessary curlicues, but she also mastered lyric writing that reveals character. In each of her theater songs, you hear a distinctive voice.

Fields wrote quickly if not always easily. She once told an interviewer that nothing was more important than the idea:

> The idea makes the song. The idea, the thought—and the enterprise and courage to present that idea in fresh, beautiful, eloquent words …. And once the words are down, the idea expressed, then of course must come the fixing, the revising, the polishing, the never-being-satisfied until you feel it's as perfect as you can make it …. I wrote the words to "I Feel a Song Coming On," but I don't believe a word of it. A song just doesn't come on. I've always had to tease it out, squeeze it out, and anyone that tells you that a song is something that's an inspiration—I hate that word—or a magic spark, or an IBM machine gets you going, has got to prove that one to me. It's hard slave labor. Ask anyone who writes—it's slave labor and I love it.

"Hey, Big Spender," the first of the score's two major songs, is actually a *noir* song, set to the beat of a striptease as the girls lie to their potential customers while taunting them to come closer: "The minute you walked in the joint, I could see you were a man of distinction, a real big spender / Good looking, so refined …." The second showstopper, "If My Friends Could See

Me Now," found life as a quintessential cheer-up song outside the show, but Charity sings it in the apartment of an Italian movie star. She can't believe how high she'srisen, although her stay at the top will prove to be dishearteningly brief "Tonight at eight you shoulda seen a chauffeur pull up in a rented limousine! / My neighbors burned! They like to die / when I tell them who is getting' in and goin' out is I!"

1968

The Windmills of Your Mind
Lyrics by Alan and Marilyn Bergman, music by Michel Legrand

Even though fellow lyricists Alan and Marilyn Bergman were born in the same New York hospital and grew up in the same section of the city, they did not meet until they were writing songs in Los Angeles. They started their careers in earnest in the late 1950s, just as Broadway and Hollywood musicals were beginning their decline. They represented a younger generation of nonrock songwriters without deep roots in musicals or the New York music scene.

Since the 1950s, most movies have had title songs. Some nonmusical films also have a single musical interlude: sometimes an ingenious comment on character and other times little more than an irritating digression. Writing incidental songs might have been a step down for a lot of older songwriters, but the Bergmans flourished writing them. Composer Michel Legrand and the Bergmans' "Windmills of Your Mind" was one of their most successful, written for a stylish caper movie called *The Thomas Crown Affair.*

Norman Jewison, the movie's director, had asked Legrand to write the score as well as a single song. Legrand in turn asked composer–arranger Quincy Jones who should write the lyrics. "There is a young couple, very gifted," Jones said, "I just finished a song with them." When they were writing a song for a movie, Marilyn explained,

> We see the film with the composer, and then we speak with the director to discuss the song's reason for being and function in the film. Then we meet with the composer and decide what style the song should be, from whose point of view, and then sometimes we'll start the process in the same room together, with one of us coming up with a line or a phrase. But ultimately we find ourselves alone in a room with a cassette.

Alan said, "When we hear a melody, we feel that there are words on the tips of those notes, and we have to find them."

For this picture about a wealthy but jaded businessman who plans an elaborate bank heist for the thrill of it, Jewison wanted a scene with the man, played by Steve McQueen, flying a glider as he plans the robbery. Marilyn said that Jewison had

> ... shot six or seven minutes of him circling in the glider—which is a dream for a songwriter: no dialogue, no sound effects, just a little shoosh of wind .... Jewison wanted a song that exposed no character, that didn't tell any plot—he just wanted the restlessness and uneasiness of the character underlined.

Legrand gave the Bergmans six different melodies to choose from. "The next morning, all three of us had independently chosen this oddball melody, almost baroque in feel. It was the opposite of what we had thought we would have chosen the night before." Alan added, "I think we chose it because it's kind of a ribbon, a circular melody that reflected the flight of a glider very well," and Marilyn concurred: "It reminded us of those moments when you're trying to fall asleep and you can't turn your mind off. Anxiety is circular, actually: 'Like a circle in a spiral / Like a wheel within a wheel ....'" Legrand, Marilyn said, "writes sequential tunes, a sequence that repeats and repeats, and if you take out one brick, it all collapses." Their lyric, in turn, creates the sense of constant spinning through its use of "ing" forms at the end of lines, enforcing the sound through words like "*in*," "with*in*," "*rings*," and "m*in*utes," and through alliteration: "like a wheel within a wheel," "running rings around the moon," and the title line: "in the windmills of your mind." The song won the three their first Oscar and, in Legrand's words, "That opened everything."

1969

Raindrops Keep Fallin' on My Head
Lyrics by Hal David, music by Burt Bacharach

Nobody wrote more hits during the 1960s than Burt Bacharach and Hal David, but they did not come fast. Bacharach told an interviewer that writing with David was "fun, both of us sitting in a room staring at each other. I'm a very slow writer. I've always been very slow. I can really labor over something. And Hal wasn't extremely fast either, so we were a good match."

During the early days of their collaboration, David recalled:

> We used to meet every day at Famous Music in New York. I'd come in with some titles and some ideas for songs, lines. Burt would come in with opening strains of phrases or what might be part of a chorus section. It was like Show and Tell: I'd show him

what I had thought of and he'd show me what he had thought of. And whatever seemed to spark the other would be the start of whatever song we started to write that day. I'd write four lines or sing lines of a lyric and he'd have a melody and, very often, we'd sit in the room and write the song together, sort of pound it out. I'd be writing lyrics and he'd be writing music and, all of a sudden, we'd have the structure of a song, which we'd keep working on. We didn't write songs so quickly that they were done overnight or that day. I'd take home his melody and he'd take home my lyrics and so, very often, we'd be working on three different songs at one time.

Near the end of the decade, Bacharach and David wrote their most famous song, "Raindrops Keep Fallin' on My Head" for the movie, *Butch Cassidy and the Sundance Kid*. When B. J. Thomas recorded it, he thought they had written it for Bob Dylan. David denies it:

We wrote the song with Paul Newman in mind. Not for him to sing but the character of Butch Cassidy. You don't write for the singer who's going to be singing over the scene. You should write for the character and what the scene has to say. And that's exactly how and why the song was written.

The song is actually a digression for a brief bucolic idyll, although the truth is that Butch loves robbing banks. He's very good at it until a relentless posse drives him, Sundance, and Sundance's mistress, Emma, out of the country. Along the way, Butch—rather than Sundance—sets Emma on the handlebars of a bicycle and does some trick riding as Thomas sings "Raindrops" on the soundtrack. David gives the lyric an offhanded quality that feels very close to the understated spinning of yarns, although the release breaks with Butch's laconic manner. It's impossible to imagine the shrewd, skeptical Cassidy ever saying, "The blues they sent to meet me won't defeat me / It won't be long 'till happiness steps up to greet me." Only in the final chorus does the lyric illuminate his determination to persist even though the Old West is fading away: "I'm never gonna stop the rain by complaining / Because I'm free, nothing's worrying me." Butch's inability to adapt gives the lie to "Raindrop's" optimism, and the song's lack of irony puts it at odds with the movie's—and Butch's—darker subtext.

1970 – 1977

1973

It's Not Where You Start
Lyrics by Dorothy Fields, music by Cy Coleman

Romantic ballads were never Dorothy Fields' stock in trade. Her gift for grounding her lyrics in blunt but expansive city talk gave them an appealingly gruff edge and an ironic sense of humor. From *Swing Time's* "A Fine Romance" to *Seesaw's* "You're a Lovable Lunatic," she wrote love songs with attitude and character, songs with bite. In *Seesaw*, the heroine sings to herself: "If there's a wrong way to do it, a right way to screw it up / nobody does it like me." To the degree that the songs reflected aspects of Fields' character, she needed them to get through the difficulties she, composer Cy Coleman, and director Michael Bennett faced while they were struggling to get *Seesaw* in shape to open. They finally dropped the librettist and director, tossed out most of the book, and replaced half the cast. The day after the opening, the producers posted a closing notice until Fields kept it going with her own money.

At one point, while the show was trying out in Detroit, Fields even stepped in to keep a chorus girl happy. The singer was a very young Amanda McBroom, who told an interviewer years later

> Everybody was really cranky, and I was really missing my boyfriend. Dorothy Fields came over, sat next to me, patted my knee and asked "What's the matter, honey?" I told her how horribly I was missing my boyfriend. She put down this enormous Louis Vuitton bag which she always carried around, pulled out a pack of Camels, lit one up, pulled out a flask, took a drag, then pulled out her checkbook, wrote me a check for $300, handed it to me and said "You get him here. Romance is important."

That same combination of sympathetic understanding and hardheaded practicality, even when it came to love, also informed the score's most important song, a rousing cakewalk called, "It's Not Where You Start." Performed by six-foot, six-inch Tommy Tune, it ends with the stage crowded with dancers knee-deep in balloons. It is one of a legion of reassuring good advice songs that always seem to find a receptive listener when it promises that "you're gonna finish on top." Because this was New York, the advice is also pretty blunt: "A hundred to one shot, they call him a klutz, / Can outrun the fav'rite, all he needs is the guts."

Send in the Clowns
Lyrics and music by Stephen Sondheim

When he was writing the score to *A Little Night Music*, Stephen Sondheim wanted a song for a man who decides he must end a rekindled love affair. However, director Hal Prince felt the song should be sung from the perspective of the rejected woman, played by Glynis Johns. Her vocal range, while not large, was perfect for something chatty and conversational. "While I was writing it," Sondheim said, "I figured it would be the man's song because the impulse for the scene, the impulse for the singing was the man's .... But Hal directed the scene in such a way that the impulse became the woman's."

In creating the song, Sondheim drew upon old theatrical traditions. When a circus performer had an accident, the call went out to "send in the clowns" to divert the audience's attention. In the song, the woman takes a ruefully comic view of her situation as a trapeze artist who has fallen to the circus floor, while her lover is still high in the air. As the clowns come in, she wonders how she could have lost her timing so late in her career and vows, "well, maybe next year."

By the time he wrote *A Little Night Music*, Sondheim had broken with the tradition of Broadway songwriters who wrote with one eye on the show and the other on the popular song market, hoping that they would become independent hits. Yet "Send in the Clowns" did just that through a signature recording by Judy Collins and became the biggest hit Sondheim has ever had.

1975

CHICAGO
Lyrics by Fred Ebb, music by John Kander

In the flamboyant yet conservative world of the Broadway musical, John Kander and Fred Ebb wrote hit shows that were startlingly, dazzlingly innovative. For *Chicago*, in 1975, they and librettist–director–choreographer Bob Fosse wrote what they subtitled, *A Musical Vaudeville*, because each song was in a particular style associated with show biz in the early twentieth century. Ebb said, "I made it vaudeville based on the idea that the characters were performers. Every musical moment in the show was loosely modeled on someone else: Roxie was Helen Morgan, Velma was Texas Guinan, Billy Flynn was Ted Lewis, Mama Morton was Sophie Tucker." Kander said they found the voice for each of the songs by listening to recordings by the old stars. "It was that unconscious process of listening to a lot of jazz from that period," he said, "letting your brain soak it in and then writing."

Adapted from Maurine Dallas Watkins' play of the same name, the sexy, cynical musical dramatized two sensational murder trials in Chicago in 1924. The real women, Beulah Annan and Belva Gaertner, found life onstage as Velma Kelly and Roxie Hart, played in the musical by Gwen Verdon and Chita Rivera. Velma and Roxie get off, thanks to the machinations of lawyer Billy Flynn, who transforms "justice" into "show biz." Once they are free, the women become, logically enough, headliners in vaudeville. The 1996 revival, originally starring Ann Reinking and Bebe Neuwirth, is still running, and the 2003 movie version won the Oscar for best picture.

Chicago's backstage story is as ferociously dark as anything onstage. Fosse suffered a heart attack soon after work on the musical began. When he returned, his manner was consistently abusive. By the time they reached tryouts, Kander turned to Ebb to say, "No show is worth dying for. Let's go home." Verdon, then married to Fosse, snapped during one of his tirades, "They can pack his heart in sawdust as far as I'm concerned."

None of the individual songs is quite a standard (though "All That Jazz," later appropriated by Fosse as the title of his autobiographical movie, probably comes closest), but the score is a stylistic whole, and the stories behind some of the songs reflect the struggle—professional as well as personal—to mount and open a new musical on latter-day Broadway. After writing "Class," the vulgar comic song for the corrupt lesbian prison matron, Mama Morton, Ebb developed substantial doubts about the song's humor: "Everybody you watch s'got his brain in his crotch ... / What became of class?" Ebb was ready to cut it before Mary McCarty as Mama ever performed it because "I never know whether a song will work when we're writing it." Basing the lyric on words that rhymed with "ass," Ebb wrote, "Last week my mother got groped in the middle of Mass." The night McCarty first performed it, Ebb said that he

… ran downstairs to the men's room to hide. Eventually I heard the audience laughing and decided to go back up. On the steps, I heard more laughter, and on the line "no one even says oops when they're passing their gas," there was a really huge laugh. Only then did I realize the song was funny.

For the show's finale, in which Kelly and Hart join forces for their night-club opening after the trial, the writers decided they wanted a cheesy act in which Velma played drum and Roxie saxophone. Kander and Ebb had written a song for each of them but were convinced neither was work-ing. Now Fosse changed his mind; he wanted the act sophisticated. With uncommon courtesy, he asked Kander and Ebb if they could write a new song, one song for both of them. Trying to look and sound reluctant as they left the room, Kander remembered that they "started skipping down the hall, laughing gleefully." They wrote "Nowadays" in no more than an hour but did not take it to Fosse until the next day. Ebb said, "We spent the entire day away just to make it look hard."

1977

New York, New York
Lyrics by Fred Ebb, music by John Kander

After coming out of temporary retirement in the 1970s, Frank Sinatra struggled to keep up with the times by singing contemporary rock and even country songs, although most of his fans would have been content for him to continue singing the classic standards of Cole Porter, Rodgers and Hart, and other songwriters of the Golden Era. Sonny Burke suggested Sinatra do something that would bridge old songs and new: a three-part album called *Trilogy* to consist of classic songs in *The Past*, more recent hits in *The Present*, and current songs in *The Future*. "We will not do another thing," Sinatra said, "until we do this."

However, *Trilogy* proved that not even Sinatra could render such songs as "Love Me Tender," "Song Sung Blue," and "Just the Way You Are" in his style. Nor could he make a hit of contemporary songs cast in the mold of classic standards, such as "Summer Me, Winter Me." An era of songwrit-ing had passed.

The one exception was the title song of a Martin Scorsese film starring Robert DeNiro as a 1940s bandleader desperately trying to bridge the musi-cal gap between Big Band swing and the new wave of be-bop. Liza Minnelli played his "canary" and sang "New York, New York" as a straightforward performance number in front of the band. Although she hoped it would become one of her great signature songs, it proved to be only a mild hit.

Sinatra incorporated the song into his opening concert medley of New York songs — following the Bernstein / Comden and Green "New York, New York," Vernon Duke's "Autumn in New York," and other metropolitan numbers. Soon the Kander and Ebb "New York, New York" began eliciting such audience response that Sinatra said, "Man, this song is getting big. We have to take it out of the overture." "New York, New York" ultimately displaced "My Way," the song that usually concluded his concerts, a song Sinatra had dubbed "kooky" upon first hearing it.

As Will Friedwald writes, "New York, New York" "exemplifies the anger and the optimism, the ambition and the aggression, the hostility and the energy, the excitement and the excrement that is New York." All those qualities also characterize the songs described in this book. In one way or another, they are songs that emanate from the dream of New York City as America's center of earthy elegance, rhythmic drive, and vernacular ease. These songs reached their peak during the years when Manhattan became the embodiment of American vitality and optimism. Fittingly "New York, New York" was the last great standard written in the style that had evolved from Broadway, Hollywood, and Tin Pan Alley.

Bibliography

Abbott, George. *Mr. Abbott*. New York: Random House, 1963.

Alpert, Hollis. *The Life and Times of "Porgy and Bess": The Making of an American Classic*. New York: Alfred Knopf, 1990.

Astaire, Fred. *Steps in Time*. New York: Harper & Bros., 1959.

Bach, Bob and Ginger Mercer, eds. *Johnny Mercer: The Life, Times and Song Lyrics of Our Huckleberry Friend*. Secaucus, NJ: Lyle Stuart, 1974.

Barrett, Mary Ellin. *Irving Berlin: A Daughter's Memoir*. New York: Simon and Schuster, 1994.

Barrios, Richard. *A Song in the Dark: The Birth of the Musical Film*. New York, Oxford: Oxford University Press, 1995.

Bergreen, Laurence. *As Thousands Cheer: The Life of Irving Berlin*. New York: Viking, 1990.

Berlin, Edward A. *Ragtime: A Musical and Cultural History*. Berkeley: University of California Press, 1980.

———. *Reflections and Research on Ragtime*. Brooklyn, NY: Institute for Studies in American Music, 1987.

Block, Geoffrey. *Enchanted Evenings: The Broadway Musical from "Show Boat" to Sondheim*. New York, Oxford: Oxford University Press, 1997.

Bordman, Gerald. *American Musical Theatre: A Chronicle*. New York, Oxford: Oxford University Press, 1978.

———. *Jerome Kern: His Life and Music*. New York, Oxford: Oxford University Press, 1980.

———. *American Operetta: From "H.M.S. Pinafore" to "Sweeney Todd."* New York, Oxford: Oxford University Press, 1981.

———. *Days to Be Happy, Years to Be Sad: The Life and Music of Vincent Youmans*. New York, Oxford: Oxford University Press, 1982.

———. *American Musical Comedy: From "Adonis" to "Dreamgirls."* New York, Oxford: Oxford University Press, 1982.

———. *American Musical Revue: From "The Passing Show" to "Sugar Babies."* New York, Oxford: Oxford University Press, 1985.

Brahms, Caryl and Ned Sherrin. *Song by Song: The Lives and Works of 14 Great Lyric Writers*. Bolton, UK: R. Anderson, 1984.

Burton, Jack. *The Blue Book of Tin Pan Alley: A Human Interest Anthology of American Popular Music*. Watkins Glen, NY: Century House, 1951.

Cahn, Sammy. *I Should Care: The Sammy Cahn Story*. New York: Arbor House, 1974.

Calloway, Cab and Bryant Rollins. *Of Minnie the Moocher & Me*. New York: Crowell, 1976.

Cantor, Eddie. *As I Remember Them*. New York: Duell, Sloan and Pearce, 1963.

Cantor, Eddie and Jane Kesner Ardmore. *Take My Life*. Garden City, NY: Doubleday, 1957.

Cantor, Eddie and David Freedman. *Ziegfeld, the Great Glorifier*. New York: A. H. King, 1934.

Carmichael, Hoagy and Stephen Longstreet. *Sometimes I Wonder*. New York: Farrar, Straus & Giroux, 1965.

Carter, Randolph. *The World of Flo Ziegfeld*. New York, Washington: Praeger Publishers, 1974.

Citron, Stephen. *Noel and Cole: The Sophisticates*. New York, Oxford: Oxford University Press, 1993.

———. *The Wordsmiths: Oscar Hammerstein 2nd & Alan Jay Lerner*. New York, Oxford: Oxford University Press, 1995.

———. *Sondheim & Lloyd–Webber: The New Musical*. New York, Oxford: Oxford University Press, 2001.

Colbert, Warren E. *Who Wrote That Song? Or, Who in the Hell Is J. Fred Coots? An Informal Survey of American Popular Songs and Their Composers*. New York: Revisionist Press, 1975.

Collier, James Lincoln. *Duke Ellington*. New York: Collier Books, 1993.

Comden, Betty. *Off Stage*. New York: Simon & Schuster, 1995.

Coslow, Sam. *Cocktails for Two: The Many Lives of Giant Songwriter Sam Coslow*. New Rochelle, NY: Arlington House, 1977.

Craig, Warren. *Sweet and Lowdown: America's Popular Songwriters*. Metuchen, NJ: Scarecrow Press, 1978.

Davis, Lee. *Bolton and Wodehouse and Kern: The Men Who Made Musical Comedy*. New York: James H. Heineman, Inc., 1993.

Dietz, Howard. *Dancing in the Dark*. New York: Quadrangle, 1974.

Duke, Vernon. *Passport to Paris*. Boston: Little, Brown, 1955.

Eels, George. *The Life That Late He Led: A Biography of Cole Porter*. London: W. H. Allen, 1976.

Ellington, Mercer and Stanley Dance. *Duke Ellington in Person: An Intimate Memoir*. New York: Da Capo, 1978.

Engel, Lehman. *Their Words Are Music: The Great Theatre Lyricists and Their Lyrics*. New York: Crown, 1975.

Erenberg, Lewis. *Steppin' Out: New York Nightlife and the Transformation of American Culture, 1890–1930*. Westport, CT: Greenwood Press, 1981.

Ewen, David. *The Life and Death of Tin Pan Alley: The Golden Age of American Popular Music*. New York: Funk & Wagnalls, 1964.

———. *American Popular Songs: From the Revolutionary War to the Present*. New York: Random House, 1966.

———. *All the Years of American Popular Music: A Comprehensive History*. Englewood Cliffs, NJ: Prentice Hall, 1972.

———. *American Songwriters*. New York: Wilson, 1987.

Feinstein, Michael. *Nice Work If You Can Get It: My Life in Rhythm and Rhyme*. New York: Hyperion, 1995.

First, William E. *Drifting and Dreaming: The Story of Songwriter Haven Gillespie*. St. Petersburg, FL: Seaside, 1998.

Fordin, Hugh. *Getting to Know Him: A Biography of Oscar Hammerstein*. New York: Random House, 1977.

———. *M-G-M's Greatest Musicals: The Arthur Freed Unit*. New York: Da Capo Press, 1996.

Freedland, Michael. *Irving Berlin*. New York: Stein and Day, 1974.

———. *Jerome Kern: A Biography*. New York: Stein and Day, 1978.

Friedwald, Will. *Sinatra! The Song Is You*. New York: Scribner, 1995.

———. *Stardust Melodies: The Biography of Twelve of America's Most Popular Songs*. New York: Pantheon, 2002.

Furia, Philip. *The Poets of Tin Pan Alley: A History of America's Great Lyricists*. New York, Oxford: Oxford University Press, 1990.

———. *Ira Gershwin: The Art of the Lyricist*. New York, Oxford: Oxford University Press, 1996.

———. *Irving Berlin: A Life in Song*. New York: Schirmer, 1998.

———, ed. *Dictionary of Literary Biography: American Song Lyricists, 1920–1960*. Detroit, New York: Gale, 2002.

———. *Skylark: The Life and Times of Johnny Mercer*. New York: St. Martin's Press, 2003.

Gavin, James. *Intimate Nights: The Golden Age of New York Cabaret*. New York: Limelight Editions, 1992.

George, Don. *Sweet Man: The Real Duke Ellington*. New York: Putnam, 1981.

Gershwin, Ira. *Lyrics on Several Occasions*. New York: Alfred A. Knopf, 1959.

Giddins, Gary. *Bing Crosby: A Pocketful of Dreams, The Early Years, 1903–1940*. Boston: Little Brown, 2001.

Goldberg, Isaac. *Tin Pan Alley: A Chronicle of the American Popular Music Racket*. New York, John Day, 1930.

Goldman, Herbert, G. *Jolson: The Legend Comes to Life*. New York, Oxford: Oxford University Press, 1988.

———. *Fanny Brice: The Original Funny Girl*. New York, Oxford: Oxford University Press, 1992.

———. *Banjo Eyes: Eddie Cantor and the Birth of Modern Stardom*. New York, Oxford: Oxford University Press, 1997.

Gottfried, Martin. *Broadway Musicals*. New York: Abradale Press, 1984.

Green, Stanley. *The World of Musical Comedy*. New York: DaCapo Press, 1980.

Grossman, Barbara W. *Funny Woman: The Life and Times of Fanny Brice.* Bloomington, Indianapolis: Indiana University Press, 1992.

Hajdu, David. *Lush Life: A Biography of Billy Strayhorn.* New York: Farrar, Straus & Giroux, 1996.

Hamm, Charles. *Yesterdays: Popular Song in America.* New York: W.W. Norton, 1979.

———. *Irving Berlin: Songs from the Melting Pot: The Formative Years, 1907–1914.* New York, Oxford: Oxford University Press, 1997.

Hammerstein, Oscar. *Lyrics.* New York: Simon and Schuster, 1949.

Handy, W. C. and Arna Bontemps. *Father of the Blues.* New York: Da Capo Press, 1991.

Hart, Dorothy, ed. *Thou Swell, Thou Witty: The Life and Lyrics of Lorenz Hart.* New York: Harper & Row, 1976.

Hart, Moss. *Act One: An Autobiography.* New York: Random House, 1959.

Hasse, John Edward. *Beyond Category: The Life and Genius of Duke Ellington.* New York: Simon and Schuster, 1993.

Hay, Peter. *Broadway Anecdotes.* New York, Oxford: Oxford University Press, 1989.

Hemming, Roy. *The Melody Lingers On: The Great Songwriters and Their Movie Musicals.* New York: Newmarket Press, 1986.

Hemming, Roy and David Hajdu. *Discovering Great Singers of Classic Pop.* New York: Newmarket Press, 1991.

Henderson, Clayton W. *On the Banks of the Wabash: The Life and Music of Paul Dresser.* Indianapolis: Indiana Historical Society Press, 2003.

Hill, Tony. "Irving Berlin," "Ned Washington," "Paul Francis Webster" in *Dictionary of Literary Biography: American Song Lyricists, 1920–1960.* Detroit, New York: Gale, 2002.

Hirschhorn, Clive. *The Hollywood Musical.* New York: Crown, 1981.

Hischak, Thomas S. *Word Crazy: Broadway Lyricists from Cohan to Sondheim.* New York: Praeger, 1991.

———. "Richard Adler and Jerry Ross," "Betty Comden and Adolph Green," "Howard Dietz," "Otto Harbach," "Harold Rome," "Meredith Willson" in *Dictionary of Literary Biography: American Song Lyricists, 1920–1960.* Detroit, New York: Gale, 2002.

Hubler, Richard G. *The Cole Porter Story.* New York: Holt, Rinehart & Winston, 1965.

Hyland, William G. *The Song Is Ended: Songwriters and American Music, 1900–1950.* New York, Oxford: Oxford University Press, 1995.

———. *Richard Rodgers.* New Haven and London: Yale University Press, 1998.

Jablonski, Edward. *Harold Arlen: Happy with the Blues.* Garden City, NY: Doubleday, 1961.

———. *Gershwin.* New York: Doubleday, 1987.

———. *Alan Jay Lerner: A Biography.* New York: Holt, 1996.

———. *Irving Berlin: American Troubadour.* New York: Holt, 1999.

Jablonski, Edward and Lawrence D. Stewart. *The Gershwin Years.* Garden City, NY: Doubleday, 1958; revised and enlarged, 1973.

Jasen, David A. *Tin Pan Alley: The Composers, the Songs, the Performers, and Their Times: The Golden Age of American Popular Music from 1886 to 1956.* New York: Donald I. Fine, 1988.

Jasen, David A. and Gene Jones. *Spreadin' Rhythm Around: Black Popular Songwriters, 1880–1930*. New York: Routledge, 1998.

Kander, John and Fred Ebb, as told to Greg Lawrence. *Colored Lights: Forty Years of Words and Music, Show Biz, Collaboration and All That Jazz*. New York: Faber and Faber, 2003.

Kane, Henry. *How to Write a Song: As Told to Henry Kane*. New York: Macmillan, 1962.

Kasha, Al and Joel Hirschhorn. *Notes on Broadway: Conversations with the Great Songwriters*. Chicago: Contemporary Books, 1985.

Kimball, Robert, ed. *Cole*. New York: Holt, Rinehart and Winston, 1971.

———, ed. *The Complete Lyrics of Cole Porter*. New York: Vintage Books, 1984.

———, ed. *The Complete Lyrics of Ira Gershwin*. New York: Alfred A. Knopf, 1993.

Kimball, Robert and William Bolcom. *Reminiscing with Sissle and Blake*. New York: Viking, 1973.

Kimball, Robert and Linda Emmet, eds. *The Complete Lyrics of Irving Berlin*. New York: Alfred A. Knopf, 2001.

Kimball, Robert and Robert Gottlieb, eds. *Reading Lyrics*. New York: Pantheon Books, 2000.

Kimball, Robert and Dorothy Hart, eds. *The Complete Lyrics of Lorenz Hart*. New York: Alfred A. Knopf, 1986.

Kimball, Robert and Alfred Simon. *The Gershwins*. New York: Atheneum, 1973.

Kreuger, Miles. *Show Boat: The Story of a Classic American Musical*. New York, Oxford: Oxford University Press, 1977.

Lambert, George Edmund. *Duke Ellington*. New York: Barnes, 1961.

Lasser, Michael. "Al Dubin," "Arthur Freed," "Mack Gordon," "Sheldon Harnick," "Frank Loesser," "Jack Yellen" in *Dictionary of Literary Biography: American Song Lyricists, 1920–1960*. Detroit, New York: Gale, 2002.

Lawrence, A. H. *Duke Ellington and His World: A Biography*. New York: Routledge, 2001.

Lax, Roger and Frederick Smith. *The Great Song Thesaurus*, 2d ed. New York, Oxford: Oxford University Press, 1989.

Lees, Gene. *Inventing Champagne. The Worlds of Lerner and Loewe*. New York: St. Martin's Press, 1990.

———. *Singers and the Song II*. New York, Oxford: Oxford University Press, 1998.

Lerner, Alan Jay. *The Street Where I Live*. New York: W.W. Norton, 1978.

———. *A Hymn to Him: The Lyrics of Alan Jay Lerner*. Edited by Benny Green. New York: Limelight Editions, 1987.

Lewens, Alan. *Popular Song: Soundtrack of the Century*. New York: Billboard Books, 2001.

Lissauer, Robert. *Lissauer's Encyclopedia of Popular Music in America: 1888 to the Present*. New York: Paragon House, 1991.

Loesser, Susan. *A Most Remarkable Fella: Frank Loesser and the Guys and Dolls in His Life*. New York: Donald I. Fine, 1993.

Logan, Josh. *Josh: My Upside Down In and Out Life*. New York: Delacorte, 1976.

Mancini, Henry and Gene Lees. *Did They Mention the Music?* Chicago, New York: Contemporary Books, 1989.

Marks, Edward B. *They All Sang: From Tony Pastor to Rudy Valèe*. New York: Viking, 1934.

Martin, Mary. *My Heart Belongs*. New York: William Morrow & Co., 1976.

Marx, Samuel and Jan Clayton. *Rodgers and Hart*. New York: G.P. Putnam's Sons, 1976.

Mast, Gerald. *Can't Help Singin': The American Musical on Stage and Screen*. Woodstock, NY: Overlook, 1987.

McCabe, John. *George M. Cohan: The Man Who Owned Broadway*. New York: DaCapo Press, 1973.

McBrien, William. *Cole Porter: A Biography*. New York: Knopf, 1998.

McBride, Patricia Dubin. *Lullaby of Broadway*. Secaucus, NJ: Citadel, 1983.

McGovern, Dennis and Deborah Grass Winer. *Sing Out, Louise: 150 Stars of the Musical Theatre Remember 50 Years on Broadway*. New York: Schirmer, 1993.

Merman, Ethel and George Eells. *Merman: An Autobiography*. New York: Simon and Schuster, 1978.

Meyerson, Harold and Ernie Harburg. *Who Put the Rainbow in The Wizard of Oz? Yip Harburg, Lyricist*. Ann Arbor: University of Michigan Press, 1993.

Montgomery, Elizabeth Rider. *The Story Behind Popular Songs*. New York: Dodd, Mead & Company, 1958.

Mordden, Ethan. *Better Foot Forward: The History of American Musical Theater*. New York: Grossman, 1976.

——. *Broadway Babies: The People Who Made the American Musical*. New York, Oxford: Oxford University Press, 1983.

——. *Rodgers and Hammerstein*. New York: Abrams, 1992.

——. *Make Believe: The Broadway Musical in the 1920s*. New York, Oxford: Oxford University Press, 1997.

——. *Coming Up Roses: The Broadway Musical in the 1950s*. New York, Oxford: Oxford University Press, 1998.

——. *Beautiful Mornin': The Broadway Musical in the 1940s*. New York, Oxford: Oxford University Press, 1999.

——. *Open a New Window: The Broadway Musical in the 1960s*. New York: Palgrave, 2001.

——. *One More Kiss: The Broadway Musical in the 1970s*. New York: Palgrave, 2003.

Morris, James R., J.R. Taylor, and Dwight Blocker Bowers. eds. *American Popular Song: Six Decades of Songwriters and Singers*. Washington: Smithsonian Institution Press, 1884.

Nolan, Frederick. *The Sound of Their Music: The Story of Rodgers and Hammerstein*. London: Dent, 1978.

——. *Lorenz Hart: Poet on Broadway*. New York, Oxford: Oxford University Press, 1994.

Ohl, Vicki. *Fine and Dandy: The Life and Work of Kay Swift*. New Haven, London: Yale University Press, 2004.

Palmer, Tony. *All You Need Is Love: The Story of Popular Music*. Edited by Paul Medlicott. New York: Grossman, 1976.

Rimler, Walter. *A Gershwin Companion: A Critical Inventory & Discography, 1916–1984*. Ann Arbor: Popular Culture, Inc., 1991.

Rodgers, Richard. *Musical Stages: An Autobiography*. New York: Random House, 1975.

Rose, Phyllis. *Jazz Cleopatra: Josephine Baker in Her Time*. New York: Doubleday, 1989.

Rosenberg, Bernard and Ernest Goldstein. "From the Lower East Side to 'Over the Rainbow,'" in their *Creators and Disturbers: Reminiscences by Jewish Intellectuals of New York*. New York: Columbia University Press, 1982.

Rosenberg, Deena. *Fascinating Rhythm: The Collaboration of George and Ira Gershwin*. New York: Dutton, 1991.

Scharfman, Rachel. "Irving Caesar" in *Dictionary of Literary Biography: American Song Lyricists, 1920–1960*. Detroit, New York: Gale, 2002.

Schuerer, Timothy E. *Born in the U.S.A.: The Myth of America in Popular Music from Colonial Times to the Present*. Jackson: University Press of Mississippi, 1991.

Schwartz, Charles. *Gershwin: His Life and Music*. New York: The Bobbs–Merrill Co., 1973.

———. *Cole Porter*. New York: The Dial Press, 1977.

Secrest, Meryle. *Somewhere for Me: A Biography of Richard Rodgers*. London: Bloomsbury, 2001.

Silvers, Phil and Robert Saffron. *This Laugh Is on Me*. London, New York: W. H. Allen, 1974.

Singer, Barry. *Black and Blue: The Life and Lyrics of Andy Razaf*. New York: Schirmer, 1992.

Spaeth, Sigmund. *A History of Popular Music in America*. New York: Random House, 1948.

Stone, Desmond. *Alec Wilder in Spite of Himself: A Life of the Composer*. New York, Oxford: Oxford University Press, 1996.

Sudhalter, Richard M. *Stardust Melody: The Life and Music of Hoagy Carmichael*. New York, Oxford: Oxford University Press, 2002.

Suskin, Stephen. *Show Tunes, 1905–1991: The Songs, Shows, and Careers of Broadway's Major Composers*. New York, Oxford: Oxford University Press, 2000.

Taylor, Deems. *Some Enchanted Evenings: The Story of Rodgers and Hammerstein*. New York: Harper, 1953.

Taylor, Theodore. *Jule: The Story of Composer Jule Styne*. New York: Random House, 1979.

Taylor, William, "Broadway: The House That Words Built," in his *Inventing Times Square: Commerce and Culture at the Crossroads of the World*. New York: Russell Sage Foundation, 1991.

Tormé, Mel. *My Singing Teachers*. New York: Oxford, 1994.

Tucker, Sophie. *Some of These Days: The Autobiography of Sophie Tucker*. New York: Doubleday, Duran, and Company, Inc., 1945.

Tyler, Don. *Hit Parade: An Encyclopedia of the Top Songs of the Jazz, Depression, Swing, and Sing Eras*. New York: Quill, 1985.

Ulanov, Barry. *Duke Ellington*. New York: Da Capo, 1975.

Waller, Maurice and Anthony Calabrese. *Fats Waller*. New York: Schirmer, 1977.

Waters, Ethel and Charles Samuels. *His Eye Is on the Sparrow*. New York: DaCapo Press, 1992.

Whitburn, Joel. *Pop Memories, 1880–1954: The History of American Popular Music*. Menomonee Falls, WI: Record Research, 1986.

Whitcomb, Ian. *Irving Berlin and Ragtime America*. London: Century–Hutchinson, 1987.

White, Mark. *You Must Remember This ... Popular Songwriters 1900–1980*. New York: Charles Scribner's Sons, 1985.

Whiting, Margaret and Will Holt. *It Might As Well Be Spring: A Musical Autobiography*. New York: William Morrow, 1987.

Wilder, Alec. *American Popular Song: The Great Innovators, 1900–1950*. New York, Oxford: Oxford University Press, 1972.

Wilk, Max. *They're Playing Our Song: From Jerome Kern to Stephen Sondheim—The Stories Behind the Words and Music of Two Generations*. New York: Atheneum, 1973.

Winer, Deborah Grace. *On the Sunny Side of the Street: The Life and Lyrics of Dorothy Fields*. New York: Schirmer, 1997.

Witmark, Isidore and Isaac Goldberg. *The Story of the House of Witmark: From Ragtime to Swingtime*. New York: Furman, 1939.

Wodehouse, P. G. *Author! Author!* New York: Simon and Schuster, 1962.

Wodehouse, P. G. and Guy Bolton. *Bring on the Girls*. New York: Simon and Schuster, 1953.

Woll, Allen. *Black Musical Theatre: From "Coontown" to "Dreamgirls."* New York: DaCapo Press, 1989.

Wood, Graham. "Ray Evans and Jay Livingston," "Bert Kalmar" in *Dictionary of Literary Biography: American Song Lyricists, 1920–1960*. Detroit, New York: Gale, 2002.

Woodbury, Paul. "Ted Koehler" in *Dictionary of Literary Biography: American Song Lyricists, 1920–1960*. Detroit, New York: Gale, 2002.

Woollcott, Alexander. *The Story of Irving Berlin*. New York: G. P. Putnam's Sons, 1925.

Ziegfeld, Richard and Paulette. *The Ziegfeld Touch: The Life and Times of Florenz Ziegfeld, Jr.* New York: Harry N. Abrams, 1993.

Zinsser, William. *Easy to Remember: The Great American Songwriters and Their Songs*. Jaffrey, NH: David R. Godine, 2000.

Index